THE FRONTIERS OF THE NEW INSTITUTIONAL ECONOMICS

THE FRONTIERS OF THE NEW INSTITUTIONAL ECONOMICS

Edited by

John N. Drobak

School of Law
Washington University
St. Louis, Missouri

John V. C. Nye

Department of Economics
Washington University
St. Louis, Missouri

ACADEMIC PRESS

San Diego London Boston New York
Sydney Tokyo Toronto

This book is printed on acid-free paper. ∞

Academic Press
a division of Harcourt Brace & Company
525 B Street, Suite 1900, San Diego, California 92101-4495, USA
http://www.apnet.com

Academic Press Limited
24-28 Oval Road, London NW1 7DX, UK
http://www.hbuk.co.uk/ap/

Library of Congress Cataloging-in-Publication Data

The frontiers of the new institutional economics / edited by John N.
Drobak, John Nye.
p. cm.
Includes index.
ISBN 0-12-222240-7 (alk. paper)
1. Institutional economics. I. Drobak, John N. II. Nye, John.
HB99.5.F76 1996
330--DC20 96-35892
CIP

PRINTED IN THE UNITED STATES OF AMERICA
97 98 99 00 01 02 BB 9 8 7 6 5 4 3 2 1

To Douglass C. North,
our colleague, teacher,
and friend

Contents

PART II ECONOMIC HISTORY

PART III INSTITUTIONS AND POLITICAL ECONOMY

Contributors

Numbers in parentheses indicate the pages on which the authors' contributions begin.

Lee J. Alston (145) Department of Economics, University of Illinois, Urbana, Illinois 61802

W. Brian Arthur (291) Citibank Professor, Santa Fe Institute, Santa Fe, New Mexico 87501

Robert H. Bates (197) Department of Government, Harvard University, Cambridge, Massachusetts 02138

Andy Clark (269) Department of Philosophy, and Philosophy/Neuroscience/Psychology Program, Washington University, St. Louis, Missouri 63130

Paul A. David (305) All Souls College, Oxford OX1 4AL, United Kingdom and Stanford University, Stanford, California, 94305

John N. Drobak (247) School of Law, Washington University, St. Louis, Missouri 63132

Stanley L. Engerman (95) Department of Economics, University of Rochester, Rochester, New York 14627

Jean Ensminger (165) Department of Anthropology, Washington University, St. Louis, Missouri 63130

Robert William Fogel (13) Graduate School of Business, The University of Chicago, Chicago, Illinois 60637

Avner Greif (57) Department of Economics, Stanford University, Stanford, California 94305

Philip T. Hoffman (31) Division of the Humanities and Social Sciences, California Institute of Technology, Pasadena, California 91125

Gary D. Libecap (145) Karl Eller Center, College of Business, University of Arizona, Tucson, Arizona 85721

Bernardo Mueller (145) Department of Economics, University of Brasilia, Brasilia, Brazil

Douglass C. North (3) Department of Economics, Washington University, St. Louis, Missouri 63130

John V. C. Nye (121) Department of Economics, Washington University, St. Louis, Missouri 63130

Jean-Laurent Rosenthal (31) Department of Economics, University of California, Los Angeles, California 90024

Warren C. Sanderson (305) State University of New York at Stony Brook, Stony Brook, New York 11790

Kenneth A. Shepsle (197) Department of Government, Harvard University, Cambridge, Massachusetts 02138

Barry R. Weingast (213) Hoover Institution and Department of Political Science, Stanford University, Stanford, California 94305

Preface

This book is the product of the contributors' deep admiration and respect for Douglass C. North and his work. The chapters were originally written for a conference held at Washington University in March 1995 to celebrate the award of the 1993 Nobel Prize in Economics to Professor North. In keeping with the spirit of Professor North's research agenda, we asked the contributors to be adventurous and explore issues at the boundaries of the new institutional economics. Our hope is that the Introduction will help the reader see these works in the context of the larger research agenda. Although the chapters in this book were originally written to celebrate Professor North's award, we did not intend to produce a typical festschrift. Rather, we have two goals for this book. We hope it will serve as an introduction to the new institutional economics not only for economists, but also for scholars of other social sciences. For those already familiar with the new institutional agenda, we hope that the book will enhance their current knowledge and generate new research.

We deeply appreciate the efforts of the contributors, both for their hard work on the conference and for their diligence in bringing this book into existence. The commentators on the chapters played an invaluable role in improving the quality of the papers and in stimulating the discussions that grew from the presentations. The commentators were Yoram Barzel, Jules L. Coleman, Lance E. Davis, Arthur T. Denzau, Thráinn Eggertsson, Robert E. Gallman, David Haddock, Ronald R.

King, Jack C. Knight, Margaret Levi, Donald N. McCloskey, Joel Mokyr, and Norman J. Schofield. We also appreciate the help of those who chaired the various sessions at the conference: Lee K. Benham, Nicholas Dopuch, Dorsey D. Ellis, Jr., Wilhelm Neuefeind, and Murray L. Weidenbaum. We give special thanks to Ronald H. Coase for his participation in the conference.

The conference, and hence this book, would not have been possible without the financial support of a number of organizations at Washington University: the Institute for the Study of Economic Performance Over Time, the Faculty of Arts and Sciences, the Business, Law, and Economics Center of the John M. Olin School of Business, the Center in Political Economy, the School of Law, and the Department of Economics. We are indebted to Jennifer Chilton Kallery for her endless efforts in making the conference run smoothly.

We appreciate the work of the anonymous referees and other readers of the various chapters who helped make this a better book. We also thank Larry Neal for introducing us to Academic Press and encouraging the Press to publish this volume. Our editors at the Press have made this a most pleasant experience.

Introduction

The "new institutional economics" is an ambiguous term. This stems in part from new institutionalism being less a distinct school than a particular set of shared concerns grounded in existing economic theories and doctrines. It does not represent a separate and heterodox branch of economics like the Marxian or Austrian schools of thought, and it has little in common with the older Institutionalists, whose research extends back to the work of Commons and Veblen. Although the new institutionalists are concerned with issues not often considered central to the mainstream of economics, they still begin with an appreciation of neoclassical price theory as a powerful tool for predicting many, but not all, economic outcomes in the real world. They tend to make use of a diverse but related set of methodologies applied to a broad range of social scientific issues, but they also believe that neoclassical price theory must be significantly augmented to become a more powerful tool for understanding the world. Often, in their focus on such issues as politics and law, interested scholars apply standard theory to nonstandard realms. In other instances, there is a greater willingness to explore the boundaries of existing models and to focus on relaxing different sets of assumptions. The interplay between institutional evolution and market forces plays a central role in their discussions. Mathematical formalism, though not unappreciated, is less important than articulating and testing issues within a coherent intellectual framework. Of late, there has been greater interest in abandoning or at least tweaking the fundamental assumptions of rationality itself. Many types of research that have gone out of fashion in the conventional economics literature, such as case studies, analyses of written contracts and legal rules, and simple cross-country comparisons, become much more important on the neoinstitutionalist agenda.

The scholars who might be labeled as "new institutionalists" generally focus on the following four areas of research:

1. transactions costs and property rights;
2. political economy and public choice;
3. quantitative economic history (usually in an institutional, microeconomic context);
4. cognition, ideology, and the role of path dependence.

Few scholars would embrace all four of these perspectives; most are parsimonious in their deviation from conventional micro theory. Further, only a subset of scholars working in these four areas would consider themselves new institutionalists.[1] Of those who see themselves as working in the new institutional economics, most are concerned with two central but very different problems: (1) how institutions affect economic growth and (2) how institutions arise.

A large group of the new institutionalists can be said to draw inspiration from the pioneering work of Ronald Coase—the 1991 Nobel laureate in economics—particularly the ideas contained in his most celebrated articles, "The Problem of Social Cost" (1960) and "The Theory of the Firm" (1937). While economists in the traditions of Marshall and Pigou have tended to characterize interactions as taking place either against a backdrop of perfect competition and first-best outcomes or in imperfect markets with an omniscient, benevolent government stepping in to impose optimal regulation, Coase has encouraged us to see transactions costs of all kinds as inherent and pervasive. Thus, the new institutionalists see no reason to speak of perfect and imperfect markets. Rather, the focus is redirected to the problem of negotiation and exchange, hence the central importance of the contract. Thus, contracting and contractual analysis, as developed by scholars like Barzel (1989) and North (i.e., North and Thomas, 1973; North and Davis, 1971), play especially prominent roles.

These scholars often point to the underexamined costs of measuring and enforcing property rights. Barzel in particular notes the tendency of neoclassical models to assume easy definitions of price and quantity even though traders in the real world devote vast resources to controling such problems. Problems such as these have inspired others to examine and characterize the multiplicity of economic structures, each with its own distinct types of transactional problems and organizational

[1] Indeed, a few of the contributors to this volume would be uncomfortable with the view that most of their work falls under the heading of the new institutionalism, although virtually all are sympathetic to some part of the new institutional agenda.

responses. Some have followed the lead of North in treating institutions as "the rules of the game" and have tried to come to grips with the broader issues of economic development within an evolving institutional and political framework.

Much of the public choice literature forms a separate branch of the new institutional framework. To recognize the importance of the political system to economic growth is to ask for a positive theory of politics and regulation. Of interest are the questions of how the political system has evolved and how different political and economic actors respond to the incentives provided by different governmental structures. The government is not seen as an omniscient planner or auctioneer—as is typical in conventional neoclassical models—but rather as a mix of institutions and organizations subject to internal pressures from a variety of constituencies. The institutionalists would further add an interest in the evolution of the political system and its relationship to economic development. Experts in the political side of political economy, such as Shepsle and Weingast, have focused on the "supply side" aspects of public choice, showing us how administrative or committee structure shapes political outcomes (see Shepsle and Weingast, 1987; Weingast and Marshall, 1988). There is thus room for discussions as broad as elaboration of a neoclassical theory of the state (begun by North, 1981, and Levi, 1988, and discussed by Nye in this volume) or as focused as a rational choice account of sovereign debt in eighteenth-century England (see Weingast's contribution to this volume).

Many of the contributors to the book have chosen to address broad questions built upon their previous work, engaging an extremely varied range of subjects. Engerman advances beyond his previous research on the economics of slavery to the role of morality and societal change in the history of involuntary servitude. Bates and Shepsle consider the role of demography in political economy, modeling at a level more typical of economists than of traditional political scientists. Greif seeks to use game theory to elaborate a thesis about clan competition in twelfth-century Italy that pushes us beyond mere formalization. Ensminger shows how anthropology can be helpful in studying the relationship between formal and informal institutions by demonstrating how informal norms undermine or complement formal rules of conduct. David and Sanderson ponder the role of persistently erroneous belief in family planning.

The new institutionalism cuts across many disciplines, such as political science, law, business, and anthropology, but perhaps its most fervent adherents lie in the field of economic history. That is to be expected given historians' concern with long-run performance and the complex evolution of economies through time. Anyone forced to consider economic growth in the medium and the long run finds it hard to take rules and institutions as fixed. While the work of the "new economic historians" or "cliometricians" has become virtually conventional, confrontation with historical issues forces cliometricians to pay more attention to structure, institutions, and the complex role of time. Whereas most cliometricians once took their cue from the research of macroeconomists on national income accounts or aggregate models of growth, the new institutional economic history has come to appreciate the value of comparative analysis, the case study, and even narrative (e.g., the recent work of McCloskey). In this context, Hoffman and Rosenthal's contribution to this volume on financing war shows links to both traditional and cliometric economic history. But this change continues to recognize the beneficial discipline that price theory and statistical exactitude provide. Thus, new institutional economists have begun to broaden the scope of economic inquiry without overturning established methodologies.

In general, the macroeconomic techniques which fueled the first few decades of the cliometrics revolution play at best a supporting role in the new institutionalism. Arguments about development derived from the income accounting paradigm are felt to be far too mechanistic for broader historical work. Perhaps the first and clearest statement of this came from North and Thomas's *The Rise of the Western World* (1973). There they noted that scholars of the Industrial Revolution who were satisfied with arguing that technological change explained the *how* of the Industrial Revolution did little to answer the question of *why*. For North and Thomas, the improvements in technology, like the Industrial Revolution itself, were different manifestations of the general problem of economic development—a problem that could be resolved only by comparing and analyzing the role of institutional change.

New institutional scholars tend to assume that the fine details of macro growth and performance are difficult to understand and measure reliably, perhaps irremediably so, despite the wealth of government statistics readily available. In contrast, the new institutionalists take for granted that we know many of the *sufficient* conditions for successful economic performance, without understanding which are truly *necessary*. Well-defined property rights, limited but strong government, the rule of law, fairly open trade, stable monetary regimes, mobility of capital and labor, and a society congenial to invention and innovation are all felt to be part of the equation. There is no consensus, however, on which of these is essential. Although neo-institutionalists assume the usefulness of microeconomics in understanding economic development, they take as unknown the range of specific applications that will emerge. Often the preferred methodology is to assume the viability of maximizing at all available margins, including political struggle, while trying to comprehend how this process of maximization within a highly constrained setting leads to adaptations that make trade and contracting possible. Some enterprising scholars have tried to apply this sort of reasoning to contracting arrangements or political structure thought to be beyond the reach of optimizing behavior. More often the focus, unlike that of much of conventional theory, is placed on developing a taxonomy of conditions and responses observed in different historical circumstances rather than on a formal elaboration of the logic.

An especially interesting set of questions surrounds the problems of enforcement and the role of legal and informal rules. Credible commitment and problems of enforcement are important in two complementary chapters in this book dealing with public debt in England and in the United States. Weingast, who deals with England, focuses on political and structural issues. Drobak analyzes credible commitment in the context of American public debt from the point of view of a legal scholar. Concern with commitment always leads to concerns about violence and the tendency of economics to simply assume away coercion. But Nye's chapter shows how North paved the way for an integrated theory of the state that incorporates coercion as a tool of government, while Alston, Libecap, and Mueller provide us with a case study of violence and conflict arising from conflicting laws governing land titles in the Brazilian Amazon.

The strong assumptions we make about rationality are generally still flexible enough to permit a variety of interesting patterns of behavior to emerge and teach us something new about commercial agreements, political conflict, or regulatory change. In some instances, however, the assumptions of standard micro theory will leave too much anomalous. In such a situation, there will be the opportunity to enlist either (a) more sophisticated theoretical formulations or (b) assumptions that put us beyond the domain of even the broadest conceptions of micro behavior, such as assuming very weak rationality, strong cultural or ideological beliefs, or historical inertia. There is a willingness to consider the latter possibilities, but as with microeconomists, the strong bias is toward situations that do not require such mental calisthenics. Indeed, with the novelty of much work in the new institutional economics, it is not unreasonable to focus predominantly on understanding behavior and organization within a rational choice context, given the comparative advantage of the economic method in this regard. Thus, the new institutionalists welcome modifications and alternatives to rational choice but remain skeptical toward these new approaches, slowly incorporating new extensions as they demonstrate their usefulness in various applications.

Of late, North and a few others have come to believe that it is important to move beyond the more conventional rationality assumptions of neoclassical price theory by using what is known of human decision making from other disciplines. For these scholars, lessons drawn from cognitive science or learning theory provide crucial insights neglected by most economists. Some have become concerned with the idea that in certain circumstances, small events may have large, irreparable consequences. This has led to concern with the notion of "path dependence" advanced by Brian Arthur (1989) and elaborated in an historical context by North (1981) and Paul David (1985). Both Arthur and David have been especially concerned with the problems of technological lock-in, in which inferior products become established by virtue of historical serendipity. North has claimed that technological lock-in is not as significant as institutional lock-in, in which path dependence (caused by rigidities in institutional and political arrangements) and divergent human beliefs explain the persistence of systematically failed economic policies. North has even argued for the inclusion of ideology and the problems of belief in the conventional calculus. Both Arthur's and David's chapters reflect the excitement surrounding the problems and possibilities of handling these controversial issues.

Perhaps the most far-reaching and interdisciplinary contribution to the book is contained in Andy Clark's chapter on economic reason. Drawing on work in both philosophy and psychology, Clark helps us understand how real-world economic institutions make possible outcomes consistent with the predictions of standard models, even when the maintained assumptions of those models are violated. Economists often speak of markets operating well despite the inaccuracy of our models of perfectly maximizing humans. Only recently have there been real efforts to flesh out the complementary mechanisms involved in ways that draw on the psychological literature. This has the promise of becoming a source of important insights in the years to come.

The papers from the conference begin with two special contributions from the co-winners of the 1993 Nobel Memorial Prize in Economics. North's contribution serves as an extended introduction to the book, providing a clear summary of institutional economics and how it builds on previous work while mixing in a number of observations on his own evolution as a scholar. Fogel's essay is not only an evaluation of North's impact on the economics profession, but also an extended meditation on the distinction between economic theory and formal mathematical modeling. He makes the case that North has been one of the great theorists of his generation.

We hope that this volume will serve as a good set of reports from the frontiers of research in the new institutional economics. We also hope that this will highlight the possibilities of profound results emerging from this coherent yet interdisciplinary social science research agenda.

John N. Drobak
John V. C. Nye
St. Louis, Missouri

REFERENCES

Arthur, B., 1989. "Completing Technologies, Increasing Returns, and Lock-in by Historical Events," *Economic Journal,* 99, 116–131.

Barzel, Y., 1989. *Economic Analysis of Property Rights.* New York: Cambridge University Press.

Coase, R., 1937. "The Nature of the Firm," *Economica,* 4, 386–405.

Coase, R., 1960. "The Problem of Social Cost," *Journal of Law and Economics,* 3, 1–44.

David, P., 1985. "Clio and the Economics of QWERTY," *American Economic Review,* 75, 332–337.

Levi, M., 1988, *Of Rule and Revenue.* Berkeley: University of California Press.

McCloskey, D. N., 1985. *The Rhetoric of Economics.* Madison WI: University of Wisconsin Press.

North, D. C., 1981. *Structure and Change in Economic History.* New York: Norton.

North, D. C., and L. E. Davis, 1971. *Institutional Change and American Economic Growth.* New York: Cambridge University Press.

North, D. C., and R. P. Thomas, 1973. *The Rise of the Western World.* Cambridge, MA: The University Press.

Shepsle, K. A., and B. Weingast, 1987. "The Institutional Foundations of Committee Power," *American Political Science Review,* 81(1), 85–104.

Weingast, B., and W. Marshall, 1988. "The Industrial Organization of Congress; or, Why Legislature, like Firms, Are Not Organized as Markets," *Journal of Political Economy,* 96(11), 132–163.

PART I

THEORETICAL FOUNDATIONS

I

Prologue

Douglass C. North

The essays in this book explore frontiers of the new institutional economics that are central to progress in the disciplines of economics and economic history. As an introduction to the essays, I would like to describe my evolution as an economist and, in so doing, point out my view of the scope of the new institutional economics and its place within the disciplines, as well as explain the part played by some of the authors of the essays in this book.[1] I set out to understand what made economies rich or poor because I viewed that objective to being the essential prerequisite to improving their performance. The search for the Holy Grail of the ultimate source of economic performance has taken me on a long and certainly unanticipated journey, from Marxism to cognitive science, but it has been this persistent objective that has directed and shaped my scholarly career.

I went to graduate school at the University of California at Berkeley—the only graduate school that would take me with my poor undergraduate record. There was no field of development in those days, but

[1] Much of the following material is drawn from "My Evolution as an Economist," a talk given in the series by Nobel Laureates in economics on their evolution as economists at Trinity College, Texas, in 1994 and forthcoming in a book titled *Lives of the Nobel Laureates: Thirteen Nobel Economists*, 3rd ed., William Breit and Roger Spencer, eds., Cambridge, MA: MIT Press, 1995.

economic history appeared to come closest to my objective of understanding how economies work. I cannot say that I learned much formal economics as a graduate student in Berkeley. My most influential professors were all outside the mainstream of orthodox economics—Robert Brady; Leo Rogin, a very influential teacher of the history of economic thought; and M. M. Knight (Frank Knight's brother) who certainly was agnostic, to say the least, about theory, but who had a wonderful knowledge of the facts and background in economic history. He became my mentor and my thesis advisor at Berkeley. But while I learned by rote most of the theory I was supposed to know, I did not acquire a real understanding of theory.

It was not until I got my first job, at the University of Washington in Seattle, and began playing chess with Don Gordon, a brilliant young theorist, that I learned economic theory. In the three years of playing chess every day from noon to two, I may have beaten Don at chess, but he taught me economics; more important he taught me how to reason like an economist, and that skill is still perhaps the most important tool that I have acquired.

I had written my dissertation on the history of life insurance in the United States and had had a Social Science Research Council Fellowship to go to the East Coast and do the spade work. That turned out to be a very productive year. I not only sat in on Robert Merton's seminars in sociology at Columbia but also became involved in the Entrepreneurial Center of Arthur Cole at Harvard. The result was that Joseph Schumpeter, who had been an intellectual source of the Entrepreneurial School, had a strong influence upon me. My early work and publications centered around expanding on the analysis of life insurance in my dissertation and its relationship to investment banking.

I next turned to developing an analytical framework to look at regional economic growth and this led to my first article in the *Journal of Political Economy,* titled "Location Theory and Regional Economic Growth." That work eventually led me to developing a staple theory of economic growth.

I was very fortunate that at a meeting of the Economic History Association I came to know Solomon Fabricant, who was then director of research at the National Bureau of Economic Research (NBER), and in 1956–1957 I was invited to spend the year at the bureau as a research associate. That was an enormously important year in my life. I not only became acquainted with most of the leading economists who passed through the bureau, but I spent one day a week at Johns Hopkins University in Baltimore with Simon Kuznets whose wise council had a lasting influence on me. During the year at the NBER I did the empirical work that led to my early major quantitative study of the balance of payments of the United States from 1790 to 1860.

Between my year at the National Bureau and 1966–1967, when I went off to Geneva as a Ford Faculty Fellow, I did my major work in American economic history, which led to my first book, *The Economic Growth of the United States from 1790 to 1860.* It was a straightforward analysis of how markets work in the context of an export staple model of growth.

By this time (1960) there was a substantial stirring among young economic historians to try to transform the field from its descriptive, institutional character to an analytical, quantitative discipline. The year that I was at the NBER, that organization and the Economic History Association had the first joint quantitative program on the growth of the American economy, a conference that was held at Williamstown, Massachusetts, in the late spring of 1957. It was at that meeting that John Meyer and Alfred Conrad presented two papers, one on methodology and the other on slavery, which were in many ways the intellectual foundation of the new approach to economic history. My paper was on the balance of payments of the United States from 1790 to 1860. This meeting was really the beginning of the new approach to economic history, which coalesced when Jon Hughes and Lance Davis, two former students of mine (who finished their graduate work at Oxford and Johns Hopkins, respectively), called the first conference of economic historians interested in developing and applying economic theory and quantitative methods to history. The first meeting was held in February 1960 at Purdue, where they were both faculty members. Bob Fogel, Bill Parker, Bob Gallman, and Dick Easterlin were amongst the pioneer economic historians who attended. This conference was highly successful and became an annual affair. The participants were a mixture of economic historians, theorists, and econometricians. There were no-holds-barred meetings, in which the speaker frequently got mauled, but we knew that we were reshaping the field of economic history. That was exciting. The reception that we received amongst economists was certainly enthusiastic. Economics departments very quickly became interested in having new economic historians, or, as we came to call ourselves, cliometricians (Clio being the muse of history). Therefore, as I developed a graduate program jointly with my colleague, Morris David Morris, at the University of Washington, we attracted some of the best students to do work in economic history. During the 1960s and early 1970s the job market was very responsive and our students were easily placed throughout the country.

In 1966–1967 I decided that I should switch from American to European economic history, and therefore, when I received a Ford Faculty grant I moved to Geneva for a year and decided to retool. Retooling turned out to radically change my scholarly life, since I quickly became convinced that the tools of neoclassic economic theory would not explain the fundamental societal change that had characterized European economies from medieval times onward.

Neoclassical theory was concerned with the operation of markets and assumed the existence of the underlying conditions that were a prerequisite to the operation of markets. It had nothing to say about how markets evolved. Moreover, it was a static theory and we needed a theory that was dynamic and could explain the evolution of economies through time. We needed new tools, but they simply did not exist. It was in the long search for a framework that would provide new tools of analysis that my interest and concern with the new institutional economics evolved. As a graduate student I had read Thorstein Veblen and John R. Commons and been impressed by the insights they provided into the workings of economies, but they did not provide a theoretical framework and we needed a theoretical structure that we could use to explain and analyze economic history. The old institutional economics, because it failed to provide such a theoretical framework, never posed a serious alternative to neoclassical theory. Marxism was explicitly concerned with institutions, asked good questions, and had an explanation of long-run change, but the model had too many flaws. Making classes the unit of analysis and the failure to incorporate population change as a key source of change were major shortcomings. The strength of neoclassical theory was its uncompromising focus on scarcity and hence competition as the key to economics, the individual as the unit of analysis, and the power of the economic way of reasoning. There had to be a way of melding the strengths of these diverse approaches into a theoretical structure. That is what others and I have set out to do in the new institutional economics.

Why focus on institutions? In a world of uncertainty they have been used by human beings in an attempt to structure human interaction. They are the rules of the game of a society and in consequence provide the framework of incentives that shape economic, political, and social organization. Institutions are composed of formal rules (laws, constitutions, rules), informal constraints (conventions, codes of conduct, norms of behavior), and the effectiveness of their enforcement. Enforcement is carried out by third parties (law enforcement, social ostracism), by second parties (retaliation), or by the first party (self-imposed codes of conduct). Institutions affect economic performance by determining, together with the technology employed, the transaction and transformation (production) costs that make up the total costs of production. Because there is an intimate connection between the institutions and technology employed, the efficiency of a market is directly shaped by the institutional framework.

My initial effort to incorporate institutions into historical economic analysis resulted in two books: *Institutional Change and American Economic Growth,* written with Lance Davis, was published in 1971, and *The Rise of the Western World: A New Economic History,* written with Robert Thomas, was published in 1973. Both were early attempts to develop some tools of institutional analysis and apply them to economic history. In our study with Lance Davis on American economic growth, we attempted to spell out the way new institutions and organizations evolved in the context of American economic growth. In our study of Europe we made the formation of property rights the key to economic performance and explored the contrasting way they evolved in the Netherlands and England, on the one hand, and in France and Spain, on the other.

Both studies were still predicated on the assumptions of neoclassical economic theory. But there were too many loose ends that did not make sense, such as the notion that institutions were efficient (however defined). Perhaps more serious, it was not possible to explain long-run poor economic performance in a neoclassical framework. So I began to explore what was wrong. Individual beliefs were obviously important to the choices people make, and only the extreme myopia of economists prevented them from understanding that ideas, ideologies, and prejudices mattered. Once you recognize that, you are forced to examine the rationality postulate critically. The long road toward a new analytical framework involved developing a view of institutions that would account for why institutions produced results that in the long run did not manage to effect economic growth, as well as developing a model of political economy that would explain the underlying source of institutions. Finally, one had to come to grips with why people had the ideologies and ideas that determined the choices they made.

It was Ronald Coase who provided a critical link that began to structure the evolving framework. In "The Nature of the Firm" (*Economica,* 1937), Coase forced us to think about the cost of economic organization. But whereas Coase was concerned with the transaction costs that determined the existence of firms, I was concerned with the transaction costs that determined overall economic performance. George Stigler had once remarked to me that he thought the efficiency of economic organization had probably been as important as technological change in historical development. I was convinced that he was right. Transaction costs provided the wedge to examine the costs of economic organization. Coase's other critical contribution, "The Problem of Social Cost" (*Journal of Law and Economics,* 1960), provided the link to connect neoclassical theory to institutional analysis. The message of that essay was that when transaction costs were positive, institutions mattered and shaped the resultant market structure. I was fortunate in having several colleagues at the University of Washington who early on took Coase's work seriously. Steven Cheung, a student of Armen Alchian at UCLA, came to Seattle after a postdoctoral fellowship at Chicago where he became acquainted with Coase. Cheung made a number of important contributions to transaction cost theory—in particular his emphasis on the costs of measurement of the multiple dimensions of a good or service, or of the performance of agents, as a critical source of transaction costs (since imperfect measurement resulted in imperfectly specified property rights). Yoram Barzel continued work that Cheung began (after Cheung left to go to the University of Hong Kong). I have learned a great deal from both of them and their influence is apparent in my next book.

In *Structure and Change in Economic History* (1981) I abandoned the notion that institutions were efficient and attempted to explain why "inefficient" rules would tend to exist and be perpetuated. In that study I began to explore the transaction costs underlying different forms of economic organization in history and also to explore the way ideologies altered free riding to influence political and economic decision making. The theoretical chapters were followed by eight historical chapters that outlined a fundamental reinterpretation of economic history from the origins of agriculture in the eighth millennium B.C. to the twentieth century.

I was still dissatisfied with our understanding of the political process and indeed searched for colleagues who were interested in developing political–economic models. Margaret Levi, a Marxist political scientist, and I had developed a political economy program but there was little interest in the subject among the faculty. This led me to leave the University of Washington in 1983 after 33 years and to move to Washington University in St. Louis where an exciting group of young political scientists (Ken Shepsle, Gary Miller and Randy Calvert) and economists (Barry Weingast and Lee Benham) were attempting to develop new models of political economy. This proved to be a felicitous move. I created the Center in Political Economy, which continues to be a creative research center (under Norman Schofield's direction).

The central theoretical puzzle about politics was reflected in the diverse and conflicting perspectives that evolved from the public choice theory that originated with Buchanan and Tullock's *The Calculus of Consent,* Mancur Olson's *The Logic of Collective Action,* and Anthony Downs's *An Economic Theory of Democracy*—three classics of the new public choice literature. Was the polity simply a leviathan to be contained as Buchanan and the Virginia school of public choice suggested? That perspective made the state little more than a giant theft machine. But how did that perspective square with the property rights argument that I had developed, which made the political creation of secure and productive property rights the key to economic growth? The problem was hardly new. *The Federalist Papers* of Madison, Hamilton, and Jay were a brilliant exposition of many of the issues. In effect, you can't do with the state, but you can't do without it either. At a deeper level of analysis, Arrow's disturbing impossibility theorem had implications for the entire process of aggregating choices. In effect, one cannot achieve collectively rational choices by aggregating the individual choices of people with diverse values and preferences.

These issues are far from resolved and pose fundamental problems for polities and therefore for economic performance. In *Structure and Change,* I developed a neoclassical theory of the state that confronted the issue of why a ruler would ever produce inefficient property rights when efficient rights would increase aggregate income and hence the revenue of the ruler. In effect, a competitive constraint (the threat of being replaced by competitors for the ruler) and a transaction cost constraint (efficient rules might have such higher costs of tax collection that the ruler's revenue would be decreased) were the sources of inefficient rules.

In "A Transaction Cost Theory of Politics" (*The Journal of Theoretical Politics,* #1, 1991), I developed a more general model of why political markets are inherently less efficient than economic markets; here I used the basic transaction cost framework I had developed to explore economic markets.

Transaction costs are the costs of measuring and enforcing agreements. Economic markets use objective criteria (size, weight, color, etc.) to measure the physical dimensions of the goods and services exchanged and legal criteria to measure the abstract dimensions of the property rights involved. Enforcement is carried out by the judicial system. Competition is a powerful force to reduce transaction costs, although economic markets are still beset by high transaction costs. But political markets are far more prone to inefficiency. What is being exchanged are promises for votes; the voter has little incentive to be informed since the likelihood that his or her vote counts is infinitesimal, there is no comparable enforcement mechanism, and competition is imperfect. The complexity of the issues (together with the lack of incentives for voters to be informed) leads to ideological stereotyping taking over. In effect, the incentives for efficiency are diluted by the structure of political markets and the complexity of the issues.

The development of a political economic framework to explore long-run institutional change occupied me during all of the 1980s and led to the publication of *Institutions, Institutional Change and Economic Performance* in 1990. In that study I explicitly attempted to evolve a theory of institutional change. The first step was to separate institutions from organizations. The former are the rules of the game, but the latter are the players. That is, organizations are made up of groups of individuals with some objective function. They are, for example, firms, trade unions, and cooperatives (economic organizations); political parties, legislatures, and regulatory agencies (political organizations); and churches, athletic associations, and clubs (social organizations). Organizations and their entrepreneurs in the pursuit of their objectives (whether a firm is attempting to maximize profits or a political party is trying to win an election, etc.) are the agents of change. The organizations themselves have come into existence because of the opportunities resulting from the incentives of the institutional framework. In the world of scarcity and competition that characterizes economies, they are in competition to survive. That competition will lead them to try to modify the institutional framework to improve their competitive position. The intensity of competition will determine the rate of institutional change, but the direction of change will reflect the perceptions of the actors—the mental models that they possess that interpret the external environment for them.

I used this framework to examine the contrasting development of the Netherlands and Britain, where polities evolved that produced the property rights underpinnings of modern economic growth, and of Spain, where secular stagnation ensued from the polity.

Economic historians were, for the most part, not impressed with the new approach. Some, like Don McCloskey, maintained that the field had always been concerned with institutions, so what was new? But most of the practitioners were confirmed neoclassical economists who saw no need to adopt a new framework. This was certainly not true of Bob Fogel, whose pioneering work in historical demography was and is fundamentally altering our understanding of population change and its impact on historical economic performance. Nor was it true of Paul David, whose pioneering work on path dependence is forcing economists to take history seriously. But they were exceptions. Gradually, however, beginning in the late 1980s, the new approach began to take hold, particularly among some young European economic historians. Phil Hoffman at the California Institute of Technology, Jean-Laurent Rosenthal at UCLA, Avner Greif at Stanford, and my young colleague, John Nye, all are doing pioneering work integrating history with both novel theoretical analysis and new sources of data, which is transforming the field.

In the 1990 book I began to puzzle seriously about the rationality postulate. It is clear that we need an explanation for why people make the choices they do; why ideologies such as communism or Muslim fundamentalism can shape the choices people make and direct the way economies evolve through long periods of time. One simply cannot get at ideologies without digging deeply into cognitive science in an attempt to understand the way in which the mind acquires learning and makes choices. Since 1990 my research has been directed toward dealing with this issue.

Herbert Simon was the pioneer who attempted to persuade social scientists to examine the actor's subjective perception of the real world. Simon maintained that if both the knowledge and computational power of the decision maker are severely limited, then we must distinguish the real world from the actor's perception if we are going to understand the choices that he or she makes. Moreover we must theorize about the reasoning processes that generated the actor's subjective representation. Simon's emphasis, however, was on bounded rationality—the limits on the computational power of the decision maker—whereas my concern with ideologies focused more on the information available to the actor and the imperfect feedback that the actor received as a result of the choices he or she made. Brian Arthur, at Stanford and the Santa Fe Institute, not only has been a pioneer (along with Paul David) on path dependence, but he also has delved into the implications of decision making under uncertainty, stimulated by John Holland's pioneering work in cognitive science at the Santa Fe Institute.

An understanding of how human learning occurs appears to be the most promising approach to the mental constructs that humans develop to explain and interpret the world around them. But the learning is not just a product of the experiences of the individual in his or her lifetime; it also includes the cumulative experiences of past generations embodied in culture. Collective learning, according to Hayek, consists of those experiences that have passed the slow test of time and are embodied in our language, institutions, technology, and ways of doing things. The accumulated stock of knowledge of past experiences is built into our learning and is the deep underlying source of path dependence—the powerful influence of the past on the present and future. Learning then is an incremental process filtered by the culture of a society that determines the perceived payoffs, but there is no guarantee that the cumulative past experiences of a society will necessarily fit them to solve new problems. The learning process then appears to be a function of (1) the way in which a given belief system filters the information derived from experiences and (2) the different experiences confronting individuals and societies at different times. Avner Greif's studies of early modern Europe have put culture front and center in exploring the contrasting development of Europe with the Muslim world.

This cognitive science/institutional approach to history offers the promise of making sense out of the economic past and the diverse performance of economies in the present. There is nothing automatic about evolving the conditions that will result in low-cost transacting in the impersonal markets that are essential to productive economies. Game theory characterizes the issue. Individuals usually will find it worthwhile cooperating with others in exchange when the play is repeated, when complete information about the other player's past performance is provided, and when small numbers of players are involved—in short, the conditions that characterize small-scale societies with personalized exchange. Cooperation is difficult to sustain when the game is not repeated (or there is an end game), when information about the other players is lacking, and when large numbers of players are involved—in short, the conditions that characterize the interdependent world of impersonal exchange of modern productive economies. Creating the institutions that will alter the benefit/cost ratios in favor of cooperative solutions is the major issue of economic performance, because it entails the creation of effective (that is, productive) economic and political institutions. Given the inherent inefficiency of political markets and the key role that political institutions play in economic performance, it is not surprising that economic performance through time has been less than satisfactory.

Two modern developments provide promise of future development. The first is the growth of cognitive science, blending research on the brain in neural sciences with research on the mind in philosophy and psychology departments. Together they have made immense progress in giving us a better understanding of how the mind works and how learning occurs. The

PNP program at Washington University under the direction of Andy Clark is an exciting program furthering such research. The second is the fascination of social scientists with game theory that has forced them finally to confront directly the rationality issue, because the foundations of game theory ultimately rest on the way human beings think and what is meant by common knowledge.

We still have a long way to go. I believe that an understanding of how people make choices, under what conditions the rationality postulate is a useful tool, and how individuals make choices under conditions of uncertainty and ambiguity are fundamental issues that we must address in order to make further progress in the social sciences. But we are making progress.

II

Douglass C. North and Economic Theory

Robert William Fogel

In recent years economic theory has often been equated with mathematical models of economic behavior.[1] The confusion between models and theory is unfortunate. Thirty years ago it was common to call courses in economic theory "economic theory" and to call courses that dealt with mathematical models of economic behavior "mathematical economics." In the 1950s and 1960s a course in economic theory was presumed to summarize the body of generalizations about the operation of the economy that economists thought were usually valid. Such generalizations were the core of the basic theory course, even though interesting but controversial generalizations were also presented. In assessing economic theories, emphasis was placed not on their intellectual elegance, much as that might be admired, but on their empirical validity.

[1] Because this interpretation of North's work and of developments in economics since the mid-1950s draws, to a large extent, on recollections and personal research experiences, I have kept references and other scholarly paraphernalia to a minimum. I have benefited from comments and criticisms of an earlier draft by Moses Abramovitz, Stanley L. Engerman, Robert E. Gallman, Lionel W. McKenzie, Robert M. Solow, and Oliver E. Williamson. Susan Jones conducted the research on which the penultimate paragraph is based and wrote note 14.

In the late 1950s and early 1960s, it was not necessary to emphasize that history was one of the principal sources of generalizations about the economy. The contribution of historical knowledge was not only evident from the way that theory was taught, but also from courses in the history of economic doctrine. After all, most of the great theorists between Adam Smith and John Maynard Keynes relied heavily upon historical information in propounding their theories. This reliance was evident not only in the work of such verbal theorists as Smith, Thomas R. Malthus, John Stuart Mill, Karl Marx, Thorstein Veblen, J. B. Clark, and Wesley C. Mitchell, but also in the work of those economists who were more versed in mathematics, such as Augustin Cournot, W. Stanley Jevons, Alfred Marshall, and Irving Fisher.

It may seem odd to younger economists that a theorist of Joseph A. Schumpeter's stature would have argued, as he did, that economic history was the most essential foundation of a sound training in economics. Schumpeter used the term "economic history" to include not only past but also present-day facts. It was not merely the need of theorists to be versed in facts that led him to make economic history primary. To theorize adequately about economies, he insisted, one had to recognize that "the subject matter of economics is essentially a unique process in historic time" (Schumpeter, 1954, p. 12). This point not only implied that the economic system was evolving over time, but that recognition of the institutional aspects of economies at particular points in time was essential to good economic analysis. The critical institutions that had to be taken into account were not, in his view, purely economic. Economic history, he argued, afforded the "best method for understanding" how economic and noneconomic institutions "are related to one another and how the various social sciences *should* be related to one another" (Schumpeter, 1954, pp. 12–13).

In emphasizing the role of historical knowledge in the formulation of theory, I do not mean to give the impression that models, either those formulated mathematically or those formulated verbally, were absent from reasoning about economic behavior until the middle of the 20th century. After all, Malthus used a very simple mathematical model in his theory of population, and Charles Davenant, Cournot, and Jevons had already formulated mathematical demand curves before Marshall so thoroughly investigated their properties within the context of a simultaneous equation system[2] (cf. Fogel, 1992a, p. 249; Jevons, 1970, p. 182; Slicher von Bath, 1963, pp. 118–119; Wrigley, 1987, pp. 92–94; on the influence of Cournot, see Creedy, 1992; Debreu, 1984; Niehans, 1990). Verbal models could be as abstract as mathematical ones, a point that Eugene von Böhm-Bawerk

[2] Davenant's (1699) curve, also called King's Law, was represented arithmetically but is

$$Q = P^{-0.403}$$

demonstrated with his stories about Robinson Crusoe. Of course, whether verbal or mathematical, these abstract models were not presumed to be an end in themselves, but a basis for arriving at valid generalizations about how some aspect of the economy actually worked.[3]

The last point needs to be emphasized. Mathematical models are not generalizations about the economy. They are, as the word implies, an abstract representation, which in engineering, physics, and chemistry is sometimes constructed in relief from clay and at other times constructed in plastic or other material to represent a variety of surfaces and objects. In economics, models are often mathematical analogies that serve to represent in a simplified way some aspect of economic behavior. Analyzing the properties of a mathematical model is not the same thing as analyzing the way in which the economy actually works. Indeed, the properties of equilibrium in the real world do not depend, as they do in some models, on whether the number of markets is odd or even. As Lionel W. McKenzie said to me in the early 1960s when he and other mathematical economists were struggling to prove the existence and uniqueness of an equilibrium within a Walrasian model, "We know that equilibria exist because markets produce them every day. The problem is that we ran into difficulties in demonstrating their existence in our models."

We study the properties of models because experience has shown that doing so yields useful, sometimes powerful, analytical tools that help to explain how the economy actually works. For example, linear programming, a mathematical procedure developed shortly after World War II as a planning instrument for the U. S. Air Force, turned out to be a powerful addition to economic analysis. One important aspect of programming is the concept of duality: for every primal problem in which the levels of linear productive activities are chosen to maximize the value added—subject to the condition that inputs of resources owned by the firm, and not purchased in the market, remain within limits of availability—there is a dual problem in which the shadow prices of these inputs are chosen to minimize their value, subject to the condition that no activity earns a positive profit. The two solutions are equal. The concept of duality, carried over to production theory,

[3] Economists sometimes tend to equate theory with generalizations that involve cause-and-effect statements. I agree that these are a very important subclass of theories, especially if one wants to probe the empirical validity of counterfactual conditional statements, as I have attempted to do in previous studies (e.g., Fogel, 1964; Fogel and Engerman, 1969). However, some theories are purely descriptive. Perhaps the most famous is the Darwinian theory of evolution, which will not support counterfactual conditional statements (cf. Blaug, 1980; Lewontin, 1970). However, even statements that will support counterfactuals are also descriptions, because they purport to describe how one or more variables will change as other variables change (cf. Fogel, 1970). On laws and law-like statements in history, see Joynt and Rescher (1961); on counterfactuals and causal statements, see Simon and Rescher (1966) and Rescher (1971).

made it possible for economic historians and other empirical students of economic growth to circumvent the paucity of data on physical inputs and outputs by using the relatively abundant data on prices to estimate technological change in various industries going as far back as 1600.

Another virtue of mathematical modeling is that it frequently makes apparent not only logical errors but also empirical errors and unwarranted conclusions that beset more informal types of reasoning. Robert M. Solow showed that the widespread belief of the late 1940s and early 1950s that physical capital formation was the key to economic growth stemmed from the assumption that the capital-output ratio and the savings rate were fixed. Using a Cobb-Douglas production function, he demonstrated empirically that in a model with two or more variable inputs, changes in the amount of physical capital (per se) explained only a small part of the record of U.S. economic growth (Solow, 1957).[4]

Thus, history and mathematical models are two productive, often complementary, ways of searching for valid generalizations about the economy.[5] Another case in point is North's use of the price dual in production theory to demonstrate his discovery that most of the productivity gains in ocean shipping between 1600 and 1850 were due not to new technologies but to institutional changes: the elimination of piracy changed the distribution of preexisting types of ships crossing the Atlantic, permitting large, lightly armed vessels with high carrying capacity and low costs to become predominant (North, 1968).

Although the application of the duality theorem provided more precision, it was North's historical research that led to the discovery that the elimination of piracy was crucial to the improvement in productivity. This striking discovery brought new attention to the key role played by the institutional context on the rate of the diffusion of existing technologies. So it is the substance of the findings, not infatuation with the methods, that is crucial in producing valid theoretical generalizations. Neither the elegance of a mathematical model nor the beauty of a literary passage in economic history by itself guarantees that the generalizations derived from each of these sources is useful in giving guidance to policy makers.

[4] One other point worth making about mathematical models pertains to empirical tests of the validity of a theory. Whether the theory comes from a mathematical model or from a study of history, it is often necessary to formulate some aspect of the theory mathematically in order to measure the key variables of the theory or to estimate key parameters. Measurement also involves modeling, although the models used to test or to explore the range of applicability of a particular theory might be quite different from the mathematical model which produced the generalization to which we apply the epithet "theory."

[5] Of course, not every valid generalization about the economy is interesting or revealing. "Food is a necessity of life," is a valid but trite generalization, unworthy of being included in the standard canon of economic theory. There are also trite models—minor variations of previous models that are unenlightening.

I have stressed the distinction between theory and models because a few years ago when I referred to Simon Kuznets as one of the leading economic theorists of the 20th century, I was criticized by some of Kuznets's admirers for exaggerating his accomplishments. Kuznets, of course, was the great empiricist of his era. The procedures he designed for the development of national income accounts and for the empirical study of economic growth still influence current work. However, he was also a theorist of economic growth and set forth a number of generalizations about modern economic growth that remain valid. One of his generalizations was that the sustained growth of per capita income coupled with a sustained increase in population was the defining feature of modern economic growth and that such growth could not have taken place regularly before the early 18th century. Another of Kuznets's generalizations was that a marked change in the structure of economic activity necessarily accompanied modern economic growth, when structure is measured either by the distribution of output or by the distribution of labor inputs.

Among the most influential of Kuznets's generalizations were those that related to population. He pointed out that the changing age distribution contributed significantly to the rate of growth of per capita income. This change in age structure was due primarily to a decline in fertility brought about by the regulation of fertility. Such regulation was promoted by the fact that the major declines in mortality down through the middle of the 20th century had come during infancy and early childhood rather than at later ages. Kuznets also argued that the reduction in completed family size and the fact that this occurred at differential rates in rural and urban areas was an important factor in the adoption of an ethic suitable for modern economic growth. The smaller family, the locus of differential rates of natural increase, and the locus of differential economic opportunities promoted a vast increase in internal migration that led to the removal of younger generations from the influence of the family and exposed them to modern ethics that promoted participation in a rapidly changing economic system. He saw this break between the ties of blood and economic rewards as a central factor in the victory of objective tests of economic performance over the more traditional basis of family and social status in the distribution of income.[6]

I have stressed Kuznet's theoretical generalizations not because I consider all of them to have been validated empirically, but because so many of them are still central to theoretical discussions about economic growth, for both the developed countries and the developing countries. By contrast, *some* of the generalizations derived from the mathematical modeling of economic growth, such as the implications of putty-clay models, ceased to

[6] The material in this and the previous paragraph is drawn mainly from Kuznets (1966), but see also Kuznets (1989).

be of interest shortly after they were put forward, despite the initial enthusiasm for them.[7]

Few theorists have made more effective use of history than Douglass C. North. The 20th-century predecessors to whom I would compare him most closely, in addition to Kuznets, are Schumpeter and Theodore W. Schultz.[8] Schumpeter was the most important growth theorist between the deaths of Smith and Malthus and his own death in 1950. His earlier work focused on long cycles in economic output, which he attributed to fluctuations in the rate of inventions and innovations. His analysis led him to single out entrepreneurs as the dynamic agents of change, to point to the equity effects of economic growth (embodied in his concept of "creative destruction"), and to make the creative clusters of innovations inherently inflationary. It is the late Schumpeter, however, rather than the early one, who is closest to North's concerns. The late Schumpeter focused on the conflict between economic concentration and competitive markets, and between the capitalist system of economic organization and the political, social, and intellectual movements that were hostile to capitalism for ideological reasons. It was these conflicts, he argued, rather than the secular diminution of investment opportunities that threatened the continuation of economic growth under a system of political democracy (cf. Rostow, 1990, especially pp. 233–242).

T. W. Schultz has received the most acclaim for his contributions to the theory of human capital. But that was only one aspect of his broader concern with economic growth and the elimination of poverty. These broader concerns led him to examine closely the impact of government fiscal policies and specific interventions into agriculture in both developed and developing countries, policies that distorted agricultural production and had perverse effects on the distribution of income. Like Schumpeter, Schultz was concerned about new sources of future income growth, and this concern led him to recognize that in the 20th century, human capital had become more important than physical capital in explaining both economic growth and the inequality of the income distribution. His theory of human capital led him to conclude that unregulated high fertility was a major factor in destabilizing the agricultural sector. Such considerations also caused him to emphasize the importance of the investment in improving nutrition and health as a key to economic growth in poor nations and to identify investment in "allocative skills" as a key to dealing with problems of disequilibria (cf. Bowman, 1980).

[7] Note that the word "some" is italicized. Schumpeter was heavily influenced by the mathematical models of Walras; Kuznets by those of Marshall, Pigou, and Gompertz; Schultz by those of Fisher.

[8] Many other leading theorists have relied heavily on historical knowledge. Milton Friedman's *A Monetary History of the United States* (Friedman and Schwartz, 1963), which was cited as part of the basis for his 1976 Nobel Prize, became an instant classic of economic history.

North, like Schumpeter, Kuznets, and Schultz, has drawn primarily on history, rather than on the properties of mathematical models, to develop his theories. As with these three predecessors, the theoretical issues that he has focused on arise from his deep concern with issues of public policy. He shares with Schumpeter, Kuznets, and Schultz a deep knowledge of history, but he is the only professional historian among them, in the sense that much of his work has been aimed at establishing what actually happened in the past. It is a measure of his historical talent that many economic historians still think of him primarily as an economic historian who has made effective use of economic theory and statistics in interpreting history. However, since his book with Lance E. Davis in 1971, *Institutional Change and American Economic Growth*, North has worked primarily as an economic theorist whose wide knowledge of both history and economics has permitted him to become one of the pioneers of the area of theory called "the new institutional economics."[9]

Each of these economists was heavily influenced in the formulation of his theory by the pressing policy issues of his era. Schumpeter was concerned with the unevenness in secular patterns of growth across nations, as well as over time and across classes within nations, an unevenness that created sharp political tensions and promoted international conflicts. Kuznets, during his early years, shared Schumpeter's concerns about the instability of economic growth in particular nations, although he recognized that after aggregating across the advanced European nations, the secular pattern of growth was much more even. Like Schumpeter, he saw technological change as the engine of economic growth but focused on the unevenness brought about by the life cycle of an innovation, the pattern of population change, and the changes in the demand for output. In his later years, during the exceptional worldwide spurt in economic growth that began early in the 1950s, Kuznets focused on the continuing potential for economic growth and the policies that would do most to promote economic growth in the developing nations.

Schultz was influenced in his thinking about human capital by his experiences with postwar reconstruction. Despite the devastation of Europe, all of the war-ravaged countries experienced rapid economic growth in the 1950s, quickly exceeding their prewar levels. This led Schultz to dwell on the key role of human capital in modern economic growth, to consider the possibility that a significant share of the so-called residual factor in economic growth was due to improvements in the quality of the inputs, particularly in the quantity of capital embodied in human labor. Although his empirical work on this question focused on education, Schultz recognized that theo-

[9] The argument of the book was sketched in Davis and North (1970). For a bibliography of North's work through 1993, see *Scandinavian Journal of Economics* 96, 195–99 (1994).

retically improvements in health, in the capacity to process information, in the development of allocative skills, and in on-the-job training might be more important than the effects of formal education per se.

In North's case it was the raging public debates over the proper role of the government in economic development that formed the background to his search for an understanding of the role of the state and of economic institutions in the process of economic growth. Although he recognized that the creation of the state was an essential precondition for economic growth, he also recognized that the state was, in many instances, the cause of economic decline. The critical issue that emerged from his analysis was the nature of the institutions created by the state and the identification of those institutions that promoted economic growth and those that hindered it.

North shares with his three predecessors a recognition of the power of neoclassical theory. All four of them employed the neoclassical price system when assessing the allocation of resources among alternative opportunities. They used the theory of production and recognized the dynamic aspects of competitive markets. They also recognized, however, that neoclassical theory, as each of them found it, was inadequate in dealing with the set of issues on which they focused. In considering the clustering of innovations, Schumpeter argued that relative prices alone could not explain such a creative process. Nevertheless, he was influenced by, and drawn to, Walras's system of general equilibrium, which he made his point of departure.

Kuznets used macroeconomic theory as his guide in working out national income accounts and brought the theory of relative prices into account in the construction of indexes of inputs and output. On the other hand, he was not only one of the early discoverers of the life-cycle pattern in wages and in savings rates, but he also made use of these patterns, as well as international differences in the way that labor markets operated, to explain the relatively high rates of inequality in third-world nations.

During the 1960s Schultz argued strongly against the widely accepted view that the marginal product of peasants in less developed nations was zero, pointing out the role of optimality and rationality in the context of traditional farming at that same time. Nevertheless, he strongly supported government action to improve education, to promote fertility control, and to advance productivity within agriculture.

The best description of North's approach to neoclassical theory is contained in his Nobel lecture. "Neoclassical theory," he writes, "is simply an inappropriate tool to analyze and prescribe policies that will induce development. It is concerned with the operation of markets, not with how markets develop" (North, 1994, p. 359). Nevertheless, in his analysis of changing institutions over time, North does not discard neoclassical theory, but modifies it. What he retained was "the fundamental assumption of scarcity and hence competition and the analytical tools of microeconomic theory." What he modified is "the rationality assumption." What he added "is the dimension of time" (North, 1994, p. 359).

I will not attempt to summarize North's contributions to the theory of economic growth and the theory of the new institutional economics since they are too well known. Instead, I want to comment on a few aspects of the development of his theories.

It is important to keep in mind how early in the post–World War II era of high rates of economic growth, North recognized the creative and dynamic role of competitive markets as an engine of economic growth. North's argument in his 1961 book that the export sector, particularly the exports of raw material from the South, was the engine that spurred U. S. economic growth during the first 40 years of the new nation, and perhaps down to 1860, was highly controversial at the time. In the late 1950s and the early 1960s much economic thought was still governed by the experiences of the interwar period, which included the widely held proposition that reliance on exports was a developmental trap that made rich countries of the world richer at the expense of the former colonial nations. In 1961 the three decades of extraordinary export-led Japanese economic growth was just getting underway, and the similar experiences of South Korea, Taiwan, and the other rapidly growing countries of South East Asia, including South China, were far in the future.

This early break with prevailing opinions played a role in North's recognition that the same stimulus did not always have the same effect and led him to focus on the role of economic institutions in shaping the capacity of economies to exploit economic opportunities. Because economic historians are above all concerned with the nature and significance of economic institutions, it was natural for him to focus on this question. Moreover, the theoretical breakthrough of Ronald H. Coase on transactions costs and North's close association with a number of economists who were attempting to develop its implications led him to work out a theory of the relationship of institutions to the emergence of modern economic growth. His 1971 book with Lance Davis demonstrated that the American experience was consistent with the proposition that capturing the gains from exchange often required changes in property rights and the invention of new institutional arrangements and forms of economic organization. That book laid the basis for a theory that institutional change was a necessary condition for modern economic growth.

Rereading the Davis-North book more than two decades after it was published, I was impressed both with how much of the current theory was already adumbrated in that book and how much had to be investigated to reach the formulations of the most recent work. In North's Nobel lecture he defined institutions as a combination "of formal constraints (e.g., rules, laws, constitutions), informal constraints (e.g., norms of behavior, conventions, self-imposed codes of conduct), and their enforcement characteristics"

(North, 1994, p. 360). This definition is far from the use of the term "institutions" that was common among economic historians in the 1960s, which tended to focus on organizations of various sorts. North's current use of the term "institution" is similar to the anthropologist's use of the term "culture," but it is more sharply focused on those aspects of culture that immediately bear on the operation of exchange and that help to produce "efficient markets."

Another important aspect of the evolution of North's theory is his link between technological change and the growth of the transactions sector of the economy. This is not an entirely new insight since what North calls the transactions sector makes up most of what Colin Clark called the tertiary sector and Kuznets called the "S" sector. Both Clark and Kuznets had established that this S or services sector, whether measured by labor inputs or by output, had become the largest sector of the economy in the United States and other rich nations by World War II or shortly thereafter. Kuznets had noted that many of these functions were originally conducted by manufacturing firms directly, but the advantages of increasing specialization led the manufacturing firms to shed them (Clark, 1951; Kuznets, 1952).

What North added was recognition of the extreme sensitivity of the cost of transactions to institutional arrangements. He also gave the transaction sector a much larger role in inducing technological change, which was not just the passive product of technological advances. To a large extent, the innovation of technological change depended on what he has called "efficient markets," markets that "are created in the real world when competition is strong enough via arbitrage and efficient information feedback to approximate the Coase zero-transaction-cost conditions and the parties can realize the gains from trade inherent in the neoclassical argument"(North, 1994, p. 360). Although such efficient markets are rarely realized, they can be more or less approximated, depending on the institutional context.

Another important contribution was North's distinction between institutions (the rules of the game) and organizations (the players). The organizations that come into being reflect the institutional inducements and the way that organizations and institutions interact to determine how receptive given societies will be to technological change. In this connection North emphasizes the role of ideology in creating a society receptive to technological change. Here again North touches on one of Kuznets's points, but unlike Kuznets, who identified the severance of the link between kinship and rewards as a function of changes in demography, North sees the change primarily in the realm of ideology and politics.

North has gone beyond his predecessors in disclosing the "unique process in historic time," to use Schumpeter's words, that yielded "credible commitment" to the type of secure property rights in which exchange could flourish. One of the high points of this work is North's 1989 paper with

Barry R. Weingast on "The Evolution of Institutions Governing Public Choice in Seventeenth-Century England."[10] This paper reveals the particular attributes that a professional historian brings to theoretical thinking. North and Weingast show how crucial the Glorious Revolution of 1688 was for the institutional changes that led to secure property rights. These institutional changes included not only limitations on the unilateral expropriations of the crown but limitations on the capacity of Parliament to act arbitrarily by establishing an independent judiciary powerful enough to curb the government's ability to renege on its agreements with businesses. North and Weingast also trace the fiscal revolution induced by these institutional changes and the impetus given to private capital markets, including the rise of banks and an increasingly differentiated set of financial instruments.

Perhaps the most far-reaching finding of this paper is the role of contingency in the institutional changes that followed from the Glorious Revolution, because these changes depended on the military victory of Parliament over the army of Charles I and the later victory of the Whig faction within Parliament. That institutional revolution did not have to take place in England during that period. The Whigs could have lost. Chance may not be important in explaining how an economic system operates, but it is, as North has emphasized, often important in explaining how an economic system got to be that way or why it subsequently changed. This, of course, is the point of the path dependency that W. Brian Arthur (1989) and Paul A. David (1985) have spelled out and that North has incorporated inventively in his theory. Recognizing that contingency often plays an important role in institutional change is part of North's rationale for questioning the use of rational choice models in explaining the evolution of institutions. It also suggests that theorists of institutional change might find models of sequential choice a more fitting framework for formulating their theories.

Models of sequential choice are not only natural vehicles for the representation of path dependency, but they allow for the incorporation of much greater complexity than do rational choice models, including sharp discontinuities. Sequential models can accommodate particular (as opposed to undifferentiated) chance events, such as those that played a large role in the defeat of Charles I and in the victory of the Whig faction over James II. When dealing with complex institutional changes, models of sequential choice involve a succession of transition matrices that give the odds at successive branching points of moving from one state to another. Transition probabilities can be estimated by using techniques such as ecological regressions. The values of these transition probabilities can then be

[10] The main title of the paper is "Constitutions and Commitment"; the portion quoted in text is the subtitle.

related to the underlying social, political, and economic factors that affected them.[11]

It is the kind of complexity permitted by models of sequential choice that North has in mind when he states that he added the dimension of time. He is, of course, aware that differential equations have been an important tool of the theory of economic growth since the 1950s and that they have been useful tools in economic history for certain aspects of the empirical study of economic growth (cf. Fogel and Engerman, 1969, 1974; North, 1968; Steckel, 1985). However, restricting analysis to equations that are continuous and differentiable creates a severe obstacle when one aims to identify, as North has, the contextually unique processes involved in institutional change. He has been concerned not only with identifying key growth promoting or inhibiting institutions, but also with analyzing those critical junctures in historical time during which such institutions either opened or foreclosed opportunity. As examples, he points to controls over economic exchanges retained by the Spanish church and state that hindered economic growth during the 17th, 18th, and 19th centuries in Spain and its colonies. By contrast the limitation of the power of church and state in economic activities during these centuries led to rapid structural change and economic growth in Britain and its colonies.[12]

The movement of British jurists and political leaders toward laissez-faire policies is intimately connected with the successes of the English Civil War and the Glorious Revolution. The codification of laissez-faire in common law by jurists, in economic theory by Adam Smith, and in statute law by Parliament may suggest a process so regular that it can easily be misinterpreted as inevitable. More detailed consideration of the historical events that led up to the laissez-faire victories reveals critical junctures, some of which are described by North and Weingast, at which hotly contested issues could easily have gone against such a development. What North means by bringing time into neoclassical theory, then, is the use of models that incorporate the historical complexity of institutional change and which recognize that the historical context in which a specific change takes place is often decisive in determining how that change unfolds.

Similarly, North's modification of the rationality assumption involves an expansion of the postulates normally employed by economists. Postulates by their nature are beyond proof. Although economists regularly

[11] See Fogel (1992b) for a fuller exposition of the case for models of sequential choice.

[12] This contrast between the economic efficacy of Spanish and British institutions has been emphasized by historians of slavery, such as Stanley Elkins (1959), Sidney Mintz (1969), Herbert Klein (1967, 1986), Degler (1971), and Eugene Genovese (1971). They called attention to institutional differences between Spain, Portugal, France, and England to explain why slavery developed so differently in the United States and in Latin American nations.

include postulates in their models, they have in recent decades shied away from those that clearly pertain to political and religious ideologies. This is a strange limitation to North and other historians who have studied the role of political and religious ideologies in shaping the development of economic institutions. The struggle to limit state intervention in economic markets was, to a large extent, rooted in Protestant radicalism, which rejected the domination of religion by bishops, as well as the proposition that only kings were divinely appointed. Radical theories of church government, developed in the 16th and 17th centuries, became secularized in the moral philosophies of the 17th, 18th, and 19th centuries, and they provided the theoretical basis for the popular democracies that emerged in the 19th and 20th centuries. The same religious radicalism—embodied in Quakerism, in the evangelical movement within the Church of England, and in the evangelicalism of the Congregationalists, Unitarians, Presbyterians, Methodists, and Baptists—gave rise to the movement that destroyed production based on slave labor, despite the profitability of that system and its high levels of productivity when conjoined with the gang system.[13]

* * *

To get some measure of the scope of North's intellectual influence, I analyzed the citations of his work in the on-line database, "Social SciSearch," which unfortunately only goes back to 1972. Between 1972 and 1985, citations of his work averaged about 50 per year. Between 1985 and 1989, the average rose to about 70 per year. During the first half of the 1990s, the annual average exceeded 130 per year. Thus North's intellectual influence has expanded remarkably. He is currently not only the most widely cited economic historian, but he is among the most widely cited economists, regardless of field.

Analysis of the disciplinary affiliations of the individuals who have been citing him during the last five years is also revealing. As might be expected, economists were the largest single group, accounting for 53 percent of all of the scholars whose disciplines have so far been identified. However, North is widely cited in the other social sciences, especially in political science and sociology, which together account for a quarter of all the citations. There were also concentrations in law, as well as in management science and public administration. The breakdown of the citations by economists was also interesting. Slightly more than one-fifth of these readers were economic historians. Another 53 percent came from the other

[13] On the role of religious radicalism in British political theory, law, and politics, see Walzer (1965), J. D. Clark (1985, 1986, 1994); compare with Brown (1991). On the influence of religious issues on Smith and other economists, see Minowitz (1993), Dooley (1995), and Temperley (1977). The literature on the role of religion in the abolition of slavery is very large. See the citations in Davis (1984), Drescher (1986), Fogel (1989, 1994), Noll (1990), and Swierenga (1990).

applied fields of economics. The remaining 25 percent were economic theorists.[14]

I close as I began, by emphasizing the importance of the historical tradition in economic theory. The return to history as a source of inspiration for theory is particularly marked in industrial organization, the main home of the new institutional economics. But it is also quite marked in the "new growth theory," which Paul Romer and others also refer to as "endogenous growth theory" (Romer, 1994; cf. Solow, 1994). It is important to note that although North is the most prominent of the theorists among the economic historians, he is not the only economic historian who is widely acknowledged for his contributions to theory. The list is too long to be enumerated here, but it includes many students and colleagues of North.

REFERENCES

Arthur, B. (1989). Competing technologies, increasing returns, and lock-in by historical events. *Economic Journal* **99,** 116–31.

Blaug, M. (1980). *The Methodology of Economics, or, How Economists Explain.* Cambridge University Press, New York.

Bowman, M. J. (1980). On Theodore W. Schultz's contributions to economics. *Scandinavian Journal of Economics* **82,** 80–107.

Brown, R. (1991). *Church and State in Modern Britain.* Routledge, London and New York.

Clark, C. (1951). *The Conditions of Economic Progress,* 2nd ed. Macmillan, London.

Clark, J. C. D. (1985). *English Society, 1688–1832: Ideology, Social Structure, and Political Practice During the Ancien Regime.* Cambridge University Press, Cambridge, UK, and New York.

Clark, J. C. D. (1986). *Revolution and Rebellion: State and Society in England in the Seventeenth and Eighteenth Centuries.* Cambridge University Press, Cambridge, UK, and New York.

Clark, J. C. D. (1994). *The Language of Liberty, 1660–1832: Political Discourse and Social Dynamics in the Anglo-American World.* Cambridge University Press, Cambridge, UK, and New York.

Creedy, J. (1992). *Demand and Exchange in Economic Analysis: A History from Cournot to Marshall.* Elgar, Aldershot, UK.

Davenant, C. (1699). *An Essay Upon the Probable Methods of Making a People Gainers in the Balance of Trade.* James Knapton, London.

[14] "Social SciSearch" produced 603 entries for journal articles in which North's work was cited (citations in books and book chapters were not included) written by 627 separate authors. Journals were classified according to the "journal subject category" field from the database. Authors were classified by discipline, based mainly on academic department or other professional affiliation. If the article entry from the database did not supply this information, other sources, such as the *National Faculty Directory* or biographical information published with other writings by the author, were consulted. In classifying the economists as economic historians, theorists, or applied economists, the database "EconLit" was often used to get a broader sample of their works.

David, P. A. (1985). Clio and the economics of QWERTY. *American Economic Review* **75**(2), 332–337.

Davis, D. B. (1984). *Slavery and Human Progress.* Oxford University Press, New York.

Davis, L. E., and North, D. C. (1971). *Institutional Change and American Economic Growth.* Cambridge University Press, Cambridge, UK.

Davis, L. E. and North, D. C. (1971). Institutional change and American economic growth: A first step towards a theory of institutional innovation. *Journal of Economic History* **30,** 131–149.

Debreu, G. (1984). Economic theory in the mathematical mode. *Scandinavian Journal of Economics* **86,** 393–410.

Degler, C. N. (1971). *Neither Black nor White: Slavery and Race Relations in Brazil and the United States.* Macmillan, New York.

Dooley, P. C. (1995). Review of *Profits, priests, and princes: Adam Smith's emancipation of economics from politics and religion,* by Peter Minowitz. *Economic Journal* **105,** 770–772.

Drescher, S. (1986). *Capitalism and Antislavery.* Macmillan, London.

Elkins, S. M. (1959). *Slavery: A Problem in American Institutional and Intellectual Life.* University of Chicago Press, Chicago.

Fogel, R. W. (1964). *Railroads and American Economic Growth: Essays in Econometric History.* Johns Hopkins University Press, Baltimore.

Fogel, R. W. (1970). History and retrospective econometrics. *History and Theory* **9,** 245–259.

Fogel, R. W. (1989). *Without Consent or Contract: The Rise and Fall of American Slavery.* Norton, New York.

Fogel, R. W. (1992a). Second thoughts on the European escape from hunger: Famines, chronic malnutrition, and mortality rates. In *Nutrition and Poverty* (S. R. Osmani, ed.), pp. 243–286. Clarendon Press, Oxford, UK.

Fogel, R. W. (1992b). Problems in modeling complex dynamic interactions: The political realignment of the 1850s. *Economics and Politics* **4,** 215–254.

Fogel, R. W. (1994). The quest for the moral problem of slavery. *33rd Annual Robert Fortenbaugh Memorial Lecture,* Gettysburg College, Gettysburg, PA.

Fogel, R. W., and Engerman, S. (1969). A model for the explanation of industrial expansion during the nineteenth century: With an application to the American iron industry. *Journal of Political Economy* **77,** 306–328.

Fogel, R. W., and Engerman, S. (1974). *Time on the Cross: The Economics of American Negro Slavery,* 2 vols. Little, Brown, Boston.

Friedman, M., and Schwartz, A. J. (1963). *A Monetary History of the United States 1867–1960.* Princeton University Press, Princeton, NJ.

Genovese, E. (1971). *In Red and Black: Marxian Explorations in Southern and Afro-American History.* Vintage Books, New York.

Jevons, W. S. (1970). *The Theory of Political Economy* (R. D. Collison Black, ed.). Penguin, Harmondsworth, UK. (Original work published 1871)

Joynt, C. B., and Rescher, N. (1961). The problem of uniqueness in history. *History and Theory* **1,** 150–162.

Klein, H. S. (1967). *Slavery in the Americas: A Comparative Study of Virginia and Cuba.* University of Chicago Press, Chicago.

Klein, H. S. (1986). *African Slavery in Latin America and the Caribbean.* Oxford University Press, New York.

Kuznets, S. (1952). Long-term changes in the national income of the United States of America since 1870. In *Income and Wealth of the United States: Trends and Structure,* Ser. 2, pp. 29–241. International Association for Research in Income and Wealth, Bowes & Bowes, Cambridge, UK.

Kuznets, S. (1966). *Modern Economic Growth: Rate, Structure, and Spread.* Yale University Press, New Haven, CT.

Kuznets, S. (1989). *Economic Development, the Family, and Income Distribution: Selected Essays.* Cambridge University Press, New York.
Lewontin, R. (1970). Discussion (with W. H. Walsh, F. I. Greenstein, and G. R. Elton) of R. W. Fogel, History and retrospective econometrics. *History and Theory* **9,** 260–264.
Minowitz, P. (1993). *Profits, Priests, and Princes: Adam Smith's Emancipation of Economics from Politics and Religion.* Stanford University Press, Stanford, CA.
Mintz, S. W. (1969). Slavery and emergent capitalism. In *Slavery in the New World* (L. Foner and E. D. Genovese, eds.), pp. 27–37. Prentice Hall, Englewood Cliffs, NJ.
Niehans, J. (1990). *A History of Economic Theory: Classic Contributions, 1720–1980.* Johns Hopkins University Press, Baltimore and London.
Noll, M. A., ed. (1990). *Religion and American Politics: From the Colonial Period to the 1980s.* Oxford University Press, New York.
North, D. C. (1968). Sources of productivity change in ocean shipping 1600–1850. *Journal of Political Economy* **76,** 953–970.
North, D. C. (1994). Economic performance through time. *American Economic Review* **84,** 359–368.
North, D. C., and Weingast, B. R. (1989). Constitutions and commitment: The evolution of institutions governing public choice in seventeenth-century England. *Journal of Economic History* **49,** 803–832.
Rescher, N. (1971). Counterfactual hypotheses, laws, and dispositions. *Nous* **5,** 157–179.
Romer, P. M. (1994). The origins of endogenous growth. *Journal of Economic Perspectives* **8,** 3–22.
Rostow, W. W. (1990). *Theorists of Economic Growth from David Hume to the Present.* Oxford University Press, New York.
Schumpeter, J. A. (1954). *A History of Economic Analysis* (E. B. Schumpeter, ed.). Oxford University Press, New York.
Simon, H. A., and Rescher, N. (1966). Cause and counterfactual. *Philosophy of Science* **33,** 323–340.
Slicher von Bath, B. H. (1963). *The Agrarian History of Western Europe, AD 500–1850.* Edward Arnold, London.
Solow, R. M. (1957). Technical Change and the Aggregate Production Function. *Review of Economics and Statistics* **39,** 312–320.
Solow, R. M. (1994). Perspective on growth theory. *Journal of Economic Perspectives* **8,** 45–54.
Steckel, R. (1985). *The Economics of U.S. Slave and Southern White Fertility.* Garland Publishing, New York.
Swierenga, R. P. (1990). Ethnoreligious political behavior in the mid-nineteenth century: Voting, values, cultures. In *Religion and American Politics: From the Colonial Period to the 1980s* (M. A. Noll, ed.), pp. 146–71. Oxford University Press, New York.
Temperley, H. (1977). Capitalism, Slavery and Ideology. *Past and Present* **75,** 94–118.
Walzer, M. (1965). *The Revolution of the Saints: A Study in the Origins of Radical Politics.* Harvard University Press, Cambridge, MA.
Wrigley, E. A. (1987). *People, Cities and Wealth.* Basil Blackwell, London.

PART II

ECONOMIC HISTORY

III

The Political Economy of Warfare and Taxation in Early Modern Europe: Historical Lessons for Economic Development

Philip T. Hoffman
Jean-Laurent Rosenthal

Douglass C. North has devoted much of his career to hunting the causes of long-term economic growth. Throughout his quest, he has urged economists to look beyond the usual sources of growth and exhorted them to pay particular attention to institutional change. Institutions, he argues, are not fixed and exogenous, and their variation is ultimately what explains why some economies remain mired in abject poverty while others manage to prosper.

Prominent among the institutions that figure in North's own work are political ones, especially the political institutions governing property rights. They take on particular significance in his argument about economic growth in Europe between the end of the Middle Ages and the 19th century—the so-called early modern period of state formation and preparation for the Industrial Revolution (for what follows, see North, 1981, pp. 146–157; cf. North and Thomas, 1973; North and Weingast, 1989). In this period, according to North, it was the growing states that determined property rights, and the property rights in turn explained whether an economy eventually grew, as in England and the Netherlands, or stagnated or declined, as in France and Spain. Whether the appropriate property rights were established resulted, in general, from a state's fiscal policies, which varied from country to country. While parliamentary regimes taxed lightly, absolute monarchies taxed heavily, undermining the incentives for growth. Of course, one other great determinant of fiscal policy existed—warfare. It was to pay for warfare that the fisc was created in early modern Europe, and when disastrous fiscal policies were imposed on an economy it was usually to defray for the costs of war.

North's argument neatly integrates warfare, fiscal regimes, property rights, and economic growth, but few scholars have really pursued it, either in early modern Europe or the contemporary world. Historians, to be sure, have written copiously about warfare and the development of the fisc, but they usually ignore the link to economic growth. As for economists, they tend to overlook politics and even more so warfare. Finally, political scientists divide their research in a way that makes integration difficult. The ones who study war are specialists in international relations and have little interest in economic growth or even in the domestic politics of taxation. That remains the domain of comparativists, who usually shun warfare. No one, it thus seems, is willing to push North's argument further.

That is what we shall begin to do here. Our aim is to evaluate North's argument and recast it using a formal model of warfare and the domestic politics of taxation in early modern Europe. Our model is admittedly simplistic, depending as it does on a particular parameterization. It certainly cannot answer all the questions about warfare, economic growth, and the politics of the fisc, even in early modern Europe. But it does reveal how warfare and the nature of political regimes shaped property rights in the era before the Industrial Revolution. The property rights in turn affected economic growth.

III.1. PROPERTY RIGHTS, THE FISC, AND WARFARE IN EARLY MODERN EUROPE

Early modern Europe offers numerous examples of the effect property rights had on economic growth. Perhaps the most vivid ones come from agriculture, the largest sector of the early modern economy, which languished when property rights shackled growth. In early modern Spain, for instance, farming suffered grievously from the depredations of the Mesta, the privileged royal sheep raisers' monopoly. The Mesta had rights to drive sheep across farmland throughout much of the country, and the damage caused by the animals discouraged improvements in arable farming (deVries, 1976, pp. 49–50; North and Thomas, 1973, pp. 4–5). Similarly, in Old-Regime France, it would have paid to drain marshes and to irrigate dry land, and agricultural productivity would have benefited greatly. Yet when entrepreneurs initiated drainage or irrigation projects, they ran afoul of overlapping property rights, and their projects were smothered in endless litigation (Rosenthal, 1992).

Why did property rights remain so wasteful and inefficient in economies that were haunted by malnourishment and even occasional famine (Fogel, 1993)? Why was it impossible to find either a private or a public solution to the problems? In the case of the Mesta, a private solution was certainly conceivable—having the arable farmers pay the sheep owners to stay away—but it required organizing the arable farmers, a diffuse and powerless group. After all, these were not peasants from the same village bargaining over access to a local pasture. They were farmers spread throughout Spain. Getting them to make payments would founder on free riding—a difficulty recognized long ago by Ronald Coase (1960).[1] As for the obvious public solution to the problem—restricting the Mesta's rights—the hurdle here was the Spanish crown. Behind the Mesta stood a powerful pressure group. More important, the Mesta was a significant source of revenue for the crown, one that could be taxed at low administrative cost (Elliott, 1963, pp. 116–117). Restricting it would have hurt the crown financially, at least in the short run, and long-run growth might not have replenished the royal coffers quickly enough. In the case of the Mesta, the state was thus the villain. With a private solution out of the question, only the state could have resolved the problem of the Mesta in favor of long-term growth, but for important political reasons it refused to do so.

The state was the villain in France as well. The ultimate obstacle there was the French legal system, which encouraged lawsuits against drainage and irrigation projects, lawsuits filed by defendants who sought to siphon off profits from the project. The suits in turn upset or discouraged private bargaining. The legal system as a whole inspired such destructive litigiousness, from the rules of evidence to the fact that judicial compensation rose with the number of cases a judge tried. Worst of all was the system's lack of finality. It was impossible to get a definitive decision, even if one appealed to the royal council, and any private bargain that resolved the property rights for an irrigation project might be upset years later in court. Why then irrigate farmland or drain marshes when private bargains were insecure and profits could always be taken away (Rosenthal, 1992)?[2]

Although complaints against the legal system were widespread on the eve of the French Revolution, reform proved politically impossible. Changing the judges' compensation would wreak havoc with the sale of ju-

[1] Organizing the farmers to pay off the sheep owners might have also had unpalatable political consequences, for once organized the farmers could more easily push for tax reductions.

[2] The state's fiscal system raised yet another barrier to drainage because much of the drained land fell into the hands of privileged landowners and hence disappeared from the tax roles. From the fisc's point of view, an undrained marsh might paradoxically be worth more than valuable drained farmland.

dicial offices, a cheap way for the French state to borrow. Streamlining courts so as to create one supreme authority at the top would break the unwritten rules of royal politics. The crown had stitched the kingdom together by according judicial privileges to powerful interest groups. Abolishing their privileges, even for the sake of judicial rationality, was out of the question. Finally, repeated legal appeals served the interests of judges, royal agents, and even the king himself. They all used the appeal process to extract revenue. It is no surprise then that legal reform required a bloody revolution.

The common thread in both examples is the state, and above all the fisc, which hindered judicial reform in France and ruled out a public solution to the difficulties raised by the Mesta in Spain. The state—and the fiscal system in particular—bore ultimate responsibility for the burdensome property rights. The two cases, it should be stressed, were hardly isolated, for there were many other instances in which the early modern state interfered with property rights to the detriment of the economy. The state might (to limit ourselves to just one other example) grant monopolies to guilds, which restricted commerce and limited technical change. The reasons, once again, were often fiscal, suggesting that the operations of the fisc ought to explain much of early modern economic performance. That European states operated inefficient fiscal systems is really no surprise; but the roots of that inefficiency and its consequences have yet to be explained.

One might suppose that the connections between fiscal regime and the economy were actually quite simple. Absolute monarchies would tax heavily to wage war, and consequently they experienced slow growth. Parliamentary regimes would hold taxes in check, and as a result their economies would prosper. That is part of North's argument, and it would win the assent of many historians. The reality, though, is that real per capita tax levels were actually high in the thriving economies of early modern Holland or 18th-century Britain, where representative assemblies restrained the fisc. Taxes were relatively low in the less prosperous economies of France and Spain, where bellicose absolute monarchs held sway. In fact, by the late 18th century, the French tax burden was not only low in absolute terms, it also took up a far lower share of per capita income—nearly half what it did in Britain (Brewer, 1989; Hoffman and Norberg, 1994; Mathias and O'Brien, 1976).

Taking our cue from this evidence, we argue that the fiscal inefficiency of early modern states derived from a widespread political equilibrium. The political equilibrium was the divided fiscal authority that characterized most states up to the 18th century, with the notable exception of Britain and perhaps Holland. In countries of divided fiscal authority, rulers could not support needed changes in property rights that undermined the tax base, because they could not create new taxes to compensate for that reduced tax base. As a result, a country with divided fiscal regimes often ended up with rigid property rights, and its property rights failed to evolve even when their inefficiency was well known, as was the case with both the Mesta and undrained marshes. Although average tax rates may have been low in such a country, the fiscal regime ended up hurting the economy. The cause was the effect that taxes had at the margin. Even though an absolutist regime collected relatively little tax revenue overall, its taxes could be disastrous at the margin. The high marginal tax rates would bring transactions to a halt in taxable sectors of the economy, and they would certainly drive resources into the large number of activities that, for political reasons, remained tax exempt. The crown's only response to the erosion of the tax base would be to enact legislation to reduce the mobility of investment. Per capita taxation would then remain low even though marginal rates were high. But in the meantime incentives would be distorted and growth undermined.

Such a process could in fact account for lower per capita tax levies under absolutist regimes. There are signs that the it was perhaps underway in parts of Germany, and it was certainly at work in France where (to consider only one of many examples) the tax-exempt elite bought up acres of farmland from tax-paying peasants.[3] The result, in all likelihood, was overinvestment in land and underinvestment in industry and commerce. Not surprisingly, France (other absolutists states were hardly different here) tried to staunch the flow of assets out of the taxable sector. Absolute monarchies passed laws and erected cumbersome bureaucracies to monitor tax compliance and limit tax evasion, leaving their fiscal systems intrusive and quite inefficient.[4]

What then motivated these fiscal policies in early modern Europe? What drove the early modern fisc? The answer is simple: warfare. Practically the only goal of early modern rulers was to wage war, whether for the glory of a monarch, as in the France of Louis XIV, or for the defense of a homeland, as in the Dutch battles against Spain. Warfare had created the European state at the end of the Middle Ages (cf. Tilly, 1990).[5] It begot the officials and the permanent taxation that paid the rising costs of armies, navies, and fortifications. Military expenses dominated state budgets: to the military expenses themselves one must add spending on foreign affairs, which amounted to subsidies granted allies, and debt service, which paid for wars past (Table III.1). By modern standards, military expenditure was already large in peace time. Not surprisingly, it loomed even bigger during

[3] Hoffman (1986) discusses the French case and also cites an example from Germany.

[4] The argument here is not novel (cf. North, 1981, pp. 147–157; Olson, 1982; de Vries, 1976).

[5] Revisionists have recently questioned this assertion; for a discussion and an effective refutation, see Lynn (1993, 1994).

TABLE III.1 Military Spending and Related Expenses as a Percent of Total Government Spending

Country	Period	Military spending alone	Military spending plus foreign affairs	Military spending, foreign affairs, and debt service
Britain	1689–1697	74	—	—
	1702–1713	66	—	—
	1739–1748	64	—	—
	1756–1763	71	—	—
	1775–1783	61	—	—
France	1628	—	47	73
	1635	—	21	95
	1651	—	15	94
	1752*	42	50	71
Habsburg Monarchy	1768*	42	—	76
Brandenburg Prussia	*ca.* 1740	≈80	—	—
	ca. 1786*	≤70	—	—
Bavaria	1760	32	—	—

* year of peace

Source: Brewer (1989, p. 40); Bayard (1988, pp. 31–36); Riley (1986, pp. 57–58); Hassinger (1978, pp. 652–655).

Note: All years are periods of warfare unless otherwise noted. Because early modern records do not clearly indicate for what purpose money was spent, all of the percentages in the table are at best approximations. In particular, they do not necessarily take into account funds spent locally that do not pass through the central treasury. In the case of France, Bayard gives figures for the years 1599–1653. Her military spending, debt, and foreign affairs, include all *comptants.* Of the years she covers, 1628 is the one with the largest fraction spent on the military and foreign affairs, 1651 is the year with the smallest fraction, and 1635 is the year France entered into open war with Spain.

hostilities, and in a continent of sovereign states battles were practically incessant. Indeed, war haunted Europe almost constantly until the nineteenth century, when diplomacy was revolutionized and states grew strong enough to quash civil war (Schroeder, 1994, pp. vii–xiv).

War itself, it is important to note, damaged the economy in ways that compounded the harm caused by the fisc. The damage that war did was both direct and indirect. The direct damage resulted from the undisciplined behavior of early modern troops, who, when funds were in arrears, would requisition supplies and lay waste even to friendly terrain. They regularly seized livestock and seed corn—both agricultural capital—and held civilians for ransom. Prudent peasants fled and stayed away if maneuvers lasted long. Meanwhile, weeds and brush quickly choked their fields, destroying years of capital invested in clearing land. Trade soon collapsed and agricultural productivity plummeted. It might take a generation to recover (Gutmann, 1980; Hoffman, 1996). Beyond the harm to agricultural trade and capital, warfare also destroyed people. Soldiers carried new diseases as they marched. Fleeing civilians did the same. In the short run, deaths soared, although the long-term effects on the population were probably small (Cabourdin *et al.,* Fogel, 1993; Walter and Schofield, 1989; Weir, 1989).

Worse still were the consequences for financial capital. With warfare, expenses shot skyward, and because taxes never kept pace, states had to borrow to meet the costs of war. At war's end, default was a tempting option, and nearly every western European country yielded to its siren call, particularly when wars lasted long. If creditors subsequently refused to lend, states resorted to a variety of expedients such as the sale of government offices—in effect borrowing from officials whose ability to pressure the government might make them willing to lend. If such expedients failed, states raised money by manipulating the currency. They debased the coinage, as in Central Europe during the Thirty Years War, or issued enough paper money to unleash rapid inflation, as in France during the Law affair (1716–1720) and the Revolution (Hoffman *et al.,* 1995; Sargent and Velde, 1995; Sussman, 1993; White, 1995).

Currency manipulation did more than just harm the state's own creditors, who (as long as their loans were voluntary) could charge a risk premium for government loans. It struck at all lenders and indeed at all parties to long-term contracts. The only way to avoid injury was to write contracts stipulating payment in specie or in kind. That escape ruled out the convenience of money, an obvious burden on long-term transactions. Worse yet, it was sometimes illegal. In France, for example, most long-term loans could not specify in-kind payment, and most long-term contracts could not demand a specified quantity of silver or gold. With no way to parry the effects of currency manipulation, investors and other vulnerable parties shunned long-term contracts. They preferred hoarding, short-term deals, or the purchase of secure physical assets such as real estate. Investment and long-term lending undoubtedly suffered as a result.

We can see as much if we look at the evolution of lending in Paris after the Law affair, when the inflation wiped out half of private lenders' capital. Not surprisingly, the financial market was devastated and lenders so terrified that they forsook long-term loans for a generation (Hoffman *et al.,* 1995). And the Paris bourse was forever overshadowed by the exchanges in London and Amsterdam.

Economic historians have not yet tallied all the long-term effects of warfare and its attendant fiscal exactions, though the evidence from agriculture alone suggests that war's impact was far from negligible. Nor shall we attempt such a full accounting here. We will turn instead to another problem—sketching a simple model of the financial trade-off that rulers faced when states went to war. We must admit at the outset our model's limitations. It will perhaps shed little light on civil strife, such as the French Wars of Religion, or on revolts and defensive wars, such as the lengthy Dutch struggle against Spain.[6] Furthermore, the sort of decision making the model assumes may not completely suit arenas like the Thirty Years War, with their Wallensteins and other independent warlords. Still, one can try to model the politics of fighting wars and of paying the bills. Contemporaries knew full well that warfare demanded money. It thus seems quite reasonable to create a model describing how politics affected the fiscal and military decisions that rulers made.

III.2 MODELING WARFARE AND TAXATION IN EARLY MODERN EUROPE

To model the fiscal constraints faced by 17th-century rulers, we must consider their primary activity—going to war. Typically, the rulers who made decisions about war in early modern Europe were monarchs, and the following model describes their decisions in a simple way. But it does incorporate three key elements: taxation and its constraints, an explicit process of military competition, and an allocation of the nonfiscal effects of war.

To keep matters from getting out of hand, we ignore a number of obvious complications. The first is that war itself can change political institutions, a problem that is dealt with elsewhere.[7] Here we take political institutions as given for each country in early modern Europe. The assumption is less restrictive than it might seem, for in Europe it was by and large domestic politics rather than international relations that drove political change (Hale, 1985, Chapter 9).

Second, we limit ourselves to the simple case of an initial decision to go to war and the ensuing stage of imposing taxes. Although a fully dynamic model would be valuable, most of the additional insights would con-

[6] Among the defensive wars that the model does not suit are battles against an invader who seeks to topple an existing dynasty. Such wars were uncommon in early modern Europe, though, at least when the existing dynasty still had control of foreign policy—the situation we are considering.

[7] For what follows, the essential assumption is that the extent of the elite's control over taxation (the parameter β defined below) is exogenous. Rosenthal (forthcoming) takes up the case of an endogenous β, which might be affected, for example, by the outcome of a war.

cern international relations—an aspect of the problem that we wish to de-emphasize. A dynamic model would yield little that is new about the problem that actually interests us—taxes.[8]

Finally, because we focus is the problem of paying for war, we neglect the issues of technological change and strategic ability. Changes in military technology, we would argue, brought temporary rather than long-term advantages to certain countries (cf. Parker, 1988). So did strategic ability, such as superior military leadership. For our purposes both simply contributed to the uncertainty surrounding the outcome of war.

Our model is a static one, focused on a ruler's decision to attack another country or at least join in a fight. The ruler makes the decision knowing that his ability to prevail in warfare hinges on the resources he commands. Those resources in turn depend on the political rules governing the imposition of taxes. In some political regimes, the ruler not only controls foreign policy but also taxation. In others, only foreign policy is under his command. And in a final type of political system, he can control some taxes but not others. When the ruler lacks complete control over taxation, we assume that raising the taxes outside his domain requires the assent of a group called the elite. We make the implicit assumption that negotiations with the elite are integrated, a simplification that often proves to be false.[9] This simplification reduces the public goods problem inherent in paying for warfare, but because we wish to emphasize the public goods problem, we start where it is minimal. Because our ruler chooses wars depending on the resources available to him, we begin by modeling the tax system.

Admittedly, our fiscal problem is imbedded in a larger strategic game in which countries choose their opponents. If political regimes vary in their ability to raise resources for war, then different regimes may well choose to fight different opponents. To complicate matters further, states usually do not engage in wars alone but within alliances, yet another layer of strategic

[8] As far as resource allocation is concerned, the dynamic case would allow for various sorts of strategic behavior—for example, a king who engaged in a suicidal war so as to get money from his estates. But the dynamic case would be most interesting in instances where the relative strength of nations changed dramatically. If we restrict ourselves to the bigger states of Europe (England, France, the Netherlands, Prussia, Spain), though, such vast swings of power were relatively rare and occurred over a very long period of time. For instance, France's challenge to Spain in the 16th and 17th centuries and England's challenge to France in the 18th century were each drawn out over more than a century. In the end no state achieved dominance, no state was eliminated, and the usual outcome of each particular war was a draw.

[9] We thus leave aside for the moment a number of important issues in early modern history: the makeup of the elite, cleavages within it, and, finally, differences between the elites of distinct countries. Such differences might prove crucial if, for example, a merchant elite wished to fight a war for commercial reasons.

interaction. Although we lay all such complications to the side here, there are historical reasons to justify such a simplification. In early modern Europe, states did have to consider the strategic implications of what regimes they fought with or against. But large states (such as France, Spain, Austria, and England) were pitted against each other in relatively stable ways. Austria and Spain fought France throughout the 16th and early 17th centuries. That conflict was then replaced by the contention between England and France. Other countries joined in on either side at different times—again in relatively predictable patterns. In the end there was a stalemate, where relatively little of French, Spanish, or British soil was acquired or lost in the two centuries before 1789. The stalemate alone suggests that we can neglect the additional levels of strategic interaction.

III.2.1 Taxation and Its Constraints

In early modern Europe, rulers usually faced constraints on the taxes they could levy. That was so, for instance, not just in the Netherlands and Britain, but in France and Spain as well (see Hoffman and Norberg, 1994). The major constraint was that rulers usually had to secure the approval of a representative institution or a law court to create new taxes or raise old ones. The constraints were not total, though, for some taxes remained under the ruler's exclusive control. In addition, the ruler usually retained a complete hold (or nearly so) over the financial system and the regulation of property rights. Thus a king could not tax at will, but he could sell monopolies, debase the currency, or raise taxes on selected groups and activities. That the constraints bound even absolute monarchs is clear from the complexity of royal tax systems and their inefficiency. But it is equally clear that monarchs could partially evade the constraints, as in 17th-century England (North and Weingast, 1989) and France (Major, 1994), where monarchs managed to create new sources of revenue without the assent of law courts or representative institutions.

We propose a simple description of how a monarch raised revenue when faced with such constraints. We begin by imagining that the economy is divided into two sectors. In the first sector, the king can tax only with the approval of the elite, which gives its assent in a law court or representative body. In the other part of the economy, the king is unconstrained. A political regime in this model therefore boils down to how fiscal authority is partitioned between the king and the elite. We denote that division by the parameter β $(0 \leq \beta \leq 1)$, which measures the extent of the elite's control over taxation. If β is 0, the crown has complete fiscal discretion; if β is 1, the crown is fully constrained.

Raising taxes is costly, so the tax burden levied to fund a war effort of size E in an economy of size Y is denoted $\tau\,(E, Y)$. Here $\tau\,(E, Y)$ is homogenous of degree 1 and it is increasing and concave in E and decreasing and convex in Y. To obtain comparative static results, we must choose a specific functional form for τ. Indeed, to characterize the evolution of taxation, we must be able to examine the third derivatives of the king's and of the elite's objective functions; in particular, we must be able to sign the third partial derivatives of τ. Because we have little insight into the behavior of these third partials, we resort to an example. We have tried several other functional forms, though, and obtained similar results.[10] For simplicity, we adopt the following formulation for the tax burden:

$$\tau(E,Y) = (EY/10)/(Y/10 - E)$$

for $0 \leq E < 0.1Y$. This formulation does seem fairly realistic: in particular, it entails declining marginal revenue for taxation and a maximum tax of less than 10 percent of output, which is about what one would expect in early modern Europe.[11]

Because taxation is in effect carried out by both the elite and the king in separate sectors of the economy, we define the tax burden τ_e that the elite needs to raise in order to fund a war effort E_e as

$$\tau_e(E_e, \beta Y) = (E_e\beta Y/10)/(\beta Y/10 - E_e).$$

The tax burden τ_k that the king needs to raise in order to fund an effort E_k is defined in an analogous way:

$$\tau_k[E_k, (1 - \beta)Y] = [E_k(1 - \beta)Y/10]/[(1 - \beta)Y/10 - E_k].$$

In our example we assume that $Y = 5{,}000$.

Given homogeneity, if the elite and the crown fund war efforts that are proportional to the size of the sector that each controls, then the taxes they raise will also be proportional. Neither will enjoy a comparative advantage in tax collection. In early modern Europe, such an assumption is far from unreasonable. Absolutist monarchs frequently complained about the inefficiency of the local tax authorities, which were usually representative institutions under elite control. On the other hand, it is often argued that such representative institutions avoided the corruption inherent in absolutist regimes (Brewer, 1989; Major, 1994, Chapter 5). In any case, as long as the

[10] The key comparative statics results concern the shape of the total tax burden after the players in our game (the king and the elite) choose optimal efforts E. The total tax burden should have a minimum for a value of β in the interior of the interval [0,1], which necessitates looking at its second derivative with respect to β. But examining its second derivative means dealing with the third derivatives of the king's and the elite's objective functions; in particular, we must be able to sign the third partial derivatives of τ. Because there is no compelling reason to sign these third partial derivatives, there is no way to derive general comparative statics results.

[11] If $E = Y/10$ then $\tau(E,Y) = \infty$.

relative efficiencies of either system are similar, our results will be unaffected.

Our specification is also consistent with many of the peculiarities of early modern fiscal systems. It reflects, for example, the distinction historians make between ordinary revenue and extraordinary revenue. Ordinary revenue consisted of the taxes that the king controlled, whereas extraordinary revenue was that beyond his control—revenues that required the authorization of a law court or representative body, or, in other words, our elite. Differences in political regimes then stem from the magnitude of ordinary revenues, with a fully constrained king having none.

III.2.2 The Technology of Warfare

The second part of our model is an analysis of a ruler's decision whether to go to war. Warfare is, of course, a repugnant subject, especially for economists. It is so not just because of its human toll, but because it violates our fundamental belief that actors will seek an efficient allocation of resources. Furthermore, warfare is driven by processes that lay squarely in the world of politics. Yet there are signs of a new interest in war in economics. Theorists have begun to explore how different political regimes survive warfare when the outcomes are driven by resources (Hirshleifer, 1995). In the spirit of such theory, we argue that warfare is not exogenous to economic activity. Rather, it is a gamble taken in a strategic context, where the level of economic activity of rival nations and the value of the expected booty figure into the decision to go to war. We deepen the analysis by studying the impact that political structures have on war, an impact that reaches far beyond the mere loss of life and destruction of capital.

The king, we assume, decides whether to go to war by weighing the probability of success, the attendant costs, the rewards in case of victory, and the penalties in case of loss. Besides victory and loss, we also allow for the possibility of draws.[12] The three outcomes are of course uncertain, but we assume that the odds of success rise as a country invests in arms, provided that other countries do not simply match the increased spending.

In this essay we have modeled the effect of expenditures on war outcomes in two very simple ways. For most of the essay, we explore an example where the effect of expenditures (E) by one country on the probability of winning or losing is strictly separable from the effects of expenditures by its opponent (E^o). The separability simplifies computation and avoids the complex issue of the impact of different opponents on a country's behavior.

[12] Draws are not crucial per se, but they do allow us to obtain an equilibrium and to get a bias in the king's assessment of the social value of war. For other ways to translate resource effort into outcomes and achieve an equilibrium, see Hirshleifer (1995).

The specific functional form for the probability of winning is as follows: if $E > c$ and $E^o > c$, then $p = a - b/(E - c) + b/(2E^o - 2c)$; if $E \leq c$, then $p = 0$; and if $E^o \leq c$ but $E > c$, then $p = a - b/(E - c)$.[13] The probability of losing q is symmetric in E and E^o. The role of c here is to create a threshold effect. It is included because in early modern Europe, considerable resources had to be invested before an army of any size could take the field, let alone prevail. As a result, a minimum level of expenditures was required before the probability of winning would be greater than zero. In the computational example we present, the war outcomes are given by

$$p = 1/2 - 4/(E - 96) + 4/(2E^o - 192),$$

and the probability of losing is symmetrically defined as

$$q = 1/2 - 4/(E^o - 96) + 4/(2E - 192).$$

Alternative specifications of the parameters *a,b,* and *c* lead to predictable results. Lowering *a* produces a greater number of draws but does not change the effort levels. Cutting *b* changes the effort level and alters the division of effort between king and elite. Finally, dropping *c* widens the range of values of β where either the king or the elite contribute nothing to the war effort, leaving the other party to foot the entire bill.

Although separability is maintained for most of the discussion, we abandon it at the end to highlight the importance of political regimes. At that point we chose an alternative set of winning probabilities:

$$p = [1 + (E - c)^{0.5}]/(N + E^o) \quad q = [1 + (E^o - c)^{0.5}]/(N + E).$$

Here N is a constant. These alternative winning probabilities yield essentially the same substantive results for taxation and war selection, so we ignore them in the initial analysis. They do shed light, though, on how different political regimes interact.

III.2.3 The Division of the Spoils

A war has three potential outcomes: a win (W), a loss (L), and a draw (D). If the king were to reap all the benefits of war and to pay all of its costs, the elite would care not a whit about the outcome and would never contribute any resources. Furthermore, because wars typically had negative social returns for a country—that was certainly true in early modern Europe when borders failed to change—kings would presumably refrain from engaging in war. Any reasonable model must therefore allocate the nonfiscal

[13] If we let the parameters other than *a* vary over all possible values, then the only possible value for *a* is ½ because $0 < p + q < 1$. If we are only concerned with the condition $0 < p + q < 1$ near equilibrium values, then $¼ < a < ½$ are possible values.

impact of war among the king, the elite, and the rest of the population. It must do so in such a way that wars occur and that distinct groups assess the value of war differently. In our model, the bulk of the population is purely passive and simply pays taxes, a situation that was common in early modern Europe. We also assume that the population gains nothing from victories and loses with draws and losses. Because the population is passive, its obvious desire for peace matters little—except for any political costs the population can impose on the two decision makers, the elite and the crown.

The elite authorizes taxes in our model, but it bears political costs for the taxes used for war at the expense of local public goods and the population's consumption. It should be stressed that the elite rarely paid such taxes in early modern Europe.[14] The elite also participated in wars directly by providing managerial talent, either as officers in the army or as officials in the royal bureaucracy, or by providing financial and commercial services. The elite thus faced three distinct sorts of consequences from a war. First, its participation required a commitment of resources that was independent of the war's outcome—what amounted to a fixed cost of war. In early modern Europe, officers often had to pay their units' expenses in advance and then wait for what might be only partial reimbursement or no reimbursement at all (Lynn, 1993, p. 310; Parker, 1972, pp. 119–120). In the meantime, they risked dying in camp or on the battlefield whether their side was victorious or not. Similarly, bureaucrats exerted themselves without additional compensation as tax rates rose and troop movements caused local disturbances.

The second consequence for the elite groups were the losses they faced in the case of both draws and defeats. Draws involved drawn-out battles that resolved nothing but were costly for the elite. In addition, the typical early modern king made promises to the elite that paid off only in case of quick victory: booty and war profits, promotions, or financial rewards to victorious officers, or reimbursement of loans, money, and supplies advanced to troops. Although the king was therefore insured against stalemates, the elite suffered, making its net return from draws D_e negative. Obviously, in defeat the elite's fate was even worse, for then it might lose property at home.

Finally, it is true that victory brought benefits to the elite, who might acquire booty, win promotions in the military, or gain new administrative positions. But because the king had to secure the conquered territory, some of the spoils of war were destined to buy off the population living there. The spoils had to be shared, and even victory would not allow the elite to improve its position in the newly acquired territory.

[14] As owners of much of the land, the elite did suffer when tax increases cut into rent, but the elite's tenants were often tax exempt (cf. Hoffman, 1986, 1991).

The final actor in our game is the king, who benefits from the added territory (and attendant prestige and power) that victories bring and suffers accordingly in defeat. He also bears fixed costs for war, but we assume that his fixed costs pale to insignificance beside the opportunities of war and the fixed costs of the elite. The final and most important assumption about the king is that—unlike the elite—he faces no penalties for draws. As we noted previously, he simply makes promises that do not have to be honored in case of a stalemate. The effect of these assumptions is ensure that the king is more aggressive than the elite, who will bear costs no matter what the outcome of the conflict. There are then occasions when the king wishes to fight but the elite does not.[15]

The outcome of wars can thus be defined as follows. For the elite, $W_e > 0$; $D_e < 0$; $L_e < 0$. For the king, $W_k > 0$; $D_k = 0$; $L_k < 0$. For the sake of simplicity, let us assume that the elite and the crown share the returns to winning and losing according to the extent of their fiscal control of the domestic economy. The elite's share, W_e, in victory is simply βW; similarly, its share in defeat is $L_e = \beta L$. In addition, the elite bears the cost of draws, $D_e = \beta D$ and $D_k = 0$.[16] Here W, L, and D are the aggregate returns to war that the elite and the crown divide ($W > 0$; $L < 0$ and $L < D < 0$). In the analysis that follows we will assume that wars only vary by the value of success ($W \in [W_l, W_h]$).

Although it may seem artificial to divide the spoils of war according to shares of fiscal power, the assumption does serve as a reasonable approximation. After all, the king cannot hog the profits from war if he expects support from the elite. In addition, if the elite controls most taxation, defeats will diminish its tax receipts. Finally, dividing the returns of war according to political power is also consistent with the reasonable notion that the sharing rules for taxes and warfare alike evolve out of the same long-term bargaining process between monarchs and elites.

III.2.4 Analysis

We begin by describing the process of war making. We first assume that some parameters are fixed: L, D, c_E, c_K, where c_E and c_K are the thresholds in the probabilities of winning and losing. Second β, the division of fiscal au-

[15] Given our assumptions, it should have been rare for early modern elites to want to fight when their kings were opposed to war. Situations of this sort do seem to have been unusual, although a true test would require a complete list of early modern wars and a detailed study of each country's diplomacy and domestic politics. The aggressiveness of our model's king also helps explain the effort that some rulers expended to get their elites to serve in the army—in Prussia, for example.

[16] The remaining cost of draws—$(1 - \beta)D$—is born by the rest of the population.

thority in the country, is assumed to be exogenous: although the political regime may vary, the king and elite take it as given The same holds for the size of the economy *Y*.

In our game, nature moves first and determines a new pair *W* (the aggregate value of winning) and E^o (opponent effort). Given that the king controls foreign policy, he then chooses a war making probability α, a random variable that is realized as α, (α = 0,1).[17] If α = 0, there is peace. If α = 1, there is war, and the king and the elite simultaneously select their levels of effort, E_k, and E_e. Finally the outcome *O* of the war is realized, with $O \in \{W, L, D\}$.

The goal of each party is to maximize the returns to war. The king has the following objective function:

$$V_k(E_k,\alpha) = (1-\alpha)0 + \alpha\{-\tau[E_k,(1-\beta)Y] + p(E_k + E_e, E_0)$$
$$(1-\beta)W + q(E_k + E_e, E_0)(1-\beta)L\}.$$

The elite chooses a level of effort E_e to provide the king so as to maximize its objective function:

$$V_e(E_e) = -\tau(E_e, \beta Y) + p(E_k + E_e, E_0)\beta W + q(E_k + E_e, \mathrm{E}_0)\beta \mathrm{L}$$
$$+ [(1 - p(E_k + E_e, E_0) - q(E_k + E_e, E_0)] D_e.$$

Because the analysis of the general case bogs down into problems of third partial derivatives, we limit ourselves to a particular example[18]:

$$V_k(E_k,\alpha) = \alpha\{-(1-\beta)E_k 500/[(1-)\beta)500 - E_k]$$
$$+ [0.5 - 4/(E_k + E_e - 96) + 4/(2E_0 - 192)](1-\beta)W$$
$$+ [0.5 - 4/(E_0 - 96) + 4/(2E_k + 2E_e - 192)](1-\beta)L - c_K\}$$

$$V_e(E_e) = -\beta E_e 500/(\beta 500 - E_e) + [0.5 - 4/(E_k + E_e - 96)$$
$$+ 4/(2E_0 - 192)]\beta(W - D) + [0.5 - 4/(E_0 - 96)$$
$$+ 4/(2E_k + 2E_e - 192)]\beta(L - D) - c_E.$$

Given β, *W*, *L*, *D*, c_E, c_K and E^o, it is easy to show that the optimization of $V_k(E_k,\alpha)$ and $V_e(E_e)$ has well-behaved solutions. Figure III.1 illus-

[17] One might assume that α is realized later—in particular after expenditure decisions are made. But that would create considerable inefficiencies, for resources would be raised to satisfy an expected war rather than a realized war, leading to a surplus of resources in peacetime and a dearth of resources in wartime. Such a political system would presumably vanish in the long run.

[18] The reason is that we want to determine the second derivative of the total tax burden after the king and the elite optimize, which entails looking at third derivatives for comparative statics.

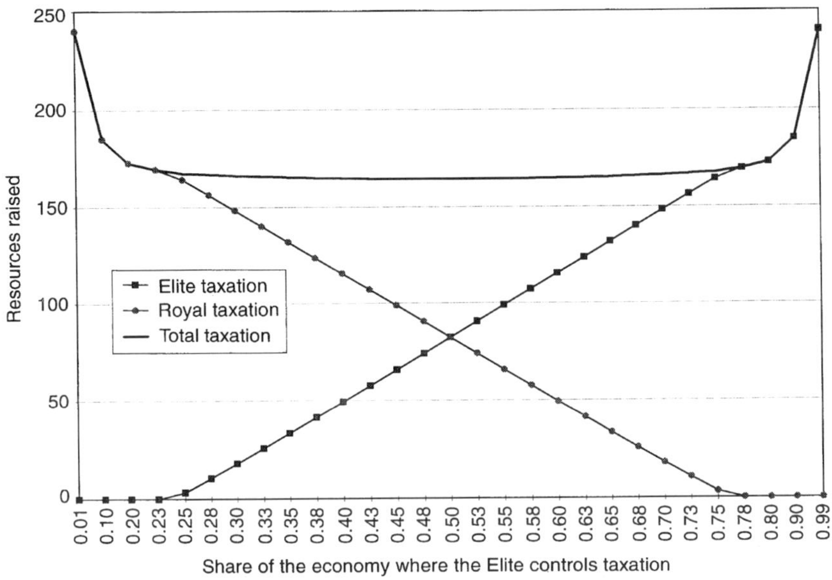

FIGURE III.1 Taxation by king and elite and control of the economy.

trates the choices of effort level by the king and the elite over the range of β, with the following set of parameters, $W = 15{,}000$, $L = -10{,}000$, $D = -400$, $c_E = 500$, $c_K = 0$, and $E^{o} = 160$.

When the division of fiscal authority is quite skewed, only one of the two parties contributes to the war effort. Such free riding forces taxes up when β is near 0 or 1 in order to pay for war. Taxes are actually slightly higher when the elite has near total control (i.e., when β is near 1) than when the fiscal system is in the king's hands. The reason is that the king stands to gain more from warfare and hence is willing to fight with fewer resources. In addition, if the king controls enough of the economy, the elite will get only a tiny portion of the spoils. It will then be the net loser in warfare and will oppose it all the more.

The second element of our model involves a selection effect on the decision to go to war. Not all potential conflicts occur, and political regimes clearly respond to warfare in different ways. In addition, government leaders in any period may behave opportunistically toward their constituents when pursuing international goals (Downs and Rocke, 1994). Such behavior is quite likely in our model because the king has a low fixed cost for waging war and bears no burden for any draws. To keep matters simple, we assume that no informational asymmetries exist between the king and the elite; war then breaks out whenever the king makes a credible announcement that hostilities are imminent.[19] His announcement is credible if either one of two following conditions is satisfied. The first condition is that both the elite and the crown want to fight the war, and for that it suffices that the elite be willing since the king is always more bellicose. The first condition thus becomes

$$-\tau(E^*_e|E^*_k) + p\beta W + q\beta L + (1 - p - q)D_e > 0.$$

Here $\tau(E^*_e|E^*_k)$ is the tax that the elite agrees to, conditional upon what the king will furnish. The second condition that makes a declaration of war credible is that the king be willing to fight without resources from the elite. In this case, we must have

$$-\tau(E^*_k|E_e = 0) + p(1 - \beta)W + q(1 - \beta)L > 0,$$

where $\tau(E^*_k|E_e = 0)$ is the tax that the king imposes when the elite furnishes nothing.

We can illustrate the effects of credibility in a figure with three curves that describe how the king and the elite react to opportunities for waging war (Figure III.2). Here the horizontal axis is β, the share of the economy where the elite chooses taxation and the vertical dimension W, the value of winning war. We define $W_e(\beta,E^*_k)$ to be the value of victory in war that makes the elite indifferent between war and peace, given that both the elite and the king contribute to the war effort and that the elite controls taxation in a fraction β of the economy. $W_e(\beta,E^*_k)$ solves the following problem:

$$p\beta W + q\beta L + (1 - p - q)\beta D = \tau(E^*_e, \beta Y).$$

Similarly, $W_k(\beta,E^*_e)$ is the value of victory required for the king to be indifferent between war and peace, given that both parties contribute to the war effort and that the elite controls taxation in a fraction β of the economy. $W_k(\beta,E^*_e)$ solves the corresponding problem:

$$p(1 - \beta)W + q(1 - \beta)L = \tau[E^*_k,(1 - \beta)Y].$$

Finally, $W_k(\beta,0)$ is the value of victory required for the king to be indifferent between war and peace, given that he alone contributes to the war effort and that the elite controls taxation in a fraction β of the economy. $W_k(\beta,0)$ solves the following problem with E_e set equal to 0:

[19] One alternative would be to write down a model where the king has the ability to commit to wars. Several possible rationales for such a model exist: kings can create "border incidents" that automatically degenerate into wars, and they have an incentive to gain a reputation for fighting all wars. But such reasoning neglects the fact that the elite was itself also a long-run player with its own reputational motives. If the elite can commit to funding levels, then it can force the crown to fight only those wars it wants to fight.

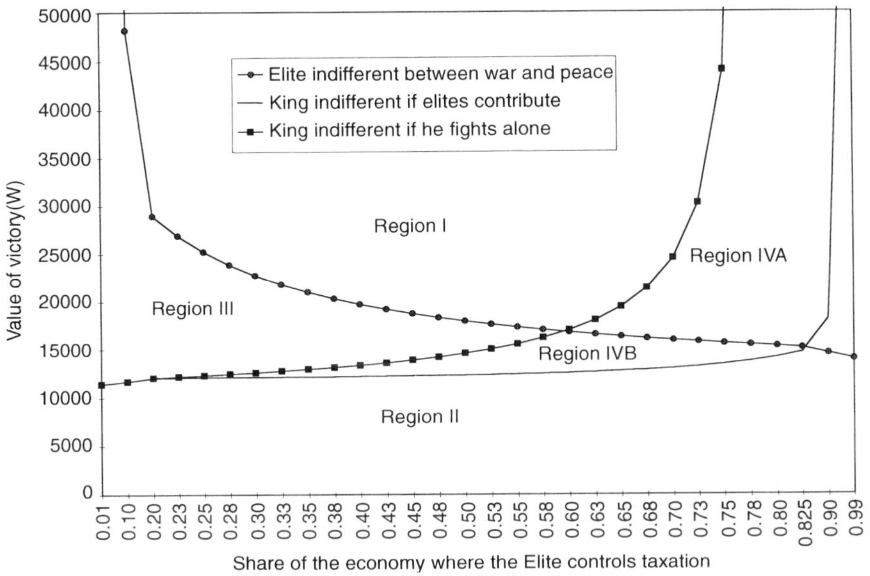

FIGURE III.2 The king's and the elite's decision to go to war.

$$p(1-\beta)W + q(1-\beta)L = \tau[E^*_k,(1-\beta)Y].$$

In the most general case the derivatives of $W_e(\beta,E^*_k)$, $W_k(\beta,E^*_e)$, and $W_k(\beta,0)$ need not be well behaved. So for Figure III.2, we returned to our specific example to solve for the three curves. In the figure, the curves $W_e(\beta,E^*_k)$, $W_k(\beta,E^*_e)$, and $W_k(\beta,0)$ define four regions. If W is large enough, both the king and the elite want to fight the war; it will occur independent of credibility (region I). If W is small enough, neither the elite nor the king want to fight the war, and peace is uncontroversial (region II). Between these two extremes we find two regions. In region III, the elite dislikes war, but the king can fight credibly on his own. Here wars occur but they are unpopular. Finally, in region IV, which has two parts—IVA and IVB—the king wants to fight but needs the cooperation of the elite because he cannot fight alone. It is in this last region that positive contributions by both parties are not subgame perfect, giving the elite significant control over taxation.

As Figure III.2 illustrates, political regimes differ in the type of wars they choose to fight. In particular, fighting wanes as the crown surrenders fiscal control to the elite and to representative institutions that weigh the social cost of war. We can think of this shift of fiscal control as movement from autocracy, through absolutism, and on to parliamentary or constitutional monarchy. In our model these three different political regimes represent different values of β, the number measuring the extent of elite control over taxation. Under pure autocracy, the king controls the entire fiscal process, so β is zero. Under a parliamentary regime, the elite has enough authority over the fisc to deny the king funds when it does not want to fight. A pure parliamentary regime corresponds to $\beta = 1$, but for our purposes parliamentarianism describes values of β above the β for which $W_e(\beta, E^*_k), = W_k(\beta, 0)$. Beyond this point the king will not fight on his own. As for absolutism, it falls between autocracy and parliamentarianism. Absolutism and parliamentarianism, unlike autocracy, are thus both forms of limited government in that the executive is constrained. The key difference between them is the extent of the constraint, but it is worth remembering that in early modern Europe absolute monarchs were indeed limited in their fiscal powers.[20]

The difference between political regimes extends beyond the selection effect in Figure III.2. It shows up as well in the intensity of taxation and the resources raised for war, and its effect on taxation is easier to see if we abandon the assumption of separability and adopt the second set of winning and losing probabilities: $p = [1 + (E - c)^{0.5}]/(N + E^o)$, $q = (1 + (E^o - c)^{0.5})/(N + E)$. With these probabilities, political regimes not only differ in their war efforts, but they also respond to their opponent's commitment (Tables III.2 and III.3). As the tables demonstrate, regimes vary greatly in their willingness to spend money on war. The sharpest contrast is not between autocrats and absolutists but rather between parliamentary and absolutist regimes. What is noteworthy in Tables III.2 and III.3 is the differences in tax burdens between the sector of the economy that the king controls and the sector that is in the hands of the elite. The difference is widest under absolutism: it is there that the gap between the king's tax rates and the elite's low rates yawns open, forcing the king to take steps to keep resources from flowing out of his sector. As we know, the result in early modern Europe was not just crushing taxation in the king's sector. It was also regulation, a crippling bureaucracy, and the wholesale abandonment of certain parts of the economy. If our model is correct, such ruinous policies derived not from indifference to the economy but from the fiscal constraints that all absolute rulers faced. It is worth keeping in mind that for economic growth the property rights that matter most are those that define income accruing to the owners of assets. The divided fiscal regime of absolutist states reduced such private streams of income in the part of the economy controlled by the monarch. It also prevented investment flows into sectors that the crown could not tax easily. Its institutional rigidity hindered the disposal of assets, yet another desirable trait of property rights. In both

[20] Our specification of political regimes differs from Olson's (1993) for whom Old-Regime France is a good example of an autocracy.

TABLE III.2 Tax Rates and Effort by Opponent Type

Opponent type							
Autocrat (β_o = 0.01)		Absolutist (β_o = 0.5)		Parliamentary (β_o = 0.99)		Same as self ($\beta_o = \beta$)	
War effort	Tax rate	War effort	Tax rate	War effort	Tax rate	War effort	Tax rate
164.9	3.3	166.9	3.34	164.8	3.30	164.9	3.30
151.8	3.0	153.60	3.07	151.7	3.03	152.5	3.05
132.2	2.6	133.56	2.67	132.1	2.64	133.4	2.67
127.6	2.6	129.10	2.58	127.5	2.55	129.0	2.58
126.3	2.5	127.71	2.55	126.2	2.52	127.7	2.55
125.9	2.5	127.32	2.55	125.8	2.52	127.3	2.55
126.4	2.5	127.82	2.56	126.3	2.53	127.8	2.56
127.8	2.6	129.32	2.59	127.8	2.56	129.2	2.58
133	2.7	134.65	2.69	133.3	2.67	134.4	2.69
153.3	3.1	155.17	3.1	153.2	3.06	153.8	3.08
166.6	3.3	168.72	3.37	166.5	3.33	166.5	3.33

Note: The values in the table were computed with the nonseparable success probabilities discussed in the text. The win loss functions are as follows: $p = (1 + (E - c)^{0.5})/(N + E^o)$, $q = (1 + (E^o - c)^{0.5})/(N + E)$. The parameter values are D = −400, W = 15,000, L = −10,000, Y = 5,000, N = 700, c = 100; $c_K = c_E = 0$.

TABLE III.3 Sectoral Tax Rates by Opponent Type

		Opponent Type							
		Autocrat (β_o = 0.01)		Absolutist (β_o = 0.5)		Parliamentary (β_o = 0.99)		Same as self ($\beta_o = \beta$)	
Regime type (value of β)		Elite rate	King rate	Elite rate	King rate	Elite rate	King rate	Elite rate	King rate
Autocrat	0.01	0.00	3.33	0.00	3.33	0.00	3.37	0.00	3.33
	0.10	0.00	3.37	0.00	3.37	0.00	3.41	0.00	3.39
	0.25	0.00	3.53	0.00	3.52	0.00	3.56	0.00	3.56
	0.30	0.25	3.54	0.24	3.54	0.29	3.57	0.28	3.56
	0.40	1.66	3.11	1.65	3.10	1.69	3.13	1.69	3.13
Absolutist	0.50	2.56	2.47	2.56	2.47	2.59	2.50	2.59	2.50
	0.60	3.18	1.55	3.18	1.55	3.21	1.58	3. 21	1.58
	0.70	3.61	0.11	3.61	0.11	3.63	0.15	3.63	0.14
	0.75	3.55	0.00	3.55	0.00	3.59	0	3.58	0.00
	0.90	3.41	0.00	3.40	0.00	3.45	0	3.42	0.00
Parliamentary	0.99	3.37	0.00	3.36	0.00	3.41	0	3.36	0.00

cases, the rules were clear—property rights were well defined—but the property rights that absolutist regimes got ended up stunting economic growth.

Albeit little more than an example, our model has three strong implications concerning political regimes. First, the willingness to engage in warfare declines as we move from autocracy to absolutism and then on to parliamentary regimes. Although ideological differences and religious cleavages not part of our model may well drive any state to fight, on average the absolute monarchs will be more bellicose than their parliamentary neighbors. The second implication is that taxes will on average be lower under absolutism than under autocracy or parliamentary government: under absolutism politics severely restricts fiscal extortion. Finally, the net returns of war will be highest under parliamentary regimes. The parliamentary regimes will limit themselves to wars that are profitable, but when they do fight they will give their armies the resources needed to win.

All three implications fit, at least roughly, much of what we know about early modern history. There were, of course, exceptions. Early modern Poland might seem to be one, at least at first glance. It was a parliamentary regime, with the elite assembled in the country's representative assembly (or national Diet), yet the Diet granted the Polish king practically nothing in taxes. As a result, in the 18th century the country was partitioned by aggressive neighbors. Keep in mind, however, that the Polish constitution was quite unusual, for any single member of the Diet could block legislation and force the very dissolution of the Diet, at least after 1652. Foreign powers took advantage of the situation by bribing the members of the Diet and paralyzing the Polish government. No other European country, as one scholar has observed, was subject to such outside interference.[21] It is not surprising therefore that taxes could not be raised in Poland: the foreign meddling and the peculiar constitution held the fisc in check. In that sense Poland is not an exception at all, and the only surprise about the country is that partitioning took so long.

In any case, much of the rest of early modern Europe does conform to the model. Absolute monarchs like Louis XIV and Philip II did seem to be aggressors, although their wars and the taxes they required sapped the French and Spanish economies. Parliamentary regimes, such as England, seemed to do much better in battle, and when they lacked the resources to compete, as in the 18th-century Netherlands, they withdrew from the international scene. Finally, the highest tax burdens were not to be found under the absolutist regimes. Rather, they were imposed by representative gov-

[21] The observations on Poland are from Birn (1992, pp. 122–124, 334–335).

ernments.[22] Absolute monarchies had high taxes rates in some sectors but low rates in others. They strangled certain sectors of the economy and had to erect stifling bureaucracies to keep resources from slipping away. In the end they collected very little, whereas the treasuries of their parliamentary neighbors were full.

III.3 CONCLUSION

Douglass North has certainly been right in linking war, taxes, politics, and property rights in early modern Europe. He is right too in arguing that the linkages affected long-term economic growth up through the Industrial Revolution. Yet while on these points we can only agree with him, our conclusions are a bit different. For us, it is not so much the level of taxation that matters, for the absolute monarchies that experienced slow growth actually raised less tax revenue per capita than parliamentary regimes. Rather, it is the effect of taxes at the margin that counts. North would no doubt concur, because he too pointed to the rigidities and distorted incentives under the absolute monarchies. What we have done, though, is explain why these rigidities persisted. Because absolute monarchs did not control the entire economy, they pushed tax rates up in the economic sectors under their domination. They then had to erect legal barriers to stem the flow of assets into sectors with lighter taxes and create bureaucracies to monitor compliance and prevent tax evasion. For their economies, the effect was, typically, overinvestment in land and underinvestment in commerce and industry. The portion of the economy that suffered most was the financial market, which was almost always under royal control.[23] The cost for long-term investment was no doubt high.

If we were to turn these historical observations into prescriptions for today's developing countries, our recommendations might also differ from North's. For us it is not so much the level of taxation, but the effect of taxes at the margin. Our advice would not necessarily be to cut taxes, but rather to pay attention to marginal rates where they strangle economic transac-

[22] One might argue that representive governments would only impose high taxes in times of war. But even in peacetime they had to pay off debts from previous wars and fund enough of an army to keep warlike neighbors at bay. Their taxes might also remain high in peacetime because they chose to spend more on public infrastructure—a point we take up next.

[23] Long-distance trade was also subject to royal taxation, and merchants in parliamentary regimes such as England and the Netherlands did seem to fare somewhat better than their counterparts in France and Spain. The problem, though, is that the assets in long-distance trade were mobile, as were many early modern merchants. An absolute monarch (or even an autocratic) could not bear down too heavily on long-distance trade. If he did, many of the merchants would take their wares and their business elsewhere.

tions and to the economic barriers that the fiscal system can impose. The effect of taxes on financial markets would be critical, because they can still fall victims to a seigniorage taxes. Just as in the past, the price for crippling financial markets will be paid in long-term investment.

Like North, we would stress the advantages that representative government has for economic growth. Our model overlooks constitutional change, but our second example does point to a great advantage that parliamentary regimes had when surrounded by warlike neighbors. They were more likely to survive and even to prosper when faced with challenges from other regimes—a sign that they possessed both political and economic strength. Their tax systems, we know, were less likely to obstruct the economy and less likely to penalize financial markets and other economic activities that are essential for growth. They may also have been more inclined to provide public infrastructure, such as roads and canals, which spawned growth. The examples of England and the Netherlands support such a hypothesis, but whether the infrastructure derived from public spending or from lack of barriers to private investment is a rich topic for future research.

ACKNOWLEDGMENTS

We would like to thank Joel Mokyr and Stanley Engerman for helpful comments.

REFERENCES

Bayard, F. (1988). *Le Monde des Financiers au XVIIe Siècle.* Flammarion, Paris.

Birn, R. (1992). *Crisis, Absolutism, Revolution: Europe, 1648–1789,* 2nd ed. Harcourt Brace Jovanovich, Fort Worth, TX.

Brewer, J. (1989). *The Sinews of Power : War, Money, and the English State, 1688–1783.* Knopf, New York.

Cabourdin, G., Biraben, J. N., and Blum, A. (1988). Les crises démographiques. In *Histoire de la population française* (J. Dupâquier, ed.), Vol. 2, pp. 175–219. Presses Universitaires de France, Paris.

Coase, R. H. (1960). The problem of social cost. *Journal of Law and Economics* **3,** 1–44.

de Vries, J. (1976). *The Economy of Europe in an Age of Crisis, 1600–1750.* Cambridge University Press, Cambridge, UK.

Downs, G. W., and Rocke, D. M. (1994). Conflict agency and gambling for resurrection: The principal agent goes to war. *American Journal of Political Science* **38**(2), 362–380.

Elliott, J. H. (1963). *Imperial Spain: 1469–1716.* New American Library, New York.

Fogel, R. W. (1993). New sources and new techniques for the study of secular trends in nutritional status, health, mortality, and the process of aging. *Historical Methods* **26,** 5–44.

Gutmann, M. P. (1980). *War and Rural Life in the Early Modern Low Countries.* Princeton University Press, Princeton, NJ.

Hale, J. R. (1985). *War and Society in Renaissance Europe.* Johns Hopkins University Press, Baltimore.

Hassinger, H. (1978). Politische Kräfte und Wirtschaft 1350–1800. In *Handbuch der Deutschen Wirtschafts- und Sozialgeschichte* (H. Aubin and W. Zorn, eds.), Vol. 1, pp. 608–657. Klett-Cotta, Stuttgart.

Hirshleifer, J. (1995). Anarchy and its breakdown. *Journal of Political Economy* **103,** 26–52.
Hoffman, P. T. (1986). Taxes and agrarian life in early modern France: Land sales, 1550–1730. *Journal of Economic History* **46,** 37–55.
Hoffman, P. T. (1991). Land rents and agricultural productivity: The Paris Basin, 1450–1789, *Journal of Economic History* **51,** 771–805.
Hoffman, P. T. (1996). *Growth in a Traditional Society: The French Countryside, 1450–1815.* Princeton University Press, Princeton, NJ.
Hoffman, P. T., and Norberg, K., eds. (1994). *Fiscal Crises, Liberty, and Representative Government 1450–1789.* Stanford University Press, Stanford, CA.
Hoffman, P. T., Postel-Vinay, G., and Rosenthal, J.-L. (1995). Redistribution and long-term private debt in Paris, 1660–1726. *Journal of Economic History* **55,** 256–284.
Lynn, J. A. (1993). How war fed war: The tax of violence and contributions during the Grand Siècle. *Journal of Modern History* **65,** 286–310.
Lynn, J. A. (1994). Recalculating French army growth during the Grand Siècle. *French Historical Studies* **18,** 881–906.
Major, J. R. (1994). *From Renaissance Monarchy to Absolute Monarchy.* Johns Hopkins University Press, Baltimore.
Mathias, P., and O'Brien, P. (1976). Taxation in Britain and France, 1715–1810: A comparison of the social and economic incidence of taxes collected for the central government. *Journal of European Economic History* **5,** 601–650.
North, D. C. (1981). *Structure and Change in Economic History.* Norton, New York.
North, D. C., and Thomas, R. P. (1973). *The Rise of the Western World: A New Economic History.* Cambridge University Press, Cambridge, UK.
North, D. C., and Weingast, B. R. (1989). Constitutions and commitment: The evolution of institutions governing public choice in seventeenth-century England. *Journal of Economic History* **49,** 803–832.
Olson, M. (1982). *The Rise and Decline of Nations: Economic Growth, Stagflation, and Social Rigidities.* Yale University Press, New Haven, CT.
Olson, M. (1993). Dictatorship, democracy, and development. *American Political Science Review* **87,** 567–576.
Parker, G. (1972). *The Army of Flanders and the Spanish Road.* Cambridge University Press, Cambridge, UK.
Parker, G. (1988). *The Military Revolution.* Cambridge University Press, Cambridge, UK.
Riley, J. C. (1986). *The Seven Years War and the Old Regime in France: The Economic and Financial Toll.* Princeton University Press, Princeton, NJ.
Rosenthal, J.-L. (1992). *The Fruits of Revolution: Property Rights, Litigation and French Agriculture, 1600–1860.* Cambridge University Press, Cambridge, UK.
Rosenthal, J.-L. (forthcoming). The political economy of absolutism reconsidered.
Sargent, T., and Velde, F. (1995). Macroeconomic features of the French Revolution. *Journal of Political Economy* **103,** 474–518.
Schroeder, P. W. (1994). *The Transformation of European Politics, 1763–1848.* Clarendon Press, Oxford, UK.
Sussman, N. (1993). Debasements, royal revenues, and inflation in France during the Hundred Years' War, 1415–1422. *Journal of Economic History* **53,** 44–70.
Tilly, C. (1990). *Coercion, Capital, and European States, 990–1990.* Blackwell, Cambridge, MA.
Walter, J., and Schofield, R. (1989). Famine, disease and crisis mortality in early modern society. In *Famine, Disease and the Social Order in Early Modern Society.* (J. Walter and R. Schofield, eds.), pp. 1–73. Cambridge University Press, Cambridge, UK.
Weir, D. R. (1989). Markets and mortality in France, 1600–1789. In *Famine, Disease and the Social Order in Early Modern Society* (J. Walter and R. Schofield, eds.), pp. 201–234. Cambridge University Press, Cambridge, UK.
White, E. (1995). The French Revolution and the politics of government finance, 1770–1815. *Journal of Economic History* **55,** 227–255

IV On the Interrelations and Economic Implications of Economic, Social, Political, and Normative Factors: Reflections from Two Late Medieval Societies

Avner Greif

IV.1 INTRODUCTION

Economic history, in contrast to neoclassical economics, has always emphasized the need to analyze economies as systems in which institutions, namely the nontechnologically determined constraints, influence economic performance. To understand economic performance, one has to analyze an economic system as one in which social, cultural, and political features interrelate with technology, endowment, and preferences. Furthermore, understanding the determinants of economic performance *over time* requires analyzing the factors that make such systems path dependent,[1] that is, the factors implying that a system's ability to change is a function of its history. In various publications, North (e.g., 1981, 1990; North and Thomas, 1973) has called attention to the need to pursue such inquiry and has provided many examples from history on the importance of this approach.

The need for analyzing economies as systems was highlighted recently by the findings of social psychologists who identified high correlations between cultural, political, and economic aspects of contemporary societies.

[1] Regarding the importance of path dependence in economic history, see David (1988). Regarding institutional path dependence, see David (1992) and North (1991).

Specifically, societies tend to be either "collectivist" or "individualist" (Bellah *et al.*, 1985; Triandis, 1990; Triandis *et al.*, 1990).[2] In collectivist societies the social structure is "segregated" in the sense that each individual interacts socially and economically mainly with members of a specific religious, ethnic, or familial group in which contract enforcement is achieved through "informal" economic and social institutions, whereas noncooperation characterizes the relations between members of different groups. In terms of their values, members of collectivist societies feel involved in the lives of other members of their group and value cooperation and contribution to the group's welfare. Finally, the political system of such societies is characterized by nondemocratic governments.

In individualist societies the social structure is "integrated" in the sense that economic transactions are conducted among people from different groups and individuals shift frequently from one group to another. Contract enforcement is achieved mainly through specialized organizations such as the court, and self-reliance, independence, and individualism are highly valued. Finally, the political system of such societies is characterized by democratic governments. Variations among contemporary societies with respect to their levels of individualism or collectivism are highly correlated with per capita income: most of the developing countries are "collectivist," whereas the developed West is "individualist."

Despite the evidence from history and from contemporary developed and less developed countries that understanding economic performance requires analyzing a system of interrelated social, cultural, political, and economic factors, rigorous comparative theoretical and historical analysis of such systems and their path dependence has not been conducted. This chapter presents such an analysis. Specifically, it provides an overview of the main findings in an ongoing research project that examines, historically and theoretically, the interrelations between, and the economic implications of, the social, cultural, economic, and political features of two late medieval societies: the Maghribi traders who operated in the Muslim Mediterranean during the 11th century and the Genoese traders of the 12th and 13th centuries who were a part of the Latin world.[3]

A comparative analysis of the emerging institutional structures of these two societies is also of interest for is own sake. The late medieval period greatly influenced the later commercial, industrial, and financial developments in Europe. "[W]estern wealth began with the growth of European trade and commerce which started in the twelfth century in Italy,"

[2] Clearly, any society has some elements of individualism and some elements of collectivism. Thus, the distinction between collectivist and individualist societies is a matter of the relative importance of these factors. (see, for example, Bellah *et al.*, (1985); Reynolds and Norman, 1988; Triandis, 1990).

[3] Relevant historical evidence are further elaborated in Greif (1989, 1991, 1993, 1994a,b, 1996).

(Rosenberg and Birdzell, 1986, p. 35). Much of the institutional framework of the West was crystallized during this period. It is also a period during which the economic decline of the Muslim world began. Hence, comparative analysis of institutional development in the Western and Muslim worlds may shed some light on the factors that gave rise to the emergence of distinct institutional trajectories in these societies and uncover sources of institutional path dependence. Indeed, it is interesting to note that the distinct institutional structures found in the late Medieval period among groups from the Muslim and the Latin worlds resemble those found by social psychologists to differentiate contemporary developing and developed economies. Hence, the findings in this chapter also suggest the historical importance of distinct institutional structures in economic development.

The rest of this chapter is organized as follows: Section IV.1 provides a short introduction to the two premodern societies under study, identifies the transaction central to their economies, and describes two economic institutions able to mitigate the related organizational problems. Section IV.2 examines the role of cultural and social factors in the selection of possible institutions. Section IV.3 discusses some of the social and economic implications of the cultural elements imbedded in these institutions. Section IV.4 examines the relationship between economic institutions, culture, and political institutions. Section IV.5 examines the emergence of distinct trajectories of organizational development, whereas Section IV.6 examines the cultural implications of distinct economic institutions and social structures. Concluding remarks follow.

Due to space limitation and because the focus of the chapter is to summarize the relevant findings, only brief substantiation of various claims regarding historical evidence and the line of causation is presented. In particular, the chapter does not provide a formal model although Greif (1993, 1994a) contains a formal model of some of the theoretical arguments made in Sections IV.2, IV.3, and IV.4. Similarly, Greif (1989, 1991, 1994b, and 1996) further elaborates on the empirical content of the arguments made in this chapter.

IV. 2 AN ORGANIZATIONAL PROBLEM AND MULTIPLE ECONOMIC INSTITUTIONS

Among the Italian cities important in the rise of European trade and commerce during the late medieval period, Genoa holds a prominent place. Furthermore, its historical records are particularly rich and go back as far as the years in which the Commune of Genoa was established, namely, around 1096. A unique historical source, known as the *geniza* (Cairo), reflects the operation of the Maghribi traders, a group of Jewish traders who operated in the Muslim world during the 11th century. The economies of the Genoese and the Maghribis were based on long-distance overseas trade. The centrality of such trade in the Genoese economy is reflected in the late medieval *maxim genuensis ergo mercator* (Genoese, therefore merchant). Similarly, trade was central to the Maghribis who were engaged in long-distance trade for centuries, locating in the area surrounding Baghdad, but who immigrated to North Africa during the second half of the 10th century due to political upheavals. After their immigration to North Africa, the Maghribis became involved in large-scale, long-distance trade all over the Muslim Mediterranean.[4]

The Maghribis and the Genoese faced a similar environment, employed comparable naval technology, and traded in similar goods. The efficiency of their trade depended, to a large extent, on their ability to mitigate an organization problem related to a specific transaction—the provision of the services required for handling a merchant's goods abroad.[5] A merchant could either provide these services himself by traveling between trade centers or he could hire *overseas* agents in trade centers abroad to handle his merchandise. Employing agents was efficient, because it saved the time and risk of traveling, allowed diversifying sales across trade centers, and so forth.[6] Yet without supporting institutions, agency relations could not be established, because an agent could embezzle the merchant's goods. Anticipating this behavior, a merchant would not hire an agent to begin with.

A neoclassical market for agents' services fails to provide an institution through which agency relations can be organized. The anonymous, discrete, neoclassical market is one in which "faceless buyers and sellers, households and firms that grind out decision rules from their objective functions (utility, profit) meet . . . for an instant to exchange standardized goods at equilibrium prices" (Ben-Porath, 1980, p. 4). In an anonymous market, conduct in a given period has no effect upon the reward in subsequent periods. Yet, as Carlo M. Cipolla has pointed out, the agent who traded using someone else's capital "could easily have disappeared with the capital or cheated in business conducted in far-off markets where none of his associates had any control" (1980, p. 198). Hence, if agency relations are governed by an anonymous market, the agent has nothing to lose by cheating the merchant. Aware of how an agent will act, however, no merchant would ever hire one to begin with.

[4] For a general introduction to Genoa's history, see Vitale (1955). For a general introduction to the Maghribis' history and the *geniza* documents, see Gil (1983b) Vol. 1 Goitein (1967), and Greif (1989, 1993).

[5] Taking a transaction as the basic unit of analysis is a methodology advanced by Williamson (1985).

[6] Among many others, De Roover (1965) noted the superiority of trading systems that employ agents.

For agents to be employed, there must be an institution—other than the market—that enables them to commit ex ante to be honest ex post, after receiving the merchant's goods. Organization theory predicts that when cooperation leads to efficiency gains that the market fails to capture, "private order" economic institutions will be established (Williamson, 1985, pp. 5, 9, 10; Joskow, 1984, p.13). Indeed, such institutions seem to have emerged among the Maghribis and the Genoese, for in both groups trade was based on agency relations among nonfamily members. Such agency relations are reflected, for example, in the first Genoese historical source reflecting agency relations, the Cartulary of Giovanni Scriba (1155–1164). It indicates that only 5.3 percent of the total trade investment did not entail agency relations, and only 6.45 percent of the sum sent abroad through agents was entrusted to family members.

When contractual relations are expected to be repeated, reputation may provide the base for an economic institution that enables trust outside the family. Theoretically, two types of reputation mechanisms related to agency relations can be distinguished (for discussion, see Allen, 1984: Rogerson, 1983,; Shapiro, 1983). The first enables an agent to signal that he is trustworthy because he fears God or has internalized an ideology of honesty. The second reputation mechanism enables an agent whose objective is to maximize his pecuniary income to establish ex ante that his most profitable course ex post is to be honest. The merchant can thus trust the agent because the agent possesses a reputation for honesty. Because an aim of this paper is to demonstrate how different institutional structures can lead to the emergence of distinct values, the analysis will concentrate for the moment on the former mechanism and will assume that an agent's objective is to maximize his pecuniary income.

When agency relations are governed by this latter mechanism, an agent remains honest out of his desire to retain his position as an agent. To make this position attractive, the merchant must create a gap between the expected lifetime utility of an agent employed by him and the agent's best alternative elsewhere. To do so, the merchant can provide an honest agent with a per-period income higher than the agent's (time-averaged) per-period income if he is fired.[7] Of equal importance is the merchant's threat to fire the agent and never operate through him again if he discovers that the agent has cheated.[8] Given a premium and the threat, a dishonest agent can earn a short-run gain by cheating, whereas an honest agent will earn a long-run gain by being paid a per-period premium over his best alternative.

[7] For such an "efficiency wage" mechanism, see Shapiro and Stiglitz (1984).

[8] Note that it is assumed that there is some positive probability that the merchant will be able to detect deviation. See the following regarding the mechanisms employed by the Maghribis and Genoese to balance the asymmetric information inherent in the relations between a merchant and an agent.

An agent acquires the reputation of being an honest agent if it is known that the long-run gain is not less than the short-run gain and hence the agent cannot increase his lifetime utility by cheating. To employ an agent, the merchant will offer the agent the *optimal premium*—the lowest cost premium for which the long-run gain is not less than the short-run gain (for the appropriate model, see Greif, 1993, 1994a).

In the reality of medieval trade, even an honest agent's employment could have been terminated due to the volatile nature of long-distance trade. Although the probability of such termination increases the optimal premium, the reputation mechanism functions also in this case. The possibility of termination, however, implies that even if honesty is induced, some agency relations are expected to be terminated and some agents would be hired each period out of the pool of the unemployed agents. The optimal premium over an agent's reservation utility will have then to take into account that he may be rehired by another merchant.

Two distinct economic institutions based on this reputation mechanism can govern merchant-agent relations and induce honesty: second-party and third-party enforcement institutions. In the former, only a cheated merchant is expected to retaliate against the cheating agent by ceasing to operate through him. In the latter, merchants who were not cheated by a particular agent are expected to retaliate by ceasing to operate through him if he cheated any merchant. (The second-party enforcement mechanism requires the support of the state as will be discussed subsequently.)

It is clear why one would expect a merchant to retaliate against an agent who cheated him. After all, when there is an equilibrium in which a second-party enforcement institution governs the relations between merchants and their agents, the wage paid to agents and the agents' unemployment rate is such that no hired agent finds it optimal to cheat. If a merchant does not retaliate by firing an agent who cheated him, however, that agent would find it optimal to cheat again (unless he is paid a sufficiently higher wage). But because the cheated merchant can hire another agent from the pool of unemployed agents, he can do better by firing the cheater and hiring a new agent.

But under what conditions would a merchant find it optimal not to hire an agent who had cheated another merchant? In the setting previously described, the expectation that all merchants would cease operating through a "cheater," an agent who ever cheated another merchant, is sufficient to motivate each merchant not to hire that agent. In other words, a "collective punishment" is self-enforcing: if it is expected to be practiced, it would indeed be practiced. This is the case because, as discussed earlier, agency relations between any particular merchant and agent can terminate even if the agent is honest.

To see the implications of termination, suppose that agency relations will be terminated after one period even if the agent is honest. If merchants practice collective punishment, cooperation is still possible if the agents are sufficiently patient. Although the bilateral relation with any particular merchant would be terminated after one period, an agent would still refrain from cheating because this implies that he would not be hired in the future by *all* the merchants. But cooperation is not possible with an agent who had cheated in the past, because he would not be hired by other merchants in the future even if he is honest in the current period. Hence, one who cheated in the past would find it optimal to cheat again if hired, expecting not to be hired in the future in any case. Anticipating that, a merchant would not hire a cheater and the collective punishment becomes self-enforcing. When agency relations are expected to be terminated with a probability lower than one, agency relations with a cheater can be established. Yet, a cheater will remain honest only if paid a wage higher than that of an honest agent. As before, a cheater—unlike an honest agent—does not consider the implications of cheating on his future relations with all the merchants. Hence, merchants strictly prefer to hire an agent who has never cheated implying that the collective punishment is self-enforcing.

Expectations of collective punishment also have implications with respect to costly acquisition and transmission of information. Suppose that each merchant can either invest or not invest in getting attached to a network of information before the game begins and his action is common knowledge. Investing requires bearing the cost of information gathering each period, in return for which the merchant learns the private histories of all the merchants who also invested. Otherwise, he knows only his own history. When collective punishment is expected, agents' histories have value and hence merchants are motivated to invest in gathering information. This is so because the wage required to keep an agent honest is a function of his history, in that an agent who cheated in the past will cheat if rehired and paid the ongoing wage.[9] Similarly, if an agent is hired by a merchant who is not attached to the information network, he would cheat the merchant unless paid a wage higher than the ongoing one. The availability of information, in turn, makes collective punishment possible. Note that the opposite is true in the absence of expectations for collective punishment. An agent's wage is not a function of his history and merchants are not motivated to invest in gathering the information. But if merchants are not gathering information, collective punishment can not be expected to be practiced.[10]

[9] This follows directly from the preceding discussion of the self-enforceability of the collective punishment. A cheater will cheat at the ongoing wage because this wage reflects the deterrence implied by the collective punishment, but a cheater is already subject to this punishment and hence the threat of such punishment does not deter cheating (see discussion in Greif, 1993, 1994a).

[10] Clearly, in reality information has many dimensions and even under second-party enforcement some information many have value. Yet, under third-party enforcement, there is an additional motivation to acquire information.

IV. 3 SELECTING AN ECONOMIC INSTITUTION: CULTURAL AND SOCIAL FACTORS

Schelling (1980) has pointed out that cultural and social factors influence the selection of alternative solutions in a multiple equilibrium game by making one rather than another a natural focal point. Were the cultural differences between the Maghribis and the Genoese such that they were likely to affect the selection of an institution from among the two self-enforcing ones just discussed? When the Maghribis began trading in the Mediterranean early in the 11th century and when the Genoese began trading toward the end of that century, they had already internalized different cultures and were in the midst of different social and political processes. Their cultural heritage and the nature of these processes suggest that among the Maghribis the second-party collectivist equilibrium was a natural focal point, whereas among the Genoese it was the first-party, individualist equilibrium.

The Maghribis were *mustarbin,* that is, non-Muslims (Jews), who adopted the values of the Muslim society. Among these values was the view that they were members of the same *umma.* This term, although translated as "nation," is derived from the word *umm,* meaning "mother," reflecting the basic value of mutual responsibility among the members of that society (see, e.g., Cahen, 1990). Further, *umma's* members shared the fundamental duty to practice good and to ensure that *others* did not practice sin (B. Lewis, 1991). In addition, the Maghribis were part of the Jewish community, within which there was a prominent idea that "All Israel is responsible for every member." Furthermore, as is common among immigrant groups, the Maghribis, who migrated from Iraq to Tunisia, probably retained social ties that enabled them to transmit the information required to support a collectivist equilibrium.

In contrast, Christianity during this period placed the individual rather than the social group at the center of its theology. It advanced the creation of "a new society based not on the family but on the individual, whose salvation, like his original loss of innocence, was personal and private."[11] Indeed, the contract through which the Genoese established their city shortly before 1099 was a contract between individuals, not between families or other social groups. Furthermore, for political reasons, the number of Genoese active in trade rose dramatically toward the end of the 12th century. While the historical records from the middle of the century reflect the operation of a few dozen traders in each trade center abroad, the records from the late 12th century reflect the operation of hundreds of Genoese in each trade center. At the same time, Genoa experienced a high level of immigration. For instance, Genoa's population increased from 30,000 to 100,000 between 1200 and 1300. In the absence of appropriate social

[11] See Hughes (1974, p. 61) and Macfarlane (1978) on English individualism during this time.

networks for information transmission, the individualist equilibrium was likely to be selected.

The distinct cultural and social conditions among the Maghribis and the Genoese were likely to direct each of these groups toward distinct equilibria. Does the historical evidence indicate such divergence? That is, was there high investment in information and collective punishment among the Maghribis and low investment in information and individualist punishment among the Genoese?

The historical evidence indicates that the Maghribis invested in sharing information and the Genoese did not. Each Maghribi corresponded with many other Maghribi traders by sending informative letters to them with the latest available commercial information and gossip, including whatever transpired in agency relations among other Maghribis. Important business dealings were conducted in public, and the names of the witnesses were widely publicized (Goitein, 1967, 1973; Greif, 1989). Information transmission was probably facilitated by the relatively small size of the Maghribi traders' group (although as discussed later, this size was endogenously determined). In 175 documents, for example, 330 different names are mentioned.[12] Although most likely not every Maghribi trader was familiar with all the others, belonging to the Maghribis was easily verifiable through common acquaintances, an extensive network of communication, a common religion, and a common language (Judaeo-Arabic).

Collective punishment is reflected in the historical records, although it was rarely used.[13] For example, in the first decade of the 11th century, Samhun ben Da'ud, a prominent trader from Tunisia, sent a long letter to his business associate, Joseph ben 'Awkal of Fustat. In the letter it is explicit that Joseph's future dealings with Samhun were conditional upon his record: "If your handling of my business is correct, then I shall send you goods." It happened, however, that Samhun did not handle Joseph's business to his satisfaction—Joseph believed that Samhun had intentionally not remitted his revenues on time. Joseph's response was to ignore Samhun's request to pay two of Samhun's creditors in Fustat. By the time Samhun found out about it "their letters filled with condemnation had reached everyone." The contents of these letters caused Samhun to complain that "my reputation (or honor) is being ruined."[14] (Goitein, 1973, pp. 26ff; Stillman, 1970, pp.267ff; for other examples and discussion, see Greif 1989, 1993)

[12] These letters are all that are available regarding trade with Sicily and Israel during the mid-11th century and the trade of Naharay ben Nissim (see Michael, 1965; Gil, 1983a; Ben-Sasson, 1991).

[13] The previous 175 contracts reflect at least 653 business ventures but only 3 cases of alleged cheating.

[14] DK 13, a. ll. 26 ff., 41.

In contrast, the Genoese seem to have held an opposite attitude regarding information sharing.[15] Lopez (1943) noted the efforts of the Genoese to conceal information and conjectured that the "individualistic, taciturn, and reserved Genoese" were not "talkative" about their businesses and were even "jealous of their business secrets" (p. 168). For example, when the Vivaldi brothers attempted in 1291 to sail from Genoa to the Far East through the Atlantic, their commercial agreements were drawn for trade in "Majorca, [and] even [in] the Byzantine Empire" (p. 169). Genoa's historical records are not explicit about the nature of punishment inflicted on an agent who cheated, but they suggest a lack of collective punishment and informal communication (De Roover, 1965, pp. 88–89; Lopez, 1943, p. 180).

Cultural factors that coordinated expectations and social and political factors that slightly altered the relevant games in the formative period seem to have directed the Maghribis and the Genoese toward different equilibria, each of which corresponds to the governance of agency relations by a distinct economic institution. To gain additional support for the conjecture that agency relations within each group were governed by distinct institutions, predictions generated under the assumption that distinct institutions prevailed are confronted with the historical records. At the same time, the nature of these predictions indicates the relationship between economic, cultural, social, and political factors in generating a society's institutional structure. The first such prediction regards social structures, as discussed in the next section.

IV. 4 THE CULTURAL CONTENT AND SOCIAL RAMIFICATIONS OF DISTINCT ECONOMIC INSTITUTIONS

Each of the economic institutions that seems to have governed agency relations among the Maghribis and Genoese reflects a distinct cultural and social heritage. Although distinct heritages provide different focal points, the related institutions enhance and give distinct content to a cultural element—cultural beliefs. Cultural beliefs are the ideas and thoughts common to several individuals that govern interactions—among these people and among them, their gods, and other groups—and that differ from knowledge in that they are not empirically discovered nor analytically proven (e.g., Bandura, 1971; Davis, 1949, esp. pp. 52ff., 192ff.). Even though the rules of the game associated with each of the enforcement institutions discussed earlier are identical, the cultural beliefs associated with each are not. Each entails different expectations with respect to actions that would be taken following cheating. In the second-party enforcement institution, members

[15] Epstein (1994) has examined the methods used by the Genoese to foster trust while retaining secrecy.

of the society hold "individualistic cultural beliefs," as merchants are expected to be indifferent to whatever transpired among other merchants and agents. In the third-party enforcement institution, members of the society hold "collectivist" cultural beliefs, as merchants are expected to respond to whatever transpires among others.

In general, following the crystallization of cultural beliefs with respect to a particular game, they become identical and commonly known through the socialization process by which culture is unified, maintained, and communicated. Hence, once a specific set of cultural beliefs crystallizes among members of a society, it has an enduring impact that may transcend the boundaries of the specific context within which it was formed. As cultural beliefs are the expectations held by members of a society, they influence a society's response when history alters the environment. Indeed, historical changes altered the environment in which the Maghribis and the Genoese operated in a manner that directly affected merchant-agent relations. Following various military and political changes in the Mediterranean, both groups had the opportunity to expand their trade to areas previously inaccessible to them (see discussion in A. R. Lewis, 1951).[16] Commercially, both groups responded similarly and expanded their trade from Spain to Constantinople. Socially, however, their responses differed: the Genoese responded in an "integrated" manner, whereas the Maghribis responded in a "segregated" manner.

The Maghribis expanded their trade by employing other Maghribis as agents. They emigrated from North Africa to other trade centers, and for generations the descendants of Maghribis continued to cooperate with the descendants of other Maghribis (Gil, 1983b, Vol. 1, pp. 200ff.; Goitein, 1967, pp. 156-159, 186-192;). For example, in the letters of Naharay ben Nissim, the most important Maghribi trader in Fustat around the mid-century, 97 different traders are mentioned but only 2 were Muslims.[17] This segregated response cannot be accounted for as a result of the Maghribis being a religious minority, because they did not establish agency relations with other Jewish traders even when these relations were (ignoring agency cost) perceived by the Maghribis as very profitable. This was true, in particular, with respect to Italian Jewish merchants (Goitein, 1973, pp. 44, 211; Greif, 1989, 1993). That this segregation was endogenous is also reflected in the Maghribis' later history when, toward the end of the 12th century, they were forced by the ruler of Egypt to cease trading. At this point they integrated into the Jewish communities and vanished from the stage of history.

The Genoese also responded to the new opportunities by emigrating abroad, and their cartularies indicate that agency relations among Genoese

[16] Among these changes were the disintegration of the Muslim Caliphate in Spain, the rise of the Fatimids in North Africa, and the decline of the Byzantine naval power.

[17] Al Qasim and Muhammad. Based on the 37 documents published by Michael (1965).

prevailed. Yet although the cartularies were written in Genoa and hence are biased toward reflecting agency relations among Genoese, they nevertheless clearly indicate the establishment of agency relations between Genoese and non-Genoese. For example, in the cartulary of the Genoese Giovanni Scriba (1155–1164), at least 18.3 percent of the total sent abroad through agents was sent or carried by a non-Genoese.[18]

The rationale behind the Maghribis' and the Genoese's different responses to the same exogenous change in the rules of the game is clear once one considers the impact of cultural beliefs on equilibrium selection. The change altered the game in a specific manner. As trade with more remote trade centers became possible, a merchant could either hire an agent from his own economy who would sail or emigrate abroad, or he could hire an agent native to the other trade center. Such intereconomy agency relations are likely to be more efficient than intraeconomy agency relations, because they enhance commercial flexibility. Furthermore, a native agent does not need to emmigrate and he is likely to possess a better knowledge of local conditions.

In deciding whether to establish intereconomy agency relations, however, a merchant's concern is profitability, not efficiency. The relations between efficiency and profitability are influenced by cultural beliefs that crystallized before intereconomy agency relations become possible. The collectivist cultural beliefs associated with the third-party enforcement institution create a wedge between efficient and profitable agency relations, leading to a "segregated" society in which efficient intereconomy agency relations are not established. This is not the case when individualist cultural beliefs prevail. In the absence of a wedge between profitable and efficient agency relations, an integrated society in which intereconomy agency relations are established will emerge.

To see why this is the case, suppose for the moment that information regarding agents' past behavior is common knowledge. Further suppose that two *identical* economies, within which either individualist or collectivist cultural beliefs prevails, become a *joint economy* in which players can identify members of their previous economy and intereconomy agency relations are possible. What will the patterns of hiring agents in the joint economy be as a function of the players' cultural beliefs? (For a formal presentation of the following argument, see Greif, 1994a.)

Intuitively, when players project their cultural beliefs on the new game—that is, when their expectations concerning others' actions in the

[18] For non-Genoese in other cartularies see, for example, Oberto Scriba de Mercato (1186, No. 9, p. 38; 1190, Nos, 138, 139), Guglielmo Cassinese (1190–1192, No. 418, p. 1325), and Lanfranco (1202–1226, No. 524). The ease of hiring non-Genoese is reflected in their use to circumvent a politically unfavorable situation in Sicily (see Abulafia, 1977, pp. 201ff.).

postchange game are the prechange expectations—these prechange cultural beliefs constitute the initial conditions for a dynamic adjustment process.[19] For example, if the prechange economies were collectivist, players would expect each merchant to hire agents from his own economy and expect that merchants of the same economy would retaliate against an agent who has cheated one of them. Yet the prechange cultural beliefs are insufficient to calculate best responses in the postchange game. To find the best response, a player must hold expectations regarding what others will do in every possible situation. In the postchange game there are situations that were not feasible before, and with respect to which the prechange cultural beliefs do not provide any guide for action. For example, the prechange cultural beliefs do not specify how merchants from one economy would react to actions taken by an agent from their economy in intereconomy agency relations. As the others' strategies are not specified, a player cannot find the best response.

To find the best response, a merchant has to form expectations about the response of the merchants from the other economy to actions taken in intereconomy agency relations.[20] Although the merchants from the agent's economy can be expected to respond in various ways, two responses predominate. For any agent's action in intereconomy agency relations, the merchants from the agent's economy can regard the agent either as one who cheated one of them or as one who did not cheat one of them. For example, in a collectivist economy the merchants may consider an agent who cheated in intereconomy agency relations as a cheater subject to collective retaliation, or they may ignore the agent's cheating. Nothing in the prechange cultural beliefs, however, indicates which of these responses will be selected for each action. Accordingly, the best that can be done analytically is to assume that in intereconomy agency relations any probability distribution over these two responses is possible.[21] Considering the prechange cultural beliefs and any such probability distributions as initial conditions enables examination of the merchants' best response (while not imposing any differences between the prechange economies apart from their cultural beliefs).

[19] For references and results regarding this type of convergence, see Milgrom and Roberts (1990). For a sociological discussion of the tendency to value cultural patterns of behavior and the tension between these values and behavior, see Davis (1949, pp. 52–53). For an economic analysis, see Geanakoplos *et al.* (1989).

[20] Because at this stage the analysis abstracts away from the relations between cultural beliefs and values, it is implicitly assumed that merchants are not expected to respond to the mere act of hiring an agent from the other economy. Note that when a merchant hires an agent from the other economy, the merchants from his economy stand to gain as unemployment rises in their economy and, hence, agents' wages fall.

[21] This probability distribution can also be thought of as reflecting a merchant's uncertainty regarding the agent's expectations concerning the responses of the merchants from the agents' economy.

What would the merchants' best response be as a function of their cultural beliefs? It is easier to present the related analysis, assuming initially that there is no efficiency gain from intereconomy agency relations. Intuitively, when intereconomy agency relations become possible between two collectivist economies, the initial cultural beliefs specify collective punishment in intraeconomy agency relations. But if there is some doubt about whether collective punishment also governs intereconomy agency relations (that is, in all but one probability distribution over the two possible responses), the optimal wage in intereconomy agency relations is higher than in intraeconomy relations, because the uncertainty about collective punishment in intereconomy relations reduces the probability that an agent who cheats in such relations will be punished. This increases the wage that has to be paid to keep the agent honest: a decline in the severity of the punishment for cheating must be offset by an increase in the reward for honesty. As the merchants' cost of establishing intereconomy agency relations is higher than the cost of establishing intraeconomy agency relations, only the latter will be initiated, and segregation is the end result. If intereconomy agency relations are more efficient, the analysis implies that merchants will initiate them only if the efficiency gains are sufficiently large.

The foregoing analysis does not hold when intereconomy agency relations become possible between two individualistic economies. Although similar uncertainty is likely to exist, the intereconomy and intraeconomy optimal wages are the same. Individualist cultural beliefs make this uncertainty irrelevant for the determination of the optimal wage. Hence, any efficiency gains from intereconomy agency relations will motivate merchants to establish them.[22]

Although a similar analysis can be conducted when a collectivist and an individualist society interact, this discussion indicates the mechanism through which cultural factors manifested through economic institutions support the emergence of distinct social structures that, in turn, reinforce the original cultural factors and economic institutions. Finally, this discussion assumes that information regarding agents' histories can be obtained without any cost. Clearly, relaxing this assumption strengthens the results discussed. In particular, if merchants do not learn about the actions taken by an agent in intereconomy agency relations, they cannot be expected to retaliate by imposing a collective punishment. Hence, this analysis indicates that cultural factors, manifested through and reinforced by economic institutions and social structure, can influence social boundaries of economic interactions.

Cultural beliefs, however, can also influence the nature of the relations within the social structures they reinforce. In the specific cases of the

[22] For a formal presentation of this argument, see Greif (1994a).

Maghribis and Genoese, this influence was to determine whether their social structures would be "vertical" or "horizontal." A vertical social structure is one in which an individual functions as either a merchant or an agent, while a horizontal structure is one in which an individual functions as an agent *and* a merchant, providing and receiving agency services.

Examining the relations between the cultural beliefs associated with the two economic institutions and social structures requires extending the theoretical analysis to allow each merchant to serve as an agent for another merchant. Suppose this is the case, and redefine the collectivist cultural beliefs to include the expectations that merchants will not retaliate against someone who cheats a merchant who has cheated any other merchant. Indeed, the historical evidence indicates that Maghribis shared such expectations; whoever was hired by a merchant who had cheated in the past was not expected to be subjected to collective punishment if he cheated that merchant. The one who cheated a cheater was not subject to collective punishment. For example, a Maghribi merchant who was accused in 1041–1042 of cheating complains that when it became known, "people became agitated and hostile and whoever owed [me money] conspired to keep it from [me]."[23]

What are the relations between cultural beliefs and the selection over vertical and horizontal social patterns of agency relations?[24] The collectivist cultural beliefs are likely to lead to a horizontal social structure, whereas the individualist cultural beliefs are likely to lead to a vertical social structure. Under collectivist cultural beliefs, a merchant's capital functions as a bond that reduces the wage required to keep him honest when he functions as an agent. A merchant who cheats while functioning as an agent is no longer able to hire agents under the threat of collective punishment. Hence, cheating by a merchant who is functioning as an agent reduces the future rate of return on that agent's capital. This implies that a merchant who had cheated while functioning as an agent had to bear a cost that an agent (who cannot function as a merchant) would not have to bear. Hence, a lower wage is required to keep a merchant honest and each merchant is motivated to hire another merchant as his agent leading, *ceteris paribus,* to a horizontal social structure. This is not the case, however, under individualist cultural beliefs. Past cheating does not reduce the rate of return on a merchant's capital. But having capital to invest *de facto* increases a merchant's reservation utility relative to that of an agent's, thereby increasing

[23] Bodl. MS Heb a 2 f. 17, Sect. D (Goitein, 1973, p. 104; see also Greif, 1989, 1993). Regarding the Italian merchants not holding such beliefs, see, for example, De Roover (1965, pp. 88–89).

[24] The basic logic of the argument developed below resembles that of Bernheim and Whinston (1990).

the wage required to keep him honest. Merchants are discouraged from hiring other merchants as their agents, leading, *ceteris paribus,* to a vertical social structure.

Differences in social structure are indeed observed between the Maghribis and the Genoese. The Maghribi traders were, by and large, merchants who invested in trade through horizontal agency relations. Each trader served as an agent for several merchants while receiving agency services from them or other traders. Sedentary traders served as agents for those who traveled, and vice versa. Wealthy merchants served as agents for poorer ones, and vice versa. Among the Maghribis there was not a "merchants' class" and an "agents' class." The extent to which the Maghribis' social structure was horizontal can be quantified by examining the related distributions of "agency measure," which is defined as the number of times a trader operated as an agent divided by the number of times a trader operated as either a merchant or an agent. It equals one if the trader was only an agent, zero if the trader was only a merchant, and some intermediate value in between if the trader was both a merchant and an agent. In 175 letters written by Maghribi traders in which 653 agency relations are reflected, 119 traders appear more than once, and almost 70 percent of them have an agency measure between zero and one. Furthermore, the more a trader appears in the documents, the more likely the trader is to have an agency measure close to one-half.[25]

The horizontal social structure of the Maghribis is also reflected in the forms of business associations through which they established agency relations, mainly partnership and formal friendship. In "partnership," two or more traders invested capital and labor in a joint venture and shared the profit in proportion to their capital investment. In "formal friendship," two traders who operated in different trade centers provided each other with agency services without receiving pecuniary compensation (Goitein, 1967, pp. 214ff.; Stillman, 1970; Gil, 1983b, Vol. 1, pp. 200ff.; for business associations, see Goitein, 1973, pp.11ff.; Gil, 1983b, Vol. 1, pp. 216ff.).[26]

In contrast, agency relations among the Genoese traders were vertical. In Italy, in general, wealthy merchants, who rarely if ever functioned as agents, hired relatively poor agents, who rarely if ever functioned as merchants (De Roover, 1965, pp. 51 ff.). Genoa's historical records reflect the operation of 1,345 agents during the 12th century. Although as many as 78 percent of them invested in trade, their total annual investments ranged from 20 to 33 percent of the total overseas trade (Krueger, 1993, p. 282). Byrne (1917) concluded that during the late 12th century, "as a rule" the

[25] This data set is defined in fn. 12. Value-based agency measure cannot be calculated for the Maghribis.

[26] Goitein (1964, p. 316) concluded that about half of the business dealings reflected in the Geniza are formal friendships.

Genoese agents were "not men of great wealth or of high position" (p. 159), and Krueger (1993) has noted that "most travelling merchants were a notch or two lower than the 'investing' merchants in the political, fiscal, and social life of twelfth century Genoa" (p. 282). Agency measures calculated from specific cartularies reflect this assertion. For example, only 21 percent of the 190 trader families mentioned more than once in the cartulary of Giovanni Scriba (1155–1164) have an agency measure between zero and one, and in value terms only 11 percent have this agency measure.[27] The vertical character of the Genoese social structure is also reflected in the forms of business associations through which they established agency relations. They mainly used *commenda* contracts, which were, by and large, established between two parties, one providing capital and the other providing work in the form of traveling and transacting overseas. The differences in the forms of business associations between the two merchant groups does not reflect diverse knowledge (Krueger, 1962; for general discussion, see, for example, De Roover, 1965; knowledge: Lieber, 1968). Rather, distinct economic institutions motivated the use of different business practices.

Another implication of vertical relation is that it is likely, in the long run, to affect a society's wealth distribution. Specifically, under individualist cultural beliefs an agent's ability to commit is negatively related to the agent's wealth and hence wealthless individuals are better able to capture the rent (above the reservation utility) available to agents. Indeed, Genoese historical sources reflect a dynamic of wealth distribution that conforms to the theoretical prediction. Wealth transfer is reflected in a declining concentration of trade investments and the increase, over time, of trade investments made by commoners (that is, nonnobles). In the cartulary of Giovanni Scriba (1155–1164), trade was concentrated, by and large, in the hands of a few noble families, and less than 10 percent of the merchants invested 70 percent of the total. In the cartulary of Oberto Scriba (1186), 10 percent of the families invested almost 60 percent. In 1376, the only year for which, to the best of my knowledge, data are available in the secondary literature, commoners who paid customs in Genoa exceeded nobles (295 versus 279), and the share of the latter amounted to only 64 percent of the total (Kedar, 1976, pp. 51–52).[28] That agency relations shifted wealth distribution is reflected, for example, in the affairs of Ansaldo Baialardo, who was hired in 1156 by the noble Genoese merchant Ingo della Volta. From 1156 to 1158, Ansaldo sailed abroad as Ingo's agent, and by investing only his retained earnings he accumulated the sum of 142 lire. (see De Roover, 1965, pp. 51–52). A house in Genoa cost about 40 lire. (see Giovanni di Guiberto, 1200–1211, Nos. 260, 261).

[27] Krueger (1957) concluded that only 6 percent (36 individuals) of the traders mentioned in Giovanni Scriba functioned as both agents and merchants.

[28] De Roover (1965) argued that agency relations in Italy facilitated wealth transfer.

IV. 5 POLITICAL STRUCTURE AND COMPATIBLE ECONOMIC INSTITUTIONS, CULTURAL BELIEFS, AND SOCIAL STRUCTURES

In a "collectivist" society such as that of the Maghribis, collectivist cultural beliefs support an economic self-enforcing collective punishment, horizontal agency relations, segregation, and an ingroup social communication network. In such a society individuals can be induced to forgo "improper" behavior—unrelated to agency relations—through a credible threat of informal collective economic punishment. If every Maghribi expects everyone else to consider a specific behavior as "improper" and punishable in the same manner as cheating in agency relations, this punishment is self-enforcing for the same reasons the collective punishment in agency relations is self-enforcing and is feasible based on the existing network for information transmission.

In an "individualist" society such as that of the Genoese, individualist cultural beliefs support a second-party enforcement institution, vertical and integrated social structure, a relatively low level of communication, and no economic self-enforcing collective punishment. In such a society a relatively low level of informal economic enforcement can be achieved due to the absence of economic self-enforcing collective punishment and networks for information transmission. In such a society a legal system based on the authority of the state is required to provide the enforceability necessary to foster exchange, support collective actions, and mitigate free rider problems.

For example, in an individualist society such as Genoa's but not in a collectivist society such as the Maghribis', a political organization with the ability to enforce its administrative and legal decisions has to supplement the operation of the individualist private order institution that governs agency relations to render it effective. This need was not reflected in the previous discussion because it was assumed that an agent's benefit from embezzling a merchant's goods resulted from increasing the agent's consumption at the period when embezzlement occurred. Although this is a standard assumption in efficiency wage models, in the historical context under consideration an agent could have used the embezzled capital for investment. That is, because any agent had the knowledge required to be an active participant in long-distance trade, the agent could have used the embezzled capital to trade each period following its embezzlement. Hence, deterring cheating requires satisfying an additional incentive compatibility constraint—an agent must be better off by remaining honest than by cheating and becoming a merchant utilizing the embezzled capital.

Whenever agency relations are governed by a collectivist punishment that induces a horizontal social structure, this problem can be mitigated without a legal system based on the coercive power of the state. The essence of a horizontal social structure is that merchants also act as agents. Hence, cheating while functioning as an agent implies increasing one's capital but reducing the expected return from *all* of one's capital, as the merchant would no longer be able to employ agents subject to collective punishment.[29] Hence, in a collectivist society even in the absence of a legal system, an honest agent can be better off than an agent who cheats and becomes a merchant utilizing the embezzled capital.

This, however, is not the case in an individualist society in which agents are not expected to be subject to collective punishment. An agent who embezzled goods would not be recruited by the cheated merchant again, but could become a merchant himself, able to utilize agents under the same conditions as the merchant he had cheated. Hence, only if agents' wages are so high that anyone prefers being an agent rather than a merchant can agency relations be established. In other words, for agents to be employed, the merchants have to pay them all the profit and a part of the capital. Clearly, there cannot be an equilibrium with such a wage. Hence, for agency relations to be established in an individualist society there is a need for an external mechanism—such as a legal system backed by the state—that restricts agents' ability to embezzle merchants' capital. (Note, however, that whenever this system has a limited ability to restrict cheating from misreporting profit expenses, and so forth, a reputation mechanism still has to be used.)

During the period under consideration, Genoa had just been incorporated into a city and liberated *de facto* from the rule of the Holy Roman Empire (e.g., *Annali Genovesi,* 1162, Vol. I; see discussion in Airaldi, 1986; Vitali, 1955). Similarly, the Maghribis immigrated to and operated within the Fatimid Caliphate, in which "the administration of their own affairs was left to themselves" (Goitein, 1971, p. 1). Hence both groups were in a position to devise their own form of authority and jurisdiction. Yet it was the Genoese who developed formal organizations to support agency relations and exchange; the Maghribis did not develop such organizations and seem not to have used the ones available to them.

During the 12th century, the Genoese ceased to use the ancient custom of entering contracts by a handshake and developed an extensive legal system for the registration and enforcement of contracts. Furthermore, the customary contract law that governed the relations among Genoese traders was codified as permanent courts were established (e.g., Vitale, 1955). These courts limited an agent's ability to embezzle a merchant's entire capital by making his family members responsible for (verifiable) illegal actions taken by him (such as outright embezzling all the merchant's capital) and requiring, at least during the 12th century, the agent to return to Genoa to settle

[29] That is, he will be able to employ agents utilizing only second-party enforcement. Hence, the wage required to keep the agent honest would be higher than it is when the agent is subject to collective punishment.

his account. Furthermore, the courts attempted to restrict an agent's ability to cheat by fixing a minimum percentage of profit that the agent was obliged to provide the merchant if he was unable to produce an account (Lattes, 1939, pp. 77, 154).[30] The emerging legal system was also important to the relations between agents and merchants from different political units. It was an integral part of a "community responsibility system" through which a merchant could reclaim his capital from an absent alien agent by holding his compatriots responsible for the damage.[31]

The Maghribi traders had access to two legal systems and the authority of both was backed by the state. Any resident in the Islamic domain could sue and receive justice from the Muslim legal system. In addition, the Jewish legal system in the Fatimid Caliphate was recognized by the state as having authority over the Jews who chose to use it. The court's decisions were backed not only by the community as a whole, but also by the state police. Yet, despite the existence of such a well-developed Jewish communal court system whose authority was backed by the state, the Maghribis entered contracts informally, used or adopted an informal code of conduct, and attempted to resolve disputes informally (see, for example, Goitein, 1967; Greif, 1989, 1993).

The different role of the government and its legal system in collectivist and individualist societies is also likely to manifest itself when collective action is required and free rider problems need to be mitigated. In the context of medieval trade, such a distinct response was likely to manifest itself in the manner in which the Maghribi and Genoese traders mitigated the need for enforcement required to support collective action in the relations between them and the rulers of the territories in which they traded.

The medieval ruler could abuse the property rights of *alien* traders visiting his territory. Theoretically, as long as the number of traders is sufficiently low, however, the relative high value to the ruler of each trader's future trade is sufficient to motivate the ruler to respect their rights. When the number of traders is large, however, this is no longer the case. A mechanism that might provide protection to traders at the higher volume of trade is for (sufficiently many) traders to respond—in the form of a trade embargo—to transgressions by the ruler against any trader. Once an embargo is declared, however, some traders can benefit from ignoring it and selling their goods in the prohibited area in times of shortage. Hence, some enforcement mechanism is required to assure that each trader will indeed respect a collective

[30] He uses evidence from the 14th century that probably originated in an earlier period. Legal development in Genoa predated the first evidence regarding agency relations among the Genoese, as it occurred during the 10th century, and concerns property rights in land.

[31] The operation of this system is reflected, for example, in the 12th-century Genoese contract preserved in Giovanni Scriba (1164, No. 1245); for discussion, see Greif (1995).

decision to impose an embargo.[32] In collectivist societies one would expect that informal enforcement mechanisms would be sufficient to ensure traders' compliance with embargo decisions. In individualist societies, however, one would expect organizations specializing in embargo enforcement to emerge.

Indeed, the historical evidence concerning the Maghribis and the Genoese is consistent with this prediction. Among the Maghribis, compliance was assured through informal means. After the Muslim ruler of Sicily abused the rights of some Maghribi traders, the Maghribis responded by imposing, circa 1050, an embargo on Sicily. It was organized informally. Maymun ben Khalpha wrote a letter to Naharay ben Nissim of Fustat (old Cairo) from Palermo (Sicily), in which he informed Naharay about the tax increase and asked him to "hold the hands of our friends [i.e., Maghribi traders] not to send to Sicily even one dirham [a low-value coin]." Indeed, the Maghribis sailed that year to Tunisia and not to Sicily, and a year later the tax was abolished.[33] There is no evidence that compliance was supported by any formal enforcement organization, although the Maghribis could have used the Jewish court system or a communal organization to this end.

In contrast, the city of Genoa functioned as a formal enforcement organization to make the threat of collective retaliation credible. After the authorities had declared that a certain area was a *devetum,* any merchant found there was subject to legal prosecution. For example, in 1340 the ruler of Tabriz (an important trade center between the Black Sea and the Persian Gulf) abused many Genoese traders, and Genoa responded by declaring a *devetum* against the city. In 1343, during the *devetum,* a Genoese merchant named Tommaso Gentile was on his way from Hormuz to China. Somewhere in the Pamir plateau he fell sick and had to entrust his goods to his companions and head back to Genoa by the shortest route. His way, however, passed through Tabriz. When this became known in Genoa, Tommaso's father had to justify the transgression before the court, which accepted the claim of an act of God and acquitted Tommaso without a penalty (Lopez, 1943, pp. 181-183).

Collectivist and individualist societies have distinct "demands" for a state. In particular, an individualist society, but not a collectivist society, requires a government with the coercive power and administrative structure required to be able to confiscate individuals' wealth and imprison them in

[32] For theoretical exposition of the traders-ruler relations, the associated commitment problem, and the role of the European Merchant Gild in assuring collective action, see Greif *et al.* (1994).

[33] DK # 22, a, ll. 29–31, b, ll. 3–5 (Gil, 1983a, pp. 97–106); TS 10 J 12, f. 26, a,ll. 18–20 (Michael, 1965, Vol. II, p. 85).

case of need. Yet, the ability for this demand to be fulfilled without undermining economic growth by its own existence depends on the process through which the government is "supplied." When a strong government exists, to advance economic exchange and performance effectively it should be able to commit to the security of private property rights. In the absence of such commitment, individuals would refrain from using the legal system to support exchange, fearing predation. This government commitment problem can be mitigated either by the government's nature or its administrative structure. When a government is effectively controlled by the members of its society—as is arguably the case under ideal democracy—commitment to property rights is trivially achieved.[34] When this is not the case, however, commitment can be achieved by a government with coercive ability if it does not have the administrative structure required to make predation profitable.[35]

An individualist society, such as that of the Genoese, requires a government having the coercive power and administrative structure necessary for an effective legal system. Hence, only if this government is controlled by the individuals it serves, economic efficiency is not undermined due to the government commitment problem. A collectivist society, such as that of the Maghribis, does not have to have a strong government, but if such a government exists, the government commitment problem can be mitigated by having a meager administration and by controlling subjects and generating revenues not directly but through the various groups that constitute the collectivist and segregated society.

It is interesting to note that the nature of the political systems within which the Maghribis and Genoese traders operated match those discussed earlier as required to foster economic efficiency. The collectivist Maghribis were governed by a strong military but administratively weak government in whose functioning they—as the middle class in the Muslim Mediterranean during this period in general—had nothing to say. At the same time, this government utilized the segregated nature of the society as its administrative structure. As was noted by Goitein (1973), "there was very little contact between the world of the [Muslim or other] traders and that of the government" (p. 10). These traders, like all the other members of the "middle class" in the Muslim Mediterranean at the time, were governed by a military elite of Turkish or Berber decent. This elite did not establish any elaborate bureaucracy, and the government's control over the population was

[34] North and Weingast (1989) argued that England's economic growth was fostered by the Parliament's ability to constrain the king.

[35] That is, it does not have the ability to obtain information regarding the distribution of wealth required for a predation profitable relative to the alternative. For the strategic use of administrative structure by the absolute kings of Spain to enhance their ability to commit to property rights, see Conklin 1993.

extended by taking advantage of existing commercial associations, such as the Maghribi traders', urban neighborhood associations, and ethnic or religious groups. The weak bureaucracy established by this elite seems to have served them well in fostering their commitment to respect the property rights of their subjects. At the same time, the segregated nature of the society enabled exchange, despite the absence of elaborate bureaucracy, and provided a mechanism for extending control over the population to the elite (for general discussion, see, in particular, Udovitch, 1988).

The individualistic Genoese had established and controlled a relatively strong and effective government. Its contractual nature is well reflected in the *Genoese Annals* written shortly after Genoa's establishment. "At the time of the fleet to Casarea [a port town in Israel], or a little before [that is, around 1096], in the city of the Genoese, a *compagna* [that is, commune or a temporarily sworn association] of three years with six consuls has begun" (*Annali Genovesi,* 1099, Vol. I, p.9.). After incorporating into a city, Genoa gradually liberated itself from the rule of the Holy Roman Empire and in 1164 its independence was *de jure* recognized by the Empire. Among other prerogatives, it gained the right to nominate its own counsuls and judges, and to impose and collect taxes (e.g., *Annali Genovesi,* 1162, Vol. I; see discussion in Airaldi, 1986; Vitale, 1955). The Genoese established a republic in which each male member had the right to vote, although only nobles could be elected to some offices prior to 1257. To enhance the impartiality of their political and legal system, in 1194 the Genoese went as far as establishing a political system in which a non-Genoese was hired for a specific (and short) period of time, during which one of his functions was to be responsible for the security of property rights and the operation of the legal system (for discussion and references, see Greif, 1994b; Vitale, 1951, 1955).[36]

The study of the general political and social processes that led to this compatibilty between these societies' economic institutions and their political systems is beyond the scope of this chapter. Yet, it is interesting to note that among the Genoese the nature of the economic institutions that governed agency relations seems to have had direct implications for the development of Genoa's political system. Specifically, as discussed in Section III, agency relations were based on a second-party enforcement mechanism leading to a dynamic of wealth distribution that increased the wealth and strength of the nonnoble Genoese. A relative increase in the wealth possessed by a subgroup within a society is likely to lead members of the subgroup to be able to achieve a greater say in political matters. This is especially true in a period when military ability was conditional on having the resources to build fortifications and acquire expensive military equipment.

[36] For the observation that in the Italian cities of the period, in general, the political system was controlled by the merchants who utilized it to advance their interests, see, for example, Cipolla, 1963, p. 397.

Indeed, the *popoli* of Genoa revolted during the 13th century against the nobility and changed Genoa's political organization to provide them with a share in Genoa's political decision making (e.g., Vitale, 1955). Genoa's political organization enabled the operation of an economic institution, which led to a dynamic of wealth distribution that eventually modified the original political organization.

IV. 6 THE EMERGENCE OF DISTINCT TRAJECTORIES OF ORGANIZATIONAL DEVELOPMENT

In the context of this chapter, organizations are viewed as factors that alter the rules of the game. Although in the short run decision makers take the rules of the game as given, in the long run the nontechnologically determined rules of the game may be changed endogenously as decision makers attempt to improve their lot by establishing organizations. Such organizations alter the rules of the game by, for example, introducing a new player (the organization itself), by changing the information available to players, or by changing payoffs associated with certain actions. This view of organizations goes back at least to Hobbes, and examples of organizational innovations of this nature are the court system, the credit bureau, and the firm. An introduction of a new organization reflects an increase in the stock of knowledge, which may be the outcome of an intentional pursuit or unintentional experimentation.

Distinct interrelated systems of economic institutions, culture, and social and political structures provide different incentives regarding organizational innovations. In particular, diverse cultural beliefs impact motivation for organizational innovations because a necessary condition for an organizational change is that those able to initiate it expect to gain from it. These expectations depend on cultural beliefs, and diverse cultural beliefs can lead to a distinct trajectory of organizational development. The distinctiveness of various organizational trajectories is likely to be reinforced by the process of modifying and refining "microinventions," which follow an "organizational macroinvention."[37] An example discussed later relates the cultural beliefs associated with agency relations with the development of the family firm. Once this organization has been invented, modifying inventions such as selling shares in the stock market and appropriate accounting procedures can further differentiate one society's organizational trajectory from another. The distinctiveness of various organizational trajectories is further enhanced as existing organizations influence responses to exogenous changes in the rules of the game. An example mentioned earlier is that of the Genoese utilizing their legal system to mitigate the collective actions problem inherent in their relations with alien rulers.

[37] Mokyr (1990) introduced this terminology with respect to technological change.

The historical records show other organizations in which the developments among the Maghribis and the Genoese differ, and this divergence can be consistently accounted for as reflecting the impact of the two distinct economic, social, political, and, in particular, cultural systems discussed previously. The history of the modern bill of lading exemplifies a development of formal organization among the Genoese but not among the Maghribis. This bill combines an earlier version of the bill of lading with a so-called bill of advice. The former was the receipt from the ship's scribe for the goods the merchant deposited on the ship. The merchant sent this receipt to his overseas agent, who then claimed the goods on the basis of the scribe's own signature. The letter of advice was sent after the ship arrived at its destination by the ship's scribe to the consignee who did not come to claim the goods. The bill of lading and the letter of advice surmounted an organizational problem related to the shipping of goods abroad.

The earliest known European bill of lading and letter of advice dates from the 1390s and relates to the trade of Genoa, whereas the Maghribi traders hardly ever used bills of lading even though the device was known to them.[38] Why did the Genoese advance the use of the bill and the Maghribis abandon it? The Maghribis rejected the bill because they had solved the related organizational problem by using their informal collective enforcement mechanism. Maghribis entrusted their goods to other Maghribis traveling on board the ship that carried their merchandise. For example, in a letter sent early in the 11th century by Ephraim, son of Isma'il from Alexandria, to Ibn 'Awkal, a prominent merchant who lived in Fustat (old Cairo), Isma'il mentions the names of the men in four different ships entrusted "to watch carefully the 70 bales and one barqalu [containing the goods] until they will deliver them safely into the hands of Khalaf son of Ya'qub.[39]

Instead of solving the organizational problem between the merchant and the ship's operator, the Maghribis circumvented it. This fact is forcefully illustrated in a letter sent from Sicily in 1057 that describes what happened to loads of merchandise whose covers were torn during a voyage. The ship arrived in port, and the owner (or perhaps the operator) of the ship started to steal merchandise. The letter writer remarked that "unless my brother had been there to collect [the goods], nothing that belonged to our friends [i.e., the Maghribi traders] would have been collected."[40] The fact that the ship's owner did not consider himself, and was not considered by the traders, responsible for protecting the goods is clear from this

[38] For information on Genoa, see Bensa (1925). For the use of the bill of lading by the Maghribi traders and possible bias in the historical records, see Goitein (1973, pp. 305ff.).

[39] TS 13 J 17, f. 3 (Goitein, 1973, p. 313). For the generality of this practive, see Goitein (1967).

[40] Bodl. MS Heb. c28, f. 61, a, 11. 12–14 (Gil, 1983a, pp. 126–133).

letter. Similarly, if goods of unknown ownership were unloaded from the ship, or if the ship did not reach its destination, it was not the captain but the Maghribi traders who took care of the goods of their fellow traders.[41] The Genoese traders, lacking an equivalent informal enforcement mechanism, could not rely on fellow traders to protect their goods, and they solved the organizational problem associated with shipping goods by using the bill of lading, the letter of advice, and the legal responsibilities they entailed.

The organizational implications of distinct cultural beliefs seem also to have manifested themselves in the development of various organizations related to agency relations. The wage required to keep an agent honest under the reputation mechanism discussed previously declines with the probability that agency relations will be terminated despite the agent being honest. That is, the more likely it is that there is a future to the relations between a specific agent and merchant, the less that merchant has to pay his agent. The magnitude of this reduction is a function of cultural beliefs. This is so because the gains from reducing the probability of such termination depend on the probability that both a cheater (an agent who cheated in the past) and an honest agent will be rehired. The lower the probability is that a cheater will be rehired, and the higher the probability that an honest agent will be rehired, the lower the gain from changing the probability of forced separation. Furthermore, when an unemployed honest agent will be rehired with probability one, the gain from changing the probability of forced separation is zero.

Collectivist cultural beliefs and the resulting segregation and collective punishment increase and may bring to one the probability that a honest agent will be rehired. Furthermore, these factors are likely to bring the probability that a cheater would be rehired to zero. Thus, under collectivist beliefs and segregation, a merchant's incentive to reduce the probability of forced separation is marginal, or even absent. In contrast, under individualist cultural beliefs and the resulting integration and second-party punishment, merchants are motivated to establish an organization that reduces the likelihood of forced separation.

The evolution of family relations and business organization among the Maghribis and the Genoese suggests that only the latter introduced an organization that changed the probability of forced separation. When the Maghribi and Genoese merchants first began trading in the Mediterranean, it was common in both groups for a trader's son to start operating independently during his father's lifetime. The father would typically help the

[41] E.g., Bodl. MS Heb., c28, f. 61, a, 11. 9–17 (Gil, 1983a, pp. 126–133).

son until he was able to operate on his own. After the father's death, his estate was divided among his heirs and his business dissolved.[42] Later developments of family relations and business organization, however, differ substantially. During the 13th century, the Genoese traders adopted the family firm, the initial essence of which was a permanent partnership with unlimited and joint liability.[43] This organization preserved the family wealth undivided under one ownership, and a trader's son, reaching the appropriate age, joined his family's firm (see discussion in De Roover, 1965, pp. 70ff.; Rosenberg and Birdzell, 1986, pp. 123–124). The Maghribi traders, after being active in trade at least as long as the Genoese, did not establish a similar organization.

It is a widely held view among economic historians, following the work of Lane (1944) on the family firm in Venice, that the family firm was established to surmount agency problems. Lacking alternative institutions, the merchant-agent relations were organized within the family in which solidarity guaranteed honesty. This assertion certainly captures some aspects of reality, but it neither provides a complete explanation nor addresses all relevant questions. Why didn't family members simply establish agency relations with each other? Why did the Maghribi traders not introduce a similar organization? Furthermore, even a superficial examination of the internal structure of the important family firms reveals that agency relations were not necessarily established between family members. For example, the Peruzzi company, probably the largest Italian company during the late medieval period, had, in 1335, 15 overseas "branch managers," only three of whom were members of the Peruzzi family. In 1402, none of the overseas employees of the Medici company was a Medici (De Roover, 1963, p. 44, Table 7; p. 80, Table 19; see also the discussion in De Roover, 1948, 1965, pp. 78–79; Herlihy, 1985).

This analysis indicates the sources of uneven development among the Italians and Maghribis. Given the collectivist cultural beliefs of the Maghribis and the resulting segregation, collective punishment, and horizontal relations, a merchant could not gain much by introducing an organization that reduced the likelihood of forced separation. Among the Italian traders, however, individualist cultural beliefs motivated merchants to increase the security of the employment they offered their agents. The family firm seems to have been the manifestation of this desire. In the Italian family firm, several traders combined their capital and formed an organization

[42] Regarding the Maghribis, see Goitein (1967, pp. 180ff.) and Gil (1983, Vol. 1, pp. 215ff.). Regarding the Genoese, see, for example, Giovanni Scriba, pp. 236, 575, 1047 for father's help, and p. 946 for a will.

[43] The family firm first emerged in the early 13th century in Piacenza, Lucca, and Siena and then spread to other Italian cities, including Genoa (see discussion, for example, in De Roover, 1965, pp. 70ff.; Rosenberg and Birdzell, 1986, pp. 123–124).

with an infinite life span and a lower probability of bankruptcy that replaced each individual merchant in his relationship with agents.[44]

The introduction of the family firm, that is, of an organization replacing individual merchants in their relations with agents, was an "organizational macroinvention" that led to modifying and refining "microinventions." Family firms began to sell units, or shares, to nonmembers. For example, the capital of the Bardi company was made up of 58 shares: six members of the family were in the possession of the majority of the shares, whereas five outsiders owned the rest. In 1312, the capital of the Peruzzi company was distrubuted among eight members of the family and nine outsiders. In 1331 the Peruzzi family lost control of the company when more than half the capital belonged to outsiders (De Roover, 1963, pp. 77–78; see additional examples in De Roover, 1965). Once shares became tradable a need for a suitable market arose, and "stock markets" were developed. Furthermore, a separation between ownership and control was introduced, which required appropriate institutions to surmount the related contractual problems and improvement in information-transmission techniques and accounting procedures.[45]

IV. 7 MORAL AND SOCIAL ENFORCEMENT MECHANISMS AND THEIR INTERRELATIONS WITH ECONOMIC INSTITUTIONS AND SOCIAL STRUCTURES

In the previous analysis, cheating had no normative content. In reality, however, various actions do have normative values, and moral considerations influence the choice of actions. Behavior may also be influenced by a social enforcement mechanism, that is, one's concern regarding others' social approval or disapproval of behavior. The importance of these factors, particularly that of values in affecting behavior, has been recognized by prominent economists and has been confirmed in experimental studies.[46] For example, Arrow (1974) proposed that values such as trust, loyalty, and truth are "commodities . . . [which] increase the efficiency of the [economic] system" (p. 23). Similarly, North (1981, 1990) emphasized the role of

[44] Additional theoretical and historical work is required to establish whether and how the family firm achieved a level of commitment above that of each of its individual members. It should be noted that agency relations in the Italian family firms were not confined to family members (e.g., De Roover, 1963, 1965).

[45] See, for example, the elaborate contractual relationships between the Medici and their managers described in De Roover (1963). For a general discussion of the European trade organization during this period, see De Roover (1965), Gras (1939), Lopez (1976), and Postan (1973).

[46] For experimental results concerning the importance of values, see Dawes and Thaler (1988), Hoffman and Spitzer (1985), and Hoffman *et al.* (1991); for discussion, see Hirshleifer (1985), Opp (1985), and Rabin (1993).

"ideology" in reducing transaction costs and directing economic behavior (see also Akerlof, 1986; Stewart, 1990).[47] In other words, values should be viewed as a component in the institutional structure of societies.

Yet integrating values in an economic analysis of the endogenous emergence of institutions is problematic. Previously, as the above quotations indicate, integration took the form of viewing values as providing a "first party enforcement mechanism." One's utility loss from acting against her values compels the individual to act in a manner that is not the most beneficial in terms of economic reward. Hence, individuals indentical in all but their values would choose different actions in the same situation. Yet simply viewing values as exogenously given is methodologically deficient in the analysis of the endogenous emergence of institutions. By appropriately defining values, every behavior can be accounted for and any difference between societies can be "explained." At the same time, ignoring values in historical comparative institutional analysis is also methodologically deficient. Arguably, values are fixed within a society over a relatively short period of time but values are neither constant over time nor identical across societies.

Accordingly, the following discussion presents a possible method for integrating moral considerations in an institutional analysis. It avoids the arbitrariness of taking values as exogenous by allowing the development of distinct values among identical individuals. Instead of taking values as exogenous, the mechanism through which values are generated is taken as exogenous and identical across societies. Examining the factors leading a given mechanism to generate distinct values in fundamentally identical societies enables examination of the endogenous process of values' formation and their interrelations with other elements in a society's institutional structure.

Sociologists have argued that individuals attempt to find moral justification for their behavior: actions that are followed are increasingly viewed as those that *ought* to be followed (Davis, 1949, p. 52; Homans, 1950; Scott, 1987, p. 16).[48] Once a value system has been formed, it constitutes part of the institutional structure of a society because it acts as a first-party enforcer. It places an additional constraint on the choice of behavior. Hence, behavior that was induced in the past and may have been optimal at that time would tend to be reinforced by the evolving value system. Such a value

[47] In these works values are viewed as an end for their own sake, that is, a factor that shapes utility functions. An alternative view of values in economics is influenced by the works of behavioral biologists such as Wilson (1975) and Dawkins (1976). This view holds that values are a means to achieve material rewards and not an end in themselves. For application of this approach in economics, see for example, Frank (1987).

[48] This view of culture as a "legitimizing" mechanism is fundamental in the works of Karl Marx and E. Durkheim. For recent economic analyses, see Sugden (1989).

system may be maintained—or at least slow to change—even when the underlying conditions render it economically inefficient. Following the development of supporting values, a larger change in the underlying conditions is required to alter behavior.

This does not imply, however, that a value system formed in the past has a permanent hold over a society and should be taken as exogenous in analyzing a subsequent historical period. Rather, as observed by the eminent sociologist Davis (1949), there is a constant interaction between actual behavior and the value system. Each is shaping and being shaped by the other and, in particular, the value system is gradually modified to accommodate actual behavior. Davis has argued that

> in human society there is what may be called double reality—on the one hand a normative order embodying what *ought* to be, and on the other a factual order embodying what *is*. In the nature of the case, these two orders cannot be completely identical, nor can they be completely disparate. The normative order acts, for example, as a determinant (though not the only determinant) of the factual order. . . . In turn, the factual order exercises an influence on the normative system, for the norms must always refer to events in the real world and take into account the factual situation. . . . . The normative system, since it aims to achieve results in the factual world, is subject to constant modification by events in that world." (pp. 52–53)[49]

Because current values are a product of current behavior and past values, whereas current behavior is determined by past values, cultural beliefs, and the economic cost and benefit of various actions, economic change can, over time, alter values.

Past behavior can influence current behavior through an additional mechanism, related yet distinct, from that of value formation. When individuals view actions that were followed in the past as those that *ought* to be followed, a second- or third-party enforcement mechanism supporting these actions may endogenously arise. This is the case when utilities are belief dependent in the sense that a deviation from an expected pattern of behavior has a direct influence on them. As recently modeled by Geanakoplos *et al.* (1989), belief-dependent utilities capture the inducement to act in an expected manner generated by emotions, such as anger or disappointment. In particular, when utilities are belief dependent a deviation from an expected pattern of behavior may induce players to respond by taking an action costly to the deviator, even if this action is economically costly to them as well. The expectations of such *ex post* response induce decision makers to *ex ante* conform to past behavior. When utilities are belief dependent, past behavior can determine current behavior.

[49] For a recent theoretical analysis of the extent to which the value of "fairness" can influence economic behavior, see Rabin (1993). In an earlier work, Rabin (1991) has examined the impact of pecuniary incentive to modify values through cognitive dissonance.

Similar analysis can also be used to examine social enforcement mechanisms, that is, the human tendency of seeking implicit or explicit social approval for conduct by conforming to established patterns of behavior. Hence, behavior can be motivated by social exchange and the expectation of emotionally prompted social approval.[50] Note that this mechanism differs from that generated by belief dependent utilities. When utilities are belief dependent, it is the knowledge that the actions of decision makers are chosen based on emotions generated by expected behavior that influences behavior. Here, behavior is motivated by one's feelings of approval or disapproval. The importance of this mechanism in inducing behavior has been recognized by economists, such as Adam Smith in his "Theory of Moral Sentiments," and sociologists, such as George C. Homans (1961).

Similarly, social enforcement mechanisms can be integrated in the analysis using an aproach similar to that discussed earlier with respect to moral enforcement. Sociologists have identified a mechanism important in determining the degree to which social approval influences behavior. Holländer (1990) noted that an individual "can obtain approval only from those who know his behavior and communicate their feelings to him" (p. 1159). In this statement he has echoed the eminent sociologist, Homans (1950), who pointed out that the more individuals interact, the more effective social enforcement is. Economic interactions among the same individuals give rise to "friendliness" among them, and the higher the friendliness level, the more effective the operation of the social enforcement mechanism. Whereas Homans reached this conclusion based on fieldwork, recent experimental studies have confirmed the importance of interaction in social enforcement (for discussion and references, see Dawes and Thaler, 1988).

The analysis in Section III demonstrated that in two identical societies, distinct social structure can emerge. A society's social structure, in turn, is important in determining the actual impact of social approval on behavior. In a society in which the social structure is such that the same individuals interact frequently and in which social mobility across groups is limited, a social enforcement mechanism will have a stronger impact on behavior. In a society in which the social structure is such that the same individuals do not interact frequently and in which social mobility across groups is high, a social enforcement mechanism will have a weaker impact on behavior.

The relations between behavior, social structure, value formation, and social enforcement suggest that among the Maghribis and Genoese, those mechanisms influencing values formation and the effectiveness of social approval were likely to yield distinctly different outcomes. The Maghribis shared a network of information transmission and had a segregated social structure with relatively frequent interactions. These were likely to lead to

[50] For economic implications of such tendencies, see Hallander (1990) and Kuran (1987).

values that elevated loyalty to the group and mutual assistance and to increase the effectiveness of a social approval mechanism. In contrast, the Genoese had a low level of information transmission and an integrated society with a relatively low frequency of interactions. These were likely to induce values that did not elevate loyalty to the group (but rather self-reliance) and to hinder the effectiveness of a social approval mechanism.

Clearly, it is difficult to assess empirically the validity of these conjectures regarding values and the effectiveness of the social approval mechanism. Any appraisal of values held by historical actors or the level of social pressure they were prone to is highly subjective. Yet it should be noted that the available evidence suggests that the Maghribis and the Genoese held attitudes consistent with these predictions. In particular, to the extent that their behavior is any indication of their values, it seems that the Maghribis held values that promoted assistance to other members of their group. Assistance was given to traders who went bankrupt, usually in the form of loans, remission of debts, and credit extension.[51] The Italian historical records of the period do not enable the examination of a similar pattern of assistance. Yet, it is instructive to note that it was the Italians who invented insurance during this period. Presumably, in the absence of mutual assistance based on group-oriented values and a social enforcement mechanism, the desire for insurance was manifested in the invention of legal substitute.[52]

More generally, studies evaluating the "character" of the Italian traders suggest that among them values and social approval mechanism did not support behavior similar to that of the Maghribis. An eminent Italian scholar of this period, Armando Sapori, concluded that

> when he [the Italian merchant] quarreled he not only used strong language, but also revealed that he had a very hard heart and paid no heed to blood ties. His disputes were often instigated by the most trivial motives and then would drag on interminably, almost always passing from the stage of reasonable discussion to that of personal invective and sheer insult. (1970, p. 10)

IV. 8 CONCLUDING REMARKS: THE ECONOMY AS A SYSTEM OF ECONOMICS; CULTURAL, SOCIAL, AND POLITICAL FACTORS; ECONOMIC EFFICIENCY; AND PATH DEPENDENCE

To the extent that a society's economic performance over time is determined by its institutional and organizational structure, comprehension of the interrelations between the various components of a society's institutional structure is required to understand economic growth and stagnation. Indeed, each of the systems analyzed in this chapter has different efficiency implications. The collectivist system is more efficient in supporting intra-economy agency relations, requires less costly formal organizations (such as

[51] See, for example, TS 10 J 16, f. 10 (Gil, 1983b, vol. 3, p. 262; Goitein, 1967, p. 204).
[52] Regarding the invention of insurance, see discussion in De Roover (1965, pp. 56–57).

law courts), and probably has a relatively effective ingroup moral and social enforcement mechanism. Yet, it restricts efficient intereconomy agency relations and, more generally, limits individual initiative and the development of "anonymous" exchange through the development of appropriate organizations such as the firm and the court of law. The individualist system does not restrict intereconomy agency relations and, more generally, promotes organizations that support anonymous exchange, but it is less efficient in supporting intraeconomy relations, requires costly formal organizations, and is less likely to have effective ingroup moral and social enforcement mechanisms. Each system also entails a different pattern of wealth distribution and each pattern of wealth distribution is likely to have different efficiency implications. This suggests that the relative efficiency of individualist and collectivist systems depends on the magnitude of the relevant parameters. Hence, although in the long run the Italians drove the Muslim traders out of the Mediterranean, the historical records do not permit any explicit econometric test of the relative efficiency of the two systems.

The analysis supports, however, the claim that trajectories of institutional structrues are path dependent. In particular, it indicates three factors that make institutional structures path dependent, hindering successful intersociety adoption of institutions. First, economic institutions are composed of two interrelated elements: cultural beliefs—how individuals expect others to act in various contingencies—and organizations—the endogenous human constructions that alter the nontechnologically determined rules of the game and that, whenever applicable, have to be at equilibrium. Because cultural beliefs are uncoordinated expectations, the capacity of economic institutions to change is a function of their history, implying that the ability of one society to use another's societal organizations is limited. A second source for path dependence is that organizational development itself is a historical process in which existing organizations and institutions impact the responses of individuals and societies to exogenous changes and determine incentives with respect to the introduction of new organizations. Hence, past organizations direct future institutional and organizational development. Finally, institutional structures exhibit path dependence because past behavior, cultural beliefs, social structures, and organizations impact the development of values and social enforcement mechanisms that inhibit flexibility in departing from past patterns of behavior.

It is interesting to note that the Maghribis' institutional structure resembles that of contemporary developing countries whereas the Genoese societal organization resembles the contemporary developed West, suggesting that institutional path dependence may have been important in the economic development of these societies. Historically then, the medieval Latin individualist society may have cultivated the seeds to the "rise of the

West." Although this conjecture should await further research regarding the extent to which the Genoese and the Maghribis represent the nature of the Latin and the Muslim societies of the period, this paper's analysis enables conjecturing about the possible long-run benefits of the individualistic system. To the extent that a division of labor is a necessary condition for long-run, sustained, economic growth, formal enforcement institutions that support anonymous exchange facilitate economic development. Individualist cultural beliefs foster the development of such institutions and, hence, permit society to capture these efficiency gains. Further, an individualist society entails less social pressure to conform to social norms of behavior and therefore fosters initiative and innovation.

ACKNOWLEDGMENTS

This chapter was prepared under a cooperative agreement between the Institute for Policy Reform (IPR) and the Agency for International Development (AID), Cooperative Agreement No. PDC-0095-A-00-1126-00. Views expressed in this chapter are those of the author and not necessarily those of IPR or AID. The chapter draws from my earlier works, particularly "Cultural Beliefs and the Organization of Society," published in the Journal of Political Economy, October 1994. The research reflected in these papers was supported by National Science Foundation Grants # 9009598 and 9223974. Donald N. McCloskey, Bent Holmstrom, and an anonymous referee provided helpful comments.

REFERENCES

Abulafia, D. (1977). *The Two Italies.* Cambridge University Press, Cambridge, UK.

Airaldi, G. (1986). *Genova e la Liguria nel Medioevo.* Utet Libreria, Turin.

Akerlof, G. A. (1986). A theory of social custom. In *An Economic Theorist's Book of Tales.* Cambridge University Press, Cambridge, UK.

Allen, F. (1984). Reputation and product quality. *Rand Journal of Economics* **15,** 311–327.

Annali Genovesi di Caffaro e dei suoi Continuatori, 1099–1240, 4 vols. (Ceccardo Roccatagliata Ceccardi and Giovanni Monleone, Trans.). Municipio di Genova, Genoa.

Arrow, K. (1974). *The Limits of Organization.* Norton, New York.

Bandura, A. (1971). *Social Learning Theory.* Prentice-Hall, Englewood Cliffs, NJ.

Bellah, R. N., Madsen, R., Sullivan, W. M., Swidler, A., and Tipton, S. M. (1985). *Habits of the Heart: Individualism and Commitment in American Life.* University of Calfornia Press, Berkeley.

Ben-Porath, Y. (1980). The F-connection: Families, friends, and firms and the organization of exchange. *Population and Development* Review **6,** 1–30.

Bensa E. (1925). *The Early History of Bills of Lading.* Stabilimento d'Arti Grafiche, Genoa.

Ben-Sasson, M. (1991). *The Jews of Sicily, 825–1068* (in Hebrew and Judaeo-Arabic), Ben-Zvi Institute, Jerusalem.

Bernheim, B. D., and Whinston, M. D. (1990). Multi-market contract and collusive behavior. *Rand Journal of Economics* **21**(1), 1–26.

Byrne, E. H. (1917). Commercial contracts of the Genoese in the Syrian trade of the twelfth century. *Quarterly Journal of Economics* **31,** 128–170.

Cahen, C. (1990). Economy, society, institutions. In *The Cambridge History of Islam.* (pp. 511–538). (P. M. Holt, A. K. S. Lambton, and B. Lewis, eds.). Cambridge University Press, Cambridge, UK.

Cipolla, C. M. (1963). The economic policies of governments. V. The Italian and Iberian Peninsulas. In *The Cambridge Economic History of Europe* (M. M. Postan, E. E. Rick, and M. Miltey, eds.), Vol. 3. Cambridge University Press, Cambridge, UK. pp. 397–429.

Cipolla, C. M. (1980). *Before the Industrial Revolution,* 2nd ed., Norton, New York.

Conklin. J. (1993). *Crown Debt, Crredibility and Mechanism for Commitment in the Reign of Philip II,* Memo. Stanford University, Stnford, CA.

David, P. A. (1988). *Path-Dependence: Putting the Past into the Future of Economics.* Stanford University, IMSSS, Stanford, CA.

David P. A. (1992). *Why Are Institutions the "Carriers of History"?* Stanford University, Department of Economics, Stanford, CA.

Davis, K. (1949). *Human Society.* Macmillan, New York.

Dawes, R. M., and Thaler, R. H. (1988). Anomalies: Cooperation. *Journal of Economic Perspectives* **2,** 187–197.

Dawkins, R. (1976). *The Selfish Gene.* Oxford University Press, New York.

De Roover, R. (1948). *The Medici Bank. Its Organization, Management, Operation, and Decline.* New York University Press, New York.

De Roover, R. (1963). *The Rise and Decline of The Medici Bank, 1397–1494.* Harvard University Press, Cambridge, MA.

De Roover, R. (1965). The organization of trade. In *The Cambridge Economic History of Europe* (pp. 42–118). (M. M. Postan, E. E. Rick, and M. Miltey, eds.), Vol. 3. Cambridge University Press, Cambridge, UK.

Epstein, S. A. (1994). Secrecy and Genoese commercial practices. *Journal of Medieval History* **20,** 313–326.

Frank R. H. (1987). If homo economics could choose his own utility function, would he want one with a conscience? *American Economic Review* **77**(4), 593–604.

Geanakoplos, J., Pearce, D., and Stacchetti, E. (1989). Psychological games and sequential rationality. *Games and Economic Behavior* **1**(1), 60–79.

Gil, M. (1983a). *The Jews in Sicily Under the Muslim Rule in the Light of the* Geniza *Documents.* Tel Aviv University, Department of Jewish History, Tel Aviv, (appeared in Italian in *Italia Judaaica,* Instituto Poligrafico e Zecca dello Stato, Rome).

Gil, M. (1983b). *Palestine During the First Muslim Period (634–1099)* (in Hebrew and Judaeo-Arabic), Vols. 1-3. The Ministry of Defence Press and Tel Aviv University Press, Tel Aviv.

Giovanni di Guiberto, 1200–1211 (M. W. Hall-Cole and R. G. Reinert, eds.), Docs. XVII-XVIII. Editrice Libraria Italiana, Turin. 1939–1940 (in Latin and Italian).

Giovanni Scriba, Cartolare di, 1154–1164 (M. Chiaudano and M. Moresco, eds.). S. Lattes and C. Editori, Torino, 1935 (in Latin and Italian).

Goitein, S. D. (1964). Commercial and family partnerships in the countries of medieval Islam. *Islamic Studies* **3,** 315–337.

Goitein, S. D. (1967). *Economic Foundations. A Mediterranean Society,* Vol. 1. University of Calfornia Press, Los Angeles.

Goitein, S. D. (1971). *The Community. A Mediterranean Society,* Vol. 2. University of California Press, Los Angeles.

Goitein, S. D. (1973). *Letters of Medieval Jewish Traders.* Princeton Universtiy Press, Princeton, NJ.

Gras, S. B. (1939). *Business and Capitalism: An Introduction to Business History.* F. S. Crofts & Co., New York.

Greif, A. (1989). Reputation and coalitions in medieval trade: Evidence on the Maghribi traders. *Journal of Economic History* **49,** 857–882.

Grief, A. (1991). Cultural beliefs as a common resource in an integrating world: An example from the theory and history of collectivist and individualist societies. In *The Economics of*

Transnational Commons (P. Dasgupta, K.-G. Mäler, and A. Vercelli, eds.). Clarendon Press, Oxford, UK.

Greif, A. (1993). Contract enforceability and economic institutions in early trade: The Maghribi traders' coalition. *American Economic Review* **83**(3), 525–548.

Greif, A. (1994a). Cultural beliefs and the organization of society: A historical and theoretical reflection on collectivist and individualist societies. *Journal of Political Economy* **102**(5), 912–950.

Greif, A. (1994b). On the political foundations of the late medieval commercial revolution: Genoa during the twelfth and thirteenth centuries. *Journal of Economic History* **54**(4), 271–287.

Greif, A. (1995). *Markets and Legal Systems: The Development of Markets in Late Medieval Europe and the Transition From community Responsibility to an Individual Responsibility Legal Doctrine.* Stanford University, Stanford, CA.

Greif, A. (1996). On the study of organizations and evolving organizational forms through history: Reflection from the Late medieval firm. *Industrial and Corporate Change*, (5).

Greif, A., Milgrom, P., and Weingast, B. (1994). Coordination, commitment and enforcement: The case of the merchant Guild. *Journal of Political Economy* **102**(4), 745–776.

Guglielmo Cassinese (1190–1192). In *Notai Liguri Del Sec. XII* (M. W. Hall, H. C. Krueger, and R. L. Reynolds, eds.) Editrice Libraria Italiana, Torino, 1938 (in Latin and Italian).

Herlihy, D. (1985). *Medieval Households.* Harvard University Press, Cambridge, MA.

Hirshleifer, J. (1985). The expanding domain of economics. *American Economic Review,* December, pp. 53–68.

Hoffman, E., and Spitzer, M. L. (1985). Entitlement, rights, and fairness: An experimental examination of subjects' concepts of distributive justice. *Journal of Legal Studies,* June, pp. 259–297.

Hoffman, E., McCabe, K., and Smith, V. (1991). *Fairness, Property Rights, and Bargaining: Some Preliminary Results,* Mimeo. University of Arizona, Tucson.

Hollander, H. (1990). A social exchange approach to voluntary cooperation. *American Economic Review* **80**(5), 1157–1167.

Homans, G. C. (1950). *The Human Group.* Harcourt, New York.

Homans, G. C. (1961). *Social Behavior. Its Elementary Forms.* Harcourt Brace Jovanovich, New York.

Hughes, D. O. (1974). Toward historical ethnography: Notarial records and family history in the Middle Ages. *Historical Methods Newsletter* **7**(2), 61–71.

Joskow, P. L. (1984). *Vertical Integration and Long-Term Contracts: The Case of Mine-Mouth Coal Plants.* Paper presented in the Economic and Legal Organization Workshop, Massachusetts Institute of Technology, Cambridge, MA.

Kedar, B. Z. (1976). *Merchants in Crisis.* Yale University Press, New Haven, CT.

Krueger, H .C. (1957). Genoese merchants, their partnerships and investments 1155 to 1164. In *Studi in Onore di Armando Sapori* (pp. 257–272). Institudo Editoriale Cisalpino, Milan.

Krueger, H. C. (1962). Genoese merchants, their associations and investments 1155 to 1230. In *Studi in Onore di Amintore Fanfani* (D. A. Graffre, ed.), Vol 1. Multa Paucis, Milan.

Krueger, H. C. (1993). The Genoese travelling merchant in the twelfth century. *Journal of European Economic History* **22**(2), 251–283.

Kuran, T. (1987). Preference falsification, policy continuity and collective conservation. *Economic Journal* **97**(387), 642–665.

Lane, F.C. (1994). Family partnerships and joint ventures in the Venetian Republic. *Journal of Economic History* **4,** 178–196.

Lanfranco (1202–1226). In *Notai Liguri Del Sec. XII e Del XIII* (H. C. Krueger and R. L. Reynolds, eds.), Societa Ligure di Storia Patria, Genoa, 1952–1954 (in Latin and Italian).

Lattes, A. (1939). *Il Diritto Marittimo Privato nelle Carte Liguri dei Scoli XII e XIII.* Citta del Vaticano, Roma.

Lewis, A. R. (1951). *Naval Power and Trade in the Mediterranean, A.D. 500–1100.* Princeton University Press, Princeton, NJ.
Lewis, B. (1991). *The Political Language of Islam.* Universtiy of Chicago Press, Chicago and London.
Lewis, D. (1969). *Convention: A Philosophical Study.* harvard University Press, Cambridge, MA.
Lieber, A. E. (1968). Eastern business practices and medieval European commerce. *Economic History Review* **21**(2), 230–243.
Lopez, R. S. (1943). European merchants in the Medieval Indies: The evidence of commercial documents. *Journal of Economic History* **3**(2), 164–184.
Lopez, R. S. (1976). *The Commercial Revolution of the Middle Ages, 950–1350.* Cambridge University Press, New York.
Macfarlane, A. (1978). *The Origins of English Individualism.* Basil Blackwell, Oxford, UK.
Marimon, R. (1988). *Wealth Accumulation with Moral Hazard.* Stanford University, The Hoover Institution, Stanford, CA.
Michael, M. (1965). *The archives of Naharay be Nissim, businessman and public figure in eleventh century Egypt* (in Hebrew and Judaeo-Arabic). Ph.D. Dissertation, Hebrew University, Jerusalem, Israel.
Milgrom, P. R., and Roberts, J. (1990). Rationalizability, learning, and equilibrium in games with strategic complementarities. *Econometrica* **6,** 1255–1277.
Mokyr, J. (1990). *The Lever of Riches.* Oxford University Press, Oxford, UK.
North, D. C. (1981). *Structure and Change in Economic History.* Norton, New York.
North, D. C. (1990). *Institutions, Institutional Change and Economic Performance.* Cambridge University Press, Cambridge, UK.
North, D. C. (1991). Institutions. *Journal of Economic Perspectives* **5**(1), 97–112.
North, D. C., and Thomas, R. P. (1973). *The Rise of the Western World, A New Economic History.* Cambridge University Press, Cambridge, UK.
North, D. C., and Weingast, B. R. (1989). Constitutions and commitment: The evolution of institutions governing public choice in seventeenth-century England. *Journal of Economic History* **49,** 803–832.
Oberto Scriba de Mercato, 1186 (M. Chiaudano and R. Morozzo Della Rocca, eds.), Doc. XI (in Latin and Italian) Turin, 1940.
Oberto Scriba de Mercatio 1190 (M. Chiaudano and R. Morozzo Della Rocca, eds.), Doc. XVI (in Latin and Italian). Turin, 1940.
Opp, K. D. (1985). Sociology and economic man. *Journal of Institutional and Theoretical Economics* **141,** 231–243.
Postan, M. M. (1973). *Medieval Trade and Finance.* Cambridge University Press, Cambridge, UK.
Rabin, M. (1991). *Cognitive Dissonance and Social Change,* Working Paper. University of California, Department of Economics, Berkeley. (Forthcoming in the *Journal of Economic Behavior and Organization.)*
Rabin, M. (1993). Incorporating fairness into game theory and economics. *American Economic Review* **83**(5), 1281–1302.
Reynolds, C. H., and Norman, R. V., eds. (1988). *Community in America.* University of California Press, Berkeley.
Rogerson, W. P. (1983). Reputation and product quality. *Bell Journal of Economics* **14,** 508–616.
Rosenberg, N., and Birdzell, L.E., Jr. (1986). *How the West Grew Rich.* Basic Books, New York.
Sapori, A. (1970). *The Italian Merchant in the Middle Ages* (P. A. Kennen, trans): Norton, New York.
Schelling, T. (1980). *The Strategy of Conflict,* 2nd ed. Harvard University Press, Cambridge, MA.

Scott, W. R. (1987). *Organizations: Rational, Natural, and Open Systems.* Prentice-Hall, Englewood Cliffs, NJ.

Shapiro, C. (1983). Premiums for high quality products as return to reputation. *Quarterly Journal of Economics* **98,** 659–679.

Shapiro, C., and Stiglitz, J. E. (1984). Equilibrium unemployment as a worker discipline device. *American Economic Review* **74**(3), 433–444.

Stewart, H. (1990). *Rationality and the Market for Human Blood,* Mimeo. University of Toronto Law School.

Stillman, N. A. (1970). East-West relations in the Islamic Mediterranean in the early eleventh century. Ph.D. Dissertation, University of Pennsylvania, Philadelphia.

Sugden, R. (1989). Spontaneous Order. *Journal of Economic Perspectives* **3**(4), 85–97.

Triandis, H. C. (1990). Cross-cultural studies of individualism and collectivism. In *Nebraska Symposium on Motivation* (pp. 41–133). (J. Berman, ed.). University of Nebraska Press, Lincoln.

Triandis, H. C., McCusker, C., and Hui, C. H. (1990). Multimethod probes of individualism and collectivism. *Journal of Personality and Social Psychology* **59**(5), 1006–1020.

Udovitch, A. L., (1988). Merchants and Amirs: Government and trade in eleventh-century Egypt. *Asian and African Studies* **22,** 53–72.

Vitale, V. (1951). *Il Comune de Podestà Genova.* Riccardo Ricciardi, Milan.

Vitale, V. (1955). *Breviario della Storià di Genova.* Società Ligure di Storia Patria, Genova.

Williamson, O. (1985). *The Economic Institutions of Capitalism.* Free Press, New York.

Wilson, E. O., (1975). *Sociobiology.* Harvard University Press (Belknap), Cambridge, MA.

V

Cultural Values, Ideological Beliefs, and Changing Labor Institutions: Notes on Their Interactions

Stanley L. Engerman

V.I

The nature of the changing frontiers in the study of economics, economic history, and economic development can be clearly seen in the work of Douglass North. Whether shifting the frontiers of analysis outward reflects more the "push" of the inadequacies of the past formulations made by the profession than the "pull" of new ideas and innovations that promise high intellectual and practical payoff, clearly interpretations of the past and of what are to be regarded as critical factors in understanding them have changed. In his 1961 book, *The Economic Growth of the United States, 1790–1860,* still in print and widely used after more than three decades, North focused on economic variables and the appropriate responses by farmers, capitalists, laborers, and investors to the various price signals provided by the national and international markets, with little discussion of why and for how long such economic behavior had existed.[1]

[1] D. C. North, *The Economic Growth of the United States, 1790–1860.* Prentice-Hall, Englewood Cliffs, NJ, 1961. North's discussion of the antebellum South, however, does suggest the impact of other sets of factors in influencing behavior and long-term economic development.

At the time of its writing, in the 1950s and early 1960s, this reliance on the presumption of market-determined, or at least strongly influenced, behavior reflected an apparent general consensus of writers concerned with economic history and economic development, whether Marxists, liberals, or conservatives, all regarding the relevant economic actors as willing and anxious to respond to economic signals, if only given the opportunity. The culture of the market was seen as widespread, or at least it could be made to be widespread, and, ideologically, economic growth was regarded as to be desired everywhere and, with appropriate policies and behavior, attainable.[2]

Even the introduction of more attention to institutional changes did not initially change this focus, because they were regarded primarily as the reaction to economic conditions and variables, and were generally seen as the response by some, if not all, members of society to more profitable economic opportunities. Collective actions via institutions were seen as a complement to private, individual actions, and although the measures taken by groups could differ from those of individuals, the motivations resembled those described in the basic model. Often more information, whether economic or cultural, was needed (for example, to help us chose between the Smith-Turner and the Domar-Nieboer models in regard to the relationship between the geographic frontier and the labor institutions that emerged), but the basic relationship between economic variables and institutional changes was accepted.[3]

As seen in the work of North (and in some measure in response to his work), much of the more recent literature on economic history and economic development has stressed the need to consider the crucial roles played, even in what might seem the narrowly economic sphere, by cultural variables, institutions, and ideology, and it has pointed to the major impact

[2] See, for example W. W. Rostow, *Theorists of Economic Growth from David Hume to the Present: With a Perspective on the Next Century.* Oxford University Press, Oxford, 1990; H. W. Arndt, *The Rise and Fall of Economic Growth: A Study in Contemporary Thought.* University of Chicago Press, Chicago, 1978; H. W. Arndt, *Economic Development: The History of an Idea.* University of Chicago Press, Chicago, 1987.

[3] S. L. Engerman, Some considerations relating to property rights in man. *Journal of Economic History* **33,** 43–65 (1973). The abundance of land led to a demand by landowners for controlled labor, although it could permit potential workers to escape from the areas of settlement, and more information on the relative importance of these supply-and-demand influences is needed for the issue to be resolved. See also S. L. Engerman and K. L. Sokoloff, Factor endowments, institutions, and differential paths of growth among New World economies: A view from economic historians of the United States. In *Why Did Latin America Fall Behind?* (S. Haber, ed.) pp. 260–304. Stanford University Press, Stanford, CA, 1996.

that these forces have had on individual and collective behavior.[4] Thus, for example, the same degree and nature of response to market signals is not apparent everywhere and at all times as a universal constant (although it may be considerably more widespread than some critics would claim), but rather the extent of this behavior has reflected individual and social cultural values, those institutions that influenced or determined the nature and limits of collective behavior and the ideologies that developed in regard to the appropriate treatment of other individuals and of natural forces. Perceptions and beliefs about what is acceptable, or at least possible, behavior do influence the economic outcomes and thus the identical stimulus provided to different individuals by the market may not lead to the same response in different places or at different times.

Among economic historians these arguments about the centrality of cultural and ideological factors have been highlighted in the most recent decades of research on the economic expansion of Europe, particularly those developments after the 16th century, in contrast with the relative stagnation of most regions of Asia, Africa, and much of the Americas.[5] Although estimates of income are obviously rather uncertain for these earlier periods, it is probable that per capita incomes were in a much narrower range internationally in the 16th and 17th centuries than they were to become afterward, reflecting the earlier onset and the more rapid economic growth of the European economies and their overseas offshoots than of the rest of the world. Raising further questions—both in the historical comparisons of Europe and elsewhere, as well as those within Europe—were the rather dramatic shifts in economic leadership over time and the significant variations in the absolute as well as the relative incomes of different nations.[6]

Explanations have been provided by numerous economists, historians, and economic historians, past and present, and ultimately most of these seem to shift from a reliance on explanations based on what some call

[4] The key works of North are L. E. Davis and D. C. North, *Institutional Change and American Economic Growth.* Cambridge University Press, Cambridge, UK, 1971; D. C. North and R. P. Thomas, *The Rise of the Western World: A New Economic History.* Cambridge University Press, Cambridge, UK, 1973; D. C. North, *Structure and Change in Economic History.* Norton, New York, 1981; D. C. North, *Institutions, Institutional Change and Economic Performance.* Cambridge University Press, Cambridge, UK, 1990.

[5] See, for example, the works by Jones, Landes, Mokyr, North, Parker, and Rosenberg and Birdzell discussed in S. L. Engerman, The big picture: How (and when and why) the west grew rich. *Research Policy* **23**, 547–559 (1994).

[6] A. Maddison, *Dynamic Forces in Capitalist Development: A Long-Run Comparative View.* Oxford University Press, Oxford, 1991.

purely economic factors to what are more traditionally regarded as those noneconomic factors influencing behavior and the adaptation to the primary environmental conditions.[7] Whereas these seemingly noneconomic forces can be related to what might be considered economic factors, it is often difficult to break out of the infinite regress where such arguments can lead. Thus, renewed attention has been given to the development and impact of cultural (and religious) factors, to the nature of and shifts in ideological views, and to the implications of differences in political power and the manner by which such power structures influenced variations in culture and institutions. Similarly, the dissatisfactions with the limited levels of income achieved by today's less developed nations has meant that the application of a broader framework to analyzing these contemporary concerns has come to be seen as necessary for the design of appropriate economic policy.

V.2

This chapter examine's some aspects of the influence of culture, ideology, and institutions on economic growth and structure, principally by focusing on the various dimensions of the labor market and of laboring activities, and the different and changing socially acceptable means of labor organization, control, or coercion. In some regards this approach to culture and ideology represents a return to older ideas concerning the basis of economic development, ideas that had helped to form economic policy planning in many places. Central to earlier debates on economic growth, the European mercantilists described what we would now call the "backward-bending supply curve of labor," the belief that low wages would lead more people to labor more than would be the case if they were to receive higher wages and thus be able to attain their basic (and limited) needs by working fewer hours.[8] The same arguments resurfaced and became central in discussions about the appropriate land, trade, and labor policies to replace slavery when it was abolished, and it was hoped that, at the least, the same

[7] See, for example, the authors noted in footnote 5, as well as the classic works on European economic change by Max Weber, Werner Sombart, Karl Marx, and various members of the German and English Historical Schools.

[8] On the mercantilist discussion, see E. S. Furniss, *The Position of the Laborer in a System of Nationalism: A Study in the Labor Theories of the Later English Mercantilists.* Houghton-Mifflin, Boston, 1919; A. W. Coats, Changing attitudes to labour in the mid-eighteenth century. *Economic History Review* **11,** 35–51 (1958); P. Mathias, *The Transformation of England: Essays in the Economic and Social History of England in the Eighteenth Century,* pp. 131–167. Columbia University Press, New York, 1979.

level and structure of output that was achieved earlier could be maintained.[9] Indeed, this type of cultural argument about labor force participation led to the development of a special subfield in British economics, tropical economics, which was based primarily on the argument that in tropical regions the labor supply curve became backward bending at a level of income below which it became backward bending in the metropolis. (After all, all individual labor supply curves became backward bending at some point. The key questions are where and why.) These cultural differences, it was argued, helped lead to many of the variations in the rate of economic growth among various parts of the world, variations that may have also related to other factors influencing labor, such as intensity of work and education achieved.

Recently Jan de Vries has focused attention on what he calls "the industrious revolution," linking the European expansion of demand for consumer goods to an increased willingness to work and to do different types of work than previously, with the resulting prospects for a more equitable distribution of income.[10] This choice, economic and culturally based, provides an important framework with which to study economic change, representing a return to some earlier historical issues but in a more sophisticated manner. The basic problem for individuals to solve regarding labor input, if choice is possible or permitted, is the selection of the desired amounts of goods and services (including those for oneself and for others, including children) and what can be described as leisure (nonwork). Adjustments might be made in response to changing real wages (whether due to higher nominal wages or to lower prices) or else to changing tastes, reflecting new cultural patterns of consumption.

The specific patterns of leisure selected can take a variety of forms as influenced by climate, nature, and crops, reflecting the patterns of the agricultural work year, as well as, in other sectors, the effects of the weather and

[9] For a theoretical analysis of factors influencing the labor supply, see Y. Barzel and R. J. McDonald, Assets, subsistence, and the supply curve of labor. *American Economic Review* **63,** 621–633 (1973); see also S. L. Engerman, The land and labour problem at the time of the legal emancipation of the British West Indian slaves. In *West Indies Accounts: Essays on the British Caribbean and the Atlantic Economy in Honour of Richard Sheridan* (R. A. McDonald, ed.). pp. 297–318. Kingston. The Press, University of the West Indies, 1996.

[10] J. de Vries, Between purchasing power and the world of goods: Understanding the Household Economy in early modern Europe. In *Consumption and the World of Goods* C. J. Brewer and R. Porter, eds.), pp. 85–132. Routledge, London: J. deVries, The Industrial Revolution and the industrious revolution, *Journal of Economic History* **54,** 249–270 (1994). For approaches to the contemporary discussions from an alternative perspective see, most recently, C. J. Berry, *The Idea of Luxury: A Conceptual and Historical Investigation.* Cambridge University Press, Cambridge, UK, 1994; E. J. Hundert, *The Enlightenment's Fable: Bernard Mandeville and the Discovery of Society.* Cambridge University Press, Cambridge, UK, 1994.

the availability of livestock, wind, and water for power. There are choices to be made about the temporal pattern of leisure—hours worked per day, days worked per week, weeks worked per year, and years worked in a lifetime—and also what might be called on-the-job leisure, whether in the form of breaks during the workday or just a lower intensity of work. The variations in such patterns differ by age, sex, and family conditions, and they can lead to differences in wage adjustments, costs, outputs, and investment opportunities. Clearly the closer potential income is to a physically defined subsistence level (itself an important culturally determined variable), the less choice would be possible, and the greater the labor input required by individuals and by society. Here we are presuming that leisure is pure consumption, but clearly one of the major concerns at early stages of development is the extent to which some leisure serves an investment purpose, to permit rest in order to regain strength and thereby enable more work and higher output.[11] One important measure of the level of potential economic development, therefore, would consider the relative amount of productive potential that has been foregone by reductions in labor force participation and the choice made for nonwork rather than the consumption of goods and services. Several recent estimates of national income and economic growth have partly adjusted for this by evaluating the magnitude of the change in leisure from a benchmark date and adding this to the traditionally measured GNP, in effect treating leisure as another economic good with a specific market value and raising the question of the desired limits to the growth in the measured output of goods and services.[12]

[11] See H. Freudenberger and J. Gaylord Cummins, Health, work, and leisure before the Industrial Revolution. *Explorations in Economic History* **13,** 1–12 (1976). For more empirical detail, see R. W. Fogel, The relevance of Mathus for the study of mortality today: Long-run influences on health, mortality, labor force participation and population growth. *NBER Historical Paper* No. 54 (1994). For a discussion of the impact of higher wages on "the industry of the common people," and how this "increases the bodily strength of the labourer," see Adam Smith, *The Wealth of Nations,* 2 vols. Oxford University Press, Oxford 1976. Vol. I, pp. 99–100 (original publication 1776).

[12] See, for example, D. Usher, *The Measurement of Economic Growth.* Columbia University Press, New York, 1980; W. Nordhaus and J. Tobin, Is growth obsolete? In *Economic Growth: Fiftieth Anniversary Colloquium V.* National Bureau of Economic Research, New York, 1972; S. S. Kuznets, Long-term changes in the national income of the United States of America since 1870. In *Income and Wealth of the United States: Trends and Structure* (S. S. Kuznets, ed.), pp. 29–241. Cambridge: Bowes & Bowes, 1952. The anthropologist, Marshall Sahlins, argued that hunter-gathers were the "original affluent society," because they were able to achieve what they wanted with limited work time and were thus able to, operating rationally, "not work hard," in terms of time and intensity [M. Sahlins, *Stone Age Economics,* pp. 1–39. Aldine Chicago, 1972].

V.3

Although this chapter is concerned primarily with the impact of culture and ideology on the labor force, this is not the only place in the study of economic history and economic development that the notion of a backward bending supply curve is significant. There is some discussion in the literature as to whether it is better in the long run for the economy to have things easy (factors abundant) or difficult (factors scarce) in order to generate economic growth. In some cases abundance early is considered desirable, but in other cases it is argued that some difficulties at the start of the growth process would lead to measures to offset major problems and thus provide for a more sustainable economic growth. Some describe the influence of slavery in the West Indies and the United States South as examples of the drawback of early, rapid growth, whereas the antebellum industrialization of the United States Northeast is given as an example of an economy that successfully overcame the problems posed by labor scarcity to achieve a dominant economic position.[13] As Hahn and Mathews suggested, however, "some sort of backward-rising curve of entrepreneurial effort is also assumed; otherwise the scarcity of labor may have the opposite effect and make the entrepreneurs throw in the sponge."[14] Thus the nature of the entrepreneurial and innovator cultures, which ensures that the appropriate degree of difficulty (neither so easy that little effort needed to be put in or so hard that economic inputs were limited) can get the desired response, needs to be understood as part of the analysis of economic change.

V.4

One key question for historical analysis is the determination of what might cause the labor supply to change over time: whether labor input is related to market wage rates (when the option is working for others) or else the returns to self-employed labor (when independence is pursued). From the point of view of a politically powerful set of "elite" decision

[13] H. J. Habakkuk, *American and British Technology in the Nineteenth Century.* Cambridge University Press, Cambridge, UK, 1962. A similar argument regarding individual talents was made by Malthus, who stated that "the exertions that men find it necessary to make . . . frequently awaken faculties that might otherwise have lain for ever dormant" [T. R. Malthus, *An Essay on the Principle of Population,* p. 208. Harmondsworth, Penguin, 1970 (first published, 1798)].

[14] F. H. Hahn and R. C. O. Matthews, The theory of economic growth: A survey. *Economic Journal* **74,** 779–902 (1964)

makers, the possibilities for coercive mechanisms to force people to work longer, more intensely, or in undesirable jobs at undesirable locations provide one set of alternatives, possibly leading to systems such as slavery and serfdom as the means to create a labor force . Slavery generally was applied to those considered outsiders and who usually had to be moved long distances, whereas serfdom arose for those countrymen already residing in the area of production.[15] Although institutions such as slavery may be argued to have had a distinct economic basis, culture and ideology also played crucial roles in their development, such as defining who could be enslaved, how they could be treated, and when and with what time trajectory slavery could be ended.

The presumably noncoerced possibility for generating a labor supply, the so-called free labor solution, meant that people would respond to changing real wages and the prospects for consumption. Those societies that have grown are generally believed to have exhibited, in an important range, a "forward-sloping labor supply curve." Thus, the way to increase the labor supply would be for employers to increase real wages (and the consumption prospects) of individuals, because the possibilities of getting higher wages and the desire to achieve more of their wants would make the increased laboring worthwhile. The economic growth problem faced in earlier (and some present) times has been to find a mechanism to shift from a "backward-bending" to a "forward-sloping" labor supply curve, one that, in effect, increases the desire for goods and services and makes workers, in the words of the 18th-century British mercantilist, Sir James Steuart, "slaves to their wants" rather than the then frequent case of being "slaves to others."[16] The cause of this transition in the labor supply curve, seen by some as a shift outward in the labor supply curve and by others as a movement along the upward sloping portion of the existing curve, has been explained in diverse ways: the attractions of new, relatively low-cost exotic goods (whether domestic or from overseas); the newfound belief in and ability to emulate others to achieve some relatively higher status by acquiring new goods; or by

[15] S. L. Engerman, Slavery, serfdom and other forms of coerced labor: similarities and differences. In *Serfdom and Slavery; Studies in Legal Bondage* (M. L. Bush, ed.). Longman, London, 1996, pp. 18–41.

[16] Sir J. Steuart, *An Inquiry into the Principles of Political Economy,* 2 vols. Chicago University Press, Chicago, 1966 (original publication 1767). On the economic impact of property rights in slaves on labor force participation and other matters, see Y. Barzel, *Economic Analysis of Property Rights,* pp. 76–84. Cambridge University Press, Cambridge, UK, 1989; and the more extensive discussion in Y. Barzel, An economic analysis of slavery. *Journal of Law and Economics* **20,** 87–110 (1977).

lowered production costs, via newer technologies or organizational innovations as well as lowered transactions costs making goods cheaper for consumers.[17]

There is also the possible impact of, to employ a word used by a number of different writers, "education" for laboring and for wants, presumably increasing the desirability of consumption and the perceived possibilities of obtaining goods, or else, via salesmanship or advertising, creating greater demands either for specific goods or for goods and services in general. This "propaganda for development," of course, has not been the only form of "education" argued for in recent years to generate an increase in the effective labor supply. The attempts to develop a "new Soviet man" provide one example of the use of patriotism and a feeling for the national interest to enhance the labor effort to get higher productivity.[18] Most modern societies in wartime have made similar attempts, as a policy to both increase production and to serve as an anti-inflationary policy, hoping to increase the labor input without a large increase in the rewards provided. To the extent that such "education" was successful, the problem of obtaining an increased labor supply could be solved, and the level of national income and economic growth increased.

V.5

Policies to increase the labor supply vary depending on whether it is believed the labor supply curve is forward or backward sloping. Within a broadly democratic framework, in which most members of society desire economic growth, it might be argued that "education" was the preferred

[17] See, for example, T. R. Malthus, [*Principles of Political Economy,* 2nd ed. p. 403. J. Murray: London, 1836] on the role of foreign goods in providing motivation for labor. Why this effect was expected to come primarily from foreign and not also domestically produced goods is unclear, but it is a frequent theme in the contemporary literature.

Moreover, there may be another, more economically based explanation for the correlation of consumption levels and hours worked, particularly at the earlier stages of the onset of economic growth. If there were members of the labor force who were producing at a low level because of limited food input, an increase in agricultural productivity would permit more, and more productive, labor input via "productive consumption." See R. W. Fogel, *The Relevance of Malthus,* for examples from modern western Europe. Similarly, declines in fertility, reducing the number of children, could free time for members of the household, permitting them to produce more goods and services for the market or for self-consumption, although the reduced number of children could also mean a reduced need for members of the family to work to provide consumption goods for children.

[18] For another possible mechanism to increase labor input without changing wage rates, paternalism, see L. J. Alston, Race etiquette in the South: The role of tenancy. *Research in Economic History* **10,** pp. 199–211 (1986).

policy, because it would permit freer choice, although the time required for such measures to achieve effectiveness might be rather long. If, however, there was a concern with the rapidity of the adjustment to higher growth, or if it is believed that such a policy to induce labor input could not be successful, then some alternative policies would be required, policies that need not be considered directly coercive because there could be elements of choice, within constraints, left to workers. Simply increasing direct or indirect taxes or else forcing taxes to be paid in cash are measures that have been utilized in various economies, increasing the gap between desires and incomes from existing work arrangements and, it is hoped, generating more work input from the population. Other mechanisms, frequently utilized, have operated by influencing the land-labor ratio in order to determine labor returns. Limitations on land availability via direct restrictions on land settlement as well as by some combinations of minimum prices, minimum acreage requirements, and credit terms have been utilized to both lower labor incomes and to influence its sectoral allocation. Encouraging or allowing large-scale immigration can have somewhat similar impacts as the controls over land settlement by leading to a direct increase in the labor force, a probable lowering of the wage for those previously resident in the country, and, if the migrants and the natives were willing to do different types of work or live in different places, a sectoral reallocation of labor (perhaps also leading to an overall increase in the labor input).

Although we have noted only some of the many possibilities, this does provide some indication of the broad range of measures that could potentially influence the labor supply and the economic returns to laborers, capitalists, and landowners. The range of feasible choices is limited, no doubt, by political, cultural, demographic, and ideological, as well as economic, factors. How these work themselves out within any set of institutional frameworks is not always certain, nor is the question of what, at any time, is to be regarded by contemporaries or later scholars as economically or otherwise optimal (and from whose point of view).[19]

V.6

In the study of various forms of coerced labor, such as slavery, the precise nature of the nexus among economic, cultural, and ideological factors poses considerable problems, both in defining what institutions exist at any time and also because of the variations in the actual manner in which

[19] R. J. Steinfeld and S. L. Engerman, Labor—Free or coerced: A historical reassessment of differences and similarities. In *Free and Unfree Labour: The Debate Continues* (Tom Brass and Marcel van der Linden, eds.). (Berne: Peter Lang, 1997). See also R. J. Steinfeld, *The Invention of Free Labor.* University of North Carolina Press, Chapel Hill, 1991.

such institutions operated. It is clear, for example, that there need be no direct correlation between the legal status of an individual and the actual material living conditions that exist.[20] Slavery, wherever and whenever it existed, was not necessarily applicable to all individuals but only to members of certain ethnicities, nationalities, religions, or races. Similarly, the timing of the abolition of slavery for these different groups also varied dramatically. It took more than only the possible existence of an economic surplus for the introduction of slavery, whereas the determination of who could be enslaved seemingly went beyond exclusively economic considerations.[21]

One of the most widely applicable generalizations about slavery is that the slave status has been reserved for those considered outsiders to the enslaving society.[22] The difficulty with this simple insider-outsider concept, however, is that the definition of who were to be considered enslavable outsiders did change over time, so that it is more exact to discuss not one but several different antislaveries over the centuries.[23] Although most recent writings focus on the abolitions in the Americas in the 19th century, when the European powers ended slavery in their colonies, and Brazil and the United States emancipated their slaves, this was really the ending of black slavery by Europeans and their descendants overseas. Not only had Europeans ended the slavery of other Europeans earlier, many of these western European nations had also ended serfdom at home, and during the

[20] For a philosophic discussion of this point, see G. Simmel, *The Philosophy of Money,* 2nd ed., pp. 297–303. Routledge, London 1990 (original publication 1900). For a suggestive argument regarding the peasantry of early modern Europe, see F. Braudel, *Civilization and Capitalism: 15th–18th Century,* Vol. II, pp. 254–272. Harper and Row, New York, 1982, and his *The Identity of France,* Vol. II, p. 138. Harper and Row, New York, 1990. For a similar argument regarding Russian serfdom, see S. L. Hoch, *Serfdom and Social Control in Russia: Petrovskoe, a Village in Tambov.* University of Chicago Press, Chicago, 1986.

[21] Important recent work on the rise and fall of slavery include D. B. Davis, *The Problem of Slavery in the Age of Revolution, 1770–1823.* Cornell University Press, Ithaca, NY, 1975, and his *Slavery and Human Progress.* Oxford University Press, New York, 1984; S. Drescher, *Capitalism and Antislavery,* Oxford University Press, New York, 1987; O. Patterson, *Slavery and Social Death: A Comparative Study.* Harvard University Press, Cambridge, MA., 1982; R. W. Fogel, *Without Consent or Contract: The Rise and Fall of American Slavery.* Norton, New York, 1989.

[22] M. I. Finley, *Ancient Slavery and Modern Ideology.* Viking, New York, 1980. This distinction was also applied to other aspects of behavior. For a discussion of the different rules of war and the differences in the treatment of captives depending on whether the foe was Christian or infidel, see M. H. Keen, *The Laws of War in the Late Middle Ages,* pp. 13, 137, 156, 189. Routledge & Kegan Paul, London, 1965.

[23] For a discussion of the evolving definition of blacks as "outsiders," see W. McKee Evans, From the Land of Canaan to the Land of Guinea: The strange odyssey of the 'Sons of Ham.' *American Historical Review* **85,** 15–43 (1980).

19th century when they were ending their slavery overseas, the nations of central and eastern Europe were also ending their serfdoms.[24]

Britain, for example, ended slavery of Britons by the 12th century and serfdom in the period after the Black Death, from the 14th to the 16th centuries, when the cartel of landowners broke down. It is doubtful that after the 12th century the British legally enslaved war captives from other European nations. Spain first ended slavery for Spaniards, but maintained slavery of whites of non-Christian religions. This ended, however, with the expanding enslavement of black Africans within Spain. The maintenance of the ending of enslavement of one's own nationals was carried forward when the European nations settled the Americas. No white Europeans were legally enslaved at any time, although periods of compulsion and sale existed for convicts and indentured servants for a limited number of years. Slavery was for life, indentured servitude for a limited period of time. Slavery was generally inherited by the children of a slave mother, while there were no such legal intergenerational aspects of indentured servitude. Given these major differences, often resting on racial factors, specific forms of punishment seem rather more similar.[25]

New World slavery was initially limited to native–American Indians, and it generally ended rather early after settlement in the Spanish colonies, as well as in most other colonies of the Europeans, but it was followed by other forms of colonial, government-imposed coercion of individuals and of communities. Slavery was then applied exclusively to Africans, purchased in Africa for the transatlantic slave trade, and to their offspring.[26] There was

[24] S. L. Engerman, Emancipations in comparative perspective: A long and wide view, In *Fifty Years Later: Capitalism and Antislavery in the Dutch Orbit* (G. Oostindie, ed.). KITLV Press, Leiden, 1995, 223–241. On the ending of serfdom in Europe, see J. Blum, *The End of the Old Order in Rural Europe.* Princeton University Press, Princeton, NJ, 1978. For discussions of the ending of slavery in medieval Europe, see R. M. Karras, *Slavery and Society in Medieval Scandinavia.* Yale University Press, New Haven, CT. 1988; P. Bonnassie, *From Slavery to Feudalism in South-Western Europe,* pp. 1–59. Cambridge University Press, Cambridge, UK, 1991; G. Bois, *The Transformation of the Year One Thousand: The Village of Lournand from Antiquity to Feudalism,* pp. 13–33. Manchester University Press, Manchester, 1992; and G. Duby, *The Early Growth of the European Economy: Warriors and Peasants from the Seventh to the Twelfth Century.* Weidenfeld & Nicolson, London, 1974.

[25] On indentured servants, see H. McD. Beckles, *White Servitude and Black Slavery in Barbados, 1627–1715.* University of Tennessee Press, Knoxville, 1989; D. Galenson, *While Servitude in Colonial America: An Economic Analysis.* Cambridge University Press, Cambridge, UK, 1981. See also D. Eltis, [Europeans and the rise and fall of African slavery in the Americas: An interpretation. *American Historical Review* **98,** 1399–1423 (1993)], for an analysis of the question of white slavery versus black slavery at the time of settlement.

[26] For the changing labor forms in Latin America, see, for example, M. A. Burkholder and L. L. Johnson, *Colonial Latin America,* 2nd ed., pp. 98–124. Oxford University Press, Oxford, 1994.

only a limited overlap of arrivals from Asia (mainly China) during the existence of slavery in specific parts of the Americas, but these Chinese came as contract laborers, not as slaves. Thus, whatever might have been the economic advantages of a broader application of enslavement, the status of slave in the Americas became narrowly restricted over time. Indeed, at the time when many of the western European powers were maintaining slavery for black Africans in the American colonies, they were generally developing at home a relatively free white labor force, with only limited numbers of black slaves, mainly in the Iberian areas, and with only some exceptions, without serfdom. This was at a time when most of Africa and much of Asia still maintained systems of slavery, and were to do so until the 20th century.[27]

V.7

The ending of slavery in the 19th century represented one of history's largest redistributions of property rights and changes in the nature of economic institutions, particularly those regarding labor. These changes in institutional arrangements generated major controversies concerning economic reforms to achieve growth. Perhaps the most explicit policy discussion regarding labor institutions emerged in the 1830s, and it centered on the question of what should be done in regard to the ex-slaves in the British West Indies after their emancipation and with the ending of the period of apprenticeship.[28] This debate included discussion of many key cultural and economic variables, among them the impact of wage rates, land-labor ratios, cultural backgrounds, ruling class ideology, institutional

[27] On slavery in Africa and Asia, see, in particular, P. E. Lovejoy, *Transformations in Slavery: A History of Slavery in Africa.* Cambridge University Press, Cambridge, UK, 1983; J. L. Watson, ed., *Asian and African Systems of Slavery.* Basil Blackwell, Oxford, UK, 1980; S. Miers and I. Kopytoff, eds., *Slavery in Africa: Historical and Anthropological Perspectives.* University of Wisconsin Press, Madison, 1977; P. Manning, *Slavery in African Life: Occidental, Oriental, and African Slave Trades.* Cambridge University Press, Cambridge, UK, 1990; A. Reid, ed., *Slavery, Bondage and Dependency in Southeast Asia.* St. Martin's Press: New York, 1983. For discussions of abolition, see S. Miers and R. Roberts, eds., *The End of Slavery in Africa.* University of Wisconsin Press, Madison, 1988; M. A. Klein, ed., *Breaking the Chains: Slavery, Bondage, and Emancipation in Modern Africa and Asia.* University of Wisconsin Press, Madison, 1993. On an even later system of labor coercion, see C. Moore, J. Leckie, and D. Munro, eds., *Labour in the South Pacific.* James Cook University of Northern Queensland, Townsville, 1990.

[28] See W. A. Green, *British Slave Emancipation: The Sugar Colonies and the Great Experiment, 1830–1865.* Oxford University Press, Oxford, 1976. See also S. L. Engerman, *The land and labour problem,* and the Colonial Office and related documents cited there. For an interesting later analysis of this problem, see S. Olivier, *White Capital and Coloured Labour,* particularly pp. 72–84. Independent Labour Party, London, 1910.

innovations, and the size and nature of the expected and desired labor force after slave emancipation.

Although in many ways the general range of policies discussed were familiar from the earlier literature of mercantilism and colonial settlement policies, it was the need to establish a new set of policies immediately that made the debate on labor policy in the 1830s so explicit and so directed. The suggested policies to obtain a satisfactory labor input from the point of view of the landowners reflected the differences in economic and demographic conditions on the various islands, and the range of policies proposed covered cases ranging from overpopulated to low-population density areas.

The problem as perceived was always the same—how to get the ex-slaves to work for others and to provide a high level of labor input. To some, the problem reflected issues unique to blacks who, it was argued, lacked the motivation to desire goods (or did not relate the consumption desired to the magnitude of productive work). The same conclusion was reached by those less racist, who believed that the ex-slaves had developed their bad working habits due to slavery. To others, however, the basic labor problem was no different in the West Indies from that among the laborers in Ireland, England, or elsewhere; that is, it was generated by the relation of desired consumption and the availability of resources that influenced worker income.[29] One intent of the period of apprenticeship (in addition to granting opportunities to owners to have a guaranteed labor force for four to six more years) was to help the ex-slaves learn about the relation between work and rewards. People, it was argued, would work only so much as was necessary to obtain the goods they desired for consumption, and the more limited their wants or the more easily they could be achieved, the less labor and, more important, the less labor for others they would be willing to undertake. Thus, the policies were to establish either (or both) of two ends. First, there was the "education," to be obtained from observing the consumption habits of others and seeing what was available in the market, which it was hoped would lead people to desire more consumption and, as a result of want creation, lead them to achieve a so-called "civilized" level of demands. Without such want creation it was believed that the labor input would be low, as would overall output. There was, however, some debate, however limited at the time, about the ultimate welfare significance of such behavior, as well its possible effects on

[29] See, in particular, H. Taylor *Paper on the Proposed Emancipation of Slaves,* CO884/1. Public Record Office, London, 1833, and *Heads of a Plan for the Abolition of Negro Slavery, and for the Continued Cultivation of the Estates by the Manumitted Slaves 17 January 1833,* CO320/8. Public Record Office, London 1833. The full title of An Act for the Abolition of Slavery, included the intent of "promoting the Industry of the manumitted Slaves."

health and life expectation. Second, there could be the reduction in the ease of acquiring goods on one's own, either by restricting the available alternatives in order to induce laboring for others or else by increasing the need to work by lowering the potential consumption to be obtained from a given amount of labor input. The first of these could be achieved by limitations on land settlement and land ownership by ex-slaves, the second by various systems of taxation, either of goods traded internationally or of domestic assets, including land.

There was also a variety of arrangements in which small acreages and housing were allowed in exchange for specified amounts of labor on the plantation, to serve as a means of attracting plantation labor and also to increase the costs and discomforts of quitting. If these policies were unable to achieve the appropriate results, resort to subsidized immigration, contract or otherwise, could be tried to increase the available labor force and more importantly, to increase the labor on plantations. Immigration was encouraged after it became clear that, for whatever reasons, ex-slaves in certain areas were unwilling to return to plantation work, and the colonial governments would not undertake the measures necessary to force their return.[30]

Discussion of the economic failure of most of the British West Indian colonies after slave emancipation contains implications regarding the nature of the labor force's orientation toward goods and leisure, and their attitude to the overall disutility of work on sugar plantations. The debate on when the ex-slaves had their "flight from the plantations" questions whether they left when freedom was initially granted, as a reaction to life as slaves or work as gang laborers, or whether it was sometime in the next decade, when the changing British sugar policy and changing world market conditions led to a decline in the world price for sugar and thus in the wages paid for plantation labor.[31] This debate highlights the importance of disagreements regarding the shape of the labor supply curve, because some argued that any attempt to raise wages would, given the limited consumption desires, have decreased rather than the increased labor input. Further, it

[30] For an overall view on the responses to emancipation in the British West Indies, see Green, *British Slave Emancipation.* For detailed examinations of some specific areas, see A. H. Adamson, *Sugar Without Slaves: The Political Economy of British Guiana, 1838–1904.* Yale University Press, New Haven, CT, 1972; D. Wood, *Trinidad in Transition: The Years after Slavery.* Oxford University Press, Oxford, 1968; D. Hall, *Free Jamaica, 1838–1865: An Economic History.* Yale University Press, New Haven, CT, 1959; C. Levy, *Emancipation, Sugar, and Federalism: Barbados and the West Indies, 1833–1876.* University Presses of Florida, Gainesville, 1980.

[31] See D. Hall, The flight from the estates reconsidered: The British West Indies, 1838-42. *Journal of Caribbean History* **10/11,** 7–24 (1978).

raises questions about the extent to which British policy regarding international trade influenced labor demands and returns, and the relation of influences on output such as differential tariffs upon input rewards and to labor input, questions important given the prolonged debates on the nature of the sugar duties at this time.

As was pointed out by Herman Merivale, professor of political economy in the University of Oxford in the 1840s, the colonies of the British West Indies can be divided into three groups related to their basic conditions and problems after slave emancipation, the basic distinctions among colonies following differences in measured land-labor ratios.[32] Although the effective land-labor ratios are obviously not determined exogenously, varying with the politics of specific areas, in this particular case the crude land-labor ratio does a much better job explaining the next half-century than does other proposed explanations. This is, perhaps, not surprising given that the same basic outcome regarding the restoration of plantation life was sought by planters in all colonies, so that differences in outcomes mainly reflected differences in the ability to achieve those desired ends. A new policy was not essential in those islands of high population density where, in effect, the ex-slaves had no land on which to settle and thus were confined to the plantations. This characterized Antigua, whose planters were sufficiently aware of the relation between density and limited opportunities that they decided to forego any period of apprenticeship and to free their slaves immediately, and Barbados, whose planters soon became concerned with the implications of outmigration and tried to legislate means to stop that outflow, attempts which were only of limited success.

An opposite case, where much productive, unused land was present and where, because of its expanse, this land was subject to only limited controls against possible settlement by ex-slaves, occurred in Trinidad and British Guiana, areas that had been rapidly expanding in output and productivity in the years immediately prior to slave emancipation. Under slavery, however, they were not able to acquire adequate labor because of British regulations regarding the transatlantic and intra–Caribbean slave trades, a labor shortage reflected in the much higher prices of slaves there than in the other parts of the British West Indies.[33] The initial policies pur-

[32] H. Merivale, *Lectures on Colonization and Colonies,* 2nd ed. Longman, Green, Longman, and Roberts, London, 1861 (1st ed. 1841); see also E. G. Wakefield, *A View of the Art of Colonization.* John W. Parker, London, 1849.

[33] The average slave prices (1822–1830) for each area are in An account of the average of sales in the several colonies affected by the act for the abolition of slavery . . . *Parliamentary Papers* **48,** 329 (1837–1838). The prices for those listed as "Praedial attached" are in H. Merivale, *Lectures,* p. 333. The British policy is discussed in S. Drescher, *Econocide: British Slavery in the Era of Abolition,* University of Pittsburgh Press, Pittsburgh, PA, 1977. pp. 92–112.

sued sought to have the ex-slaves work on the plantations by setting high prices for land, imposing high minimum acreage requirements, and placing taxes on land and on food imports. Nevertheless, the ability to force the ex-slaves onto plantations was rather limited, and another source of labor—and the use of a rather different form of institutional supply—was seen to be required. Attempts at receiving voluntary migration and of the subsidization of European settlers did not prove successful, leading to the opening for contract labor immigration, mainly from India but also from China, Portuguese Madeira and Cape Verde, and Africa.[34] With contract labor brought in to work on the plantation, the movement away of the ex-slaves was now less costly to planters, and if the indentured laborers did not return to their homelands after the contracted period had ended, there was a further benefit to landowners via the increase in the overall labor supply. Given that part of the costs of the migration were paid by the planters hiring the laborers and part were paid out of the general tax funds of the colonies, this meant that the plantation owners were being provided a subsidy, part of which was, in effect, being paid by the ex-slaves. The importation of contract labor for work on sugar plantations was successful in maintaining and expanding plantation agriculture until a new moral attack emerged, particularly within India and Britain, that forced the end of the Indian indentured labor movement overseas in 1917, a time when the system was still working well economically and desired by planters as well as by migrants. As was the case with New World slavery, indentured labor was ended ultimately on ideological grounds, not as a result of any economic failures, and this ending took place with only relatively limited input from the workers.

The rest of the British Caribbean, including Jamaica, had its plantation labor force leave for smaller plots of land, as was done by the ex-slaves in Trinidad and British Guiana. Lacking as potentially profitable a plantation sector, however, the planters in those islands were not able to benefit from their attempts, necessarily limited, at attracting contract labor. Output remained relatively stagnant in these areas, while the attempts, via land and tax policies, to force the ex-slave workers back onto the plantations did not succeed. Whether a more draconian colonial policy could have succeeded economically remains unclear, as are the reasons why such a policy was not attempted, since force, compulsion, and the use of military power were not unknown policies at that time.

[34] For discussions of the issues regarding indentured labor in the late 19th century, see H. Tinker, *A New System of Slavery: The Export of Indian Labour, 1830–1920.* Oxford University Press, Oxford, 1974; K.O. Laurence, *A Question of Labour: Indentured Immigration into Trinidad and British Guiana, 1875–1917.* Ian Randle, Kingston, 1994.

V.8

In examining these responses to emancipation on the British sugar islands, certain cultural and ideological, as well as economic, issues are raised concerning the choices made by the workers and by the political elite. Even now, little is definitely known about the incomes of those ex-slaves not working in the plantation sector, so whether there was a cost to them in terms of material goods of choosing nonplantation rather than plantation work is not certain. That such a cost of moving to farms with fewer controls existed in the United States in the immediate postbellum period is probable, based on comparisons of cotton plantation wages and small-farm incomes. What is certain is that in few cases in the Americas, except on the overpopulated islands of Barbados and Antigua, were ex-slaves "willing" to work on plantations.[35] The only other successful post-emancipation plantations in the British Colonies were those based on using contract labor from poorer countries, often under governmental supervision and with the legal terms of the contract being strictly enforced. The British and their West Indian planter class, however racist and uncaring about the blacks and however severe the military measures taken against civil disorder at various times over the next century, were not willing to take measures necessary to force the ex-slaves back onto plantations and, instead, they were forced to draw upon labor taken from halfway around the world. That this 19th and 20th century contract labor was seldom white, unlike the indentured labor of the 17th and 18th centuries, may be explained in part by differences that had developed in relative international income levels and their variance, but other factors, such as climate, disease, ethnic composition, and working conditions, no doubt had some impact.

Other adjustments to the ending of slavery provide somewhat different patterns than do those of the British West Indies but involved drawing upon a new source of labor to maintain the production of staple crops. These adjustments often did not maintain the same scale of production that had been possible with the use of slave labor, but they relied on changes in the technology and the organization of crop production, with reductions in the optimum observed scale of producing units. In some cases, these reductions in size meant some loss in efficiency, but in the cases of cotton and coffee the reduction was somewhat less dramatic than would have been the case for sugar at that time. In sugar production throughout the world during most of the 19th century, whether in areas where sugar

[35] See, for example, W. G. Sewell [*The Ordeal of Free Labor in the British West Indies.* Sampson, Low, Son, & Co., London, 1861], who was typical in considering Barbados to be the demonstration of the success possible with slave emancipations while believing most other colonies were still suffering from problems of adjustment.

had previously been produced with slave labor or in areas where sugar production began without a prior existence of slave plantations, there seemed no possibility of effective small-scale units able to compete with plantations. For cotton and coffee, smaller production units were possible. Thus, in the U.S. South after 1865, while many ex-slaves remained in agriculture and still were producing cotton, both whites and blacks were generally working on small farms, with a perceived lower level of intensity of labor input and measured efficiency than on the prewar plantations. The postbellum expansion of cotton production was achieved by the entry (or expansion of production) of white farmers, on small farms, moving into the market production of cotton, a shift made possible by the avoidance of plantations by the ex-slave, causing the disappearance of these more productive units.[36] Even the prospect of strong positive inducements, however, did not lead many ex-slaves, or whites, to work on plantations in the postbellum era. Such distaste for plantation work has long been, understandably, a widespread phenomenon, and the desire of those who are free and with high enough incomes to avoid such working conditions is what has led to the existence of various systems of labor controls, including slavery, when that was legally possible.

A pattern somewhat similar to that of the U.S. South emerged with the final ending of slavery in Brazil in 1888. European labor had been sought as a substitute for black slave labor on coffee plantations since the 1850s, but such attempts were not successful. Few, if any, whites remained as plantation laborers and small coffee farms were not successful in competition with plantations, which continued as long as slavery existed. With the ending of slavery, however, it appears that the ex-slaves left the plantations and plantation regions, whether voluntarily or otherwise (and whether in response to the immigration of Europeans or rather preceding that and thus leaving room for them). Coffee remained an important crop after the ending of slavery, but production was achieved by using the subsidized labor of immigrants from Europe, mainly Italy and Spain, workers who labored mainly on relatively small farms, not on plantations.[37] It appears that, with the preference to avoid gang-type work, the level of efficiency in production fell with the size of the farms, but the smaller European immigrant-operated farms seemed to be the only way to maintain the market produc-

[36] See the material summarized in S. L. Engerman, Economic adjustments to emancipation in the United States and British West Indies. *Journal of Interdisciplinary History,* **13,** 191–220 (1982).

[37] T. H. Holloway, *Immigrants on the Land: Coffee and Society in São Paulo, 1886–1934.* University of North Carolina Press, Chapel Hill, 1980; G. R. Andrews, *Blacks and Whites in São Paulo, Brazil: 1888–1988.* University of Wisconsin Press, Madison, 1991.

tion of coffee once the ex-slaves had left the plantation and the plantation regions.

Another variant of the adjustments to the end of slavery, one resulting from an unexplained lag in technological change and innovation, and one that similarly had a marked influence on the ethnic composition of the labor force, is seen in Cuba, where slavery ended in 1886, and in Louisiana, where slavery had ended in 1865.[38] Prior to the last decades of the 19th century almost all the world's sugar, with the major exception of that produced in India, involved large plantations, combining the grinding mill with the cane fields. With the development of larger central mills, and with the expansion of railroads to move sugar rapidly from the fields to the mill, it became possible for cane to be grown on smaller units as well as plantations, and in some (but only some) areas there was a transition permitting smaller farms to produce some proportion of the cane. In the cases of Cuba and of Louisiana, these smaller farms were operated almost exclusively by whites, in the case of Cuba often immigrants from Spain, while on the remaining plantations black labor predominated.

Thus in the adjustments to the end of slavery, where technology and tastes regarding the nature of the labor process permitted, a shift to smaller-scale production was possible, although with some probable decline in measured productivity. Such changes in scale often led to the use of white labor to work on smaller farms, whereas they generally did not want to, and could not be made to, work on plantations. Despite legal instruments such as vagrancy laws, to "encourage" people to work, the ex-slaves were seldom forced back onto the plantations. Their work on smaller units, whether these were self-owned or not, generally meant an involvement with market production (as opposed to self-subsistence farming). While the political forces in the ex-slave societies worked to limit the rights and freedoms of the freedmen, some limits were accepted on the nature of the economic adjustments—if not by all individuals, at least by the governments.

V.9

Whereas most discussions of labor institutions relate to circumstances where individuals hire, own, or coerce other individuals, subject to state-provided legal codes, the coercive (and other) labor practices of the state as an active power have clearly played a major role in economic change. The

[38] See, on Cuba, R. J. Scott, *Slave Emancipation in Cuba: The Transition to Free Labor, 1860–1899.* Princeton University Press, Princeton, NJ, 1985, and, on the Louisiana sugar industry, see J. C. Sitterson, *Sugar Country: The Cane Sugar Industry in the South, 1753–1950.* University of Kentucky Press, Lexington, 1953.

state has had the legal power to coerce individual citizens into particular preferred activities, but in the past the state has also drawn labor by paying individuals, using individuals being punished for having violated some behavioral norm of society, or using military captives from foreign countries. The basis for selection among these methods reflected society's attitudes concerning individuals and their rights, in contrast to the interests of the collective unit, as well as the nature of the political bargaining process that had emerged among members of society. From early despotisms to nations with socialist or communist governments, some central control over allocation of the labor force, for either an economic or a noneconomic end, has long persisted. Even governments in those societies with large private sectors resorted at times to nonmarket mechanisms to coerce labor to perform specific functions. Most frequent has been the use of labor for military purposes, with forced drafts from the population to serve various military functions, often with low or no pay (at least none besides the provision of necessary consumption items). Formal drafts for military service in democratic societies, substituting implicit taxes on special individuals for general taxation, are a relatively recent institution. In some cases the coercive nature of the forced service led to arguments for the replacement of the draft by a voluntary army, recruited by paying market wages for those laborers with desired characteristics, a return to the earlier system based on the hiring of mercenaries, who often came from foreign nations. In some cases, such as in the U.S. Civil War, a draft did not necessarily lead to service by the drafted individual, who could either pay a fee to avoid military duty or provide a substitute to fulfill his military obligations.[39]

In other places and times, the form of compulsion to service was more direct than the somewhat more randomized procedures in democratic societies, with more explicit tactics used to force service and its completion and, frequently, more severe punishments than only a term of imprisonment if service was rejected.[40] Yet, there was often a combination of domestic com-

[39] For excellent surveys of the military volunteers and conscription policies of the United States and of the major European powers, see the essays by J. L. Rafuse, United States' Experience with Volunteer and Conscript Forces, and J. M. McConnell, European experience with volunteer and conscript forces: Involvement in domestic issues, in *Studies Prepared for the President's Commission on an All-Volunteer Army.* Government Printing Office, Washington, DC, 1970. Rafuse (p. III-1–41), pointed out that in the United States between 1865 and 1965 the ratio of average "annual military pay and allowances" to "manufacturing earnings" fell from 1.041 to .581.

[40] For background on these questions related to military recruitment see, among many works, G. Parker, *The Military Revolution: Military Innovation and the Rise of the West, 1500–1800.* Cambridge University Press, Cambridge, UK, 1988; W. H. McNeill, *The Pursuit of Power: Technology, Armed Force and Society since AD 1000.* Oxford University Press, Oxford, 1982; P. Contamine, *War in the Middle Ages.* Basil Blackwell Oxford, 1984; J. Keegan, *A History of Warfare.* Vintage Books, New York, 1994.

pulsion applied to citizens and the use of the market to obtain additional needed military power by the hiring of mercenaries. While at times slaves were not permitted to serve in the military, or else were not entrusted with weapons, slaves did sometimes form the basis of a military corps and even its fighting force, either while still enslaved or after receiving their freedom from slave status in exchange for the performance of military duty.[41] The benefits of coercive recruitment for the government (and the taxpayers) were from obtaining desired labor at a lower cost to them than they would have been required to pay using the market alternatives. This, however, meant laboring in an occupation with a high disutility to the laborers, forced to suffer a loss in welfare. The nature of compulsory service also influenced the variety of incentives and punishments. Because discharge of recruits could be rather costly, because much of the laborers's income was provided in kind, and because imprisonment in lieu of service was seen as self-defeating, resorting to physical punishments such as whipping persisted longer in the military than in many other parts of the labor market (except, of course, slavery).

The construction of government public works sometimes utilized hired labor, but often depended on taxed or forced draft labor for limited times. In addition, criminal or convict labor was employed for the specified period of punishment. Whether or not the definitions of criminal activities varied specifically with the government's desires for labor, as opposed to its desire for social control, such use of convicts did serve to obtain labor input while reducing the costs of internment. Why such means of punishment were chosen rather than torture, hanging (or other means of death), enslavement, or exile no doubt reflects some combination of economic, cultural, and ideological forces.[42] The use of convicts by the British to settle new regions, such as the United States and Australia, provided an alternative to indentured labor, and a difference in these two forms of labor was apparently recognized because the period served by convict labor generally exceeded that of the laborers coming under indentures.[43] Criminals were often regarded as

[41] See, for example, the case discussed by R. N. Buckley [*Slaves in Red Coats in the British West India Regiments, 1795–1815.* Yale University Press, New Haven, CT, 1979], which resulted in the manumission of those slaves purchased by the British to fight in the West Indies.

[42] See the interesting discussion in J. H. Langbein, *Torture and the Law of Proof: Europe and England in the Ancient Régime,* pp. 27–44. University of Chicago Press, Chicago, 1977.

[43] On the convicts to Australia, see A. G. L. Shaw [*Convicts and the Colonies: A Study of Penal Transportation from Great Britain and Ireland and Other Parts of the British Empire.* Faber and Faber, London, 1966], and on the earlier movement of convicts to the North American colonies, see A. R. Ekirch [*Bound for America: The Transportation of British Convicts to the Colonies, 1718–1775.* Oxford University Press, Oxford, 1987]. The early fights (and successes) of convicts and former convicts for equality of rights in Australia are described in D. Neal [*The Rule of Law in a Penal Colony: Law and Power in Early New South Wales.* Cambridge University Press, Cambridge, UK, 1991].

legally similar to slaves, and the lack of rights of both, although for differing lengths of time, was explicitly recognized by the United States government in the Northwest Ordinance and, again, in the Thirteenth Amendment which ended slavery.

V.10

The conditions that generated the supply of labor required to meet the demand for free labor and for slaves and other coerced labor in different societies reflected patterns of cultural and ideological belief that influenced economic behavior. Voluntary slavery (at least voluntary from the family's view) of children was one way to meet the problems of famine and low income, and this was a frequent pattern in Asia and Africa. In Europe, however, voluntary slavery was limited in its frequency, but there was resort to infanticide and abandonment (which, if recovery was anticipated, could have meant an outcome similar to voluntary enslavement, but presumably at lower cost to the enslaver, whereas if recovery was not expected, this could be tantamount to infanticide). Involuntary slavery often originated with the sale to others or the keeping for one's own use of military captives, who had not been killed either in battle or after capture. The capture of foreign soldiers could have been turned to financial gain also by the ransoming of captives to their areas of origin rather than selling them to other nations, or else by keeping them as slaves, rather than either killing them or else just freeing them.[44] Given the historical frequency of wars and of wartime captives, and the frequency of wars among contiguous or close-by nations, an examination of the economic and ideological factors influencing the choice made between sales to foreign areas in contrast with ransoming or merely freeing to return to areas of origin provides some interesting comparative perspective, as does the differential use, military or otherwise, of those captives not returned. Military captives were a major source of those slaves who were sold to the Americas, whereas prisoners of war of western European nations were by the Middle Ages more generally ransomed or otherwise returned to their countries of origin, after the end of

[44] B. S. Frey and H. Buhoffer, A market for men, or There is no such thing as a free lynch. *Journal of Institutional and Theoretical Economics* **142,** 739–744 (1986). The scales of ransom prices are discussed in G. Parker, ed., *The Thirty Years' War,* pp. 203–204. Routledge & Kegan Paul, London, 1984, and his *The Army of Flanders and the Spanish Road, 1567–1659: The Logistics of Spanish Victory and Defeat in the Low Countries' Wars.* pp. 169–170. Cambridge University Press, Cambridge, UK, 1972. See also W. E. S. Flory, *Prisoners of War: A Study in the Development of International Law.* American Council on Public Affairs, Washington, DC, 1942.

the fighting, and not made a part of either a trans-European or the transatlantic slave trade.[45]

V.11

These examples of changing labor institutions indicate the complexity in the interaction of economic, cultural, and ideological factors, a point that has been advocated in the recent writings of Douglass North. A distinct separation of motives is no doubt quite difficult, since the effects of culture and ideology are seldom completely independent of the costs they impose on society and, as Adam Smith suggested regarding the Quakers and slavery in Pennsylvania, even the demand curve for morality could be regarded as downward sloping.[46] Correspondingly, the forces that lead individuals to financially income maximize or seek what we might regard as economic ends, in contrast with the drive for power, domination, or for just a quiet and/or lazy life, reflect certain cultural values, whereas the rules of society and the emergence of new institutions are influenced by the ideologies accepted by the rulers and the ruled.

To deal with traditionally economic questions without attention to the manner in which cultural and ideological forces can influence the nature of economic behavior can lead in some misleading directions. The problems we have in understanding the patterns of culture and ideology, and how

[45] On military captives used as slaves, see, among other sources, D. J .E. Maier, [Military acquisition of slaves in Asante. In *West African Economic and Social History: Studies in Memory of Marion Johnson* (D, Henige and T .C. McCaskie, eds.), pp. 119–132. University of Wisconsin Press, Madison 1990], on one of the major slave-capturing societies in Africa (the author also noting the periodic use of "human sacrifice" during "state ceremonies" and other occasions); R. Bartlett [*The Making of Europe: Conquest, Colonization and Cultural Change.* Princeton University Press, Princeton, NJ 1993], on episodes of captives in military actions used for slave labor, and, on a different issue, the granting of freedom to encourage migration (pp. 123–132); and P. W. Bamford [*Fighting Ships and Prisons: The Mediterranean Galleys of France in the Age of Louis XIV,* pp. 138–199. University of Minnesota Press, Minneapolis, 1973], on the acquisition and use of galley slaves, including a brief discussion of the late 17th-century option available to some rebellious citizens to "obtain release by supplying a slave (or the price of a slave) to take their places at the oars" (pp. 176–177). These patterns may also reflect differences in the attitudes toward warfare and the willingness of military foes to communicate with each other.

[46] Adam Smith, Wealth of Nations, Vol I, p. 388. On the other hand, Smith argued that the persistence of slavery was due to "the pride of man," which "makes him love to domineer," a trait for which slaveowners were presumably willing to pay a price and that suggested to Smith a rather long future for slave societies.

> The love of domination and authority and the pleasure men take in having every (thing) done by their express order, rather than to condescend to bargain and treat with those whom they look upon as their inferiors and are inclined to use in a haughty way . . . will make it impossible for slaves in a free country to recover their liberty.

they change over time, present difficulties for attempts to describe changing labor and other institutions over time and space, and things then seldom appear as determinate as desired for analytical purposes. Nevertheless, to exclude cultural and ideological factors from being among the explanatory variables for large-scale changes in institutional forms may limit our ability to understand such changes, whether these cultural and ideological factors have impacts via the formal structures of a society (as in laws), the informal structures of society (as with social norms), the effects of values, expectations, and aspirations on individual decisions, or from the interactions of these various elements. Although the newest frontier for economies may be one of greater analytical complexity rather than one with an increased simplicity of analysis and explanation, it should lead to a rather more interesting and useful intellectual study of important questions.

ACKNOWLEDGMENTS

John H. Munro Professor of Economics and Professor of History, University of Rochester. I have benefited greatly from the detailed comments of Yoram Barzel at the conference. In addition, I have been helped by the discussion at the conference, as well as by remarks from Lance Davis, Seymour Drescher, David Eltis, David Galenson, Sherwin Rosen, Kenneth Sokoloff, Robert Steinfeld, and Ralph Shlomowitz.

The slaves' condition, though not necessarily the prospects for freedom, also seemed better under absolute, arbitrary governments. [Adam Smith, *Lectures on Jurisprudence (Report of 1762–3),* p.186. Oxford University Press, Oxford, 1978].

For a rather explicit evaluation of the costs of the "White Australian" policy ending the use of Kanaka contract labor in the production of sugar, and substituting white producers with the use of tariff and bounty payments, see the comments of the Australian Royal Commission Report on the Sugar Industry in 1912. They commented:

> A white community which prefers to grow its own sugar in its own territory with white labor, rather than purchase from abroad sugar grown by cheap coloured labor, must face the responsibility of making good the increased cost of production under the higher standard of living and reward. Either the consumer or the taxpayer must pay. In Australia . . . the cost is paid by the consumer.

A Sydney commercial agent, in testifying before the Commission, estimated a yearly charge of 6s. per person per annum—about $\frac{1}{2}$ of 1 percent of GDP (see *Report of the Royal Commission on the Sugar Industry,* xxi, xx, and 553. Government of the Commonwealth of Australia, 1912).

Interesting cases of apparently ideologically influenced changes in government and private policy that led to dramatic changes in the nature of labor markets in the 20th-century United States are the changes described in R. J. Butler, J. J. Heckman, and B. Payner [The impact of the economy and the state on the economic status of blacks: A study of South Carolina. In *Markets in History: Economic Studies of the Past* (D. W. Galenson, ed.), pp. 231–346. Cambridge University Press, Cambridge, UK, 1989] and in C. Goldin, [*Understanding the Gender Gap: An Economic History of American Women,* pp. 160–179. Oxford University Press, New York, 1990] dealing, respectively, with hiring practices toward blacks and toward married women.

VI

Thinking about the State: Property Rights, Trade, and Changing Contractual Arrangements in a World with Coercion

John V. C. Nye

> *"Who governs?" and "How well?" are the two most basic questions of political science.*
>
> *—Robert Putnam* (Making Democracy Work, *1993, p. 63*)

VI.1 INTRODUCTION

The influence of economic ideas on political economy has come about through an understanding that competition in politics has many of the characteristics of market competition. However, the problem with extending market analysis to politics, particularly the theory of the state, has seemed to be the problem of coercion—that is, trades that are not voluntary and mutually beneficial. But it is rarely understood that abandoning the assumption of voluntary trades only undermines the normative theory of economic analysis. In virtually every other respect, the positive analysis of economic markets can be carried over to a positive theory of the state.

Stigler once argued that there is no inherent reason for economists to assume that transactions in daily life are free of fraud or coercion. He reasoned, "I conclude that we economists have customarily excluded fraud and coercion because we have thought that they are not empirically significant elements in the ordinary economic transactions of an enterprise economy"

(Stigler, 1982, p. 24). But, of course, this empirical assertion, whether or not it applies to "ordinary economic transactions" is manifestly false when considering the interaction between politics and economics and the importance of both coercion and positive economic theory in viewing the rise of the modern state.

This is the central insight contained—though not fully elaborated—in the work of Douglass North, as well as that of Yoram Barzel (1996), Margaret Levi (1988), and Mancur Olson (McGuire and Olson, 1996). Both the zero transactions cost versions of the standard theory and the positive transactions cost theory as suggested by Coarse (1937) have their direct analogs in the political economy literature. It is the purpose of this chapter to discuss this expanded political economy framework and to show how a variety of historical applications, including many pioneered by the scholars previously mentioned, are part of a coherent rational choice view of the state. Then the dynamics of state relations can be sketched out roughly by considering the historical changes in economic and military technology and their impact on the basic problem of general trades, which includes the possibility of coercion.

VI.2 FORCE AND THE MARKET

Surprisingly enough the presence of coercion or power in and of itself is not enough to affect the "efficiency" or rather "surplus maximizing nature" of competitive outcomes. It is the nature of attendant transactions and monitoring costs of various sorts that really changes the analysis.

The case of perfect coercion with zero monitoring costs on all margins is analogous to that of the perfect monopolist who can price discriminate. In standard price theory, the efficiency of the output/price levels chosen is unaffected by the existence of a perfect monopoly so long as the monopolist can perfectly price discriminate. A rational choice theory of power should begin from similar premises. Rulers who can perfectly and costlessly extract all surplus from their subjects will do so without affecting the "efficiency" of the final outcome. What will be affected are the distribution of gains in equilibrium. The only correction that needs to be made is in the use of the term *efficiency.* Because efficiency assumes voluntary trade and Pareto optimally we need a different sort of term here. Perhaps it is better to speak in terms of surplus maximizing outcomes, but the analogy to standard price theory should be obvious.

As with the standard theory, the problem faced by the Ruler is twofold: trades and monitoring of behavior are not costless activities, and the Ruler's position is not that of a perfect monopolist—rulers too are subject to competition of one sort or another, and the manner in which they control their subjects will not only affect the amount and type of surplus they extract, but it also affects their capacity to remain in charge.

The point I am making here is one that has been variously made by North and Barzel but with greater emphasis on how much of the standard theory has analogs in political economy. Just as Coase postulated the purposely unrealistic zero transactions cost world as a benchmark within which to frame debates about the effects of different constraints on firm behavior, so too does rational choice theory seek to explore the limits of a market-oriented approach to political economy by starting from a perfectly competitive world with complete markets and then relaxing the assumptions to conform to the particulars of a given time or place.

It is striking that North implicitly acknowledged the importance of violence and force in his work (North, 1981; North and Thomas, 1973) through his thorough discussion of the resources devoted to military capacity throughout history without integrating coercion directly into his model. By simply taking a competitive model based on voluntary transactions and applying it to politics, North demonstrated how salient the basic positive analysis is without getting at the complications introduced by non–Pareto-improving exchanges. Thus, North's views on the inefficiency of existing political institutions derive primarily from three problems: imperfect information, transactions costs of various sorts, and the consequence of additional actors (such as the role of the state's agents in enforcement or nonenforcement of property rights). All three could very easily be applied to a standard study of business transactions in a market economy. What makes the last point—the role of the state—interesting above and beyond simple market analysis is the introduction of coercion.

But North in particular erred when he spoke of the state as having a monopoly on coercive authority. It is certainly the case that modern states tend to *claim* monopoly power on the legitimate use of force within their national boundaries. However, we know that historically the veracity of such claims was not always coincident with their ex ante or ex post legitimacy. States often laid claim to areas over which they had no control, and legitimate and illegitimate communities rose up from organizational structures often imposed from without. Furthermore, the idea of the state's legitimate rights to the exclusive use of force was something that governments struggled to establish as late as the 17th or 18th centuries in Europe (cf. Anderson, 1988). One can therefore think of the surviving political units as equilibria in some rough sense of the term.[1] The particular scale of these

[1] Although this would take us outside of the scope of this chapter, it is easy to see how James Anderson's observation that with the original nationalisms "the state as a territorial entity predated and helped to create the nation" and it was only late in the 19th century that national movements developed independent of the "natural" territorial boundaries (Anderson, 1988, p. 129). This would be consistent with a view that technological limits of all sorts—on both transportation and administration—would have made it much more difficult in earlier times to promote and develop the sort of territorially independent nationalisms of the last century or two.

units will interact with the possible choices in the sphere of production to dictate what the nature of relations will be between the Ruler and the Ruled.

If we treat the struggle for political power as a market, then we need to understand the winning Rulers in terms of the market structure that emerges depending upon how competitive the political market is. The Ruler of a region or nation with extremely open economic and political markets having few constraints on the movement of its subjects and facing many potential challenges to the leadership will have very little power to discriminate or even to bargain. Hence, it would be proper to treat the resultant state equilibria as being more deterministic and the problems facing the state as being more decision theoretic in nature than those of a secure Ruler with the ability to control which people remain subjects and who may enter or leave the state. Such a Ruler may not only act as a monopolist but may also have more room for bargaining with his or her subjects. Where a few individuals or groups of individuals are involved, and strategic considerations therefore become paramount, the situation may be less deterministic. Then game theory will become more relevant (e.g., the essay by Avner Grief in this volume). But in a sufficiently competitive market, the strategic issues are unimportant.

We can think of the struggle for power as itself subject to competitive forces bounded by existing technologies and a relative scarcity of resources. Monopoly in the control of force is only one possible—and often unlikely—market structure among many possible variants. The relevant issue for the new institutional economic historian is to determine the dynamics of why certain types of political institutions proliferated at one time and not another, leading to inquiries into how the specific technologies of control, force, and production evolved and affected the development of various historical economies.

VI.3 TRADING IN FORCE

There is no reason why force should be viewed differently from any other commodity except for the following: First, from a normative standpoint, trades may occur that are not mutually beneficial, with at least one party to the trade doing so involuntarily. Second, the extent to which force—or more precisely, the technology of force—will or will not change the standard analysis depends on the degree to which it can be traded and properly "priced" on the open market. The more complete and well-developed markets are, and the easier it is to buy and sell force from those with an initial endowment in it, the less of an effect it will have on the final equilibrium outcome although it will affect the final distribution of surplus/rents. In essence, this is the zero transactions cost version of the Coase theorem with tradeable force added to the list of commodities that can be exchanged.

We can therefore state how force should be integrated in a rational choice view of the state by suggesting an analogous conjecture to the original Coase theorem:

In a world with well-defined property rights, complete markets, and zero transactions costs, the capacity to use and exercise force will accrue to those with the highest value of force regardless of the initial allocation of force.

However, where these conditions do not hold or are poorly approximated, then the final use of force and the manner in which it is disposed may *depend on the initial allocation of force and upon the specific nature of the interactions among the individuals in society.*

Those with the highest value for a particular technology of force will pay the highest prices for it. At the margin, the different uses of force will reflect the underlying valuation of the goods that are being protected or fought over (where goods refer to the whole panoply of desirable states and services and not simply physical commodities). Thus, to make a point I will elaborate later, involuntary slavery would not be viable in most instances since almost no one would presumably value their freedom as much as the slave, and he would pay the most for the force necessary to keep out of slavery.

One confusion that often arises in these discussions concerns the concept of trades where force is concerned. Some might ask, "Why would any trades take place in the presence of coercion?" "How can we talk about property rights in a world with force?" Actually it does not make sense to talk about property in a world without enforcement. However we will not engage in a discussion of whether or not the use of that force is legitimate or desirable. Rather we should note that the initial configurations of property rights throughout history have usually derived from positions that (1) could be defended with the existing technology or (2) came about after those with the capacity to take from others took what they could and then arrived at a position they could defend. Let us return to the problem of how these trades take place.

In discussing the tradability of force, we are of course concerned with problems regarding the ownership of the instruments of force or, more generally, the capacity for coercion and surplus extraction. To the extent that such capacity is tradable, we would be able to extend the logic of the Coase theorem. Whoever has the most to gain from a given capacity is likely to end up with the force if transactions costs are low and the instruments of control are easily observable and well defined. The simplest way to understand this is the following: Imagine someone who owns the only gun in town. Having the gun may make him powerful enough to force others to do much of his bidding and permit him to rob people at gunpoint. However, if someone can manage to do even more with the gun than the initial recipient of the weapon, there will be an incentive for a trade to take place, either directly, through someone offering the gun owner a high price for the gun, or indirectly, through the gun owner hiring out his services to someone who could offer him more than he could possibly make simply working for himself. As it will emerge, this analysis will be helpful even in instances (like natural physical strength) in which the capacity for coercion or force cannot be directly given away but in which the persons or groups with such capacity can hire themselves out to others. Indeed trade, in the sense of exchange, need not even take place, so long as there is a competitive mechanism that permits the most effective users of force to prosper and drive out the less effective.

However, when there are barriers to such trades taking place, or when it is not possible to credibly engage in such exchanges, or when uncertainty regarding who might benefit from transfers of authority exists, we find that the initial allocation of force will have an almost arbitrary importance, and competitive forces may not move us to a surplus maximizing equilibrium. Furthermore, the process of adjustment, which may include costly battles and conflicts to demonstrate who truly has the greater force and who stands to benefit from reallocation, will dissipate much of the rent that is to be gained from a more efficient arrangement.

This final configuration thus will depend very crucially on the nature of possible exchanges and coalitions, as well as on the technology of force and the degree of competition in both the economic and political/military spheres. When there are no economies of scale in firepower or administration, there is little incentive for those with force to band together, and one should observe autonomous units of small size dominated by bandits, warlords, or even self-sufficient families engaged in limited self-defense. When the military technologies or administrative arrangements permit the exploitation of large economies of scale, one would expect to see political units of much larger size. Smaller groups would either be defeated in battle, be bought out by other communities, or be expanded through conquest or consolidation to form the minimally sized units that are stable both politically and economically.

The possession of force or the instruments thereof does not give the Ruler unlimited power. Indeed, in many cases those having been granted the capacity to coerce may not be the most "efficient" users of said force, even in the most narrowly self-interested of terms. The logic of the Coase theorem would lead us to believe that whenever it is possible to trade in force or when the holders of force can hire themselves out, they will combine or work with those better capable of extracting surplus. The Ruler need not be, and rarely is, the physically strongest individual. The strongest military states are not arbitrarily powerful. Rather a set of decisions is made and conflicts are engaged that over time lead to organizations that all reflect some equilibrium configuration involving trade-offs of strength versus material productivity, administrative efficiency versus loss of control, the benefits of homogeneous groups versus the strength of extensive coalitions, and so on.

Thus when I invoke the concept of "trades" I am thinking of the evolution of states and communities as political entities, in the same way that Alchian discusses the evolution of firms in the market over time. Purposive, conscious exchange is not central to the argument. Competitive conflict in which survival is the minimal requirement for a viable political grouping may be sufficient to produce equilibrium outcomes that would emerge from fully conscious maximization. Thus, Alchian acknowledged that firms arise for various reasons and often behave in fashions quite different from that postulated in textbooks. Most are not in fact profit maximizers (at least not consciously so) most of the time. Some bad firms survive for long periods, internal considerations of hierarchy or bargaining may dominate some firms' concerns vis-à-vis market competitiveness, and the emergence or disappearance of many firms may be difficult to analyze or seem incongruent with market trends. However, over the long haul, and given sufficient entry and exit, we expect those firms that do survive to exhibit survival traits consistent with market demands and existing supply constraints. Moreover, even when entry and exit is limited and competition apparently minimal, there should still be some movement, if rather attenuated and haphazard, in the direction of enhanced efficiency.

I argue then that the same is true in general for nations and states. It makes sense for political scientists and historians to focus on many of the peculiar aspects of various states on the special qualities of individuals or conflicts that arose out of historical accident. But the rational-choice scholar should and must come to grips with the competitive forces that underlie long-run change and the nature of the obstacles that impede or distort competition. I would also argue that the issues discussed in this essay bring us closer to an explanation consistent with the economizing framework that many authors have chosen to use. The new political economy thus adds market competition to the centuries' old attempt to analyze political dynamics.

We need to understand how the capacity for coercion and control changes the possible outcomes in the standard analysis with only voluntary trades. In general the person or group with the ability to extract rents from the rest of society will do so in a fashion that maximizes their revenues/income in the broadest sense of the word. This means that the Ruler will want the people being exploited to maximize their surplus conditional on the Ruler's capacity for rent-extraction to be unaffected by the choice of production methods on the part of the citizens. Obviously when the choice of production methods that increase the potential rents to be extracted leads to a lowered capacity on the part of the Ruler to extract rents, the Ruler will choose to weigh the trade-offs between control and income in a fashion to maximize expected gains. The higher the transactions cost of monitoring alternate mechanisms of production, the more that revenue extraction and control is tied to specific activities on the part of the subjects, and the smaller the potential gain from the people's use of the "optimal" production technology, the more likely is the Ruler going to force the people to work and produce in a fashion that is not first best for them and that does not maximize their surplus, although it allows for easy control.

The possibility of coercion and force in this world does not necessarily imply the existence of overt conflict such as warfare. Although violence may be the most effective form of exerting coercing groups or individuals in any specific instance, most of the time we can view overt conflict as resulting from uncertainty or incomplete information. Because warfare and violence are costly, both for the stronger and the weaker side, one should not expect any conflict to arise with perfect information. The stronger should simply demonstrate his or her capacity to coerce and the extent to which such coercion will lead to gains, and the coerced will comply up to the limit of his or her capacity to resist. This fanciful situation does in fact cover the majority of situations in which one group exerts power over another. When it is useless to resist, it may be in both sides' interest to settle down into their accustomed roles. In many cases, however, there is no way to credibly determine in advance who the winner of a given conflict will be or whether the gains outweigh the losses for both the winner and the loser from a particular fight, hence the existence of armed struggle and warfare as the only credible means of establishing winners in many conflicts. Warfare will also serve as one social mechanism by which more "efficient" or effective political units come to dominate or displace less effective political units.

VI.4 THE RULER AS PREDATOR AND AS MANAGER

So far we have assumed that the relationship between the Ruler and the People has been entirely negative or, in the terms of Margaret Levi (1988), predatory. However, that is often not the case. Democratic representative governments ideally choose leaders because they see them as engaged in certain functions that are necessarily or best-handled through the political process. To a certain extent, the ideal republican government (viewed purely from a positive, efficiency-maximizing perspective) would have only those civil servants whose functions cannot be carried out more effectively or efficiently in the purely private sector.[2] Even the most laissez-faire, libertarian economic traditions from Adam Smith onward have recognized the basic role of government in establishing necessary rules and institutions to facilitate the workings of the marketplace. Furthermore, even rulers and states who are most parasitic have provided a variety of services to the populations that they govern—this may have ranged from services as minimal as providing protection from rulers even more despotic than themselves to far-sighted monarchs who established an effective police and judicial system for the settling of disputes and the maintenance of law and order as well as the building of roads, bridges, and other aspects of social overhead capital.

In this light I propose to distinguish between two extremes: the first is the predatory, or what I prefer to call, the parasitic aspects of rule, well-developed in the work of Levi (1988), and the second might be referred to as the public goods aspect or, my preferred term, the managerial aspects of governmental activity. In so doing, we can correct one of the oversights in Levi's work—the lack of a precise definition of predatory rule.

Thus, we can define a pure parasitic action as one that leaves at least one party strictly worse off and that is undertaken involuntarily for the benefit of the Ruler. Moreover, a parasitic Ruler is one who engages in activity with the People in such a way that the People's welfare would be Pareto-improved if the predatory Ruler did not exist.

A purely parasitic action involves an exchange in which the People gain nothing from their interaction with the Ruler. They would be better off without the "trade." However, in its purest form, a parasitic action cannot simply be refused, and the People have to expend resources in order to avoid participating or to try negating the unwanted interaction.

Conversely, the purely managerial Ruler can be seen as providing a service like any other and the goods the ruler provides are what are often referred to in the profession as public goods. However, this may be a misnomer because many private actions have public goods aspects as well.[3] What is important is to observe, given our tendency to distinguish

[2] I am entirely aware that even within the narrow liberal tradition that there are other purposes to the state that may override efficiency considerations. It makes my task simpler just to ignore these issues and to focus on efficiency considerations while being aware that a truly comprehensive positive and normative theory of the state would take all this into account. However, it should be noted that many liberal justifications for the state—particularly those having to do with public goods and the problems of social externalities—inadverdently are concerned with the provision of such goods from an efficiency perspective. That is, the state is needed because it does a better job than the private sector and this would be found desirable even by the most libertarian individuals.

[3] To take a simple textbook example, if in painting my house and beautifying my front yard I help make the neighborhood beautiful, the neighborhood benefits even if my motivations were purely self-centered.

between private market and political activity, that pure managerial functions in an efficient political system are undertaken by those who are least-cost providers of these services, whether that political activity is explicitly labeled governmental or not. To take an elementary example, dispute arbitration can be provided by private individuals or state-run courts. In either case a particular service is needed and should be undertaken by the most "efficient" (in a constrained, positive-transactions cost world) provider. We can then think of this aspect of a ruler's behavior as making a positive contribution to the welfare of the people. This argument is much in keeping with Ronald Coase's work on the appropriate way to view externalities (cf. Coase, 1960). Again, transactions costs, missing markets, and uncertainties of various types make the attainment of the efficient system difficult.

Perhaps the classic example of hiring an outside authority for what I call managerial duties was the medieval institution of the *podesta.* The podesta was an outside executive administrator hired by communes and city-states in the 12th and 13th centuries to settle local disputes and to serve as an intermediary between communes and the emperor. He had a limited amount of what I call force, in the form of police power and military command, but he was a temporary official with a limited term in office and restricted scope of activity. The ideal podesta would have been purely a managerial ruler, although all such men were likely to have acquired some coercive authority after attaining office. In the best case, the podesta acted as perfect manager and intermediary with the emperor; in the worst, the podesta came to acquire strong parasitic tendencies.

Of course, the two sets of capacities may be difficult to unbundle (once more drawing analogies from the transactions cost literature on organization). The complication induced by violence and other forms of coercive authority is that its asymmetric distribution within any given population makes it difficult to separate rulers and governments into those that are purely parasitic and those that are managerial or purely servile. Even in a world that begins from nearly ideal representative government, if the least cost providers of governmental services are also those who would tend to become more capable of parasitic behavior once in power then we are faced with choosing between making insufficient provision for governmental activity in the efficient servicing of the People versus providing all the necessary goods and services at the risk of creating a person or group of people with force potential for parasitically extracting rents from the People in the future. Hence, the inevitability of some parasitic behavior and the threat of greater rent-extraction becomes part of the price that is to be paid for services rendered by the State. The possibility of parasitic activity increasing becomes an inevitable by-product of creating a State apparatus with enhanced authority and power to undertake benevolent activity. Ultimately, whether the Ruler is parasitic or managerial in equilibrium depends on the structure of the political economic market and the preferences of the Ruler.

Additionally, there are many circumstances under which representative government is difficult and perhaps impossible to establish in any stable way. In such a case, a least-bad parasitic/predatory ruler may be the only route to the establishment of order (cf. Machiavelli's discussion in *The Prince* of the disadvantages of democracy vis-à-vis monarchy, in which he emphasized democracy's instability and hence impracticability as a political system). In other situations, the choice of being left alone may not be available to the people. In amending his original work on the manorial system (North and Thomas, 1973), Douglass North (1981) conceded that the exchange of labor services and rents for protection and order between the serfs and their lords may have been a choice of the least of many evils on the part of the serfs who might have been better off had there been no lords and no threat of further invasion or enslavement from outside factions. However, given the circumstances, the arrangement was, in North's view, a stable equilibrium that endured for hundreds of years in medieval Europe mainly because no preferable alternative was viable.

Interestingly enough, the idea of the state as predator has become prominent in economics through the rise of the public choice school of Buchanan, Tullock, and Niskanen, and through related writings of Stigler, Pelzman, and Becker. To a large extent, this work's implicit theory of the state suffers from partial equilibrium procedures that do not attempt to flesh out what accounts for the observed set of political market structures. Typically, Pelzman, Stigler, Buchanan, and the others begin with a rule that says, for example, that politicians are maximizing votes, or the state is trying to expand its power, or the political structure permits transfer to be made from one group to another, without asking how we arrived at a situation in which such rules of thumb are reasonable approximations. In this we again echo the Coasian problem of the proper explanation for the existence of the firm. Whereas Marshallian theory presupposes atomistic profit maximizing firms so as to get to mathematically interesting issues of the dual problem of cost minimization/profit maximization, Coase and the related transactions cost literature see the firm as inevitably a solution to a more general problem of maximization in which cost minimization, profit maximization, and so on within the firm are secondary to the general issue of characterizing the choice of an equilibrium set of contracts (the firm) designed to satisfy the utility maximizing desires of individuals engaged in mutual trade. Much of what North (1981) did, which I have further elaborated in this chapter, was to extend this logic to the political problem of what determines the equilibrium political units and from there to discuss the problem of ruler/subject relations within the nation-state (political "firm").

When Coase asks, "Why is not all production carried on by one big firm?" (1937) we can ask the same questions about the state and the economy. In the limiting case, the all-powerful ruler with only slaves as subjects essentially represents the case in which all transactions are taking place, so to speak, under one roof. Thus the question can be amended to "Why aren't all organizations subsumed in one giant master-slave, predator-prey arrangement?" The answer as with Coase depends on the nature of transactions costs of organization and exchange, the presence or absence of economies of scale, and I would add, the costs of enforcing and monitoring coercive control. As with Coase, marginal analysis works well. The issue is what about dynamic factors, and it is thus to the historical circumstances that we need to turn for answers to the questions about long-run dynamics.

Perhaps a greater tension in the public-choice school derives from the decision to model the state in contractarian terms while deriving a predatory element almost exclusively from the aggregation procedures, the structure of the bureaucracy or through the force of redistributionist pressures via the mechanisms of majority government. They have succeeded in bringing to light a richer view of state-economy interactions by endogenizing the behavior of politicians using the rational actor model rather than by treating the state as an all-knowing, benevolent despot, as was common previously. But again they do not ask why these particular configurations have emerged at this time. Where I believe that my synthesis goes further is in extending this analysis to an even more general consideration of the role of force and violence in a world of rational actors and market exchange and through a consideration of the endogenous factors that affect the evolution of the modern state in historical context. In so doing, I see us returning to a mainstream tradition that includes not only Hume, Hobbes, and Locke, but also the general historical considerations of social philosophers from Machiavelli to Marx and Weber. Where the public-choice school makes a unique contribution is in developing the normative agenda of a contractarian political philosophy, especially notable in the work of James Buchanan.

VI.5 SOME CASES FROM THE LITERATURE

Let us consider some classic examples from the work of North and others to see how they fit within a consistent rational actor theory of the state and to get a flavor of how an expanded Coasian framework can be used to describe economic and political history.

Let us begin with a relatively familiar example: the rational choice literature on slavery. As writers such as Barzel (1996) have observed, in a world of sufficiently complete markets, it almost never makes sense for people to be physically enslaved (leaving aside the pathological case of those who derive utility from becoming slaves). There are two reasons for this.

First we presume that no one would value a slave's freedom more than the slave himself and thus, with perfectly complete markets he would consequently buy off his freedom by paying the Ruler more as a free man than the Ruler could earn by keeping the subject in slavery.[4] Second, any Ruler with the capacity to extract rents in a world without monitoring costs but limited ability to dictate production would never interfere in the forms of production or would end up making the slave do what he would have done anyway. If welfare and thus consumer plus producer surplus were maximized by a particular arrangement of production and exchange in the no-Ruler world, it would be in the Ruler's best interest to permit the same arrangements while simply transferring as much of the surplus as he could from the subjects to himself. But of course, monitoring, control, and rent extraction are not undertaken in a world without transactions costs.

Slavery, as we have observed it throughout history, can only be understood in a world in which the effective exercise of Force by the Ruler is limited to certain mechanisms of control and in which there are usually no easy ways to exercise this control for very complicated production arrangements. Consequently slavery has usually involved a very large deadweight loss—not just to the slaves, but to the rulers as well. In most instances, it is likely that slave owners would have preferred their slaves to have had greater physical freedom and a wider range of choice in their output decisions if the rulers could have been assured of collecting at least as much revenue (in the broadest sense of the term) with comparable control as they obtained under the slave arrangements that were typical. Indeed it is certain that they would have tolerated a much lesser degree of control for the certainty of a high income stream (including political and military services). Lacking such guarantees and lacking the markets necessary to arbitrage the massive deadweight losses involved, the Ruler could not often tolerate many alternate working arrangements that might have produced higher returns. Conversely, the slave, while having a potentially higher output as a freedman, did not have a credible mechanism for trading on this lost output in exchange for greater freedom and a better standard of life.

The employment of rational choice reasoning is made clearest by contrasting periods of widespread slavery with medieval serfdom. North and Thomas (1973) made the following point:

> Some might ask why in feudal times the lords did not simply make slaves of the peasants, owning them outright. For one reason, it was not difficult for an oppressed peasant to flee to a neighboring castle where he might hope for a better bargain, since labor was scarce and lords were in competition for its use. Second, it would have been costly to direct and supervise slaves in the many types of tasks involved in making the self-sufficient manor a viable economic system. (p. 20)

[4] Whether payment is in goods, services, or something else is irrelevant because we are presuming perfectly enforceable contracts in a world with complete markets.

Viewed critically, the first argument is somewhat weakened by the obvious evidence that rulers in ancient Egypt or Rome were in competition for labor as well, yet resorted to slavery, and we need to ask why labor markets functioned better in medieval Europe rather than simply presuming that the threat of escape was sufficient to limit slavery. The more interesting argument is the second one for what is implicit rather than directly argued.

If the technology of production in the middle ages was such as to permit more technologically advanced and complex processes that precluded easy monitoring, then slavery became costly because the opportunity costs in terms of lost output was higher than in the classical period. Hence, the core of the North and Thomas view needs to be restated so that it was possible for slavery to be imposed, but that it was more profitable to engage the peasantry in a labor relationship that, although partially coercive, was not as all-encompassing as the slave state.[5] In the end, the North and Thomas claim regarding the choice between slavery and feudal manorialism must ultimately rest on the importance of a greater gap between the output of peasants who were relatively free and the more closely monitored slave farming, and hence it must make claims regarding the progressivity of medieval agriculture.[6]

More generally, the equilibrium arrangement involving the Ruler and the Ruled will depend predominantly on the following:

1. The nature and costs of establishing a variety of exchange and coercive relations between the Ruler and the Ruled.
2. The degree of competition (including political and military conflict) for the position of Ruler.
3. The technology of production, especially its complexity and the gap between productive activity by free and exploited individuals.
4. The extent of competition and completeness in all relevant markets.

Between the absolute slave and Ruler and the relationships between free equals in a competitive market, all sorts of intermediate positions are possible. Consider the problem of property rights and its provision.

Property rights are often seen as necessary conditions for economic growth and development. However, their establishment, definition, and enforcement are costly and are troublesome to implement. For a Ruler capa-

[5] I do not wish to address the question of whether serfdom was the "optimal" configuration in the middle ages. Suffice it to say that it had adaptive advantages in the middle ages and that it tended to prosper even in conditions where slavery was both feasible and occasionally attempted.

[6] This is not unreasonable, given the current research that suggests that medieval Europe was indeed more technologically progressive in matters of production than ancient Greece or Rome (cf. Mokyr, 1990).

ble of enslaving a group of individuals, the provision of property rights is a departure from the direct prescription of production. It has the benefit of permitting greater exchange and of making promises not to extract all of the surplus earned by the people more credible. However, aside from the direct costs of setup, the Ruler must give up some control or Force in setting up a credible system. The long-run gains in income must be set against the long-run loss of control. When competition between political and economic groups is strenuous, one is much more likely to observe such change. Not only is it in the interest of the sovereign to do so, but the inability to make such an adjustment will mean losing out in the long run to a neighboring state that can draw upon a larger set of resources in both military and economic conflict.

In order to take this rough framework and convert it into a fully developed theory of the evolution of control, one would need to make stronger assertions about the order in which technology developed and its interaction with economic control and material production.

As a first guess, I would hazard that the early stages of Ruler-People relationships are likely to be characterized by hierarchies resulting from coercion that stems from differential access to the technology of violence. The authority may stem from natural relationships such as kinship (the family and extended families) or religion. Given the asymmetric, initial distribution of power, the limited capacity for trading this power, and the limited opportunities for encouraging productive activity and, hence, the lower opportunity of inefficient production methods, it is likely that authority relations will focus on control, direct provision of labor services for production or warfare, enslavement, personal attachment, and fairly simple routine activities. Only as monitoring improves or as more complex production possibilities raise the opportunity cost to the Ruler of maintaining routine, easily monitored production will the gains from permitting autonomy overcome the fundamental problems of monitoring and the need to maintain control. Only in a more developed society, where individuals are relatively safe from appropriation because of a weak state or technology that favors individual control, will the possibility of a contractarian arrangement, as Barzel (1996) envisioned, emerge.[7] Without well-developed contracts and with no way of enforcing agreements between groups with differential access to power and force, it is unlikely that specialization will

[7] In his recent and still unpublished work on the subject, Barzel (1996) elaborated the logic of specialization in defense as we move from a state of nature to a state of authority. Although his discussion of the comparative statics of such trades is admirable, I find his reliance on a contractual metaphor somewhat inappropriate unless one specifically acknowledges the peculiar role of force. Then detailing the evolution of control becomes less an issue in contractual specialization in control versus defense, but rather should be directed to a discussion of the evolution of monitoring technology and the enforceability of contracts between groups with differential access to force.

emerge in forms conducive to production but requiring greater autonomy on the part of the weak and exploited. The rise of trade and a growing market make possible larger scale control but also provide more opportunity and benefits to all from escaping or relaxing such control. Obviously, this is an empirical issue that needs to be tested through thorough analysis of the historical record.

VI.5.1 What Happens as We Approach the Modern State?: Britain and France from 1600 to 1800

We can further our understanding of how the comparative statics of state management vary by moving forward in time to an example when coordination and control issues became more complex, namely, the rise of the modern state in Britain and France. Britain and France in the period from about 1600 to 1800 can be seen as representative cases for the period in state evolution when the technology of control and the relationships between the ruler and people had evolved to make central government viable, and even desirable. Hence, they provide insight into the process of transition whereby the relatively weak and decentralized arrangements of the various smaller states, counties, and provinces that made up premodern Britain and France were integrated into a system of control stemming from a bureaucratic central authority with a greatly enhanced capacity for managing affairs at a national level. The economic analogy would be understanding changing industrial structure, mergers, and other forms of organizational adaptations in the light of large-scale innovations in technology and changing market conditions.

Recent work on the interrelationship between political decision making and the fiscal condition of the two nations has emphasized how much of the evolution of institutions in Britain and France had less to do with differing preferences and much more to do with differential success in augmenting the state's revenue by credibly committing to sound fiscal policy in the form of enhanced property rights, stable monetary policy, and limited confiscation (cf. North and Weingast, 1988; Levi, 1988; Brewer, 1988; Root, 1994). What remains to be fleshed out is why one state, Britain, was so successful in creating a stable and fiscally able central administration while the other, France, was not.

I have elsewhere suggested (Nye, 1992) that the British and the French sovereigns should not be viewed as being fundamentally different either in their attitudes toward the economy or the state. I intend to explore some of the ideas from that piece at greater length in other work but for the purposes of this chapter my views can be summarized as follows:

The overall goals of the two monarchies (where "goals" are understood to be in the economic as-if sense) were probably quite similar, but the specific approaches they took were heavily conditioned by the very dissimilar political conditions that the two states faced. These political conditions were in turn strongly influenced, occasionally decisively so, by the given geography, population, and specific historical conditions each faced. There was much interaction and even intermarriage between the ruling classes of both countries, and there was virtually full information regarding the administrative and political experiments in both nations. However, the opportunity costs of undertaking various actions and the creation of various organizations and institutions were rather different in the two nations.

For one thing, their size was quite different. In both land mass and population, France was several times larger than Britain in the 17th century and thus posed a greater problem for the ruler in terms of the most basic concerns of military control, tax collection, regulation, and so on. Militarily, Britain was fairly secure. Despite her involvement in various wars, her island status coupled with the evolution of naval technology favored her continued independence. Although conquering Britain was not out of the question, it was liable to have been a costly undertaking fraught with extreme risk and leaving the potential conqueror with future headaches with respect to colonial administration. The French, much more than the British, had to fear both the encroachment of her Continental neighbors as well as the ever-present possibility of revolution, or what was perhaps worse, the dissolution of the French state. Indeed, under Louis XIV, Colbert's greatest administrative accomplishment was to bring the great tax farms within the purview of a central financial administration and to begin the process of creating a set of universally applicable laws. But the cost of such unification was higher than in Britain, hindering as it did any 18th century attempts by Louis XV and Louis XVI to create a central fiscal structure that more closely resembled the English by ceding tax-collecting and regulatory authority to local and regional controllers. The different constraints on the British and French crown thus led to systematically different choices (in many cases, not consciously) with respect to the nature of regulation and its implementation. We should also bear in mind that although Britain was of great strategic importance as early as the 15th century, it was not considered one of the great powers in Europe until the 18th century at the very earliest. Conversely, the French were preoccupied with their great rivals the Spanish. Indeed, whatever the eventual costs of the 17th-century administrative system put into place by Louis XIII and Louis XIV, contemporaries certainly viewed France's political ascendancy vis-à-vis Spain as being tied to the French crown's capacity to encourage economic development, collect large revenues regularly, and pay for her standing armies.

To simplify, it might be said that given a choice by the respective rulers to provide greater freedoms or guarantees thereof in exchange for enhanced production and the promise of future revenue, accompanied by a weakening of central control in the short run, the British were more likely than the French to guarantee greater freedoms for more revenue. Ironically the French would have paid for greater short-run control both in the form of restrictions that limited economic growth by imposing higher dead-weight costs on the economy (state monopolies, price controls, less secure property rights) and weaker long-run control and decreased flexibility in the creation of an administrative apparatus (through the sales of office, tax farming, and the complex social structure that emerged from Louis XIV's court as a means of overseeing the nobility). This also leaves open the possibilities that there were situations where weak central control meant more autocratic local regulations and vice versa, since one should not assume a one-to-one correspondence between a strong central authority and restrictive regulations at the village level.

In time, the two governmental structures tended to converge as their economic and demographic situations became more similar and as technologies of administration and production changed further to favor the creation of bureaucratic central administrations and to weaken the importance of geographic factors in conditioning economic and political development. Such an assertion may seem odd to those used to readings histories that stressed the great differences in British and French economic development during the period of industrialization. But in truth many of these differences were functions of the divergent demographic patterns in the two nations which led both to converge to similar total populations (cf. O'Brien and Keyder, 1978). Furthermore technological innovations stemming from the British Industrial Revolution were fully assimilated and diffused throughout both nations by the end of the 19th century. Even their commercial patterns became more similar by the late 1800s than they had ever been, with export shares being virtually identical in the last third of the 19th century (Nye, 1993). On the eve of World War I, Britain and France were both fairly well-off, modern industrial nations with well-developed central bureaucracies, but the time paths up to then were very different, and I believe that much of this difference was conditioned by the very different demographic and political conditions that confronted the two states in the early 17th century. Both had well-developed market economies, with high levels of per-capita income and a free citizenry. Neither was essentially laissez-faire, although the technology of control would shift in the 12th century to make political redistribution and bureaucratic control an even more pervasive feature of Western life.

Thus, state developments were partially conditioned by the differing political costs of administrative innovations, but in the long run they were dominated by the evolution of the economy and the technology of administrative control.

VI.5.2 Do Developed Economies Lead to Free States?

Does all this mean that the evolution of market institutions and the economic development of modern states should inevitably lead to less parasitic, more representative, and more "progressive" democratic institutions? Unfortunately, the answer is no. Even if we assume that people prefer freedom to slavery and decentralized autonomy promotes greater productivity, one cannot assume that the technology of control will favor greater liberty.

Such an answer might seem surprising given the emphasis in the earlier part of this chapter on the efficiency characteristics of low transactions cost and complete markets worlds. Yet remember the crucial issue is not the development of the markets per se but their relationship to the development of the technology of control. Even in the base case, in which markets are complete and perfectly efficient but one Ruler has constant control, there would be few changes in the People's activities relative to the no-Ruler situation. However, the *ruler would extract most of the rents from the People.* In the standard jargon, the distribution of gains would have changed, although not the amount of total surplus. In practice, however, the most unproductive and distorted outcomes from the asymmetric relationships of control we observe stem not just from the distributional concerns, but from the way in which deadweight losses to both the Ruler and the People are an inevitable by-product of strong rule with costly monitoring and uncertainties regarding current and future control. Remember that physical slavery and most servile relationships we have observed throughout history were in no way first best, even when considered strictly from the Ruler's point of view. The potential gains in an evolving economy to permitting greater freedom by abandoning direct control were such as to create a coincidence in the development of progressive freedoms and productive efficiency. But this coincidence need not go hand in hand.

Second, there will be a move toward more individual freedom to the extent that markets develop and individuals value that freedom more than anyone else. As in the case of slavery, if there were perfectly enforceable contracts in all states of the world, and sufficiently complete markets, the slave would buy his freedom because he could promise his owner more output when freed than the owner could possibly obtain from one who was enslaved and forced to work. However, in the real world, such an arrangement would be neither credible nor enforceable in most circumstances.[8] But once high wage opportunities were established as a realistic alternative to slavery, with a credible mechanism of obtaining revenues and rents from the worker, it no longer made sense for most employers to enslave workers (in the traditional manner), even if it were legal to do so. Thus, we should also observe that greater incomes and market freedoms should lead to greater individual freedom if people value freedom and can pay for that valuation.

But, even in a thriving, well-developed market economy, it is possible

[8] Of course, the variety of voluntary servitude arrangements testified to the range of employment alternatives that were possible, even given the very limited and unpleasant lives led by many of the poor in the 17th and 18th centuries.

for the technology of control to change so as to make greater control more viable and involuntary rule more pervasive. Let us take a couple of large-scale, macro examples of this. It has been readily observed that the size and the influence of the state—when measured in monetary terms—have grown steadily as a function of GNP in all Western nations and most everywhere else since the late 1700s (see, e.g., the discussions in Atkinson and Stiglitz, 1980; Lindert, 1994). It is unclear from current research whether this growth is demand driven (i.e., people want more from the state, or else the state is the best provider of more goods and services than before) or whether it is supply driven (i.e., it is easier for the state to do many more things than before and, more importantly, it is easier for the state to extract revenues than before). Some versions of the demand argument suggest that the modern state acts in the managerial rather than the parasitic sense with the state's functions becoming more important in the 20th century. However, it is important to acknowledge that it has not been easy to explain the growth of the state in terms of the typical demand explanations (cf. Lindert, 1994).

Some variants of the supply argument may fit this story, although most people are reluctant to conclude that the state has become more efficient in providing its services. A more plausible alternative is that one of the costs we have had to tolerate as demand for the state has grown is a higher degree of lost revenue due to an increase in the parasitic potential of government. From this standpoint, exemplified by the work in the public-choice school of analysis, government has become a mechanism for channeling redistributionary demands by various groups that collectively impose greater costs on everyone. If we think about this in terms of the mechanisms of control for a moment, and assume a constant tendency for predation over time, the government or its agents need not have a stronger desire for revenue extraction. It may simply be true that in the tug of war between the Ruler and the People, it has become easier for the Ruler to take from the People as the technology of control has evolved and as states have been granted a wider leeway to become involved in the private sector.

Thus, it is entirely possible that the state has not become monotonically more intrusive over time, merely that the *measured* extent of state involvement is greater than before. Just as likely is that the forms of state intervention have changed but not necessarily their intensity (or rather not in any systematically increasing way). This may seem perplexing in the light of the rising expenditures and revenue/GNP trend that I cited for the last two centuries. But we must remember that nominal revenue and expenditure measures hardly capture the totality of a state's involvement in the economy. A government dictate that imposed price controls on agriculture and expropriated grain in favor of the cities (as was common in early modern Europe) might be as intrusive or more so as a policy that openly taxed farmers to subsidize the cities, but the latter policy would show up in greater measured taxation and expenditure, while the former would not. Similarly we have no quantitative estimates of the extent to which price regulations, employment restrictions, business rules, and monetary controls of all kinds affected the economies of the world before the mid-19th century. Most scholars would agree that government expenditures would have been a very poor proxy for the degree of state involvement in the French economy, for example, during the reign of Louis XIV. In the contemporary United States, this issue has emerged most prominently in the political debate over the effect of unfunded federal mandates in skewing the distribution of state and local taxes and expenditures.

These decisions would not be neutral with respect to their effects on the economy. Even holding (without loss of generality) the parasitic tendencies constant might still lead to different policies with very different deadweight costs and very different consequences for the long-run configuration of the ruler-people relationship. Even starting from the assumption that state involvement is a constant share of the economy, we would still observe that the forms of intervention and hence their observable and measurable characteristics would vary with changes in the economy and developments in the technologies of administration and production.

Any change in the capacity of the Ruler to control, or more importantly, any changes in the shape of the production function of control and force, would affect the equilibrium patterns of rights, order, security, and individual freedoms. From this perspective, one might view the rise in the instruments of control and the efficiency of massive armies backed by powerful bureaucratic administrations as supporting the rise of the various forms of totalitarian and dictatorial regimes throughout the world. Changes in technology that favor the individual or smaller political configurations (including perhaps improvements in computing, personal information, telephone service, fax machines, radio and TV, and so on, as well as easier travel) would work against the success of large-scale bureaucratic control. At the national level, improvements in competition in international capital markets may constrain the types of fiscal and monetary policies that governments can run, limiting for example the extent of inflationary policies, or punishing more swiftly those regimes that attempt to diverge from world-market pressures. This will have the positive consequence of restraining certain types of control (inflation being only the most obvious). However, to the extent that political control and parasitic tendencies remain, the state will search for second-best means of attaining its policy goals, including a return to direct regulation and hidden subsidies rather than more visible taxation and expenditure (e.g., requiring companies to provide health care or education rather than paying for it directly). To the extent that political and national independence are viewed as socially desirable in and of themselves, such market pressures will prove inimical to the welfare of certain groups.

REFERENCES

Anderson, M. S. (1988). *War and Society in Europe of the Old Regime 1618–1789.* St. Martin's Press, London.

Atkinson, A., and Stiglitz, J. (1980). *Lectures in Public Economics.* McGraw Hill, New York.

Barzel, Y. (1996). *Property Rights and the Evolution of the State,* unpublished manuscript. University of Washington, Seattle.

Brewer, J. (1988). *The Sinews of Power.* Harvard University Press: Cambridge MA.

Coase, R. (1937). The nature of the firm. *Economica* **4,** 386–405.

Coase, R. (1960). The problem of social cost. *Journal of Law and Economics* **3,** 1–44.

Epstein, R. (1993). *Bargaining with the State.* Princeton University Press, Princeton, NJ.

Levi, M. (1988). *Of Rule and Revenue.* University of California Press, Berkeley.

Lindert, P. (1994). The rise of social spending, 1880–1930. *Explorations in Economic History* **31,** 1–37.

McGuire, M., and Olson, M. (1996). The economics of autocracy and majority rule: The invisible hand and the use of force. *Journal of Economic Literature* **35,** 72–96.

Mokyr, J. (1990). *The Lever of Riches.* Oxford University Press, Oxford.

North, D. C. (1981). *Structure and Change in Economic History.* Norton, New York.

North, D. C., and Davis, L. E. (1971). *Institutional Change and American Economic Growth.* Cambridge University Press, Cambridge, UK.

North, D. C., and Thomas, R. P. (1973). *The Rise of the Western World.* Cambridge University Press, Cambridge, UK.

North, D. C., and Weingast, B. (1988). Constitutions and commitment: The evolution of institutions governing public choice in seventeenth-century England. *Journal of Economic History,* Vol. XLIX, No. 4, December, 803–831.

Nye, J. V. (1992). Guerre, commerce, guerre commerciale: L'économie politique des échanges franco-anglais. *Annales: Economies, Societés, Civilisations,* No. 3, May–June, pp. 613–632.

Nye, J. V. (1993). Reply to Irwin on free trade. *Journal of Economic History* **53**(1), 153–158.

O'Brien, P., and Keyder, C. (1978). *Economic Growth in Britain and France 1780–1914.* Allen and Unwin: London

Putnam, R. (1993). *Making Democracy Work.* Princeton University Press, Princeton, NJ.

Root, H. (1994). *The Fountains of Privilege.* University of California Press: Berkeley.

Stigler, G. (1982). *The Economist as Preacher and Other Essays.* Chicago University Press, Chicago.

PART III

INSTITUTIONS AND POLITICAL ECONOMY

VII Violence and the Development of Property Rights to Land in the Brazilian Amazon

Lee J. Alston
Gary D. Libecap
Bernardo Mueller

VII.1 INTRODUCTION

The process of sustained economic development requires institutions to adapt to large changes in relative prices. Institutions are the formal and informal rules that motivate or constrain behavior. Douglass North has successfully drawn the attention of his colleagues in economics, economic history, and other social sciences to the role of institutions in determining economic performance (see especially, North, 1990; for a summary of Douglass North's contributions, see Libecap, 1992). If institutions do not adapt to reflect new scarcity values and economic opportunities, then distortions will emerge in the economy that will dissipate much of the potential rent from resource use.[1] One form of dissipation is violent conflict over the access and use of valuable assets. But violence need not result if institutions adapt quickly so as to funnel behavior into growth-enhancing economic activities.

[1] For example, North and Thomas (1973) argued that the failure of Spain to maintain a lead role in economic growth in the 16th and 17th centuries was due to the failure to adopt new institutional forms that encouraged competitive market activities.

In this chapter, we examine the circumstances under which violence might occur.

Among the most fundamental institutions in a society are the set of laws that determine property rights, which define or delimit the range of privileges granted to individuals with specific assets, such as parcels of land. Property rights generally include the right to exclude nonowners from access, the right to appropriate the stream of rents from use of and investments in the resource, and the right to sell or otherwise transfer the resource to others. As such, property rights not only provide the incentives for investment and other types of economic behavior that affect the performance of the economy, but they also determine who are the economic actors in a society and define the distribution of wealth (for discussion of property rights institutions, see Barzel, 1989; Libecap, 1989; Eggertsson, 1990; North, 1990; Alston *et al.,* 1996).

The effectiveness of property rights institutions in molding behavior toward productive use of assets depends on both the nature of definition and enforcement. A well-defined rights structure will have little impact if it is not enforced. Under these circumstances, competition for control over valuable assets with rent dissipation will occur in a manner similar to open-access conditions (for discussion of open access, see Gordon, 1954). Strict enforcement of a very narrow range of rights also may leave many margins open for competition and rent dissipation.

Because property rights assign wealth through the control of valuable assets, they are controversial and can be subject to intense, and perhaps violent, competition for control. Violent conflict can occur if rights are either incompletely defined or incompletely enforced. Definition and enforcement involve both informal, private actions and formal laws. Informal and formal actions are not separable; that is, based on the level of formal definition and enforcement, individuals choose an appropriate level of private activities to claim assets or to protect their holdings.

Property rights necessarily are political institutions. Political forces, both past and present, determine the nature and enforcement of the existing rights structure, and changes in property rights arrangements involve collective action in the political arena to reach concensus on assignment and enforcement. These negotiations may be informal within a small group, or a part of a more formal political process involving organized constituent groups, politicians, and other government officials. Property rights have been the subject of a variety of studies that most often focus on their distributional implications (for summary of some of the literature, see Furubotn and Pejovich, 1972; North, 1978; De Alessi, 1980; Libecap, 1986). Nevertheless, despite the importance attributed to property institutions we know surprisingly little about the institutional changes underlying their emergence and modification.[2] Further, there has been little systematic research on whether the process of defining rights will be smooth or whether it will involve violent conflict.

Frontiers are an ideal setting for addressing these questions and analyzing the emergence of property rights arrangements to land. The frontier is defined with respect to distance from a market center, and it is the point where the net present value of land use just covers the opportunity costs of the claimants. We can examine the rise in land rents with movements from the frontier toward a market center, the associated increase in demand for property rights, and the response of local organizations and governments in providing tenure services. Land close to the frontier is often associated with conflict over property rights to land or other assets. Battles between "claim jumpers" and miners and between cattle raisers and sheep herders are part of the historiography of the 19th century American West (for a related discussion of conflict over land, see Alston *et al.,* 1995d). More recently, popular accounts of settlement in the Brazilian Amazon point to widespread violence over land (see Human Rights Watch, 1991). Yet, conflict in the assignment of property rights is not inevitable. Indeed, if tenure institutions are supplied smoothly as land rents rise, then the assignment of property rights on the frontier can be routine with few disputes. Violence dissipates rents, and hence, it is in the interest of claimants to avoid such disputes. By contrast, if tenure is not provided and enforced in a timely manner as land rents rise and the number of competing claimants increases, then violent conflict is possible. Violence not only can reduce the value of the disputed asset in the short run, but it can have longer term price effects if the conflict leaves a legacy of uncertain control. Hence, it is important to determine the circumstances under which violence occurs in the development of property rights institutions.

We focus our analysis on the development of property rights to land in the Brazilian Amazon using both secondary sources: the Brazilian censuses from 1975 through 1985 and survey data from 249 small holders in the state of Pará collected in 1992 and 1993. Government land in Brazil is open for private settlement and claiming, much as in North America in the 19th century. Large-scale migration from the South and Northeast to the Amazon began in the late 1960s with the construction of the TransAmazon and

[2] Recently there has been a renewed interest in institutional analysis to understand the development of property rights arrangements (see Alston *et al.,* 1996). The revival was sparked by a variety of sources but the most important was the collapse of the economies of the former Soviet Union and its satellites. This collapse brought about a need to understand the role of institutions in moving from collective to market economies.

Belém-Brasília highways and the initiation in the early 1970s of federal settlement projects. For example, the population of the large, northeastern Amazonian state of Pará doubled between 1970 and 1985, growing from 2,167,018 to 4,318,400 (IBGE, Anuário Estatístico do Brasil, 1990, pp. 180, 183). The land in farms doubled in the 1960s and the 1970s, and the number of farms rose sharply. As much as a half of the farms established from 1970 to 1985 were without title in some of the censuses.[3] Further, the settlement of the region has been portrayed as involving considerable violence. For example, the regional office of the Pastoral Land Commission in Conceição do Arguaia

> registered from 1982 to 1989 a total of 774 death threats, 834 rural workers arrested or detained, 558 rural workers injured or beaten, 2,514 *posseiro* (squatter) families expelled, 704 farms burned or destroyed, and 2,735 workers kept in conditions of slavery in the diocese of Conceição do Araguaia (Human Rights Watch, 1991, p. 72). By contrast, our surveys of six frontier sites in Pará suggest that settlement and tenuring has been comnparatively peaceful. (For discussion of settlement at four sites, see Alston *et al.,* (1995a.)

Accordingly, the extent of violence in the assignment of property rights to land is unclear. In this chapter, we extend the analysis of institutional change pioneered by Douglass North to examine the assignment of property rights to land in the Amazon to determine the circumstances under which violence occurs.

VII.2 ANALYTICAL FRAMEWORK FOR ANALYZING VIOLENCE AND THE ASSIGNMENT OF PROPERTY RIGHTS

Individuals desire secure property rights to land in order to increase and to capture the rental stream from land use. In agricultural societies, rental streams from land are determined by the innate fertility of the soil, availability of other inputs such as labor and capital, and access to markets. Even so, land rents increase more with secure property rights. Long-term investments require the assurance provided by secure rights to land, and title can serve as collateral for accessing capital markets. Rents also increase

[3] IBGE, Censo Agropecuario—Pará, Rio de Janeiro, 1970, 1975, 1980, 1985. There has not been an agricultural census since 1985. The actual percentage of agricultural establishments without title are 47 percent (1970), 49 percent (1975), 41 percent (1980), and 32 percent (1985). The situation seemingly has not changed. We conducted a survey of small-scale farm establishments in 1993 and found that only 56 percent of the settlers in our sample of 249 had a definitive title. For related discussion, see Alston *et al.* (1995a). In that paper we combined definitive and provisional titles.

as private enforcement costs fall with supplemental monitoring and enforcement by the government. Finally, rents increase as land markets are extended with the adoption of formal property rights. State-enforced title, which is the principal formal property right to land, signals security of ownership to potential purchasers who do not have local knowledge. Hence, the market is broadened from reliance on local buyers to include more remote purchasers.

These effects of title, however, can be muted if land is very abundant, transportation costs to markets are high, and prices are low. Under those conditions, there is less incentive to invest in land-specific investments, competition over claims is limited, and land markets are local. Hence, the returns from title are small. If there are private costs to obtaining formal title, such as meeting recording requirements, complying with administrative rules, and lobbying government agencies to provide surveying and other titling services, then claimants will rely on informal arrangements when land values are very low.

In frontier areas, distance to market is a major determinant of land value. Assuming that land fertility is constant, we illustrate the relationships among land rents, property rights, and distance in Figure VII.2.1. In the figure, the horizontal axis represents distance from the market/administrative center and the vertical axis represents the rental value of land use. In panels a and b, line AB reflects the rental value of land with completely defined

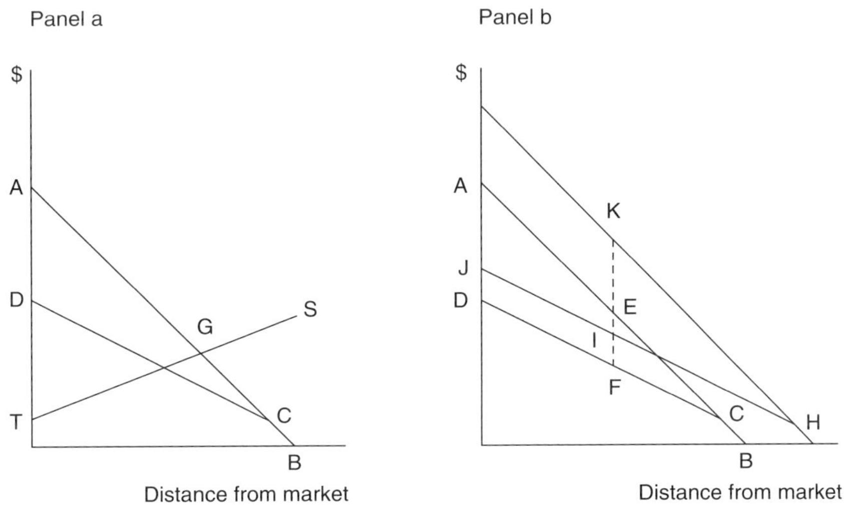

FIGURE VII.2.1

and enforced formal property rights minus any private enforcement costs. Land sufficiently far from a market center does not generate sufficient economic rent to attract claimants. This land is beyond the economic frontier. We define the economic frontier at point *C* as occurring where the rental stream from land use is equal to the opportunity cost of the marginal claimant.

The implication is that the frontier will be settled by those with low opportunity costs. Because of low land values at the frontier, there will be little competition for claims and little demand for formal title. Moreover, because of higher transportation and administrative costs for assigning and enforcing titles at the frontier, titles will not be supplied. Accordingly, land on the economic frontier will be occupied by squatters and held with informal land claims.

In panel a, line *CD* reflects the rental value of land when property rights are privately defined and enforced. These costs are low near point *C*, involving occasional patrolling and limited marking of boundary lines. Moving to the left of point *C*, closer to market, land values rise and individuals have incentive to make rudimentary investments. To do so they require more definite and costly property guarantees that can be provided privately among local farmers (squatters) through informal ownership agreements. These "claims clubs," or *sindicatos* in Brazil, are respected by locals, who will band together to defend squatters' rights against outside intrusions. Exchanges of squatter holdings take place with the buyer receiving a receipt from the seller and the transaction witnessed by others. Hence, land exchanges and the development of local markets are promoted by informal property rules. These informal arrangements are more costly to individuals than if the government defined and enforced the property rights of individuals; the difference to private individuals of net benefits is represented by the area between *CD* and *BA*. Even so, these costs are still likely to be low and the deviation between the two rental streams small when land values are low.

As land rents rise closer to market from the economic frontier, new settlers are attracted with higher opportunity costs who may buy the informal rights or squatter claims of the initial settlers. Exchanges may take place because the initial settlers may value the land less than the new arrivals if they are less likely to be able to obtain a formal title. The same low human capital attributes that induced them to settle land at the frontier reduce their political capabilities to secure formal titles: illiteracy, limited wealth, and a lack of experience in using government. In addition, new arrivals with more human and physical capital cannot only better access capital markets but also may be more aware of the highest valued use of the land. This pattern of sequential development of squatters with low opportunity costs selling to more affluent arrivals will be smooth as long as the change in rental values changes slowly, and informal claims are recognized by the new arrivals.[4]

Even closer to market, however, the higher rental streams associated with lower transportation costs will generate increased competition for the land, and informal, private property rights will become more difficult to enforce and will be less satisfactory for claimants. Informal arrangements will not provide collateral, nor the security needed for long-term investments and consolidation. Additionally, because they are neither recognized beyond the locality or enforceable in the courts, local property rights will not support broader land markets. By contrast, formal title signals government recognition of individual ownership and thereby encourages entry by outside purchasers. In the figure, the growing losses of land rent because of the absence of formal title are shown by the increased area between *AB* and *CD*.

In terms of the supply of formal tenure services, the marginal administrative, assignment, and enforcement costs of providing tenure, including survey, demarcation, and processing land claim applications, rise with distance from the market center toward the economic frontier. In panel a, these costs are shown for convenience as rising along the line *ST* and intersecting *AB* at point *G*. As drawn, it would be socially optimal for government to supply the tenure services demanded at that point.

In Figure VII.2.1, panel b, we illustrate some complexities in the assignment of property rights to land that may increase the likelihood of violent competition and increased dissipation of land rents. Suppose that government does not assign formal property rights until point *E*. Between points *C* and *E* potential rents with title exceed those without title, but title is not provided.[5] The triangle *CFE* represents rents that will be competed for and potentially dissipated as a result of the lack of title.[6] Nevertheless, this situation may be socially optimal if the costs to government of providing title are very high. If government delays providing title beyond point *E*, perhaps for political reasons, then ownership competition and costly disputes will follow with increased rent dissipation.

A further complication that may lead to violence is the shift in land

[4] Most Latin American countries give significant rights to squatters—even if they squat on private land they are to be compensated for improvements. Nevertheless, conflict may arise over the level of compensation that is decided by the courts. For discussion of the development of land markets, see Alston *et al.* (1995a).

[5] For now, we are ignoring political considerations and assuming that the government provides title at the point where marginal social costs equal marginal social benefit or demand.

[6] Dissipation would occur not only due to competition among claimants (greater labor and capital devoted to marketing and patrolling claims, violent conflict) but also due to foregone opportunities, such as increased market sales and investment.

rents, as shown in panel b. Land rents might shift due to a variety of events, including construction of new roads, rise in output prices, or the subsidized recruitment of new settlers. Two of these activities result from policy choices of the government. In the case at hand, squatters who were on the economic frontier at point *C* are now on inframarginal holdings. With the shift in land rents, the frontier moves outward and settlement is attracted to the new frontier at point *H*. Previous, informal arrangements appropriate for settlers at *C* are now insufficient to provide security of claims, and farmers desire formal title. Indeed, the area of potential dissipation is now *HIK*, which is larger than *CFE*. With more at stake, there will be greater potential conflict and associated efforts to obtain private and government recognition of land claims. The likelihood of violence is enhanced because the increase in rental streams brings in settlers with different characteristics who may be unfamiliar with the informal norms of behavior in operation. Heterogeneity of settlers also implies that the gain from redistributive efforts increases. We emphasize that a lack of formal property rights alone does not lead to conflict and violence, but rather the interaction of informal rights and increasing land rents.[7]

VII.3 THE SETTLEMENT OF THE BRAZILIAN AMAZON

Before analyzing the incidence of violence in the assignment of property rights to land, it is important to describe the settlement of the Brazilian Amazon to understand how claimants could obtain title and to see how government programs encouraged a discontinuous shift in land rents and thereby promoted violence. Land that is neither in private hands or used by governments is known as *terra devoluta*. Before this land can be transferred to private parties, it must be surveyed and mapped after which a document is created for it in the land registrar. The land is registered in the name of the state or federal government depending on who has jurisdiction.[8] At this point the land is eligible for transfer according to the land policy of the state or federal government. When transferred, the name of the new owner is added to the document, which is kept in the office of the land registrar, thus chronicling the succession of owners.

Private individuals can acquire government land through purchase or through *posse* (squatting). An individual who resides and cultivates a plot

[7] Over time informal institutions might adjust to provided sufficient security but at least in the short-run institutions are not so malleable.

[8] Until 1971 jurisdiction of the public domain was in the hands of the states, with the exception of a strip of land bordering other countries. Following 1971 both state and federal governments had jurisdiction over parts of the public domain. States initially received jurisdictional control in 1888 at the founding of the Brazilian Republic.

of unclaimed *terra devoluta* for at least a year and a day can then file a petition with the land agency to receive title for the land, having to pay only for demarcation and titling services. Individuals can also squat on unused private land and receive title to the land if they reside on and improve the land for five years.[9] Even if squatters are evicted from the land, by law they are entitled to compensation for improvements. Whether and how much compensation occurs depends on the political power of the parties involved and the disposition of the local court. Though squatters tend not to be powerful on their own, when organized in a *sindicato* or backed by the church, they can rival the more wealthy landowners in political clout.

Squatting on private land may be somewhat strategic in that squatters may hope to hasten the process of receiving rights to land by having the government expropriate the private land and give it to the squatters. Governments may do so in an effort to avoid violent conflict. If the price for the expropriation is sufficiently high, landowners may welcome the expropriation.

The most recent development of the Amazon began in the late 1950s with the construction of the Belém-Brasília highway, linking the capital of the state of Pará with the capital of Brazil. The idea was to integrate the Amazon with the more populous and developed southern states. Road construction dramatically increased the rental value of land located near the new road and initiated migration to the area. During the 1960s development plans for the Amazon escalated in response to a concern that other countries would invade the Amazon for its timber and mineral wealth (Fearnside, 1986, pp. 15-18; Ianni, 1979, p. 67). The military government in 1965 initiated Operation Amazonia with the goal of encouraging settlement and thereby securing its borders.

Beginning in 1966 the federal government, under the auspices of SUDAM (Superintendency for the Development of the Amazon), provided tax and credit incentives for private firms for investment in specific areas in the Amazon.[10] SUDAM subsidies were cyclical. Gasques and Yokomizo (1986) divided the actions of SUDAM into phases that included 1966–1972, when 86 projects were approved, 1973–1979, when 19 projects were approved, and 1980–1985, when 148 projects were approved. In addition to providing direct incentives for establishing ranching operations, the government built roads to provide access to the ranches. The result was that the areas became attractive for squatters because of the dramatic increase in

[9] Five years in the residency requirement as set down in the Constitution of 1988. The conditions for receiving title are that the *posseiro* have no other land, that his occupation is not contested, that he resides on the land, and that the area claimed be 50 hectares or less.

[10] Gasques and Yokomizo (1986), Schneider (1994) and Yokomizo (1989), provide the best analysis of the impact of the fiscal incentive program.

rents, the large size of the projects, and the often limited presence of the owners. For example, Gasques and Yokomizo (1986) found that from a sample of 29 SUDAM subsidized cattle ranches between 1974 and 1985, 14 of the cattle projects sold no cattle at all, and only 2 projects reached more than 50 percent of their target production. The average size of the projects was 16,334 hectares.

In addition to the continued SUDAM fiscal incentives, the federal government increased its involvement in the Amazon in other ways, most notably through colonization projects. However, before the federal government could directly settle people, it had to acquire control of the land. This was achieved through the military decree law 1164 in 1971, whereby jurisdiction passed from state governments to the federal government over a 100-kilometer strip of land on both sides of all federally constructed highways, federal highways under construction, or highways planned in the Amazon. With this measure, 311 of the 499 million hectares of land in the Amazon region were seized by the federal government. The federal government delegated the administration of land policy to its newly created (1970) land agency, INCRA (the National Institute for Colonization and Agrarian Reform).

In the early 1970s, the federal government initiated a series of ambitious large-scale programs (PIN, POLOAMAZONIA, PROTERRA, POLONOROESTE, CARAJAS) with the objective of accelerating the occupation of the Amazon. These programs included the construction of roads and infrastructure, private and public colonization projects, exploitation of minerals, and continued fiscal incentives for large-scale agricultural projects. The colonization projects were an effort toward land reform and had an initial goal of settling 100,000 families in the Amazon. Although INCRA never achieved its initial settlement goal, the new roads provided access and high returns to spontaneous migration, particularly peasants from the poor Northeastern region.[11] The large migratory flows greatly exceeded the capacity of INCRA to grant titles expeditiously to the claimants. Rather than initiating settlement, INCRA was forced into a position of responding to spontaneous migration and informal land claims.[12] In part this was due to declining budgets for INCRA after 1976. In essence, the government was in a situation described in panel b of Figure VII.2.1, in which

[11] For discussion of the settlement of the Amazon in general see C. Mueller (1992), Santos (1984), Sawyer (1984), and Wood and Wilson (1984). For Pará, see Foweraker (1981), and Moran (1984, 1989b), and Schmink and Wood (1992). The leading number of states for migrants to Pará for the period 1970 to 1980 were Maranhao, Goias, Ceara, and Minas Gerais (IBGE, 1991, p. 190). These are all states in the northeast or central region of Brazil. The private and public colonization projects generally attracted settlers from the south.

[12] C. Mueller (1992, p. 6) discusses the situation in the Amazon in general. For a more specific analysis of titling difficulties in Rondonia, see C. Mueller (1980).

titling activities were not increased despite an increase in migration and rental streams. ITERPA, the land agency in Pará, was in a similar responsive situation. Other migrants, though not large in number, came to the Amazon to capture the continued fiscal incentives and subsidized mineral wealth.

It is important to stress the different characteristics of migrants and their different objectives. *Posseiros,* or squatters, were poor, with little education. They migrated in search of land for settlement and exchange. Corporations from southern Brazil bought land in the Amazon to receive tax credits available for developing the region. They were wealthy and had considerable political connections.

In addition to an array of government programs that shifted expected land rents, uncertainty over property rights in the Amazon also occurred because of the variety of government agencies involved in settlement. First was the jurisdictional dispute between the federal government and the state governments over the control of public land. Additionally, within the federal government, different agencies competed with one another for jurisdiction. Moran (1981) argued that more than 51 separate bureaucratic entities took part in the development and settlement of the Amazon in the 1970s. The most notable were INCRA and SUDAM, but other agencies included BASA, the regional development bank, and FUNAI, the federal Indian agency. Additionally, there were ITERPA, the state agency in Pará, the armed forces, the state and local police, and the courts, local, state, and federal. With the myriad of players involved it is no wonder that there was uncertainty over the processing of property rights to land.[13]

As a result of the government programs and the migratory flows, the rental stream from land increased dramatically in the 1970s. The price of land per hectare in Pará in constant 1970 *cruzeiros* rose from 37.0 in 1960 to 41.4 in 1970 and then skyrocketed to 98.7 in 1975 and 152.6 in 1980 (IBGE, 1960, 1970, 1975, 1985). As described in panel b of Figure VII.2.1, the rapid increase in land rents and a coinciding slow response in the provision of titles by the land agencies, especially INCRA, resulted in violence.[14] But violence was not uniform across Pará. In most areas, land values remained so low, effectively near *C* in Figure VII.2.1, that informal rules prevailed and the absence of formal titles did not contribute to conflict. In specific areas, however, there was violence, and we now turn to the characteristics of those settlement regions to determine why.

[13] For an examination of the bureaucratic organizations involved with the development of the Amazon, see Bunker (1985b).

[14] Although INCRA recognized the importance of titling and tried to quicken the pace of titling, the high costs of demarcation and sorting through fraudulent claims to land thwarted its efforts (Yokota, 1981).

VII.4 CONFLICTS OVER LAND IN THE AMAZON

VII.4.1 Settlement with Conflict

A lack of formal property rights alone is insufficient to generate conflict. In a survey that we conducted in 1992 and 1993 of small holders in Pará we found very little evidence of conflict over land, though those with informal claims invested resources in solidifying their claims.[15] Settlers kept their boundaries clear, worked their plots, and lobbied officials for title. The informal claims had value, and there were sales of informal claims. Conflicts between squatters and large landowners have received the most press, but they often are not violent. The settlement of Colonia Reunidas in Pará illustrates conflicting claims to land and why they occur. In 1973 a group of 115 squatters settled on an unoccupied area that they suspected of being *terra devoluta.* Some months later they received a court order to leave the area because it was titled to a cooperative farm in southern Brazil. The cooperative compensated the squatters for the clearing and other improvements. In return, the squatters signed documents agreeing not to return. At this time, land values were low and did not merit entrenched conflict by either group. Ten years later, after highways had been improved and overall settlement of the region had increased, the area was still held in absentee ownership and unoccupied. It was reinvaded by some of the old squatters along with new recruits. Again, there was a court order in favor of the cooperative, but the squatters refused to leave. The local police tried to forcefully evict the squatters. Tension mounted and several armed conflicts arose. The squatters hired a lawyer to represent them with INCRA, who had jurisdiction in the area. In 1985 INCRA expropriated (with compensation) the area from the cooperative and turned the area into a land reform project. INCRA provided demarcation, infrastructure, and credit. The agency also promised title, though by 1993 formal definitive titles had not yet been received by the squatters. In this case, neither the squatters nor the initial landholders lost. The squatters received the land and initial landholders were compensated. This win-win situation was at the expense of taxpayers.

In general, violence in Pará was centered around areas where one federal land agency SUDAM provided subsidies for cattle ranching while other agencies were constructing roads and promoting settlement by small holders. All of these activities led to sharp shifts in land rents, dramatic increases in migration to the area, and conflicting claims to land. Whether the land agencies did not provide clear title because of jurisdictional disputes,

[15] For a description of the survey and an analysis of settlement and turnover, see Alston *et al.* (1995a).

overlapping mandates, or insufficient budgets and staffs, the result was that property rights were unclear. This setting corresponds to the HIK area in panel b of Figure VII.2.1, in which potential land rents in the absence of clear title led to violent conflict and rent dissipation.

VII.4.2 A Test of the Determinants of Violence

As discussed in Section VII.2, the likelihood of conflict and violence increases when land values rise quickly without a commensurate increase in titling activity; there is considerable absentee landownership; and landholdings are highly concentrated. In this section we test some hypotheses concerning the causes of deaths related to land conflicts. Though death is the most extreme manifestation of violence, our results are invariant to this variable or the number of evictions. The model follows:

$$\begin{aligned}\text{Deaths/Rural Population} = {} & B_0 + B_1 \text{ Squatters} + B_2 \text{ Land Values} \\ & + B_3 \text{ Squatters } X\% \text{ Increase in Land Values} \\ & + B_4 \text{ Concentration of Landholdings} \\ & + B_5 \text{ SUDAM Fiscal Incentives} + E\end{aligned}$$ [16]

Our data is at the *municipio* level, and the dependent variable is the cumulative number of deaths from 1970 to 1985 resulting from conflicts over land divided by the rural population in 1980. Our variable measuring the uncertainty in property rights is the percentage of farm establishments occupied by squatters. Higher levels of squatting place you in the contested area of Figure VII.2.1. As such we expect $B_1 > 0$. We include land value as a control measure for the rent gradient, but we do not have a prediction for B_2. With increases in land values, for any level of squatting, there will be more competition for the rental stream from land and conflict is more likely to occur. In particular, if land values increase rapidly, governments may not be able to respond immediately and the interaction between uncertain property rights and relatively high rental streams should lead to violence; $B_3 > 0$. Higher concentration of landholdings implies that enforcement costs of property rights increase. One means of enforcement is violence, which leads us to predict $B_4 > 0$. SUDAM Fiscal Incentives are measured as the cumulative area of projects that received SUDAM fiscal benefits from 1970 to 1985 as a percentage of the area in farms. SUDAM project areas seem ideal for conflict: the projects covered a large area so that claims and infringements on them would be difficult to monitor; roads were built raising the rental streams from farming the land; the area was either used

[16] We recognize that violence may also reduce land values and that violence, with a lag, may prompt titling activity by governments. We are addressing this simultaneity issue in ongoing research.

sparsely or not all (the famous phantom ranches); and yet the rental stream from the fiscal incentives caused the owners to defend their property rights when it was discovered that their rights were threatened by the presence of squatters—$B_5 > 0$. In Table VII.4.1 we present descriptive statistics and in Table VII.4.2 we present our regression results.

We estimated the equation stated previously with a Tobit procedure. We have 82 observations at the *municipio level*—63 limit observations (zeros) and 19 nonlimit observations (nonzeros). To correct for heteroskedasticity, we multiplied all variables by the square root of the rural population in 1980. After weighting the variables, we fail to reject homoskedasticity.

In a Tobit estimation, the effect of a change in X_i on the value of Y above the limit is not B_i (McDonald and Moffit, 1980). The total marginal effect on Y is found by multiplying the coefficients by the probability of being above the limit. In turn, the marginal effect can be decomposed into (1) changes in the probability of having any deaths in a *municipio* weighted by the expected value of deaths above the limit and (2) changes in the percentage of deaths in those *municipios* that had deaths, weighted by the probability of being above the limit.

Following the decomposition suggested by McDonald and Moffit, we find that changes in the percentage of deaths accounts for 71 percent of the total change in the percentage of deaths resulting from a change in the independent variables, whereas changes in the probability of having any

TABLE VII.4.1 Descriptive Statistics

	Mean	Standard deviation	Minimum	Maximum
Deaths/Rural Population	0.34	1.55	0	13.07
Squatters	38%	18%	4%	85%
Land Value	Cr$1,500	CR$1,650	Cr$270	Cr$10,090
Squatters × Increase in Land Values	69%	96%	−41%	487%
Landholding Concentration	17%	23%	0	94%
SUDAM Fiscal Incentives	6%	14%	0	93%

Definitions and sources: Deaths: Cumulative number of deaths associated with rural land conflicts, 1970–1985 divided by the rural population in 1980) × 1000 (IDESP, 1990; IBGE, 1980). Squatters: Average percentage of farm establishments occupied by squatters in 1970, 1975, 1980, and 1985 (IBGE, 1970, 1975, 1980, 1985). Land value: Average price per hectare of land in 1970, 1975, 1980, and 1985 in 1985-Cruzados (IBGE, 1970, 1975, 1980, 1985). One cruzado is equal to 1,000 cruzeiros, the former currency. In December 1985, ten cruzados was equal to approximately one dollar at the prevailing exchange rates of IBGE (1985). Land holding concentration: Area in farms in 1985 greater than 5,000 hectares as a percentage of total farm area (IBGE, 1985). SUDAM fiscal incentives: Cumulative area in projects receiving SUDAM fiscal incentives as percentage of total area in farms in 1985 (personal correspondence with SUDAM in Belem, Pará and IBGE, 1985).

TABLE VII.4.2 Coefficients of the Determinants of Violence Dependent Variable: Deaths from Land Conflicts as a percentage of Rural Population × 1,000

Variable	Coefficient	Asymptotic t-statistic	Marginal effect dE_y/dX_i	1/2 Standard deviation impact
Constant	−3.07	2.08		
Squatters	1.60	0.69	0.28	0.7
Land Value	−0.66	1.09	−0.12	−1.7
Squat × Land Value Increase	0.75	2.82	0.13	2.1
Land Concentration	2.11	1.02	0.37	0.9
SUDAM	5.48	2.00	0.97	1.7

Notes: N = 82; log-likelihood function = −67.35; Tobit estimation with 63 limit observations and 19 nonlimit observations. E_y is the expected value of cumulative deaths for all observations. The impact from a 1/2 standard deviation effect is reported in the absolute number of deaths.

deaths in a *municipio* accounts for remaining 29 percent of the marginal effect. Put another way, marginal changes in the percentage of deaths accounts for most of the response in death rates rather than changes in the probability of having any deaths at all in a *municipio*.

Overall, the results are consistent with the implications from the model developed in Section VII.2. Neither the levels of land values nor squatting per se offer as much explanatory power as the interaction between increasing land values and insecure property rights. This is consistent with the notion that closer to the frontier, where land values were increasing rapidly and thus attracting squatters, the government could not title fast enough; they were overwhelmed by in-migrants fighting over the increased land rents. The presence of SUDAM subsidies in a *municipio* increases violence. The result suggests that the SUDAM subsidies attracted ranchers to the areas who were willing to defend their property rights against intrusion from squatters who were attracted to the SUDAM subsidized areas by the roads that SUDAM built. Once it gave the subsidies, the government erred in not enforcing ranching activity or property rights on the frontier.[17] High concentrations of land ownership also led to more deaths, though the reliability of the coefficient is low. High concentrations of land are more difficult to defend and lead to a greater likelihood of invasion and the potential for violence.

To give more intuition to our results, we calculated the impact on total deaths from a one-half standard deviation change from the mean of the independent variables (see Column 5 in Table VII.4.2). The average rural

[17] This results support the conjecture presented by Schneider (1994).

population per *municipio* is 38,381 and at the mean value of the independent variables, the absolute number of cumulative deaths from 1970 to 1985 is 4.5. For the Squatters × Increase in Land Value variable, we held the level of squatting at its mean and calculated the impact from a one-half standard deviation change in the percentage increase in land values from 1970 to 1985. This change has the biggest impact on deaths, slightly more than 2. The same change in SUDAM subsidies raises deaths by 1.7. Changes in squatting levels and land concentration have a lesser impact and the reliability of the coefficients is low. Increases in land value decrease the number of deaths by 1.7, but again the significance level is low.

VII. 5 CONCLUDING REMARKS

Modern economic growth has been with us for only about 150 years and then only for a small part of the world. Part of the reason, continually stressed by Douglass North, has been the institutions of society:

> In fact, one of the most evident lessons from history is that political systems have an inherent tendency to produce inefficient property rights which result in stagnation or decline. (1987, p. 422)

By "inefficient" property rights, North means that under the existing rights structure, potential rents are not realized but instead are foregone with missed opportunities or dissipated through redistributive activities. In particular, North has argued that the institutions of a society must continually adapt to changes in relative prices for growth to occur.

Our contribution in this chapter has been to provide a case study of the importance of institutional change in response to increases in the potential rent from land in the Brazilian Amazon in order to limit violence over land conflicts. We found that a lack of formal property rights alone on the frontier did not produce violence, but rather it was a lack of formal property rights coupled with an increase in rental streams that prompted violence. Rental streams from land began to increase dramatically in the 1970s as a result of investments by the Brazilian government in roads, colonization projects, mining projects, and fiscal incentives for ranching projects. This investment activity directly and indirectly brought settlers to the Amazon to capture the increased land rents. Unfortunately, the increase in rent was not matched by an commensurate increase in titling activities. The land agencies lagged behind in assigning titles, as well as enforcing those titles that it assigned. Violent conflict was all too often the result. But violence was not the norm; deaths over land occurred in fewer than one-quarter of our sample *municipios*. Violence was most prevalent where land concentrations were high and absentee ownership likely, where the government provided fiscal incentives for ranches without either enforcing ranching activity or the property rights of ranchers, and in those regions where land rents increased and property rights were uncertain.

What does our analysis portend for future settlement of the Amazon? Currently only about 11 percent of the Brazilian Amazon is deforested, so there is room for considerable settlement. Given the fiscal situation in Brazil in the late 1980s and early 1990s, there was little investment in the Amazon. With the economic picture looking rosier in Brazil, there is renewed talk of developing the Amazon. The policy implications of our results are clear: investment must be coupled with increased titling and enforcement activities in order to avoid the violent conflicts that marked the 1970s and 1980s.

ACKNOWLEDGMENTS

We acknowledge gratefully the financial assistance provided by the National Science Foundation Grant SES 92113603 and The World Bank. We thank Robert Schneider for insights on the causes of violence in the Amazon. For comments, we thank David Fairris, Jack Knight, Jean-Laurent Rosenthal, Tomas Nonnenmacher, Ken Sokoloff, participants at the Conference on the Frontiers of Economics and at seminars at University of California at Riverside, University of California at Los Angeles, University of Southern California, California Institute of Technology, and the Institute of Behavioral Studies at the University of Colorado.

REFERENCES

Alston, L. J., Libecap, G. D., and Schneider, R. (1995a). Property rights and the preconditions for markets: The case of the Amazon frontier. *Journal of Institutional and Theoretical Economics* **151**(1), 89–107.

Alston, L. J., Libecap, G. D., and Schneider, R. (1995d). The demand and supply of property rights on the frontier: The Case of North America and Brazil. In *The Privatization Process: A Worldwide Perspective* (T. Anderson and P. J. Hill, eds. pp. 203–236).

Alston, L. J., Eggertsson, T., and North, D. C., eds. (1996). *Empirical Studies in Institutional Analysis.* Cambridge University Press, Cambridge, UK.

Barzel, Y. (1989). *Economic Analysis of Property Rights.* Cambridge University Press, Cambridge, UK.

Bunker, S. G. (1985b). Misdirected expertise in an unknown environment. In *The Frontier After a Decade of Colonization* (J. Hemming, ed.), pp. 101–118. Manchester University Press, Manchester.

De Alessi, L. (1980). The economics of property rights: A review of the evidence. *Research in Law and Economics* **2,** 1–47.

Eggertsson, T. (1990). *Economic Behavior and Institutions.* Cambridge University Press, Cambridge, UK.

Fearnside, P. M. (1986). *Human Carrying Capacity of the Brazilian RainForest.* Columbia University Press, New York.

Foweraker, J. (1981). *The Struggle for Land: A Political Economy of the Pioneer Frontier in Brazil, 1930 to Present.* Cambridge University Press, New York.

Furubotn, E., and Pejovich, S. (1972). Property rights and economic theory: A survey of recent literature. *Journal of Economic Literature* **10,** 1137–62.
Gasques, J. G., and Yokomizo, C. (1986). Resultados de 20 años de incentivos fiscais agropecuaria da Amazonia. *ANPEC, Encontro Nacional de Economia,* pp. 47–84.
Gordon, R. S. (1954). The economic theory of a common property resource: The fishery. *Journal of Political Economy* **62,** 124–42.
Human Rights Watch (1991). *Rural Violence in Brazil.* Human Rights Watch, New York.
IBGE (Fundação Instituto) (1990). Anuário Estatístico do Brasil, pp. 180–183.
IBGE (Fundação Instituto Brasileiro de Geografia e Estatística) (1960). *Censo Agropecuario.* Pará, Rio de Janeiro. Volume II, Tomo II, pp. 76, 100–101.
IBGE (Fundação Instituto Brasileiro de Geografia e Estatística) (1970). *Censo Agropecuario.* Pará, Rio de Janeiro. Volume III, Tomo IV, pp. 118–121, 178–181.
IBGE (Fundação Instituto Brasileiro de Geografia e Estatística) (1975). *Censo Agropecuario.* Pará, Rio de Janeiro. Volume I, Tomo IV, pp. 132–137, 264–269.
IBGE (Fundação Instituto Brasileiro de Geografia e Estatística) (1980). *Censo Agropecuario.* Pará, Rio de Janeiro. Volume II, Tomo III, pp. 154–159, 282–287.
IBGE (Fundação Instituto Brasileiro de Geografia e Estatística) (1985). *Censo Agropecuario.* Pará, Rio de Janeiro. No. 6 pp. 148–153, 276–278.
IBGE (1991). *Geografia do Brasil-Região, Norte,* Vol. III. Rio de Janeiro. p. 190.
IDESP (1990). Belém *Pará Agrário,* Conflitos Rurais, Numero Especial. pp. 6–20.
Ianni, O. (1979). *Colonização e Contra-Reforma Agrária na Amazônia.* Editora Vozes, Petropolis, Brazil.
Libecap, G. D. (1986). Property rights in economic history: Implications for research. *Explorations in Economic History* **23,** 227–252.
Libecap, G. D. (1989). *Contracting for Property Rights.* Cambridge University Press, New York.
Libecap, G. D. (1992). Douglass C. North. In *New Horizons in Economic Thought: Appraisals of Leading Economists* (W. J. Samuels, ed.). Elgar, Aldershot, UK.
McDonald, J. F., and Moffitt, R. A. (1980). The uses of Tobit analysis. *Review of Economics and Statistics* **62,** 318–321.
Moran, E. F. (1981). *Developing the Amazon.* Indiana University Press, Bloomington.
Moran, E. F. (1984). Colonization in the Transamazon and Rondonia. In *Frontier Expansion in Amazonia* (M. Schmink and C. H. Wood, eds.), pp. 285–303. University of Florida Press, Gainesville.
Moran, E. F. (1989b). Government-directed settlement in the 1970s: An assessment of transamazon highway colonization. In *The Human Ecology of Tropical Land Settlement in Latin America* (D. A. Schumann, and W. L. Partridge, eds.), pp. 172–197. Westview Press, Boulder, CO.
Mueller, C. (1980). Frontier based agricultural expansion: The case of rondonia. In *Land, People, and Planning in Contemporary Amazonia* (F. Barbira-Scazzocchio, ed.), Occas. Publ. No. 3. Cambridge University, Center of Latin American Studies, Cambridge, UK.
Mueller, C. (1992). *Colonization Policies, Land Occupation, and Deforestation in the Amazon Countries,* Working Paper No. 15. Department of Economics, University of Brasilia.
North, D. C. (1987). *Institutions, transaction costs and economic growth.* Economic Inquiry **25,** 419–428.
North, D. C. (1990). *Institutions, Institutional Change, and Economic Performance.* Cambridge University Press, New York.
North, D. C., and Thomas R. P. (1993). *The Rise of the Western World: A New Economic History.* Cambridge University Press, New York.
Pará Pastoral Land Commission (1989). *People Killed in Land Conflicts.* Pará Pastoral Land Commission, Belem.
Santos, R. (1984). Law and social change: The problem of land in the Brazilian Amazon. In *Frontier Expansion in Amazonia* (M. Schmink and C. H. Wood, eds.), pp. 180–284. University of Florida Press, Gainesville.

Sawyer, D. R. (1984). Frontier expansion and retraction in Brazil. In *Frontier Expansion in Amazonia* (M. Schmink and C. H. Wood, eds.), pp. 180–284. University of Florida Press, Gainesville.

Schmink, M., and Wood, C. H., Eds. (1992). *Contested Frontiers in Amazonia.* Columbia University Press, New York.

Schneider, R. (1994). *Government and the Economy on the Amazon Frontier,* Latin America and Caribbean Technical Department, Regional Studies Program Report No. 34. World Bank, Washington, DC.

Wood, C., and Wilson, J. (1984). The magnitude of migration to the Brazilian frontier. In *Frontier Expansion in Amazonia* (M. Schmink and C. H. Wood, eds.), pp. 142–152. University of Florida Press, Gainesville.

Yokomizo, C. (1989). *Incentivos Financeiros e Fiscais na Pecuarizacao da Amazonia,* Texto Para Discussao, No. 22. Institute de Planejamento, Outubro.

Yokota, P. (1981). *Questão Fundiána Brasileira.* INCRA, Brasilia.

VIII Changing Property Rights: Reconciling Formal and Informal Rights to Land in Africa

Jean Ensminger

VIII.1 INTRODUCTION

Policy planners in Africa confront an intriguing puzzle. At the same time that many African societies are changing social norms and indigenous rights in property to more individualistic systems approaching privatization, we find increasing numbers of societies backing away from government sponsored formal systems of freehold land tenure. Even more curious, we often find that the very same societies that evolved indigenous privatization are now shunning government programs. Obviously something about the supply of formal rights imposed by governments is not meeting the demand for property right change at the local level. Some simple economic explanations provide partial answers: the transaction costs of the registration process are high and lagging markets in essential complementary factors of production (particularly capital) may be constraining growth rather than land. But these explanations are not the whole story. Most agricultural production in Africa is still kin-based and highly risky. Lineages are not just kinfolk, they share some of the characteristics of corporations: they cooperate in labor, risk management, and investment. Fundamental to the high level of trust and cooperation that such systems enjoy are basic guarantees of subsistence in the short run—through access to land-and the long run—through inheritance of that land. Property right changes that violate this complex of complementary interdependencies are doomed to fail. One need not interpret this failure as violation of a sacred "moral economy"; one can as well impute a cost-benefit calculus to farmers' demands for property rights. But one *must* include in this equation the costs and benefits as they are realized by the farmer, that is, filtered through the calculus of kinship. The fit between formal and informal institutions is key to the former's success.

New institutional economists have long appreciated the significance of the role of institutions in economic performance (Eggertsson, 1990; North, 1981). Over the years the challenge to be all-inclusive has moved further from the domain of institutions with obvious bearing upon economics, such as property rights (North and Thomas, 1973), into the realm of informal social institutions (North, 1990), and finally culture itself (Denzau and North, 1994; Greif, 1994; Putnam, 1993). Anthropologists should applaud this trend, as it not only highlights the significance of their comparative advantage in the stock of knowledge, but it also reiterates the position taken by many of them, including the substantivists who debated the formalists in the 1960s. North (1990) brought informal institutions to the fore because they are important constraints on economic behavior-they both determine the calculus through which the all-important incentives of formal rules will affect choice and they provide for much of the enforcement that is essential to any economy. In North's words (1990, p. 36),

> formal rules, in even the most developed economy, make up a small (although very important) part of the sum of constraints that shape choices; a moment's reflection should suggest to us the pervasiveness of informal constraints. In our daily interaction with others, whether within the family, in external social relations, or in business activities, the governing structure is overwhelmingly defined by codes of conduct, norms of behavior, and conventions. Underlying these informal constraints are formal rules, but these are seldom the obvious and immediate source of choice in daily interactions.

The need to better understand informal constraints is highlighted by the fact that

> the informal constraints that are culturally derived will not change immediately in reaction to changes in the formal rules. As a result the tension between altered formal rules and the persisting informal constraints produces outcomes that have important implications for the way economies change."
>
> (North, 1990, p. 45)

This last point is beautifully illustrated by the evidence of formally imposed private property rights in African land. An examination of the process of land tenure change in Africa clearly reveals the importance of *complementarity* between informal and formal institutions. When formal systems are imposed upon a society with which they are out of accord, self-enforcement may erode and externally engineered incentives may fail to yield the predicted results.

Africa provides a fascinating laboratory for testing theories of property rights. The vast majority of the continent still recognizes customary rights to land (generally in the form of commons in pastoral areas and lineage or chiefly control in farming areas), but there is also no shortage of experiments in government and locally initiated privatization. Yet at the same time that new government initiatives furthering privatization are underway, there is increasing evidence from anthropologists and Africanists (Fleuret, 1988; Haugerud, 1983, 1989; Okoth-Ogendo, 1986; Shipton, 1988) that even the longest running national privatization efforts are unraveling, reverting to customary rights, and show few, if any, investment and productivity benefits over indigenous systems (Bruce and Migot-Adholla, 1994). Does this mean, as one might conclude by reading between the lines of the anthropologists' reports, that Africans are communitarian and privatization is just inconsistent with their values, social norms, and social organization? Perhaps to a degree, but this ignores the forces of demographic and economic change, which have driven changes in those very same values and social norms and have led to indigenous movement toward greater privatization in the absence of state programs. But the alternative is not to conclude that freehold property rights can be simply transplanted in Africa. Imported property rights are often poorly matched with the demand driven by the costs, benefits, and preexisting distribution generated by local institutions. As many anthropologists have noted and new institutional economists have accepted, "Property rights are always embedded in the institutional structure of a society, and the creation of new property rights demands new institutional arrangements to define and specify the way by which economic units can cooperate and compete" (North and Thomas, 1973, p. 5). As a consequence, when not properly embedded, new rights become unimplementable and unenforceable. As Eggertsson (1994, p. 19) put it, "The weakness of property rights analysis is its limited understanding of informal institutions, how they evolve and how they relate to formal institutions."

We know a great deal about African land tenure in the colonial, postcolonial, and contemporary eras. The cases are sufficiently numerous and detailed for us to make some real headway in understanding the place of property rights in African development and even to make some suggestions for policy implications. A recent volume (Bruce and Migot-Adholla, 1994) of quantitative studies on the effects of tenure security on agricultural performance also provides us with much needed cross-cultural work from a unified and rigorous framework. I shall argue in this chapter that the basic assumptions of property rights theory (Demsetz, 1967, p. 350; North and Thomas, 1973) are correct—as relative prices change (perhaps through demographic pressure, expanded commercial opportunities, or new technologies), new social norms and property rights emerge to internalize the beneficial and harmful effects and adjust to the new cost-benefit position. There is strong evidence that under these conditions of changing relative prices, African societies have moved toward increasing exclusivity of land rights since before colonialism. Some even go so far as to see a convergence in this direction (Bruce, *et al.,* 1994, p. 262). But Demsetz (1967, p. 350) also reminded us that the gains from property right change must exceed the costs in order to justify change. Further, for new property rights to exist, the owner must possess "the consent of fellow men to allow him to act in particular ways. An owner expects the community to prevent others from interfering with his actions, provided that these actions are not prohibited in the specification of his rights" (p. 347). Increasing evidence from Africa is calling into question both of these conditions: (1) whether the gains of new property rights justify the transaction costs and (2) whether the fit between customary tenure, social norms, and the new property rights is sufficient to lend legitimacy to their enforcement. If these conditions are not met, then privatization and titling do not necessarily yield more secure property rights. To understand why this is the case we must examine the cost-benefit structure of property rights and the incentives they provide in the social context.

Imposed property rights are not endogenous, and as a consequence, they may fail to "connect" with other complementary indigenous norms and institutions. This is evidenced in Africa today in the most extreme case—when people with title deeds place so little value on them they do not bother to update their own titles, thus yielding a failure of self-enforcement.

In this chapter I begin by tracing the evolution of indigenous property rights in the absence of formal land tenure reform. The evidence provides strong support for the proposition that social norms and institutions respond in ways economists would predict to exogenous changes in relative prices. The trend in Africa also appears to be well established in the direction of increased privatization. I turn next to the evidence of the effects of land titling on investment in the land and agricultural productivity. Here the evidence is not so simply explained, as titling does not appear to lead to positive gains in economic performance. Next I examine the evidence that formal titling in Kenya, the country with the first and most comprehensive titling program, is unraveling. Evidence indicates that part of the failure can be attributed to the transaction costs of maintaining the titling system and lagging factor markets in capital and labor. But I shall argue that there is equally compelling evidence that the formal system is conflicting with the needs and interests of farmers as defined by their current production strategies founded on largely lineage-based systems. Finally, I consider the Kenyan government's response to these failings and discuss the implications for the theory of property rights and institutional change more generally.

VIII.2 CUSTOMARY LAND TENURE IN AFRICA

One of the most interesting findings from a survey of indigenous systems of land tenure in Africa is the degree of similarity one finds in land tenure across comparable agro-climatic zones on the continent (Migot-

Adholla and Bruce, 1994, p. 5; Migot-Adholla *et al.,* 1994a, p. 99).[1] One can capture the underlying principles of a few general types relatively simply, which is surprising on a continent made up until recently of over 1000 independent ethnic groups with autonomous institutions. A common characteristic in almost all African customary systems is for use rights to be assigned at the household level, whereas transfer rights are assigned at a higher level such as the lineage, clan, or chiefdom (Matlon, 1994, p. 65).

The major types of land tenure in Africa can be crudely lumped into common property (managed either by all members of the ethnic group or some recognized large subset), lineage controlled, and chief-controlled. Typically one finds common property where land is used by hunters and gatherers or pastoralists. Such areas are generally arid and have low population density, rendering more restrictive control costly due to the high transaction costs.

Lineage or clan control is especially prevalent in Africa. Generally the person who cleared the land first is entitled to use it and pass it down to his descendants (through the male line in patrilineal systems and through the sister's son in matrilineal systems). Over time, such lineages become large, as do the areas of land that they control. Generally, the head of the lineage has authority to allocate land to those with need, thus there is a tendency for land to be relatively efficiently matched in people-land ratios.[2] This system also affords the easy accommodation of newly married wives without necessarily having to deprive existing wives in a polygynous household. Typically a husband allocates each wife (or son's wife) separate parcels over which she has near complete control in farm management decisions. Upon the death of the father it was typical for the land to be subdivided among sons or for the eldest or youngest son to inherit the fathers' land, whereas the lineage allocated unoccupied land to the other sons. Until relatively recently, and still in many parts of Africa, frontier land was available. Once lineage lands became inadequate, sons set out to the frontier to break new ground and begin the process once again. The lineage system puts a premium on *use* of the land rather than transfer rights. Those who fail to use the land risk losing it.[3] In some areas this provided people with an incentive to plant cocoa and coffee very sparsely over the plot, not for their economic

[1] For a recent overview of African land tenure, see Shipton (1994).

[2] Matlon (1994; p. 47) demonstrated that this by no means ensures equality even under customary tenure. He found that average holdings varied by four-fold per capita in Burkina Faso. This was a result of historical sequencing and political influence. On the other hand, despite high population density, Blarel (1994; p. 78) found that in Rwanda the incidence of absolute landlessness was rare under customary tenure.

[3] Matlon (1994; p. 54) noted that in Burkina Faso as land pressure increases people fear to lend land for more than one season.

value but in order to lay claim to the land (for Cote d'Ivoire, see Koby, 1979; Cameroon, see Levin, 1976; Zanzibar, see Middleton, 1961, cited in Feder and Noronha, 1987, p. 153). Once the frontier was gone, social norms sometimes changed to allow for equal shares to sons, and this has necessitated the subdivision of parcels.

In more politically centralized African societies that had chiefs, paramount chiefs, and kings, transfer rights in land ultimately rested with the central authority, who allocated use rights to households. When land failed to be used, it reverted to the control of the centralized authority. Such systems shared many of the attributes of the lineage systems, but they were open to more widespread abuse by higher authorities once land became salable (see Firmin-Sellers, 1966, for Ghana). One distinguishing characteristic of most of these systems is that prior to colonialism and the advent of cash cropping, land was rarely if ever recognized as a commodity over which individuals could sell their rights. But another general principle of such systems was enormous flexibility to respond to a wide range of shocks. Far from being conservatively timeless and unable to change, indigenous systems were dynamic and responded in quite predictable ways to the forces of demographic and economic change.

VIII.3 ENDOGENOUS DEMAND FOR PRIVATIZATION IN AFRICA

Just as there appears to be consistency in the form of land tenure rights across Africa, with the least-privatized systems found in the sparsest environments with the lowest population density and least commercial value, so too were there patterns in the transformation of indigenous systems. In general, we find evidence that areas with the highest population pressure, the greatest returns to commercial agriculture, and the greatest accessibility to technological advances, moved most quickly in the direction of exclusivity of some rights if not outright privatization (cf. Boserup, 1981). In many, if not all cases, this was accompanied by complementary changes in social norms and social organization, which restricted the size and obligations of the kinship group (cf. Hecht, 1985; Parkin, 1972). What is more, this trend is apparent both in pastoral areas making the transition from commons to some form of relatively small group or individual control, and in farming areas making the transition from lineage or chiefly control to individual tenure. One must bear in mind, however, that such transitions are still the exception in Africa, and more classic commons and lineage land rights still prevail in most areas. Nevertheless, the tendency for property rights to move in the direction of exclusivity with the increasing value of land is clearly consistent with, and provides powerful support for, the theory of property rights as elaborated by North and Thomas (1973) and Demsetz (1967).

It is worth examining some of these cases of endogenous change in property rights in order to better understand how property rights change in Africa. One should bear in mind though that land "sales" did not always mean the same thing, nor did incipient privatization of land represent the same bundles of rights in Africa as it did or does in Europe (Berry, 1988; Okoth-Ogendo, 1986).[4] For example, among the Kikuyu, Meru, Mbeere, and Luo of Kenya, land "sales" appear to have been accompanied by an understanding of redeemability on the part of the seller (Brokensha and Glazier, 1973, p. 191, Coldham, 1978; Glazier 1985, p. 200; Homan, 1963, pp. 226–229) and sometimes required the approval of members of the land-holding lineage (Brokensha and Glazier, 1973, p. 191).

Perhaps the earliest examples of land sales come from Ghana, where commercial crops such as palm oil led to the development of a land market even prior to colonial rule (Feder and Noronha, 1987, p. 154). There is also evidence of land sales in Nigeria prior to colonial rule in 1861. Further evidence of an indigenous land market comes from the densely populated areas of Kenya including Kikuyu-land prior to the turn of the century (Leakey, 1977; Muriuki 1974, p. 70), Taita before colonialism (Fleuret, 1988, p. 14), Luo before World War II (Coldham, 1978, p. 95), and in the coffee and tea zones of Mbeere and Kisii well before national land litigation (Brokensha and Glazier, 1973). The Taita and Luo cases are especially well documented in that we have cross-sectional data from within each group showing that the more populated areas involved in cash crop production changed their property rights first. In Tanzania land sales were also common in the areas most involved in commercial production. Dobson (1954, cited in Ault and Rutman, 1979) found that among ten Tanzanian societies, those with individual rights were the ones experiencing land pressure. Hailey (1957, cited in Feder and Noronha, 1987, p. 155) reported that among the Sambaa of Tanzania land sales did not even require the consent of kin. In one of the richest studies of this process, Netting (1965, 1968) provided an analysis of two sites over time. The Kofyar of Nigeria who farmed intensively on the plateau had individual ownership of plots, whereas in the areas where the same ethnic group practiced shifting cultivation there were no individual rights. By the 1980s when the Kofyar were also farming the plains intensively, they had developed a market in land there as well

[4] Berry (1988) discussed at length the issue of multiple and overlapping bundles of rights in land, as well as the symbolic battles over "meaning" associated with property rights in Africa when these rights are altered. Barzel (1989) provides a theoretical framework to understand why some rights are specified, and some are not in different contexts and cost environments.

(Netting, 1993). Colson (1971) documented the same trend associated with increased commercialization in southern Africa.

Interestingly, the pressure for land privatization was so great that a land market developed in some areas, even though it was expressly outlawed under colonial rule. In some areas where active land markets were operating prior to colonialism, they were stopped by the colonial authorities; this was the case among the Sukuma of Tanzania, whose pre-1891 land market was stopped after the German occupation (Malcolm, 1953, p. 12, cited in Feder and Noronha, 1987, p. 155). In Kenya the colonial government engaged in a debate over whether to contain the indigenous pressures toward individual rights among the Kikuyu by shoring up communitarian institutions such as the council of elders. Others argued for allowing the continued development of individualism in social norms as well as property rights as a necessary precondition for economic growth (Chanock, 1991, pp. 72–74; Sorrenson, 1967, pp. 52–71). Eventually, the colonial government of Kenya led the way in national privatization (see below).

In a nicely documented case of the development of an indigenous land market in the Ivory Coast, Hecht (1985) described the process whereby the Dida made the transition from lineage-based rights to individual rights in the cocoa-growing zone from 1940–1980. This is an especially interesting case as it involves the transfer of land to immigrants or other "African strangers." In many of the examples discussed previously, the transfers were within ethnic groups, but it is arguably far more difficult to secure property rights and contracts across ethnic groups, at least in the absence of commonly shared national institutions. Yet the Dida managed to do this without the formal recognition or backing of the Ivorian government (Hecht, 1985, p. 333).

Hecht's description is valuable because of the detail he provided on the changes in social organization that preceded the changes in property rights. Under the pressures of export crop production, Dida lineages began to fragment as brothers split into separate families and sons kept their wages for their own nuclear families rather than turning them over to their fathers or the head of the lineage. Hecht (1985, p. 324) reported that

> Marriage transactions ceased being a lineage affair and took on an individualistic character, with young men arranging their own matches.
>
> Local attitudes and practices related to land followed this larger pattern of change in the rural economy. Before 1945 planted, fallow and virgin forest land alike was all viewed as part of the lineage patrimony; membership in the lineage and use of lineage land were synonymous. After the second world war, however, land began to be regarded as belonging to individual conjugal households, independent of lineage affiliation, and subject to purchase and sale only by the conjugal units directly involved in the transaction.

Although most of the instances of indigenous development of land markets occurred as a consequence of land pressure or recent commercialization, Allan (1965, p. 369) provided an example driven by technological change:

> In the maize-growing parts of the southern and central provinces of Northern Rhodesia cash transactions in land have emerged in the form of payments for improvements, a development which appeared first among the Plateau Tonga with their comparatively long history of plough cultivation and maize marketing. Where the plough is used land must be stumped, at much greater labour or cost in wages of labour than in the case of normal hoe cultivation. Stumped land thus acquires a special value, easily assessed in money terms, which is independent of the scarcity or abundance of land in general. Nowadays when land is transferred, payment is commonly asked for the value of stumping and for such other permanent improvements as houses, out-buildings, wells, fencing, and fruit trees. This practice is not confined to the land-hungry Tonga: a very similar pattern of payment for improvements has appeared among the Soli and Sala and other comparative newcomers to the maize market who are not yet short of strong and fertile land. On the other hand, cash transactions in land appear to be unknown in the greatly overcrowded lands of the Ngoni where the plough is not used and land is not stumped.

National programs for formal land titling are still the exception rather than the rule in Africa. Consequently, we find the same pressures at work today for change in indigenous property rights that have prevailed in some parts of Africa for at least 150 years (Migot-Adholla et al., 1994a, p. 102). One gets a flavor for the more contemporary era from the following passage in Feder and Noronha (1987, p. 155):

> Independence has not put a stop to land transactions. In Tanzania, Pitblado (1981) reports that in one village in the North Mkata Plain, some 16 percent of land was acquired by purchase; in another, the figure was 36 percent. In Lesotho, where land cannot be legally sold (and where urban and rural lands have equal value in the eyes of the law), Mosaase notes that as a result of land scarcity 'a clandestine land market had developed and the indiscriminate selling of arable land for residential and commercial sites has become uncontrollable' (1984, p. 90). In Mali, land is inalienable in theory. In practice, though, sales of less fertile lands to stronger farmers take place, even though it is difficult to obtain data on such sales. In Niger, sales of land are increasing, although indigenous rules say that land cannot be sold (University of Arizona, 1979). Ega's (1979) survey of three villages in Zaria, Nigeria, showed that 18 percent of those surveyed had obtained their lands by purchase. He notes that 'there is a significant prevalence of illegal commercial transactions in land and considerable mobility of land. In particular, purchase has become an important means of acquiring land' (1979, p. 291). Of the Volta region of Ghana, Nkunya says that 'outright purchase . . . is becoming more and more common these days'.
>
> (1974, p. 4)

Some recent quantitative studies are also evidence that commercialization and population pressure continue to provide incentives for indigenous change in property rights. Migot-Adholla and colleagues (1994a) found that although all three regions they studied in Ghana are highly commercialized, the one with high population pressure had 82.5 percent of "complete transfer" parcels (defined as the highest tenure security) as opposed to 76.7 percent and 70.3 percent in the other two regions. The effect of commercialization on privatization was demonstrated in a Rwandan study (Blarel, 1994), where in two regions of comparable population density, the one with greater commercialization had 81.5 percent of permanently held parcels with "complete transfer" rights as opposed to 57.6 percent and 46.7 percent in less commercialized regions.

Although pastoral lands are considerably less developed in many parts of Africa, one sees similar trends in areas where population pressure, commercialization, or technological advances have provided an incentive to privatize the gains from investment. One of the best-documented instances of the move toward greater exclusivity of rights on pastoral lands comes from Peters' work (1992) among the Bakgatla of Botswana. This is one of the most technologically developed pastoral systems in Africa, where diesel-powered boreholes are common and there is beginning to be talk of fences. Peters (1992, p. 414) reported that the push to introduce private property in water supplies (which determine access to land) began in the early 1930s, following the drilling of deep bore wells in the late 1920s and early 1930s. Between 1936 and 1976 the human population increased nearly threefold while the livestock population increased nearly twofold, contributing further pressure for revised property rights. Particularly well-documented in this case is the parallel change in indigenous social organization. Syndicates own the boreholes, which effectively limit access to the land. Syndicate rules limit heirs to one son and place constraints upon the use of the range by dependents of members. Such limitations run in strong contradiction to African norms of large, polygynous, extended families where sons often have expectations of equal inheritance. In fact, it was also common among the Bakgatla for sister's sons to be treated as classificatory sons, but such relationships are disappearing under resource pressure. Peters (1992, p. 421) noted how pressures have caused, "individuals and groups within syndicates to redefine conventionally accepted statuses and rules that govern claims to resources, and to reduce the degree of negotiability of those definitions. The outcome is a narrowing of the social orbit of syndicate organization and growing exclusivity." Peters (1992, p. 430) concludes that, "Changes in the relative economic costs of ranching compared with open-range herding, in the use of cattle to express and validate social or political links, or in the diversity of use of available resources, are all likely to increase the trends toward exclusion."[5]

These cases of indigenous response to changing relative prices provide strong evidence of the ability of societies to adapt to exogenous forces. We see complementary changes occurring simultaneously in both social organizations and property rights. The complementarity of these simultaneous adjustments is crucial to their success in coping with both the constraints and opportunities of a changing world. I shall later argue that it is currently extremely difficult for top-down national mandates to achieve this same level of complementarity with informal institutions. The demographic and commercial changes that Africa is currently experiencing are of such a rapid and intense nature that some greater level of stability may need to be reached before imposed change can be effective. African social norms and informal institutions are currently a rapidly moving target. In this context, I turn now to an examination of the fate of one formal government effort at property rights change in Africa.

VIII.4 KENYA: A CASE STUDY IN LAND TITLING IN AFRICA

Given the many endogenous efforts at privatization around the continent in the precolonial and early colonial days, it is not surprising that colonial governments, and later independent governments, experimented with nationalized tenure programs. In Kenya at least as long ago as 1933,

[5] The Kgatla case is a more ìpureî example of endogenously driven efforts to privatize pastoral common lands than are many others that are confounded by interethnic competition for grazing lands (for the Orma, see Ensminger, 1992; Ensminger and Rutten, 1991; for the Boran, see Hogg, 1990; and for the Maasai, see Galaty, 1980). One of the problems associated with commons when there is interethnic competition for the land is that the ethnic group is dependent on the state to enforce their common property rights against the claims of competitors. States have proven themselves to be particularly unreliable in this regard, perhaps because they are ambivalent about standing up for ethnic institutions (including those that manage the commons) while they are attempting in other arenas to downplay ethnicity and create a common national identity (Ensminger and Knight, 1997). Yet the failure of governments to defend the boundaries of ethnic commons effectively turns such commons into open access and a recipe for the ravages of overgrazing. As a consequence, we find an increasing tendency for pastoral populations to push for greater privatization in order to "preempt" other claims to their land. While Hogg (1990) for the Boran and Ensminger and Rutten (1991) for the Orma have argued that the endogenous forces for increasing privatization were also evident, it is all but impossible to separate out the independent effects of the external threat. In the Kgatla case, however, it is clear that it is the underlying demographic and economic forces that are driving changes in norms more of social organization and more exclusive definitions of property rights.

the Carter land commission heard evidence arguing that communal tenure was retarding agricultural development and some advocated private tenure in the interests of development. Belief in the efficacy of fee-simple property rights was also shared by the African leaders of newly independent states. President Banda of Malawi told the Parliament in 1967 that the absence of individual title was the main obstacle to development, "No-one is responsible for the uneconomic and wasted use of land because no-one holds land as an individual. Land is held in common" (Malawi Parliamentary Debates, 1967, cited in Chanock, 1991, p. 71).

Kenya was the first colony to initiate a nationwide effort to register land, known as the Swynnerton plan (1954).[6] Kenya has also experienced marked stability in government policy toward privatization, with the independent government of Kenya (since 1963) remaining deeply committed to land registration. As noted earlier, there were already areas in Kenya where customary tenure was moving in the direction of individualization and where land markets were developing. The Swynnerton plan attempted to speed up and formalize these efforts by imposing a system based on 1925 English land law (Okoth-Ogendo, 1986, p. 79). The consolidation and registration began in Kikuyu areas in the 1950s, and much of that area was registered by the end of the decade; Luo-land and Western Provinces were nearly completed by the mid-1970s. By 1981 more than 6 million hectares had been registered nationally (Barrows and Roth, 1990, p. 269). Okoth-Ogendo estimated in 1993 that 90 percent of all land in farming districts had been privatized.

The goals of the Swynnerton plan (1954) were to promote cash-crop agriculture by consolidating scattered strips into units of "economic" size,[7] securing titles so as to encourage investment in the land, facilitate the extension of credit by use of title deeds to secure loans, reduce land disputes, and ease transfer. In fact, the planners consciously anticipated that titling would facilitate the concentration of land in the hands of farmers better able to farm more profitably. It was understood and accepted that this would create a landless class, who were expected to labor on the larger farms and in industry. The intention was that once consolidation, adjudication, and registration were complete, land would no longer be subject to customary law and would resemble English freehold tenure (Pedraza, 1956; Sorrenson, 1967).

[6] For a discussion of the privatization efforts in Uganda and Zimbabwe, see Barrows and Roth (1990).

[7] "Economic" size was defined locally according to the carrying capacity of the land. Local committees seem also to have given some consideration to the potential numbers of people who would have been rendered landless if the size was set too high (Haugerud, 1983; p. 73).

Brokensha and Glazier (1973, p. 198) described the process of land adjudication in Mbeere:

> Land adjudication committees, provided for in the Act, are to be established in each Sub-location, and will include at least one representative of each clan which has land claims, giving a total membership of twenty to thirty-five. Clans will select their own representatives. . . . The committees in conjunction with the demarcation officer must settle clan boundaries. In committee proceedings neither the traditional oath nor modern lawyers will be allowed.
>
> Once clan borders have been determined and final maps drawn, the committee will then face its second Herculean labour, the hearing of cases on individual rights. This may prove to be less difficult for the adjudication committee than for the clan committee which has the task of deciding on individual grants of land. Men who are unsatisfied with their new plots can appeal to the adjudication committee.

A colonial land tenure officer of the day, Derek Homan (1963, p. 237) described the process of land consolidation under Swynnerton as follows:

> Briefly, the whole process is carried out by committees of elders which first adjudicate as to the nature and extent of each man's rights to land in the area concerned, and then, after deducting a percentage from each for land required for 'public purposes' (roads, schools, markets, etc.), re-allocate all land in the area so as to give each man, in one piece, the equivalent of the total he previously had in a number of fragments.

Although Kenya's program is the best researched and most extensive in Africa, many other governments have attempted private titling, especially the Ivory Coast and Malawi, but with variations: Botswana, Cameroon, Ghana, Lesotho, Liberia, Mali, Senegal, Sierra Leone, Somalia, South African reserves, Sudan, Swaziland, Uganda, and Zimbabwe (Feder and Noronha, 1987, p. 150; Shipton, 1994, p. 365). Meanwhile, socialist regimes have attempted collectivized land tenure in Ethiopia, Tanzania, and Mozambique with fairly disastrous results (see Shipton, 1994, p. 365, for case study references). Nigeria and the francophone countries proceeded by first declaring all lands as the property of the state, thus undermining lineage and chiefly claims and leaving the way open for outright land grabs by elites (Shipton, 1994, p. 365).

Whereas those coming from a property rights tradition will easily discount the failures of socialized and nationalized efforts at land reform, explaining the unexpected consequences of the Kenya land reform and others like it (which most parallel the British system of freehold property rights) is more problematic. Not only have scholars failed to find strong evidence for the expected investment, productivity, and security effects from land titling, but there is considerable evidence of reversion to customary tenure in titled areas, even those areas that prior to titling were experiencing indigenous shifts toward privatization.

VIII.4.1 Evidence of the Effects of Land Titling

Bruce and Migot-Adholla (1994) just published a volume reporting on the effects of land tenure security in eight country studies from Africa. These articles represent four World Bank studies (Burkina Faso, Ghana, Kenya, and Rwanda) focusing upon indigenous customary tenure and the degree to which it does or does not discourage investment and limit increased agricultural production. Four other studies were carried out by the Land Tenure Center at the University of Wisconsin (Kenya, Senegal, Somalia, and Uganda) and focus on the effects of individualized tenure systems on investment and agricultural productivity. In a similar study, Feder and Onchan (1987) found a significant correlation between land titling in Thailand and improvements in the land in the form of bunding and clearing of stumps. In the Thailand study, titles were also associated with greater access to credit and higher capital formation in two provinces, but not in a third where informal credit was readily available. Given the positive correlation in Southeast Asia, it is particularly striking that in none of the eight country studies in Africa found unequivocal empirical support for any of the performance outcomes examined.

One of the tenure effects that these studies looked at closely was improvements in the land. Blarel (1994, pp. 88, 93) did find that Rwandans with higher tenure security improved the land more, but this was not correlated with higher productivity because the very poor (with less tenure security) have higher yields on short-term land. Migot-Adholla and associates (1994a, p. 107) found no effect in Ghana of type of tenure on land improvement. They suggest that this is because those without title already in fact enjoy the same security as those with title. In the World Bank Kenyan study by Migot-Adholla and colleagues (1994b, p. 137), they found that after controlling for other possible variables, neither title nor tenure security (operationalized independently) were related to terracing or perennial tree crop planting in three of the four in-country sites. In Somalia (Roth *et al.*, 1994, p. 224), titling had no statistically significant effects on investments in agriculture. The studies also considered the use of agricultural inputs, but like the effects on land improvement, the data were inconclusive at best (Bruce *et al.*, 1994, p. 255).

With regard to effects on agricultural productivity (Migot-Adholla *et al.*, 1994, p. 137), the World Bank Kenyan study found no effects of titles on yields in any of their regressions.[8] Furthermore, the authors noted (Bruce and Migot-Adholla, 1994, p. 255) that these findings, "cannot simply be dismissed as the result of noisy yield data, because the results for many other variables included in the regressions were satisfactory, both in terms of statistical significance and expected signs." In an analysis of the Ghanaian,

[8] The authors specifically suggested that this is probably related to the failure to use credit.

Kenyan, and Rwandan data sets together (Place and Hazell, 1993, pp. 16–18), the authors also found that with few exceptions land rights were not significantly related to whether farmers made land-improving investments or used yield-enhancing inputs. This led to their conclusion that either all current types of land tenure are equally constraining (which might be surprising given their variation) or that some other constraint is binding agricultural productivity (p. 18). The authors also noted that in the Kenyan case a possible explanation for the lack of difference between the customary tenure systems and the titled areas is that the titled areas have in practice reverted to customary tenure, thus eliminating difference in the independent variable. I turn now to this most curious and unexpected phenomenon.

VIII.4.2 The Unraveling of Formal Title Systems in Kenya

Given that many African societies have been evolving systems of more privatized land tenure since the colonial days, one might expect the formalization of these changes at the national level to have been well received and effective. However, there is considerable evidence, much of it collected in detailed case studies by anthropologists, that things have not gone the way they were expected to go.

Data are mounting that what is occurring on the ground bears less and less resemblance to what is documented in land registries. Typically, parcels are subdivided among sons without them having legal title to the plots. What is more, even once the fathers die, the succession claims are often not registered. A government officer named Homan (1963, cited in Coldham, 1979, p. 618) reported that in the early 1960s "after about four years of full registration in Kiambu District [arguably the most developed in Kenya], over 3,000 titles are still registered in the names of deceased persons." Coldham (1979, p. 618) himself observed that in East Kadianga (Luo-land in western Kenya) during 1966–1973, not more than 3.4 percent of successions (1 out of 29) had been registered, and in Gathinja during 1963–1974, not more than 21.4 percent (9 out of 42). Even more puzzling is the failure to register changes in title upon sale of the land. Coldham (1979, p. 618) reported that in East Kadianga during 1966–1973, "at least 30 per cent of all sales of land (13 out of 42) were unregistered, while in Gathinja during 1963–1974, the equivalent figure was 15 per cent (2 out of 13)." In Embu (Kenya), Haugerud (1983, p. 73) found similar evidence in 1979, 20 years after adjudication. Approximately 20 percent of her sample households occupied land registered in the name of an individual who was not a household member. Three-fifths of these (12% total) were living on land registered to a deceased person. She also found that refragmentation was common (1983, p. 74): 58 percent of sample households owned two or more parcels of land, 12 percent owned at least three parcels, and 6 percent owned at least four parcels. She noted that this degree of fragmentation approached that of the preconsolidation era.[9] Another study of a site in Luo-land (Migot-Adholla *et al.,* 1994, p. 138) found that although 75 percent of the parcels in Kianjogu were titled, only 8 percent of the owners reported that they could be sold, thus implying that customary norms prevented them from doing so.

Mirroring many of North's (1990, p. 45) statements about formal and informal institutions cited earlier, Coldham (1979, p. 619) stated the situation regarding customary versus formal land tenure clearly in the following passage:

> The fact that a title is registered, and that therefore the land ceases to be governed by customary law, is unlikely in itself to affect the behaviour of those concerned. Customary controls will continue to be exercised; customary institutions-like the 'redeemable sale' or the '*muhoi* tenancy' among the Kikuyu—will continue to exist; customary rules and procedures governing the transfer or inheritance of land will continue to be observed.

The literature leaves little doubt that formal land titling is not having the intended effects of increasing agricultural investment and productivity by providing greater security, or even, given its failure to replace customary norms of succession and transfer, of creating a land market. Why?

VIII.4.3 Understanding the Failure of Land Titling in Kenya

I shall argue that the failure of formal land tenure change in Kenya is the result of the transaction costs of the registration process, the failure of complementary factor markets, and, especially, incompatibility with the all-important social norms and organizations without which people cannot produce or enforce anything. I stop short of the position taken by some Africanists, however, whose tone sometimes suggests that customary systems suffer none of these limitations. We have seen considerable evidence earlier that Africa has been and continues to experience enormous demographic and economic pressure on social systems and property rights institutions. Inheritance patterns are changing as land pressure intensifies, and these changes will drive further changes in customary land tenure. The real policy questions for Africa are when to leave customary systems to accommodate these changes and how to intervene if customary systems appear to no longer guarantee tenure security?

[9] Similarly, in Rwanda Blarel (1994; p. 89) found evidence that even shortly after registration land was being sold and subdivided without a record of the transaction being made or the "title" being updated.

Transaction Costs

The studies cited in Bruce and Migot-Adholla (1994), which fail to find compelling economic benefits as a result of land titling, certainly call into question whether the economic returns to society justify the transaction costs of the registration system. The costs from the point of view of Kenyan farmers themselves also appear to be prohibitive to some in both time and money.

Okoth-Ogendo (1986, p. 88, see also Coldham 1979, p. 618) describes the process of land registration as it related to succession, which under the original adjudication act was limited to five heirs. It should be borne in mind that in polygynous Kenya, which in the 1980s had the highest population growth rate in the world, men often had more than five heirs.

> The administration of this qualification [that only five heirs may succeed to any parcel of registered land], however, was turned over to local chiefs and courts rather than to the indigenous institutions or in consultation with them. As a result, the system turned out to be patently absurd, for *inter alia* its implementation depended very heavily on the active co-operation of potential heirs, particularly in the transmission of all relevant information relating to property left by intestate owners. For example, they were expected to report to their local chief the death of persons from whom they expected to inherit land. The chief was then required to transmit that information to the local court for the issuance of a certificate of succession. In that certificate, the court was required to indicate who the heirs and their respective shares were and, where the number exceeded five, to determine who among them would be allowed to succeed and how the rights of those excluded would be dealt with.
>
> To the extent that no provision was made for the participation of indigenous institutions, for example, family councils, clan elders, etc., in this procedure both at its reporting and allocative stages, it remained to all intents and purposes a dead letter. Besides, to the extent that the procedure was patently inequitable, it became the cause of a great deal of *de facto* subdivision that was not reflected in the register. It is not surprising, therefore, that so very few applications for certificates of succession ever came up to the local courts.

This passage by Okoth-Ogendo captures both the cumbersome nature of the bureaucracy, and also the unacceptable distributional consequences associated with disinheriting some of one's children.

Wangari (1990, p. 70), writing on the land registration process in Embu, Kenya, also pointed to the inadequacy of the administrative structure and the simple logistical problems for rural families getting to towns in order to keep up their titles. Such trips can be extremely costly in time and money, and those who have lived in rural Africa will appreciate the fact that every trip to a government office does not necessarily result in finding the appropriate official, much less accomplishing the intended objective.

Many of the costs of land registration are the same regardless of the size of the parcel. It is not surprising, therefore, that the owners of larger parcels maintain their titles more often than do the owners of small (Feder and Noranha, 1987). From their Kenyan study, Migot-Adholla and colleagues (1994, p. 133) reported that only 31.6 percent of households with less than $400 annual income have titles, whereas 87.9 percent of households with income of more than $2,250 per year have titles.[10] Time constraints, fees, and, in resettlement areas, the failure to have fully repaid purchase loans, may explain the variation by wealth in use of titling. Haugerud (1989, p. 84) for Embu, Blarel (1994, p. 90) for Rwanda, Migot-Adhollaand colleagues (1994, p. 102) for Ghana, and Ault and Rutman (1979, p. 177) all suggested that the transaction costs of the registration process are not justified by the economic returns. The Land Tenure Center's comparative data (Bruce *et al.,* 1994, p. 256) estimate that survey and registration costs in smallholder agriculture run at least $50 to $100 per parcel, also calling into question the economics of this process from the point of view of African governments.

Although transaction costs are clearly a relevant issue, they are not the whole story. Large landholders do appear to believe that titling is worth the expense, implying that there is some value (at least to some categories of farmer) in the process of registration. I turn next to the subject of lagging factor markets, which have also been suggested by many people as an explanation for the failure of titling to have positive economic effects.

Lagging Factor Markets in Capital and Labor

If land is not the constraining factor of production, it stands to reason that more formal property rights will accomplish little and probably not recoup their transaction costs. One can assume that the original architects of the Swynnerton plan in Kenya believed that title deeds must precede the widespread availability of credit because commercial lending institutions would require collateral. However, as innumerable researchers have noted, the development of capital markets in Africa, even in land-adjudicated countries like Kenya, has not lived up to expectations (Collier, 1983). Barrows and Roth (1990, p. 276) made the cogent point that when capital is limited by other factors, titling will merely *redistribute* the inelastic supply.

Capital for agricultural investment is the key to the whole success of land registration. Titles were to provide sufficient collateral to open up commercial loans for investment in land improvement and purchase of necessary complementary inputs to raise agricultural productivity. The data on credit in Kenya are not altogether clear. Haugerud (1983, p. 83) reported that only 15 percent of titles from one portion of the Embu coffee and cotton zones had current loans charged against them. However, if one takes into account the fact that households had multiple parcels (46 percent with two, 6 percent with three, and 6 percent with more than four), we arrive at

[10] In Somalia (Roth *et al.,* 1994; p. 225) also found that whereas *all* large farms had title deeds, the same was not true of smaller farms.

an estimate of 26.4 percent of households holding loans in a given year—arguably a healthy credit market. This higher figure seems more consistent with the fact that Haugerud (1983, p. 83) and others have noted that the price of land is "inflated" in part due to the borrowing power that it confers. Highly pertinent, however, is the fact that many of these loans were not used for agricultural development, as has also been reported by others; loans often go for school fees, bridewealth, subsistence, luxury goods, or to purchase more land.

Shipton (1992, p. 374) reported a far lower rate of loans for Luo-land in Kenya. By 1991, 16 years after land registration, only 6 percent of the registered parcels had ever been mortgaged to any financial institution. Okoth-Ogendo (1986, p. 81) reported that in "Kisii and South Nyanza [Luo-land] districts, little more than 2 per cent of registered smallholders were able to obtain secured or unsecured credit in any single year between 1970–1973." Migot-Adholla and associates (1994, p. 134) found a similar level of borrowing in their four Kenyan sites, where from 1987–1988 between 1 and 10.7 percent of households were currently borrowing. But of the 28 formal loans they recorded, only 12 were secured by land title. Citing Odingo's 1985 work, Barrows and Roth (1990, p. 275) report that he

> found that farmers were reluctant to use land as collateral because of fear of losing it. About one-third of those sampled in Machakos had applied for credit, but very few had approached the commercial banks or used land as collateral. Only one per cent had sought credit in Nakuru.

In their quantitative Kenyan study in Njoro, Carter and associates (1994, p. 159) found that capital was the limiting factor constraint for small farms, whereas labor was the limiting constraint for large farms.

One of the most interesting questions raised by these findings is why titles have not led to an increase in the supply of credit. In order to address this question we must delve more deeply into some norms and social practices in African societies. This brings us to the general question of the complementarity between informal institutions and formal land law.

VIII.4.4 Complementarity between Formal and Informal Institutions Regulating Land

Property rights in Africa are intimately wrapped up with kinship relations and rights over people. As Watts (1993, p. 161) put it, "Rights over resources such as land and crops are inseparable from, indeed are isomorphic with, rights over people; to alter property rights is, as Robert Bates (1987) says, to redefine social relationships." On the frontier, pioneers opened land as a means of attracting and controlling large numbers of dependents and followers (Kopytoff, 1987). African agricultural production was and is lineage based in most places. Formal land legislation conflicts with many of the social norms and relationships of production that are still crucial to agricultural success. We have seen the effects of these conflicts in a number of the studies cited earlier; they fall into the following domains: consolidation was inconsistent with the ecological need for scattered strips and broke up cooperative work units, the restrictions on the minimal allowable "economic unit" and the limit on heirs was inconsistent with indigenous norms of inheritance, household composition was highly fluid over time, asymmetries in information were great and meant that the educated were able to manipulate the system and gain what was perceived by others as illegitimate advantage, and, finally, the new property rights reduced the rights of many over the customary system while enhancing those of the single titled "household head." To the extent that formal land tenure change failed to take account of these necessities of sound agricultural management, as well as "prevailing distributional norms" and the "vested interests they create" (Libecap, 1989, p. 116), it failed to take hold and became mired in dispute and, worse yet, disuse.[11]

Lack of Ecological Complementarity: Fragmentation and Consolidation

As originally conceived, the Swynnerton plan in Kenya put a great deal of emphasis on the consolidation of fragments into one "economic unit" per household. A number of authors (including Bates, 1989) have examined the political motivations of the colonial officials who promoted this practice. Although couched in the economic logic of efficiency and agrarian development, there is good reason to believe that consolidation also allowed the British to use land reform as a means of rewarding their friends, that is, the loyalists who fought against the Mau Mau during Kenya's war for independence, which also precipitated land reform. Although consolidation actually appears to have been welcomed later on in some politically less sensitive areas where it was also no longer an ecological necessity (Fleuret, 1988), the Embu experience is probably more typical. Haugerud (1983, p. 74) found that much of the work of consolidation had been undone by the time of her survey in 1979, by which time 58 percent of households had more than one parcel. Embu is an area with high ecological diversity, ranging from the rich tea zone on the slopes of Mount Kenya, through the lucrative coffee area, to the far more arid cotton zone in the low-lying areas that are also good for cattle and where land is less scarce. Historically, households have split their holdings as a form of insurance. Given the re-creation of this pattern, one can only surmise that it still offers benefits that outweigh the costs of travel and dual maintenance.[12]

[11] Watts (1993) has documented exactly such a case study for the Gambia.

[12] In the only quantitative study of which I am aware in Africa on the costs and benefits of fragmentation, Blarel (1994; p. 91) found in Rwanda that the labor loss of walking due to fragmentation is more than compensated by the gains; furthermore, analysis reveals that farm fragmentation is not related to yields.

Fleuret (1988, pp. 149–152) noted that in the Msidunyi area of Taita, where they do not have irrigation, there is a high degree of fragmentation, with the mean number of parcels at 13. Fragmentation is a risk management strategy and there was much resistance to consolidation. In the nearby Iparenyi area of Taita, in contrast, the climate is much more favorable to cash crops such as coffee and there is water for irrigation. As a consequence, agriculture is less risky, farms are less fragmented, and consolidation (along with adjudication and registration) were compete by 1967, only four years after the start of the program in that area. Nevertheless, Fleuret (1988, p. 149) noted an important problem associated with consolidation even in this area:

> [Traditional irrigation is] highly dependent on kinship relations and on the expression of those relations in landholding patterns for its success, in particular the proximity of close agnates due to the partitioning of their father's holdings into individually held portions for each heir. But, in Iparenyi, the act of consolidation has seriously disrupted the landownership pattern on which traditional water management rests. . . . Because the land reform program has as one of its consequences that close agnates no longer necessarily have holdings contiguous to one another, the basis for irrigation management has been transformed. Those who cooperate in such a system in Iparenyi now are business partners whose relationship is commercial rather than consanguine. Of the six existing systems, three are characterized by serious disagreements between the partners which inhibit the availability of water, and one has become privatized.

We see in this case a perfect instance of the trade-off between the economic rationale for consolidation (economies of scale) and the obvious increases in transaction costs due to the loss of kin connectedness that had benefited cooperation.

In a highly analogous situation, land adjudication among Maasai pastoralists has also led to ecologically unviable units under management regimes that have no basis for traditional legitimacy (Coldham, 1979, pp. 620–623). The Maasai were the earliest Kenyan pastoralists to be targeted with land tenure changes aimed at controlling overgrazing and the tragedy of the commons. Coldham (1979; 624) catalogs the misfit with indigenous norms as follows:

> [The group ranch] introduces an alien system of land tenure: it creates boundaries which not only conflict with customary grazing patterns, but are the source of novel distinctions between members, invitees, and trespassers; and it establishes a new system of authority, and calls for the adoption of unfamiliar procedures based on election, representation, delegation, and the majority vote. In practice, as we have seen, the desired changes of behaviour have not occurred. The Masai continue their semi-nomadic existence in search of pasture regardless of ranch boundaries.

Lack of Complementarity with Social Organization: The Problem of Succession

The Swynnerton plan placed a great deal of import on the need to maintain economically viable units of land, and thus it forbade the titling of units below a certain size (determined by local carrying capacity). The number of heirs was also limited to five to prevent rapid fragmentation of parcels through subdivision. As we saw earlier, one response to these limitations was for families to subdivide the land anyway and merely fail to register the subdivisions, thus undermining the entire exercise (Okoth-Ogendo 1986, p. 88). The conflict between the formal system and customary inheritance patterns was great, and in this instance, social institutions clearly outsurvived formal innovation. As Coldham (1979, p. 617) noted, sometimes people were attracted to adjudication as a means to demarcate clear boundaries in areas where disputes were getting out of hand, but they did not intend to buy into a system that would also change their practices of conveyance.

Haugerud (1989, p. 70) made the important point that indigenous household composition was highly fluid and not well suited to the inflexibility of title deeds. Only 20 percent of the households in her sample were nuclear families, which fit best with land registration, while about a quarter of the sample households had considerable changes in membership over her 20-months of fieldwork. Domestic conflict changed the composition of 27 percent of the sample households by one or more members. One of the advantages of customary tenure systems, where transfer rights were retained by the lineage, was the ability to respond quickly and frequently to needs for the reallocation of land.

Lack of Complementarity in Distribution: The Problem of Asymmetries of Information

In the early days of land adjudication in Kikuyu (Sorrenson, 1967) and Embu (Brokensha and Glazier, 1973; Glazier, 1985), there is considerable evidence that the educated elite took advantage of their position to secure far better and larger holdings than their less sophisticated kin. As Bates (1989, pp. 30–31) put it, the educated had strong incentives for changes in property rights, they faced lower costs in pushing legal claims, they spoke the language of the colonizers, and the colonizers were dependent on them for insight into local law and custom. Haugerud (1983, p. 79) described how mere knowledge of the implications of land registration and what was to come were used by the well informed to gain advantage. In the early days, before most people understood what was happening, an assistant chief, his father, and other elders of his clan staked out claims in lowland Embu where the population density was relatively low and rights to land more ambiguous than in the tea and coffee zones. Because of his office, the assistant chief knew what evidence the land boards would consider legitimate for land claims, and the men were able to stake claim to much land prior to adjudication. These men wound up with parcels five to ten times the average size for that zone and also retained large claims in the richer zones.

As Libecap (1989, p. 28) warned, "Distributional conflicts will be intensified if there are known serious information asymmetries among the competing parties regarding the evaluation of individual claims." This was certainly the case in Kenya's past and quite likely in the present. Although the population of Kenya is today quite literate by African standards, there are still large numbers of illiterate farmers (more of whom are women than men), who are vulnerable in the courts as a consequence of their lack of familiarity with legal procedures and their lack of literacy. This is one argument for keeping as many adjudication decisions regarding land as possible closer to the village and out of the courts; in the village, information regarding claims will be greater and the playing field more level (all other things being equal).

Lack of Complementarity in the Distribution of Rights within the Household

When property rights are changed there are always winners and losers. But it stands to reason that the closer the fit between the new and old systems, the less the injustice to prevailing distributions. Libecap (1989, pp. 3–4) suggested that the net social gains from changes in property rights will be modest specifically because the difficulty involved in resolving the distribution conflicts that result is so great. There is ample evidence from the Kenyan situation to support his argument.

We have already noted that the limitation on the number of heirs resulted in disinheritance. So abhorrent was this perceived miscarriage of social justice that households merely let titles lapse rather than disinherit family members. But there were other mismatches of rights between customary tenure systems and formal registration. Most notably, women do most of the farming in Africa, and under customary tenure they were granted considerable control over farmland in the form of usufruct rights and managerial control over the plots allocated to them by the household head. In the absence of a land market, women's access to and control of property was considerable. With land adjudication, this changed markedly. Land was now registered solely in one person's name and this was almost always the male household head. Only 5 percent of parcels in Kenya are registered in women's names, and rarely do sons have registered land while their fathers are still living. With the development of a commercial credit market and a land market, the potential now exists for titled heads of households to sell their land (or lose it through loan default) and thus extinguish all of the usufruct rights of women and the traditional lineage inheritance rights of sons.

Although the Kenyan registration process has always provided some protection for the interests of others against sale of land, the potential for mortgage foreclosure was not guarded in the original law. The protection against sale was built into the law in that the land boards, which had to approve land sales, were specifically entrusted to act paternalistically to look out for the best interests of the landowner and his or her family (Okoth-Ogendo, 1986, p. 84). This meant that they had the authority to reject sales (and frequently did) if they deemed them not to be in the interest of the family on the grounds that the land was the sole source of support for the family or that the remaining holding would be too small a parcel to sustain the family. The boards were also supposed to consult with other interested family members (especially wives and sons) prior to granting sale approval.[13] However, no such control over loss of land due to loan default was built into the system (Okoth-Ogendo, 1986, p. 85).

I would argue that mortgage foreclosure, while it is an emotive issue anywhere, has been especially so in Kenya because of the failure of formal land law to adequately capture the full range of customary rights in land held by other parties. The fact that one member of a family can unilaterally extinguish those claims has caused enormous outrage. This is but one of the many examples in Africa in which an inappropriate model based on the assumption of a unitary household utility function has led to unexpected consequences (cf. Guyer, 1981). Although it may be the most extreme case, the Luo are worth considering in this context, as it is a well-documented case of mortgage foreclosure.

Under customary tenure, Luo households were free to use the land, but a man could not transfer the rights of the lineage or his heirs by sale or gift to a stranger (Coldham, 1978, p. 94). Although Luo-land was one of the areas in Kenya that moved to greater privatization before land reform, land sales were rare and usually to clansmen. Shipton (1992, p. 380) explained that the Luo have a segmentary lineage system and each genealogy is literally reflected in the landscape by the pattern of burials on local farms. Like many African peoples, the Luo revere the ancestors, who are buried on the family plot. To the Luo (p. 375), "mortgaging the land is mortgaging the ancestors." Bank efforts to foreclose on land consistently meet with resistance or violence. People suspect that witchcraft is used against those buyers who try to settle but eventually leave (p. 377). As one women commented, "If you want to make an enemy for life, mess with a dead Luo" (p. 377). Land auctions have often been canceled for fear of violence or political repercussion, and for 13 months the AFC suspended its loan recovery program altogether (p. 378).

Under these circumstances, it is not surprising that banks place rela-

[13] It is not clear how much local variation there was in practice concerning this stipulation.

tively little value upon title deeds as collateral for loans. They have learned that the prospects of foreclosure, at least in some areas, are too low to warrant the risk. Obviously this must affect the supply of credit and account at least in part for the failure of the anticipated increase in credit that was expected to flow from land registration. Thus, we see that what might appear as a "lagging factor market," has its roots more deeply in a failure of social complementarity between formal and informal norms and social organization. But is the root of the problem here really the segmentary lineage system of the Luo (as Shipton suggests) or the failure to properly acknowledge and give legal authority to the rights of all vested parties—namely, wives, widows, and sons—who may have had greater tenure security under customary law?

VIII.4.5 Government Response—Revision in the Formal Law

Over the years there have been efforts on the part of the Kenyan government to respond to many of the perceived failings of the original land law, but these have never resulted in reversal of the general trend toward greater privatization. Interestingly, changes in the land law have been consistently in the direction of greater fit with customary law.

In 1968 the land act was revised and, most notably, compulsory consolidation was abandoned (Okoth-Ogendo, 1986, p. 83). Given the highly political as opposed to economic motives for the original consolidation initiative under colonialism (see Bates, 1989), it is not surprising that this was one of the first inconsistencies with customary practice to go.

In 1972 the government also repealed the limit on the number of heirs who could inherit registered property (Sections 120 and 121 of the Registered Land Act, Government of Kenya, 1989, p. 58; see also Okoth-Ogendo, 1986). Although this constraint undoubtedly dissuaded some people from trying to register successions that would have been deemed illegal, its repeal by no means led to complete registration of subdivisions. Most of the studies cited earlier that documented the failure to register successions were carried out after the change in the law.

One of the most far reaching and potentially interesting changes in land law is still underway. In 1991, by decree, President Moi ordered that all land foreclosures must be approved by the provincial administration, a more cumbersome process than the courts (Shipton, 1992, p. 378). This formalized a policy that he had been promoting since the late 1980s in public meetings and the press. In the late 1980s an increasing number of mortgage foreclosures were making it into the popular press (Laban Gwako, personal communication). In populist fashion, the president made an issue of standing up on the side of the innocent who were rendered landless when kin defaulted on loans over which they had no control.

Wangari (1990, p. 92) cited a newspaper account from the most widely read Kenyan English-language paper (*Daily Nation,* June 21, 1989) that captures the tone of the president's position, and he specifically remarked on the failure of formal law to adequately account for customary law. On this occasion the president called upon the courts to "consider the traditional tenets of [a] particular society, especially when passing judgment [in] matters that affect land." At issue in this case was a foreclosure and sale of land due to the default on a large loan by the eldest son who inherited the titles to all of his father's land as trustee for his mother, her cowife, and his brothers. Due to the foreclosure and subsequent sale, all were rendered landless. President Moi personally refunded the purchase price to the new buyer and issued new title deeds to the one surviving widow and one son of each widow. The rest of the article describes the speech by President Moi upon his visit to the community:

> Respect Traditions, Moi Tells Courts
>
> President [Moi] said that through generations, people had acquire[d] traditional and social norms in which their lives were deeply rooted. He said that if written laws negated against the traditional aspects of life, or caused distress after failure to consider them, then injustice is done.
>
> The president observed that this particular case was a classic example of acute suffering and haplessness of a family due to hasty judgments delivered without considering their wider implications.
>
> President Moi said the ordinary people could easily be exploited due to their ignorance of legal technicalities adding that it was unfair to take land cases to courts.
>
> He said the provincial administration and elders ought to consult and find the root cause of any land dispute with a view to solving the problem amicably.
>
> The President added that in settling such a dispute, the traditional aspects of land ownership should be catered for.

This change in land policy is actually more significant than it may appear. Two things are happening simultaneously: more land transactions are being moved out of the courts and back to the local land boards and those boards are under more pressure than before to hear evidence from wives, sons, and other parties with legitimate customary rights in the land, prior to authorizing any land sale (Richard Kisiara, personal communication).[14] Both the movement of land cases from the courts to the local level, and the

[14] Richard Kisiara was carrying out research in Uasin Gishu District, Kenya in 1993–1994. He reported that title holders wishing to sell land had to bring their wives and sons to the chief, who wrote a letter to the land board in that location verifying that the sale was agreed to by the family. This, of course, does not prevent the intimidation of wives, which was common. In one case followed by Kisiara, the wife did refuse the sale, the chief refused to authorize it, and the wife was badly beaten by her husband.

increased emphasis on consent of the family in all land matters could represent subtle but far-reaching departures from past practice.

It was noted earlier that the educated elite have distinct advantages in the court system. At the village level, however, not only do those advantages diminish, but they have some actual disadvantages. As elites, their ties may be more solidly rooted in the urban areas and they may not be as versed in customary law as their less-educated kin who have lived their entire life in the village. The shift from the courts to the village-level also affects the level of information that is brought to bear on land cases. No one knows the facts better than those closer "to the ground."

There is much support in the theoretical literature for leaving control of property rights to local communities (Ostrom, 1990). One reason for this is that information is greater at the local level and this facilitates rapid synchronous adjustment (Ault and Rutman, 1979, p. 171) as well as better cooperation and easier resolution of disputes. We have seen that communities all over Africa evolved more private property rights without the intervention of national governments and these systems often functioned remarkably effectively. However, the same pressures that drive the choice of increased privatization often bring a dissolution of community and a failure of local enforcement (Ensminger and Rutten, 1991). Fleuret (1988, p. 142) reports that land disputes under customary tenure rose in Taita in the 1940s with the increasing value of land (cf. Coldham, 1978, p. 95). Brokensha and Glazier (1973) have a beautiful description of the demise of the traditional oathing practice, which was used by the Mbeere to resolve land disputes prior to adjudication. Increasing inequality in that community had undermined the traditional system. Once it was known that land adjudication was coming, people stored up their grievances for the anticipated land board that was to be put into place for land registration rather than use the traditional oathing ritual (which had lost effectiveness) or the courts (which they distrusted). Here we have a case where the indigenous system appears to have no longer been capable of handling the pressure of increasing land values.

VIII.5 CONCLUSION

Anthropologists talk of the need for "contextual fit" in policy development (Shipton, 1992, p. 381), sociologists talk about "embeddedness" (Granovetter, 1985), and institutional economists talk about the need for formal institutions to build upon informal institutions (North, 1990). I suspect all of these theorists are talking to some degree about the same thing, but the abstractness of this language can obscure a great deal. There are, in fact, significant similarities and differences in the theoretical positions of all of these authors. I believe that by applying the concepts and theory to empirical case studies we are better able to move the debate forward and clarify points of agreement and difference.

I attempt in this chapter to show that "contextual fit," or what I refer to as the complementarity between formal and informal institutions, really is crucial to successful property right change. But in my analysis I do not abandon a rational choice framework in which farmers make calculated choices concerning property rights under the constraints of prevailing distributional norms and their production systems. It just so happens that in Africa a large number of these constraints are connected to social relationships and kin. However, unlike some anthropologists, I am less persuaded that ideological issues such as attachment to the ancestors in the ground are such strong constraints on choice regarding major economic decisions such as those dealing with property rights. Violation of distributional norms, on the other hand, is a powerful motivation, perhaps too often overlooked by economists (see Knight, 1992). Equally, embeddedness does not for me mean resistance to change, as I believe is well brought out in the evidence of the indigenous narrowing of social orbits and embrace of privatization in the face of rising land values. For me, embeddedness means synchrony in change. During periods of rapid and intense exogenous shock, such as prevails in much of contemporary Africa, such adjustments may best be left to indigenous local institutions. However, there is ample evidence that these same exogenous shocks lead to increasing inequality and local heterogeneity, which eventually erode community and the cooperation, low transaction costs, and high self-enforcement that it affords (Taylor and Singleton, 1993). Once this occurs, indigenous institutions may no longer be able to cope effectively and could benefit from national formal institutions designed as carefully as possible to fit with prevailing relations of production and distributional norms. Identifying the proper point and means of intervention is obviously *the* challenge for policy planners, and it will demand a deep understanding of indigenous norms and local institutions.

ACKNOWLEDGMENTS

The author thanks Yoram Brazel, Thráinn Eggertsson, Andrew Rutten, and Barry Weingast for detailed comments on this paper; helpful comments were also received from the audiences at Washington University in St. Louis, the University of California at Berkeley, and the University at Los Angeles, where this paper was presented.

REFERENCES

Allan, W. (1965). *The African Husbandman.* Greenwood Press, Westport, CT.

Ault, D., and Rutman, G. (1979). The development of individual rights to property in tribal Africa. *Journal of Law and Economics* **22**(1), 163–182.

Barrows, R., and Roth, M. (1990). Land tenure and investment in African agriculture: Theory and evidence. *Journal of Modern African Studies* **28**(2), 265–297.

Barzel, Y. (1989). *Economic Analysis of Property Rights.* Cambridge University Press, New York.

Bates, R. (1987). The agrarian origins of Mau Mau. *Agricultural History* **61,** 1–28.

Bates, R. (1989). *Beyond the Miracle of the Market: The Political Economy of Agrarian Development in Kenya.* Cambridge University Press, New York.

Berry, S. (1988). Concentration without privatization? Some consequences of changing patterns of rural land control in Africa. In *Land and Society in Contemporary Africa* (R. E. Downs and S. P. Reyna, eds. pp. 53–75). University Press of New England, Hanover, NH.

Blarel, B. (1994). Tenure security and agricultural production under land security: The case of Rwanda. In *Searching for Land Tenure Security in Africa.* (J. Bruce and S. Migot-Adholla, eds. pp. 71–95) Kendall/Hunt Pub. Co., Dubuque, IA.

Boserup, E. (1981). *Population and Technological Change.* University of Chicago Press, Chicago.

Brokensha, D., and Glazier, J. (1973). Land reform among the Mbeere of Central Kenya. *Africa* **43**(3), 182–206.

Bruce, J., and Migot-Adholla, S., eds. (1994). *Searching for Land Tenure Security in Africa.* Kendall/Hunt Pub. Co. Dubuque, IA.

Bruce, J., Migot-Adholla, S., and Atherton, J. (1994). The findings and their policy implications: Institutional adaptation or replacement? In *Searching for Land Tenure Security in Africa* (J. Bruce and S. Migot-Adholla, eds. pp. 251–265). Kendall/Hunt Pub. Co., Dubuque, IA.

Carter, M., Wiebe, K., and Blarel, B. (1994). Tenure security for whom? Differential effects of land policy in Kenya. In *Searching for Land Tenure Security in Africa* (J. Bruce and S. Migot-Adholla, eds. pp. 141–168). Kendall/Hunt Pub. Co. Dubuque, IA.

Chanock, M. (1991). A peculiar sharpness: An essay on property in the history of customary law in colonial Africa. *Journal of African History* **32,** 65–88.

Coldham, S. (1978). The effect of registration of title upon customary land rights in Kenya. *Journal of African Law* **22,** 91–111.

Coldham, S. (1979). Land-tenure reform in Kenya: The limits of law. *Journal of Modern African Studies* **17**(4), 615-627.

Collier, P. (1983). Malfunctioning of African rural factor markets: Theory and a Kenyan example. *Oxford Bulletin of Economics and Statistics* **45**(2), 141–172.

Colson, E. (1971). The Impact of the colonial period on the definition of land rights. In *Colonialism in Africa* (P. Duignan and L. Gann, eds.), Vol. 3. Cambridge University Press, Cambridge, UK.

Demsetz, H. (1967). Toward a theory of property rights. *American Economic Review* **57**(2), 347–359.

Denzau, A., and North, D. C. (1994). Shared mental models: Ideology and institutions. *Kyklos* **47**(1), 1–31.

Dobson, E. B. (1954). Comparative land tenure of ten Tanganyika tribes. *Journal of African Administration* **80**(6).

Ega, L. A. (1979). Security of tenure in a transitory farming system: The case of Zaria villages in Nigeria. *Agricultural Administration* **6**(4), 287-297.

Eggertsson, T. (1990). *Economic Behavior and Institutions.* Cambridge University Press, Cambridge, UK.

Eggertsson, T. (1994). *Property Rights, Economic Analysis and the Information Problem. Workshop in Political Theory and Policy Analysis.* Indiana University Press, Indiana.

Ensminger, J. (1992). *Making a Market: The Institutional Transformation of an African Society.* Cambridge University Press, New York.

Ensminger, J., and Knight, J. (1997). Changing social norms: Common property, bridewealth, and clan exogamy. *Current Anthropology* **38**(1) (in press).

Ensminger, J., and Rutten, A. (1991). The political economy of changing property rights: Dismantling a pastoral commons. *American Ethnologist* **18**(4), 683–699.

Feder, G., and Noronha, R. (1987). Land rights systems and agricultural sevelopment in Sub-Saharan Africa. *Research Observer* **2**(2), 143–169.

Feder, G., and Onchan, T. (1987). Land ownership security and farm investment in Thailand. *American Journal of Agricultural Economics* **69:** 311–320.

Firmin-Sellers, K. (1996). *Custom and Capitalism: The Transformation of Property Rights in the Gold Coast, 1927-1957.* Cambridge University Press, Cambridge, UK.

Fleuret, A. (1988). Some consequences of Tenure and Agrarian Reform in Taita, Kenya. In *Land and Society in Contemporary Africa* (R.E. Downs and S.P. Reyna, eds. pp. 136–158). University Press of New England, Hanover, NH.

Galaty, J. (1980). The Maasai Group-Ranch: Politics and development in an African pastoral society. In *When Nomads Settle* (P. C. Saltzman, ed.), pp. 157–172. Praeger, New York.

Glazier, J. (1985). *Land and the Use of Tradition Among the Mbeere of Kenya.* University Press of America, Lanham, MD.

Government of Kenya (1989). *The Register Land Act.* Government Printing Office, Nairobi, Kenya.

Granovetter, M. (1985). Economic action and social structure: The problem of embeddedness. *American Journal of Sociology* **91**(3), 481–510.

Greif, A. (1994). Cultural beliefs and the organization of society. *Journal of Political Economy* **102**(5), 912–950.

Guyer, J. (1981). Household and community in African studies. *African Studies Review* **24,** 114.

Hailey, W. (1957). *An African Survey.* Oxford University Press, London.

Haugerud, A. (1983). The consequences of land tenure reform among smallholders in the Kenya highlands. *Rural Africana* **15/16,** 65–89.

Haugerud, A. (1989). Land tenure and agrarian change in Kenya. *Africa* **59**(1), 61–90.

Hecht, R. (1985). Immigration, land transfer and tenure changes in Divo, Ivory Coast, 1940–1980. *Africa* **55**(3), 319-336.

Hogg, R. (1990). The politics of changing property rights among Isiolo Boran pastoralists in northern Kenya. In *Property, Poverty and People: Changing Rights in Property and Problems of Pastoral Development,* (P. Baxter and R. Hogg, eds.), pp. 20-31. University of Manchester Press, Manchester.

Homan, F. D. (1963). Succession to registered land in the African areas of Kenya. *Journal of Local Administration Overseas* (London) **2**(1).

Knight, J. (1992). *Institutions and Social Conflict.* Cambridge University Press, Cambridge, UK.

Koby, A. T. (1979). Projection des formations sociales sur l'espace: Example du pays Odzukru en Côte D'Ivoire. In *Maitrise de l'espace agraire et developpement en Afrique tropical.* ORSTOM, Paris.

Kopytoff, I. (1987). *The African Frontier: The Reproduction of Traditional African Societies.* Indiana University Press, Bloomington.

Leakey, L. (1977). *The Southern Kikuyu Before 1904.* Academic Press, New York.

Levin, M. (1976). Family structure in Bakosi: Social change in an African society. Ph.D. Dissertation, Princeton University, Princeton, NJ.

Libecap, G. D. (1989). *Contracting for Property Rights.* Cambridge University Press, New York.

Malcolm, D. M. (1953). *Sukumaland: An African People and Their Country.* Oxford University Press, London.

Matlon, P (1994). Land tenure security and agricultural performance in Africa: Overview of research methodology. In *Searching for Land Tenure Security in Africa.* (J. Bruce and S. Migot-Adholla, eds. pp. 41–70). Kendall/Hunt Publ. Co., Dubuque, IA.

Middleton, J (1961). *Land Tenure in Zanzibar,* Colonial Res. Stud. No. 33. H.M. Stationery Office, London.

Migot-Adholla, S., and Bruce J. (1994). Introduction: Are indigenous African tenure systems insecure? In *Searching for Land Tenure Security in Africa.* (J. Bruce and S. Migot-Adholla, eds. pp. 1–13). Kendall/Hunt Publ. Co., Dubuque, IA.

Migot-Adholla, S., Benneh, G. Place, F., and Atsu, S. (1994). Land, security of tenure, and productivity in Ghana. In *Searching for Land Tenure Security in Africa.* (J. Bruce and S. Migot-Adholla, eds., pp. 97–118). Kendall/Hunt Publ. Co., Dubuque, IA.

Migot-Adholla, S., Place, F., and Oluoch-Kosura, W. (1994). Security of tenure and land productivity in Kenya. In *Searching for Land Tenure Security in Africa.* (J. Bruce and S. Migot-Adholla, eds., pp. 119–140). Kendall/Hunt Publ. Co., Dubuque, IA.

Muriuki, G. (1974). *A History of the Kikuyu 1500–1900.* Oxford University Press, New York.

Netting, R. (1965). Household organization and intensive agriculture: The Kofyar Case. *Africa* **35**(4), 422–429.

Netting, R. (1968). *Hill Farmers of Nigeria: Cultural Ecology of the Kofyar of the Jos Plateau.* University of Washington Press, Seattle.

Netting, R. (1993). Smallholders, Households: Farm Families and the Ecology of Intensive, Sustainable Agriculture. Stanford University Press, Stanford, CA.

Nkunya, G. K. (1974). *Land Tenure and Agricultural Development in the Angola Area of the Volta Region.* Land Tenure Center Paper No. 120. University of Wisconsin, Land Tenure Center, Madison.

North, D. C. (1981). *Structure and Change in Economic History.* W. W. Norton, New York.

North, D. C. (1990). *Institutions, Institutional Change and Economic Performance.* Cambridge University Press, Cambridge, UK.

North, D. C. and Thomas, R. (1973). *The Rise of the Western World: A New Economic History.* Cambridge University Press, New York.

Odingo, R. S. (1985). *The Dynamics of Land Tenure and of Agrarian Systems in Africa: Land Tenure Study in the Nakuru, Kericho and Machakos Areas of the Kenya Highlands.* U.N. Food and Agriculture Organization, Rome.

Okoth-Ogendo, H. W. O. (1986). In The perils of land tenure reform: The case of Kenya. In *Land Policy and Agriculture in Eastern and Southern Africa.* (J. W. Artzen, L. D. Ngcongco, and S. D. Turner, eds. The United Nations University, Tokyo.

Okoth-Ogendo, H. W. O. (1993). Agrarian reform in Sub-Saharan Africa: An assessment of state responses to the African agrarian crisis and their implications for agricultural development. In *Land in African Agrarian Systems.* (T. Bassett and D. Crummy, eds.), pp. 247–273. University of Wisconsin Press, Madison.

Ostrom, E. (1990). *Governing the Commons: The Evolution of Institutions for Collective Action.* Cambridge University Press, New York.

Parkin, D. (1972). *Palms, Wine, and Witness: Public Spirit and Private Gain in an African Farming Community.* Chandler Publishing Co., San Francisco.

Pedraza, G. J. W. (1956). Land consolidation in the Kikuyu areas of Kenya. *Journal of African Administration* **8,** 82–87.

Peters, . (1992). Manoeuvres and debates in the interpretation of land rights in Botswana. *Africa* **62**(3), 413–434.

Pitblado, J. R. (1981). *The North Mkata Plain, Tanzania: A Study of Land Capability and Land Tenure.* University of Toronto Press, Toronto.

Place, F., and Hazell, P. (1993). Productivity Effects of indigenous land tenure systems in Sub-Saharan Africa. *American Journal of Agricultural Economics* **75,** 10–19.

Putnam, R. (1993). *Making Democracy Work: Civic Traditions in Modern Italy.* Princeton University Press, Princeton, NJ.

Roth, M., Unruh, J., and Barrows, R. (1994). Land registration, tenure security, credit use, and investment in the Shebelle Region of Somalia. In *Searching for Land Tenure Security in Africa* (J. Bruce and S. Migot-Adholla, eds. pp. 199–230) Kendall/Hunt Publ. Co., Dubuque, IA.

Shipton, P. (1988). The Kenyan land tenure reform: Misunderstandings in the public creation of private property. In *Land and Society in Contemporary Africa* (R. E. Downs and St. Reyna, eds. pp. 91–135). University Press of New England, Hanover, NH.

Shipton, P. (1992). Debts and trespasses: Land, mortgages and the ancestors in western Kenya. *Africa* **62**(3), 357-388.

Shipton, P. (1994). Land and culture in tropical Africa: Soils, symbols, and the metaphysics of the mundane. *Annual Review of Anthropology* **23,** 347–377.

Sorrenson, M. P. K. (1967). *Land Reform in the Kikuyu Country: A Study in Government Policy.* University Press, London.

Swynnerton, R. J. M. (1954). *A Plan to Intensify the Development of African Agriculture in Kenya.* Nairobi: Government Printer.

Taylor, M., and Singleton, S. (1993). The communal resource: Transaction costs and the solution of collective action problems. *Politics & Society* **21**(2), 195–214.

University of Arizona, Arid Lands Natural Resources Committee (1979). *Etude sur la commericalisation du bétail et de la vivande dans le département de Zinder, Niger* (prepared by Amould Kinni). University of Arizona press, Tucson.

Wangari, E. (1990). Effects of land registration on small-scale farming in Kenya: The case of Mbeere in Embu District. Ph.D. Dissertation, The New School for Social Research, New York.

Watts, M. (1993). Idioms of land and labor: Producing politics and rice in Senegambia. In *Land in African Agrarian System.* (T. Bassett and D. Crummy, eds.), pp. 157–193. University of Wisconsin Press, Madison.

IX Intertemporal Institutions

Robert H. Bates
Kenneth A. Shepsle

> *The population of approximately six hundred was divided into rather sharply divided age grades with the old gray-haired men constituting a governing body. They were promoted to the office on the basis of age, relieved of physical labor, provided with food from the common stock, and placed in control of the distribution of food. Consequently, the choicest diet was often reserved for them.*
>
> (*Simmons, 1945; p. 31*)

IX.1 INTRODUCTION

Traditionally, anthropologists study societies that are non-Western, agrarian, and poor. They return from their labors to challenge those who make universal claims. Anthropologists challenge moral philosophers who propound notions of what is universally right and good; what is moral in one society, they reveal, is not in another (Mead, 1942). Anthropologists challenge psychological theorists, marshaling evidence of the contrasting emotional responses of persons in different cultures (Whiting and Child, 1953), and they challenge economists, whose claims of "universal laws" they refute with evidence drawn from precapitalist societies. From the vantage point of anthropology, few patterns are universal; human behavior is shaped by the idiosyncracies of social context.

Two features of the anthropological critique of economics stand out. One is their claim that in non-Western and underdeveloped societies, economic processes remain "embedded" within social relations; production and exchange do not take place in the autonomous, anonymous marketplace.[1] As stated by Dalton (1971; pp. 204–205):[2]

> Unlike the economist who can analyze important features of industrial capitalism (such as price and income determination) without considering social relationships, the economic anthropologist concerned with the *organization* of primitive economies finds there is no separate economic system that can be analyzed independently of social organization.

A second is that in non-Western and underdeveloped societies, the allocation of resources is not the result of decisions taken by isolated individuals; rather, it is taken by individuals acting in family and kinship units. Thus Sahlins (1972; p. 187), writing on "stone age economics," devoted two of his book's six chapters to "the domestic mode of production," and in a third he wrote:

> exchange in primitive communities has not the same role as the economic flow in modern industrial communities. . . . The bias is that . . . of a domestic mode of production: of household producing units, division of labor by sex and age . . . , [and] production that looks to familial requirements. . . . It is the bias . . . of societies ordered in the main by kinship.

The anthropologists' challenge to economists extends to political scientists as well. Economists might expect to find the operations of the market standing independent of the kinship system, and, anthropologists demonstrate, they would be wrong. Political scientists might expect to find an autonomous sphere of politics, and, anthropologists reveal, they too would be wrong. Just as there is no autonomous operation of market forces in many agrarian societies, there are often no states (Evans-Pritchard, 1940; Fortes and Evans-Pritchard, 1940). Rather, in many societies, political "functions" are performed by kinship structures.[3] Anthropologists have studied the politics of societies that lack states, and they have shown the way in which kin relations enable such societies to furnish themselves with collective goods, such as defense, peace, and the enforcement of property rights (Fortes and Evans-Pritchard, 1940).

In this chapter, we respond to the challenge posed by anthropologists. Although we employ economic forms of reasoning, we embed rational agents within a social structure that resembles that of a family. Within this

[1] The father of this position is, of course, Karl Polanyi (1957). For a more recent treatment, see Dalton (1967, 1971).

[2] Dalton took an extreme position, but one echoed by others. See, for example, Berry (1985) or Guyer (1995). For an influential exposition of this position, see Granovetter (1985).

[3] The language is that of A. R. Radcliffe-Brown (1952). It was, of course, taken up by political scientists, most notably in Almond and Coleman (1960).

structure, rational agents begin as infants, mature into young adults, and then achieve senior status. When they die, they are replaced by the next generation. Employing this framework, we find that, as anthropologists contend, societies based on kinship, rather than on markets or states, can produce goods, including public goods such as defense, peace, or security. We argue that this simple structure helps to explain why in areas with low population densities, public goods are provided by kinship systems, while in areas with dense populations, they are more often provided by states. It also helps us to understand why, in a given area, governance based initially on kinship may later be provided by bureaucracies. The analysis also offers insight into the internal structure of modern organizations—bureaucracies, firms, and legislatures—in which there is a division of labor, and of rewards, between seniors and juniors. The important implication of our analysis is that diversity, as celebrated by anthropologists, need not imply the absence of "universal" processes.

IX.2 AN APPROACH TO INTERTEMPORAL INSTITUTIONS

The starting point for our analysis is a demographic model in which there is a group consisting of T generations, each of which has N members. At each time period t, the oldest generation "dies" (or otherwise retires from the group) and a new generation is "born" (or otherwise enters group life). Thus, at any time period there are NT members.[4] Each member of the oldest generation at time t, born $t - T + 1$ periods ago, has only the current period remaining in the group; the members of the youngest generation have $T - 1$ periods remaining after the current one. Their interactions in each period constitute a game in which the members of each generation must decide whether to contribute to the production of a public good, such as defense.

This setting, which may be generalized or specialized in any number of ways (some of which we pursue shortly), is modeled by Cremer (1986) as a multiperiod prisoners' dilemma involving overlapping generations of players. To provide the reader with intuition, we present an especially clean version crafted by Cooper and Daughety (1989). Cooper and Daughety model the provision of a public good the production of which varies linearly with member contributions, which we call "effort." Let $e_t^{i\tau} \in \{0, 1\}$ be the level of effort contributed by member i of generation τ at time t. Thus, the amount

[4] Most of the insights of our argument are conveyed in the setting in which every generation is of the same size, N. But, as we will show when we examine what happens when there is a demographic "shock" (a baby-boom generation), the qualitative conclusions go through with generations of different population size.

of public good provided at time t is $\sum_{k=0,T-1}\sum_{j=1,N} e_t^{j,t-k}$. Effort is costly; in particular, in units in which the public good is calibrated, individual effort costs α. Consequently, for any member of generation τ, his or her *period* t *payoff* is

$$\Pi_t^{i,\tau} = \sum_{k=0,T-1}\sum_{j=1,N} e_t^{j,t-k} - \alpha\, e_t^{i,\tau}. \tag{1}$$

For $\alpha > 1$, the cost of effort exceeds the benefit to its contributor, so that it is not rational to contribute in any stage game with payoff function (1). However, for $\alpha < NT$, it would be desirable for everyone to "do the irrational" and contribute, since $\Pi_t^{i,\tau} > 0$ for all i in this circumstance. Thus, for $1 < \alpha < NT$, equation (1) gives the payoff function of an n-person prisoners' dilemma: if everyone contributes, all enjoy positive benefits; but $e_t^{i,\tau} = 0$ is a dominant strategy.

Our analysis begins with an intertemporal setting conceived as one of overlapping generations of individuals repeatedly engaged in the game, the stage-game payoff of which is given in (1). Note that this structure of repeated interactions among members of overlapping generations "fits demographic reality" (Cooper and Daughety, 1989, p. 4) better than conventional finite and infinite horizon repeat-play formulations. A standard method for explicating the prisoners' dilemma, and resolving the tension therein between individual rationality and social optimality, is to examine it in repeated play by *infinite*-lived individuals. But people are not infinitely lived; it therefore does not follow that the punishment strategies that induce the provision of public goods by infinite-lived agents holds for their finite-lived brethren. The overlapping-generations framework with finite-lived players, developed by Cremer (1986) and Cooper and Daughety (1989), provides an alternative specification. In such a framework, people clearly possess incentives to "defect" in the last period of their lives (since there is no "future" in which to punish them). Likewise, the prisoners'-dilemma incentive to free-ride remains. Nonetheless, it may be shown that societies of rational individuals, embedded in overlapping generations, can achieve the positive provision of public goods as a subgame perfect equilibrium.[5]

Consider a putative equilibrium in which any member of the group contributes effort for the first T^* periods of her life and then shirks thereafter; thus, a member from generation τ contributes in periods τ, τ +

[5] The second conventional treatment of the repeat-play prisoners' dilemma game involves *finite*-lived individuals. Because it lacks an overlapping-generations demographic structure, all individuals are effectively members of the same generation. In this setting, the equilibrium is one in which none of the public good is produced. From the logic of backward induction, the repeat-play situation "unravels" with no individual making a positive contribution in any period.

$1, \ldots, \tau + T^* - 1$, and then shirks from period $\tau + T^*$ until she dies after period $\tau + T - 1$. In a slight emendation of the Cooper and Daughety formulation, we suggest that this behavior can be sustained by the (credible) threat of ostracism: if any agent younger than T^* shirks, she is banished from the group, a circumstance yielding her a subsequent per-period utility of zero.[6] Cooper and Daughety prove the following proposition:

Proposition 1 (Cooper and Daughety): For the game with period t payoff function (1) in which $1 < \alpha < NT$, if (i) $(T - T^*)T^* = (\alpha - 1)/N$ and (ii) $T^2/4 \geq (\alpha - 1)/N$, then there exists a T^* such that the intertemporal strategy in which every member of each generation contributes for his or her first T^* periods and shirks thereafter is a subgame perfect equilibrium.

A sketch of the proof begins by noting that an agent from generation τ would not wish to defect when she reached age $\tau + T^* - 1$, her last period of contribution. If she continues to follow the stipulated equilibrium behavior by contributing effort for one more period, then she receives $NT^* - \alpha$ that period followed by $(T - T^*)$ periods in which she receives a utility of NT^* (assuming in all these periods that everyone else contributes who is supposed to). This amounts to a total payoff from that point on of $(T - T^* + 1)NT^* - \alpha$. If, on the other hand, she defects by failing to work and is ostracized by the group from the next period of her life until its end, her payoff is $NT^* - 1$, followed by zero thereafter. These payoffs are equal when condition (i) of Proposition 1 is satisfied, so that an agent exactly $(T^* - 1)$ periods old is indifferent between following and deviating from the equilibrium path. However, an agent one period younger will definitely contribute since, if he does not, the punishment period will be a period more and the periods of reward from social cooperation will be one less. (By parallel argument, an agent one period older will definitely shirk.) So, if a T^* exists satisfying (i) in Proposition 1, social production of the public good can be sustained. Condition (ii) of the proposition gives the requirement for such a T^* to exist.[7]

From (1) it is straightforward, albeit notationally inelegant, to compute the lifetime utility of any group member from generation τ as $\Sigma_{t = \tau, \tau + T - 1}$

[6] Cooper and Daughety showed that trigger strategies sustain this equilibrium: if any one person shirks before he or she is T^* periods old, *everyone* stops contributing thereafter and the group effectively disbands. Ostracism, with group interaction continuing minus the ostracized individual, is thus *a fortiori* credible. We revisit the issue of credible enforcement in the concluding section.

[7] The proof is found in Cooper and Daughety (1989). In effect, condition (ii) gives the requirement for the graph of the function defined on the left-hand side of (i) to intersect the graph of the (constant) function on the right-hand side, rather than lie entirely below it.

$\Pi_t^{i,\tau}$, appropriately discounted if necessary. It is easy to show that this is a (weakly) monotonic function of N (the size of each generation). Monotonicity is a consequence of two effects. First, for the given equilibrium number of contribution periods, T^*, more individuals are contributing as N increases, thereby increasing per-period utility as given in (1). Second, T^* increases with N (the value of T^* that solves (i) in Proposition 1 is monotonic in N and (ii) holds a *fortiori*). Thus we have the following corollary:

Corollary to Proposition 1: Suppose that the generation born at τ is of size $N_\tau > N$. The equilibrium level of production of the public good remains an equilibrium (indeed, higher levels may now be sustainable), and lifetime utility of every generation alive during τ's lifetime is increased.

IX.3 AN ILLUSTRATION

To see how this demographic framework provides a sustainable means of providing public goods,[8] consider the case of a group in which life expectancy is three periods ($T = 3$)—young, middle-aged, and old. Suppose further that the steady state in this group is one in which each generation consists of a single individual ($N = 1$). Thus, at any time t there are three generations alive (of one person each), as displayed in Table IX.3.1. This ongoing situation is picked up there at time $t = -3$ when the young, middle-aged, and old generations are G_{-3}, G_{-4}, and G_{-5}, respectively. At the beginning of period $t = -2$, G_{-5} dies and is replaced by G_{-2}. A similar replacement occurs at $t = -1$. The first three rows of Table IX.3.2 display the equilibrium of Proposition 1. During the steady-state population periods,

TABLE IX.3.1 Cross-sectional and Longitudinal Display of Generations

	Time (t)								
	−3	−2	−1	0	1	2	3	4	5
Generations									
Y	G_{-3}	G_{-2}	G_{-1}	$\mathbf{G_0}$	G_1	G_2	G_3	G_4	G_5
M	G_{-4}	G_{-3}	G_{-2}	G_{-1}	$\mathbf{G_0}$	G_1	G_2	G_3	G_4
O	G_{-5}	G_{-4}	G_{-3}	G_{-2}	G_{-1}	$\mathbf{G_0}$	G_1	G_2	G_3

[8] For an earlier study of the sustainability of such systems, see Chapter 5 of Legesse (1973).

TABLE IX.3.2 Equilibrium Strategies and Payoffs

	Strategies			Payoffs		
	e_t^y	e_t^m	e_t^o	Π_t^y	Π_t^m	Π_t^o
Time (t)						
−3	1	1	0	$2-\alpha$	$2-\alpha$	2
−2	1	1	0	$2-\alpha$	$2-\alpha$	2
−1	1	1	0	$2-\alpha$	$2-\alpha$	2
0	2	1	0	$3-\alpha$	$3-\alpha$	3
1	1	2	0	$3-\alpha$	$3-\alpha$	3
2	1	1	0	$2-\alpha$	$2-\alpha$	2
3	1	1	0	$2-\alpha$	$2-\alpha$	2
4	1	1	0	$2-\alpha$	$2-\alpha$	2
5	1	1	0	$2-\alpha$	$2-\alpha$	2

each member's (undiscounted) lifetime utility is $6 - 2\alpha$ derived from working while young and middle-aged and shirking while old; this payoff is positive for $\alpha < 3$, thus illustrating the claim of Proposition 1. Even in the absence of formal political institutions, then, a *demographic structure*—one based on birth and death with persons progressing through generations—yields the provision of public goods.

Let the demographic process proceed. What is striking is that in societies organized in overlapping generations, increased population leads to the *strengthening* of incentives to provide public goods.

Return to Table IX.3.1 and note that a perturbation occurs at $t = 0$, disturbing the steady-state demographic pattern of exact population replacement. The new generation, G_0, consists of *two* individuals. Thereafter, the earlier population pattern reemerges, with one person per generation in subsequent periods. The generation born in $t = 5$ is the first to be born into a society in which no generation had been alive when the population-blip (baby-boom?) generation lived. Now consider Table IX.3.2. The baby-boom generation produces a *positive* externality of one extra unit of defense per period during the periods its members work, and it consumes the public good at no cost to the group throughout its lifetime (since its enjoyment of the public good is nonrivalrous). Thus, the lifetime utility of the generation old at $t = 0$ is $7 - 2\alpha$, of the generation middle-aged at $t = 0$ is $8 - 2\alpha$, and of each member of the baby-boom generation is $8 - 2\alpha$, all exceeding the lifetime utility of generations born during steady-state circumstances. It is easy to check that at no point along the equilibrium path does it pay one of these generations alive with the baby boomers to defect if it did not pay for a generation alive during steady-state (non-baby-boom) circumstances to defect.[9]

IX.4 DISCUSSION

The Cooper and Daughety framework enables us to provide a formal model of what anthropologists call the "domestic domain" and of the way in which this domain—whether a family, a clan, or a tribe—can provide public goods (see Evans-Pritchard, 1940; Bates, 1983, Chapters 1 and 2; Fortes and Evans-Pritchard, 1940). It also illuminates the limits of their arguments and of this alternative to the state.

As long ago argued by Fortes (1958), one of the leading students of kin-based societies, the domestic domain is dominated by the fact of time. Individuals age and the composition of a family alters as its members pass through their life course. Families organize the relationships between generations; the rules of descent structure the transmission of wealth and property. Families also structure the transmission of authority in societies in which kinship organizes the distribution of power. Simmons (1945) provided illustrations from the anthropological record, gleaned from Oceana, North America, Central America, and Africa. It is the examples from Africa that are most relevant for our argument.

Many societies in Africa—the Zulu, the Nyakusa, the Gusi, the Nandi, the Pokot, the Samburu, and the Maasai, to mention but a few (see Baxter and Almagov, 1978)—are organized into age grades. The young men specialize in military arts; serving as warriors, they provide the public good of defense. Prior to their induction into the warrior age grade, the young men serve as herdsmen for their families. When they reach an appropriate age, the elders conduct initiation rites and the youths pass from workers for their families into servants of the tribe. In some societies, the warriors move into military camps—for example, into *manyatas* in the case of the Maasai

[9] An old person never deviates from the equilibrium, whether alive during steady-state times or baby-boom times (since that person never contributes to the public good). A middle-aged person in steady-state times sticks to the equilibrium path if his expected payoff in his two remaining periods ($2 - \alpha$ and 2, respectively) exceeds his defection payoff of 1 (only the young generation of size one contributes in this circumstance), that is, if $\alpha < 3$. A middle-aged person alive when there are baby boomers working, on the other hand, will defect if the expected payoff in her two remaining periods ($3 - \alpha$ and 3, respectively) exceeds her defection payoff of 2 (only the young baby boomers contribute in this circumstance), that is, if $\alpha < 4$. Hence baby-boom time middle-agers will not deviate if their steady-state counterparts did not deviate. Finally, young generations in steady-state times will not deviate from the equilibrium if their lifetime payoff of $6 - 2\alpha$ exceeds the defection payoff of 1, that is, if $\alpha < 5/2$. Baby boomers when young will not defect if their lifetime payoff of $8 - 2\alpha$ exceeds their defection payoff of 1, that is if $\alpha < 7/2$. Again, baby-boomer youngsters will not defect if steady-state youngsters do not.

(Spencer, 1988)—from which they defend the tribal territory against encroachment by man and beast, thereby defending the wealth and livelihood of other members of the polity.

With the passage of time, the warriors graduate to the next age grade, that of elderhood. Elderhood is marked by the accumulation of status, power, and wealth. As Spencer (1965) recounted for the Samburu; "The voiced ambitions of . . . elders are to build up herds, to marry several times, and to have direct control over a large and growing family, to have cordial friendships with a large number of clansmen, age mates, and others" (p. 84). Elders accumulate cattle, wives, and children—the socially sanctioned forms of wealth in many of these societies. In elderhood, men thus turn from community service to the reaping of the private rewards that tribal life has to offer.

Our exploration of the Cooper and Daughety model suggests how such a system can be sustained politically. The society secures defense; the sacrifices incurred by individuals in their youth are compensated for by rewards when they become elders;[10] and the fear of ostracism ensures that youths will not renege on obligations prior to their formal induction into elderhood. A demographic structure can thus sustain the provision of public goods. Family structures can serve as polities.

IX.5 EXTENSIONS

The argument suggests both the strengths and limitations of this system. In so doing, it provides insight into other themes studied by anthropologists: segmentation (e.g., Turner, 1957), state formation (Brumfiel, 1994; Carneiro, 1970; Fried, 1967; Service, 1975), and the tendency for the state to replace kinship systems with the passage of time and the growth of populations (consult the references in Bates, 1983; also see Stevenson, 1968).

Linking these phenomena is the contrast in the scale economies governing the provision of public and private goods. It may well be, as we have assumed, that the provision of public goods is roughly linear in effort over large ranges, so that the growth in group size provides increased benefits in terms of defense of person and property.[11] Nonetheless, production is not linear in the *private* economy; factor inputs for the production of private

[10] Accounts of the attractions of life in the *manyatas* may make one wonder if rewards for community service are really deferred until elderhood. What is required by our model is that $\alpha > 1$, or that the individual cost of effort exceed the private benefits. This requirement is particularly likely to be fulfilled when the benefits take the form of public goods. In such situations, it is often difficult for an individual to detect the impact of his or her contribution, even though he or she may be fully aware of the costs.

[11] Indeed, North (1981) and North and Thomas (1973) argued that the provision of defense is characterized by *increasing* returns to scale.

goods typically encounter diminishing returns. In agrarian societies, for example, as the number of persons increases, good lands become settled and crowding leads to diminishing marginal products. So too does the movement of persons to the extensive margin of less rich soils.

The interplay between nondecreasing and decreasing returns to scale in the public and private economies, respectively, casts light on how kinship systems enable human populations to "boot strap" up from small size and low levels of income in initial periods of their existence to greater specialization, wealth, and trade in later periods. Early in a society's history, as its population grows, marginal returns in private production decline as resources become inferior and crowded. If the production of public goods continues to remain roughly linear in effort, however, the society may be able to compensate for the effects of decreasing private returns. It may do so by providing public defense to enable and sustain far-flung trade. That is, as persons are driven by decreasing private returns from the territorial core to new regions, they encounter different factor endowments. The provision of defense and security enables this more dispersed society to reap gains from specialization and trade. The provision of public goods thus underpins the attainment of higher incomes as gains from trade compensate for the losses from decreasing private returns (North and Thomas, 1973). In short, the model shows how economic growth can emerge in kinship systems.

In later periods, however, decreasing marginal returns most probably begin to affect the production of public as well as private goods. With large populations dispersed over wide territories, the additional inhabitants yields greater costs than benefits in the provision of public goods. Thus, the onset of diminshing returns in both public and private goods lowers average income. The kinship system that facilitated economic growth in periods of little population now constrains economic growth as population reaches larger size.

Without explicitly assuming income maximization as an objective of behavior, anthropologists have studied the resultant responses of human societies.[12] One such response is *segmentation.* Africa supplies numerous examples, ranging from the splitting of villages (Turner, 1957) to the dispersal of kingdoms such as the Luanda and Nguni (Cunnison, 1959; Barnes, 1954). The movement of population constitutes a basic feature of African society, especially in the precolonial period, prior to the introduction of national boundaries and territorially defined nation-states (Kopytoff, 1987). As argued by Colson (1969), spatial dispersion represents a rational response to the abundance and relative uniformity of Africa's land. The model we provide suggests that it represents as well a rational response to the incentives that structure the provision of goods by family systems.

A second response to decreasing returns in public good production is

[12] We wish to thank Avner Greif for suggesting this elaboration of our argument.

state formation. Given the logic of our argument, we expect this response to take place in societies from which exit is unattractive. Were the society to abut inferior lands, for example, then its members would be reluctant to escape the impact of decreasing returns by dividing into smaller segments and exiting from the initial location. Rather than "replicating" themselves in another location, they might instead *innovate,* as by providing defense and security in ways less subject to diseconomies of scale. They might, in other words, centralize their institutions in the form of states.

Africa again provides apt illustrations, and data collected from the African files of the Human Areas Relations Files (Bates, 1983) help us to assess this argument. The measures of political centralization include whether or not there were central bureaucracies; whether the political system was based upon kin relations, local chieftancies, or centralized monarchs; and whether or not there existed a national army, and one unified under a central command. As shown in Table IX.5.1 the regions with higher densities, such as those with favored land endowments, tended more frequently to possess centralized bureaucracies, a national army, and one that was commanded centrally. The political system of African societies with low population densities, on the other hand, were more frequently based on kinship systems.

IX.6 CONCLUSION

This essay has explored a demographic model of the provision of public goods. Employing an overlapping generations model, it has shown how, given the threat of ostracism and the prospect of free-riding in old age, younger persons can be induced to contribute to the public welfare.

TABLE IX.5.1 Population Density and Political Centralization

Political Structure			**Central Bureaucracy***			**National Army****			**Army Commanded at****		
	Low[a]	High[b]		Low	High		Low	High		Low	High
Kinship	33	25	Absent	56	29	Absent	75	29	Local	75	29
Chiefs	22	25	Present	44	71	Present	25	71	Regional	0	0
Central Monarchs	44	50							National	25	71
$N =$	9	8		9	7		8	7		8	7

* $p < .10$, Fisher exact test
** $p < .01$, Fisher exact test
[a] Low: 40 persons or fewer per square mile
[b] High: More than 40 persons per square mile

We have only briefly focused on various features of this model that, in fact, require some additional investigation. Of special interest in this respect is the punishment mechanism. In conventional analyses of repeat-play prisoners' dilemma games, punishment takes the form of retaliation. In the public goods setting we are exploring, however, retaliation is problematical, since the defector may continue to enjoy any of the public good that actually is produced. Exclusion provides an alternative; hence our model depends on the ability of the group to *ostracize* those that defect from the cooperative bargain. Only through physical removal from the domain over which the public good may be enjoyed can a defector be sanctioned. This, in turn, makes it imperative that defectors are identifiable, that their noncooperation is verifiable, and that it is physically possible to remove them from the physical domain of the public good. As limitations in monitoring, verification, and removal technologies accumulate, ostracism becomes less viable.

A related theoretical requirement of the ostracism option is the credibility with which it can be threatened. We stipulated its credibility in the body of the chapter, but the corollary to Proposition 1 makes an issue of this. If, as that corollary asserts, lifetime utility for group members is monotonic in the size of the group, then group members will be loathe to ostracize individuals who otherwise could contribute to their welfare. After a period of defection, for example, a defector could claim to have had a momentary lapse that will not be repeated if only the group will not ostracize her. In effect, this means that the group will be cross-pressured about implementing ostracism threats.

We intend to focus on the equilibrium implications of potential slippage in credibility in a future paper. For now, however, several interesting aspects of this problem may be noted. First, the threat of ostracism will surely be credible against possible defection in a member's final work period (period T^*). Why? Because the group loses *nothing* by ostracizing that member since, according to the equilibrium in Proposition 1, that person may be expected to shirk after period T^* anyhow. If credibility were given a continuous representation, then this suggests that the threat of ostracism is more credible to those nearing age T^* than it is to those considerably younger. This, in turn, would provide an explanation for the difficulty often encountered in trying to discipline the young, an implication that accords well with verbal accounts of unruly behavior by youths who provide public goods in kinship societies (see footnote 10). In a complementary fashion, it may be noted that the opportunity cost of ostracism borne by the group is, in fact, *not* borne at all by elders of age T. Because this is their last period, they will not bear the burden of lost services if a defector is subsequently ostracized. This would suggest that the rendering and implementing of punishments is more credible if vested in the most senior members of the group, an empirical expectation of our theory that we intend to explore further.

Though couched as an essay in political anthropology, this chapter implies two additional lessons. One pertains to the literature on public goods. Olson's pioneering work, *The Logic of Collective Action* (1965), highlighted the problem of public goods supply, namely the incentive to free-ride. Based on the folk theorem of noncooperative game theory, a revisionist literature treats the provision of public goods as far less problematic (Fudenberg and Maskin, 1986). Our argument constitutes an amendment to both positions. We concur with the revisionists' criticism: rather than being problematic, as at least an unadulterated version of Olson would have it, cooperation in the provision of public goods can be sustained in equilibrium. Indeed, we demonstrate that such cooperation can result from relationships that naturally occur in family settings. We disagree, however, with the revisionist game theorist's solution to the perverse logic of collective action. The revisionists assume that players are infinitely lived, or at least as long lived as the game itself; we instead assume them to be mortal, or at least shorter lived than the game. A stunning implication of this assumption is that the more players there are—up to the point of inflection in the marginal product curve—the less problematic the provision of public goods. Up to this critical point, in other words, our model arrives at a conclusion different from Olson's size principle. Large groups are "privileged," to use Olson's term.[13]

Our argument generates implications for the study of institutions as well. We have explored a demographic model and its implications for the behavior of families. But the logic of the model inheres not only in families but also in formal institutions. Young people enter such institutions, serve apprenticeships within them, and later reap the rewards of senior status. The institutions are longer lived than their members, and they provide collective goods. A contribution of this chapter has been to demonstrate how generationally based incentive systems elicit, in equilibrium, socially regarding behavior from private individuals (Huntington, 1968), behavior compatible with the continued maintenance of such institutional arrangements.

[13] Let us be clear, as at least one reader has urged us, that our model, with its dependence on a technology of punishment (ostracism), differs from Olson's original model but shares features in common with his "by-products" theory. Indeed, our punishment technology may be thought of as the negative of Olson's "selective benefits." If a group, in other words, is armed with the capability to discriminate selectively between contributors and noncontributors, punishing the latter with ostracism, then it may sustain the positive production of public goods; moreover, this sustainable level increases, for a while at least, with the size of the group.

REFERENCES

Almond, G., and Coleman, S. (1960). *The Politics of Developing Areas.* Princeton University Press, Princeton; NJ.

Barnes, J. A. (1954). *Politics in a Changing Society.* Oxford University Press, London.

Bates, R. (1983). *Essays on the Rural Economy of Africa.* University of California Press, Berkeley and Los Angeles.

Baxter, P. W. and Almagov, U. (1978). *Age, Generation, and Time.* St. Martins Press, New York.

Berry, S. (1985). *Fathers Work for Their Sons.* University of California Press, Berkeley.

Brumfiel, E., ed. (1994). *The Economic Anthropology of the State.* University Press of America, Boston.

Carneiro, R. L. (1970). A theory of the origins of the state. *Science* **169,** 733–738.

Colson, E. (1969). African society at the time of the scramble. In *Colonialism in Africa, 1870–1960.* (L. H. Gann and P. Duignan, eds.). Cambridge University Press, Cambridge, UK.

Cooper, R. and Daughety, A. (1989). *Cooperation in Infinite Horizon Games with Finitely Lived Players,* Working Paper Series 89–19. Department of Economics, University of Iowa, Iowa City.

Cremer, J. (1986). Cooperation in ongoing organizations. *Quarterly Journal of Economics* **101,** 33–49.

Cunnison, I. (1959). *The Luapula Peoples of Northern Rhodesia: Custom and History in Tribal Politics.* Manchester University Press for the Rhodes-Livingston Institute, Manchester.

Dalton, G. (1967). *Tribal and Peasant Economies.* Natural History Press, Garden City, NY.

Dalton, G. (1971). *Economic Development and Social Change.* Natural History Press, Garden City, NY.

Evans-Pritchard, E. E. (1940). *The Nuer.* Oxford University Press, Oxford, UK.

Fortes, M. (1958). Introduction. In *The Developmental Cycle in Domestic Groups* (J. Goody, ed.). Cambridge University Press, Cambridge, UK.

Fortes, M. and Evans-Pritchard, E. E., eds. (1940). *African Political Systems.* Oxford University Press, Oxford, UK.

Fried, M. (1967). *The Evolution of Political Society.* Random House, New York.

Fudenberg, D., and Maskin, E. (1986). The folk theorem in repeated games with discounting or incomplete information. *Econometrica* **54,** 533–554.

Granovetter, M. (1985). Economic action and social structure: The problem of embeddedness. *American Journal of Sociology* **91,** 481–510.

Guyer, J., ed. (1995). *Money Matters.* Heinemann, Portsmouth, NH.

Huntington, S. P. (1968). *Political Order in Changing Societies.* Yale University Press, New Haven, CT.

Kandori, M. (1992). Repeated Games Played by Overlapping Generations of Players. *Review of Economic Studies* **59,** 81–92.

Kopytoff, I., ed. (1987). *The African Frontier.* Indiana University Press, Bloomington.

Legesse, A. (1973). *Gada.* Collier-Macmillan, London.

Mead, M. (1942). *And Keep Your Powder Dry.* Morrow, New York.

North D. C. (1981). *Structure and Change in Economic History.* Norton, New York.

North D. C., and Thomas, R. P. (1973). *The Rise of the Western World.* Cambridge University Press, Cambridge, UK.

Olson, M. (1965). *The Logic of Collective Action.* Harvard University Press, Cambridge, MA.

Polanyi K. (1957). *The Great Transformation.* Beacon, Boston.

Radcliffe-Brown, A. R. (1952). *Structure and Function in Primitive Society.* Cohen and West, London.

Sahlins M. (1972). *Stone Age Economics.* Aldine, Chicago.

Salant, D. J. (1991). A repeated game with finitely lived overlapping generations of players. *Games and Economic Behavior* **3,** 244–259.

Service, E. (1975). *Origins of the State and Civilization.* Norton, New York.
Shepsle, K. A. and Nalebuff, B. (1990). The commitment to seniority in self-governing groups. *Journal of Law, Economics & Organization* **6,** S45–S72.
Simmons, L. W. (1945). *The Role of the Aged in Primitive Society.* Yale University Press, New Haven, CT.
Smith, L. (1989). *Folk Theorems in Overlapping Generations Games,* Mimeo. Department of Economics, University of Chicago, Chicago.
Spencer, P. (1965). *The Samburu: A Study of Gerontocracy in a Nomadic Tribe.* University of California Press, Berkeley and Los Angeles.
Spencer, P. (1988). *The Maasai of Matapato.* Manchester University Press for the International African Institute, Manchester.
Stevenson, R. F. (1968). *Population and Political Systems in Africa.* Columbia University Press, New York.
Turner, V. (1957). *Schism and Continuity in African Society.* Manchester University Press for the Rhodes-Livingston Institute, Manchester.
Whiting, J. W. M., and Child, I. L. (1953). *Child Training and Personality.* Yale University Press, New Haven, CT.

X The Political Foundations of Limited Government: Parliament and Sovereign Debt in 17th- and 18th-Century England

Barry R. Weingast

X.1 INTRODUCTION

The fall of socialism and the ensuing struggles for economic and political reform have forced economists and political scientists to inquire more deeply about the foundations of their approaches. These arduous struggles demonstrate that establishing democracy and markets requires far more than establishing the appropriate electoral rules, legislatures, central banks, and systems of property rights. It reveals our remarkable ignorance about how to maintain limited government.

It is now common for students of the transition to observe that both democracy and markets require limited government, a government capable not only of enforcing political, individual, and economic rights against intrusions by others, but also one that respects these rights as limits on its own action (see, for example, Levy and Spiller, 1994; North, 1990, 1993; Przeworski, 1991; Williamson, 1994; Weingast, 1995). Yet how is limited government assured? Enforcing the limits inherent in markets and democracy requires that political officials find it in their own interest to abide by these limits, that is, that these limits be self-enforcing (North and Weingast, 1989; Ordeshook, 1993; Przeworski, 1991; and Weingast, 1995). But how do states achieve the credible commitments required to assure adherence to these rights?

The Frontiers of the New Institutional Economics

To learn something about these issues, this chapter investigates how particular states in the developed West addressed one aspect of the problem—that concerning the institutional foundations of sovereign debt in 17th- and 18th-century England. North and Weingast (1989) emphasized the role of Parliament in helping to achieve commitment of the Crown to limits on its behavior. In this chapter, I return to that problem and develop a specific model that provides further insights into the issue.

Most medieval and early modern European sovereigns—as with modern developing countries—had problems making credible commitments to honor their agreements (North, 1990, 1994; see also the essays in Hoffman and Norberg, 1994). The lack of such commitments is clearly observed in the history of sovereign debt, in which repudiations were common. The central problem is that it is difficult to sue a sovereign in his own courts. One of the central challenges in developing the modern state, then, was engineering such commitments. But what made sovereigns honor their agreements?

The economic theory of sovereign debt provides considerable insights into this problem. Economists emphasize that the principal constraint on sovereign behavior concerns the penalty, *P*, that lenders can impose on a sovereign (see, e.g., Bulow and Rogoff, 1989; Eaton *et al.*, 1986).[1] When the sovereign must decide whether to honor the loan agreement (that is, to return the funds with interest), his main consideration concerns the size of the penalty he will suffer in the event of default. Put simply, the sovereign will honor the agreement only if the penalty, *P*, is larger than the cost of repayment. Knowing this, lenders will not provide funds beyond this amount, regardless of the promised interest rate. *Credit-rationing* is therefore central to this theory. An absence of the ability to sanction the sovereign does not lead to indiscriminate reneging, but to an absence of credit.

The perspective further implies that any increase in the penalty that can be imposed on the sovereign will increase the amount of credit available. Although this discussion leaves the nature of these penalties abstract, the comparative statics result has striking implications for political institutions. To the extent political institutions can affect the penalty that lenders can impose in the event of reneging, the sovereign is not only more likely to honor his loan agreements, but his credit limit will rise.

The following model takes up where the economists leave off. I begin by adapting the model of Greif *et al.* (1994) to this problem, and ask: What is the nature of the penalty that lenders can impose on the sovereign? The most important source of penalties concerns reputation. When relations between the sovereign and the lenders are ongoing, lenders can potentially punish the sovereign by withholding future funds. Bulow and Rogoff suggested one reason hindering the reputation mechanism, namely that credit

[1] The economics of sovereign debt is discussed in Section X.3.

boycotts hurt lenders as well as borrowers. A second reason, studied here, concerns the observation that, as the total loans available increases, the value of the loans starts to decline after some level.

This perspective yields a series of results about sovereign debt and political institutions. The declining marginal productivity of capital implies that the sovereign is indifferent between obtaining and not obtaining the last loan. The sovereign's indifference implies that the lender of the last loan cannot harm the sovereign by withdrawal of future funds. Because defaulting on the agreement by confiscating the funds is valuable to the sovereign whereas the threat of a boycott by this lender is not, the threat of sanctions cannot deter the sovereign from reneging. As we will discuss, the history of sovereign debt is replete with illustrations of the principle.

The result can be stated another way: Unless the entire community of lenders can coordinate their actions and participate in a credit boycott in the event of a default against any one of them, the threat of a credit boycott by those who have been harmed by the sovereign cannot sustain honorable behavior at the optimal level of debt. The argument provides for the role of institutions. To the degree that institutions help coordinate the behavior of all lenders-in particular, to enforce a complete credit boycott—they can help sustain honorable sovereign behavior at higher levels of debt.

This brings us to the Glorious Revolution in late 17th-century England. Prior to this revolution, loans to the sovereign remained at the discretion of the sovereign in the sense that the sovereign had unilateral authority over whether to adhere to the terms of the loans. As predicted by the theory, the royal record with respect to honor debt agreements was miserable, and thus they remained debt constrained.

After the Glorious Revolution, loans became laws of Parliament. Altering the terms of a debt agreement therefore required a new act of Parliament. Thus, adhering to the loan was no longer at the discretion of the sovereign, but required the cooperation of Parliament. As Parliament represented, in part, those holding government loans, cooperation between the Crown and Parliament was hardly assured.

More broadly, sovereign debt was embedded in the larger constitutional system, with important consequences. The constitutional revisions following the Glorious Revolution altered the penalties that lenders could impose on the sovereign in two ways. The institutional changes help foster the coordination of lenders, in part by threatening the Crown with removal for violating the laws of Parliament. Unilateral reneging by the sovereign on a loan agreement therefore threatened a penalty larger than credit boycott. In terms of the economic theory of sovereign debt, the changes following the Glorious Revolution markedly increased the penalties lenders could impose on the sovereign in the event of default, thus greatly changing the sovereign's incentives to adhere to debt agreements. Moreover, these institutional changes address the credibility problem raised by Bulow and Rogoff, namely that, because a credit boycott hurts lenders as well as the sovereign, a full credit boycott is unlikely. In contrast, deposing the sovereign transfers the burden of these costs from lenders to the entire nation.

Finally, the approach yields predictions about sovereign debt. Increases in the punishments on the sovereign should increase the sovereign's credit limit, with dramatic increases in penalties leading to dramatic increases in the funds available. The historic record reveals exactly such a pattern (Brewer, 1989; Dickson, 1967; North and Weingast, 1989). Prior to the Glorious Revolution the Stuarts were remarkably credit constrained, rarely having a debt of more than £2 million. Nine years after the Glorious Revolution, government debt had increased an order of magnitude, to £17 million. It reflected an increase in debt from about 5 percent to around 40 percent of GNP in nine years.

My approach has considerable implications for the larger question of how limited government becomes self-enforcing on political officials.[2] By altering the sovereign's incentives, institutional change following the Glorious Revolution changed the nature of sovereignty in English society. Beyond a coup, the revolution resulted in a unanimous agreement on a set of new principles about the relationship among the sovereign, Parliament, and the citizens. The rights of citizen representation in Parliament and of Parliament's authority over legislation and taxes became sacrosanct.

Central to the success of self-enforcing limited government following the Glorious Revolution was the agreement of citizens, not on values about the state, but on trigger strategies focusing on the behavior that should motivate withdrawal of support from the sovereign. The potential massive withdrawal of support in the event of a transgression threatened the sovereign with a huge penalty for violating these limits. When this threat is credible, sovereigns will typically be deterred from violating fundamental rights. Representative institutions thus played a central role in the onset of self-enforcing limited government in 17th- and 18th-century England.

This chapter proceeds as follows. The next section provides some background for 17th-century England. Section X.3 turns to the problem of sovereign debt and develops the model. Section X.4 summarizes the credit history of 17th- and 18th-century England, showing the dramatic increase in credit available to the English government following the Glorious Revolution. Section X.5 contains my conclusions. Finally, an appendix develops the formal model proving the results discussed in Section X.3.

[2] This perspective is pursued at greater length in Weingast (1994).

X.2 THE PHENOMENA TO BE EXPLAINED: POLITICS AND INSTITUTIONAL CHANGE IN 17TH-CENTURY ENGLAND

England in the 17th century witnessed a civil war, the abolition of the monarchy and the beheading of the king, the restoration of the monarchy, and finally the Glorious Revolution of 1688–1689. A number of issues were at stake, including the relationship between the state and the economy, between Parliament and the Crown, religion, and foreign relations. During the decade following the revolution, the English decisively settled their political questions, allowing England to emerge as one of the most powerful states in Europe.

X.2.1 Enduring Political Divisions in 17th-Century England

Seventeenth century England was a deeply divided nation. A useful set of distinctions concerns the tripartite division between sovereign and two separate sets of citizens, one I will call the "commercial nexus" and the other, the "countryside." The commercial nexus included a variety of groups with strong economic ties. First and foremost were the great trading interests in the city of London whose economic activities spanned the continent and the oceans. Also included were many of the agricultural regions along England's rich set of inland waterways and coastlines, for as London grew in both population and wealth, many of the coastal and especially riverine areas came to specialize in commercial agriculture, as Thursk (1987), Brenner (1976) and others have described.

These economic ties correlated their political interests. As their wealth derived from commerce, they favored policies that would protect and promote it, for example, secure property rights and low and stable taxes. In foreign affairs, they favored strong state promotion of their interests, including war to protect trade routes and colonies from foreign rivals. By and large these regions sided with the parliamentarians opposing the Crown during the Civil War.[3] Late in the century, their political representatives in parliament became known as the Whig opposition.

In opposition to the commercial nexus stood the more traditional elements of society, having their biggest support in the countryside. By and large these areas supported the Crown during the Civil War[4]; by the Glorious Revolution, these interests comprised some primary components of the Tories. They tended to oppose foreign wars and entanglements, government debt, and taxes on their main source of wealth—land. They also had the strongest ties to the Church of England.

[3] Hochberg's (1984) analysis shows that they did so by a margin of three to one.

[4] Hochberg's (1984) analysis shows they did so by a margin of about three to one.

The political divisions among the citizenry played a strong role in the events leading up to and following the Glorious Revolution. In the decade preceding the Revolution, the Whigs strongly and often bitterly opposed the crown, while the group later called the Tories provided the Crown's support.[5] This division endured after the Revolution.

> It is an oversimplification to see the Whigs as the party of business and the Tories of seigneurial power. Some of the greatest aristocrats were resolute Whigs, and some of the keenest battles in the City of London were fought between rival groups of businessmen with Whig and Tory backing. But one can safely contrast emphasis on commerce as a point in the Whig profile, and emphasis on agriculture as a point in the Tory one. So, too, the Whigs tended to internationalism—to "Dutch finance" under William and "no peace without Spain" under Anne; while the Tory was inward-looking and protectionist. . . . The Whig favoured immigration, especially of refugee Protestants, the Tory deplored the admission of "useless and necessitous foreigners"; the Tory tended to peace, the Whig to war. (Carswell, 1973, pp. 40–41)

X.2.2 The Events Leading to the Revolution

Prior to the Glorious Revolution, reciprocal mistrust characterized the relationship between the Crown and Parliament, especially the Whigs in that body. A large number of Whigs believed that if they provided sufficient finances to the Crown, the Crown would raise a domestic army to force higher taxes and more onerous policies. Possessing no apparent means to ensure that the money would be spent in acceptable ways, parliament kept the Crown short of revenue.[6] Only by this method did its members have some influence over the Crown, since forcing the Crown to ask for money provided a forum that allowed them to bargain for concessions. The liability of this strategy was that it also forced the Crown to seek ways around parliamentary constraints. This took several forms under the late Stuarts. First, the Crown attempted to convince Parliament of the need for funds for one purpose and then used them for another. Second, James secured funds by secret negotiations with Louis XIV. Third and seen as the most egregious, the late Stuarts attempted to pack the constituencies.

From the Crown's point of view the difficulty was one of being hobbled by a system that provided inadequate revenue with the problem centering around a parliament that wanted too central a role in the government. Revenue constraints meant, first, foregoing highly desired goals, second, going into greater debt than otherwise warranted—usually via costly means such as tax farming—and third, attempting to deceive Parliament.

[5] Although these labels later came to denote political parties in the modern sense of the term, in the late 17th and early 18th century, they were not so organized (see Plumb, 1967; Hill, 1976).

[6] The members of Parliament did not act with one voice. Obviously, this discussion refers to the majority of those in Parliament, and ignores Parliamentary divisions for the sake of exposition. The effects of the latter are not analyzed here.

As a consequence the system of mutual mistrust proved self-reinforcing. Neither party acting alone could get out of the dilemma; yet by persisting in its behavior each ensured the other would behave in the manner it found inimical.

Two major political events occurred against this background in which first one side then the other sought to undermine its opponent's political basis. The first began in the late 1670s and is known as the "exclusion crisis" in which the Whigs attempted to exclude the king's brother, James, from line of succession to the crown. This move not only failed to achieve its ends, but raised sufficient support for the Crown that it enabled the latter to undertake a much more serious institutional attack on the Whig opposition. Known as the campaign to "pack the constituencies," this plan sought to alter the political basis of local representation in a manner that disenfranchised the opposition, enabling royal supporters in these localities to gain political control. The campaign proved remarkably successful, at least in the short run. Of the 104 members elected to Parliament in the mid-1680s from the constituencies receiving new charters, only one Whig was elected. The effect was dramatic, converting "what had been a formidable, aggressive and highly organized opposition party into an impotent collection of a few individuals" (Jones, 1972, pp. 47, 50).

In the midst of this campaign, James II became king in 1685. Having succeeded in disenfranchising the opposition, James sought greater control over political decisions and immediately began squabbling with his own supporters. Two sources of dispute were the following. First, James's support for Catholicism alienated many of his own Tory supporters (Carruthers, 1990). Second, James sought to build a Catholic army in Ireland. The Tories refused to cooperate. In reaction, James turned his rechartering campaign against them. At the same time, he attempted to manipulate the judges to gain approval. In *Godden versus Hales,* "the judges had laid it down that 'there is no law whatsoever but may be dispensed with' by the King, for reasons of which he is sole judge" (Hill, 1980, p. 204).[7] Had the late Stuarts' institutional strategies been successful there would have been few limits on James's authority. Not only would he have had a compliant judiciary, an army with which to bully the citizenry, but a compliant parliament.[8]

The rechartering campaign almost succeeded; indeed, it would have had not an extraordinary set of events occurred. James's actions sufficiently alarmed the Tories that the entire country rose in opposition to him, inviting William, Prince of Orange and the leader of the Dutch state, to take the crown. In large part, James's attack on the basis of political representation

[7] Moreover, according to Hill, "four judges were dismissed before *Godden versus Hales* came up for trial."

[8] This has led many to conclude like Western that, "After 1680 England seemed to be moving inexorably towards absolutism and only the events of 1688 led to a change of direction, perhaps at the last possible moment" (1972, p. 3).

led to his demise. Had it succeeded, it would have centralized power in the hands of the monarchy, leaving the traditional political means of protection of "property and liberty" substantially weakened.[9]

Historians have argued for 300 years about the wisdom of James's actions, debating whether he was inevitably doomed to failure or whether his actions represented an intelligent gamble.[10] This important issue will not be answered here. For my purpose, the key is that James made his attempt, leading to the revolution.

X.2.3 Political and Institutional Change

The Glorious Revolution was more than a simple coup. The perpetrators of the revolution also sought to alter decisively the relationship of the monarchy, Parliament, and the citizen. The principal institutional reorganization entailed three phases: the Revolution Settlement of 1689 transferring the crown to William and Mary and including the Bill of Rights; legislation throughout the early 1690s creating new institutional practices and conventions; and the Act of Settlement in 1701. These refashioned the English state.

The institutional changes fall into several categories. Strong limits on royal authority were imposed. Over the long run, the royal control over the judiciary was abolished, creating the so-called "independent judiciary." Parliament gained considerable powers and rights: control over its own elections; the right as sole agent controlling taxes; the right to elections at least every three years and to limits on the length of any Parliament; and new role in governmental decisionmaking, appropriating money, and administration. Strong safeguards for personal liberty were also ensured, notably, prohibitions on excessive bail and on cruel and unusual punishment. The army was brought under Parliamentary control in the Mutiny Act. The exercise of marital law and the collection of revenue were illegal without Parliamentary consent. The Toleration Act guaranteed a degree of religious toleration. Finally, the Settlement Act excluded a Catholic from becoming king.

Although historians have debated whether the consequences of these changes were "inevitable" or foreseen, they do agree on many aspects of

[9] "The universality that permeates the Revolution of 1688 arose . . . because of [James's] outright onslaught on the very basis of political power, which if successful would have made the Stuarts as absolute as their French or Spanish cousins. It is this attack on the natural leaders of society in their country neighbourhoods that must be regarded as the most fundamental cause of the Revolution of 1688" (Plumb, 1967, p. 62).

[10] Whig historians, for example, have long considered the Stuarts inept, James II included (e.g., Macaulay, 1848, p. xx). Others see this move as an intelligent gamble that, while risky, nearly succeeded (see, e.g., Jones, 1972).

the transformation. "None of its architects could have predicted its effectiveness in securing the liberties, religion, property and independence of the nation after so many previous attempts had failed" (Jones, 1972, p. 6). In spite of claims by Whig historians that many of these changes were inevitable, none of the institutional changes or their far-reaching effects appears to have been preordained.

X.2.4 Consequences of the Revolution

The revolution ushered in a period of greater political protection of domestic property rights, economic activity, religious freedom, and personal liberty. It also thrust England into a new set of international relationships. Making William king entailed war with France, in part a war of political independence. Had France won, the Stuarts would undoubtedly have been restored to the throne. Moreover, rivalry with France also involved economic issues such as trading routes, colonies, and access to the world's resources. The outcome and consequences of this war could hardly have been foreseen. Not only did England survive these wars, but it emerged as a major international power. The success in royal-parliamentary cooperation, while hoped for, was not inevitable.

As Brewer emphasized, these new arrangements produced a state sufficiently strong to raise resources in an efficient manner on an unprecedented scale. They promoted the strong presence of Britain in international relations, the creation of a major world empire, and ultimately an absence of potential challengers.

The English political divisions emphasized previously remained after the revolution and had an important effect on both institutions and policy. First, the menacing international powers gave the upper hand to those favoring a more aggressive foreign policy, that is, the Whigs.

> For the Whig the Revolution meant pluralism and a limited monarchy; for the Tory it had been a painful necessity which had hazarded the due and proper relationships of society. When the Whig referred to the Revolution he tended to speak of "honesty", meaning the frank recognition of the fact that parliament had altered the succession to the Crown; and of "liberty and property", meaning that the sanctity of private property was the only effective guarantee of individual liberty. The Tories attitude was summed up in the slightly different phrase, "religion and property". The property factor . . . is common to both; but the emphasis is very different. For the Whig, the relevance of property is to connect self-interest and the stability of society; for the Tory, it is to symbolize habit and tradition as the guarantees of order. (Carswell, 1973, p. 40.)

Second, in a change of roles, the Tories were among those strongly favoring limits on state behavior, both to confine the growth of the state within well-defined limits and to limit the growth of their own taxes. As the fiscal-military state grew, the proponents of smaller government and limited war did not give in, fighting to limit the domestic effects of the new state.[11]

The results are well known. In two wars fought in close succession—the Nine Years War, 1689–97, and the War of Spanish Succession, 1701–1714—the more powerful French failed in the first to vanquish Britain and its allies and were defeated in its goals regarding the succession in Spain and the fate of the remaining Hapsburg territories in the second.

X.2.5 Constitutional Changes

The Glorious Revolution and the decade following abounded in constitutional changes. These revisions began with the Revolution Settlement. One of its principal components was the Bill of Rights, passed by Parliament in early 1689. It was composed of several parts, the first of which contained two lists. The first enumerated a set of violations of the rights of citizens by James II, and began

> Whereas the late King James The Second, by the assistance of divers evil counsellors, judges, and ministers employed by him, did endeavour to subvert and extirpate the protestant religion, and the laws and liberties of this kingdom (quoted in Williams, 1960, pp. 26).

The list contained 12 items by which James had done so, including "By assuming and exercising a power of dispensing with and suspending of laws, and the execution of laws, without consent of parliament"; levying money without parliamentary approval; "raising . . . a standing army within this kingdom in time of peace, without consent of parliament"; "By causing several good subjects, being protestants, to be disarmed, at the same time when papists were both armed and employed, contrary to law"; and "By violating the freedom of election of members to serve in parliament" (quoted in Williams, 1960, p. 26). A second list, paralleling the first, provided for a set of limits on royal authority, making it clear that the powers abused by James II were beyond royal authority.

The significance of the Bill of Rights' enumerations lies in stating a set of relatively unambiguous principles defining boundaries on the Crown's behavior.[12] Agreeing on these limits in advance—and assuring that they became part of the constitution via the Bill of Rights—provided an explicit mechanism for coordinating members of society. Although gray areas could never be fully eliminated, the Bill of Rights improved the ability of citizens

[11] "The war against the state helped to shape the changing contours of government: limited in its scope, restricted its ambit and through parliamentary scrutiny, rendered its institutions both more public and accountable . . . *[P]aradoxically, this success made the fiscal-military state stronger rather than weaker, more effective rather than more impotent.*" (Brewer, 1989, p. xix, emphasis added.)

[12] The conclusions stated in this paragraph are derived in Weingast (1994).

to coordinate their judgments that a transgression had taken place and that a reaction was required. The fact that these limits were produced under time of relative consensus rather than by one group within society forcing them on another made them credible as the focal point of national attention with respect to the king's future behavior. Thereafter, citizens could coordinate their reactions based on whether the Crown overstepped one of these boundaries, not on their separate, diverse judgments about whether one of the Crown's actions constituted a transgression. This narrowed considerably the ability of the Crown to exploit this diversity of opinion among the citizenry because it made the withdrawal of his minimal support more likely. Put another way, the explicit agreement represented by the Bill of Rights improved the capacity of the community to penalize certain actions by the Crown, in turn, making these less likely. Violating constitutional enumerations would come at the Crown's own peril.

In addition to an attempt to clarify and produce consensus about the limits on royal authority, parliamentarians initiated a series of institutional changes designed to promote their goals. The first and foremost concerned the Parliament itself. The Glorious Revolution ushered in the era of the "King in Parliament." No longer would the Crown demand obedience by appealing to the divine right of kings. The new prescription was implemented in a series of steps that were designed to make Parliament a full participant in the decision-making and management of the government.

When designing the new institutions in 1689, Parliament sought to prevent the Crown from living on its own by granting it much less revenue, thus requiring the Crown to appear regularly before Parliament in order to ensure adequate funds. This system attempted to foster cooperation between the Crown and Parliament and to forestall attempts by the former to end-run the latter. Moreover, to make the principle explicit, the new arrangements proscribed any attempt by the Crown to rule without Parliament by calling for frequent elections.[13]

One of the beneficial affects of the new arrangements resulted from the creation of multiple "veto" centers over policy (Ekelund and Tollison, 1981; North and Weingast, 1989). Policy required approval not only of the Crown, but of Parliament. Because each had its own interests and constituents, the three veto centers—the Crown, lords, and commons—had different preferences over policies. Several consequences followed. First, any attempt to change the status quo had to gain the support of a larger segment of society than before. Second, those represented in Parliament could more readily block undesirable policy initiatives of the Crown.

In relatively short order, this system evolved into one in which Parliament gained considerable power over the policies of the government.

[13] Specifically, they put in place legal constraints about the calling of Parliament, including a clause in the Bill of Rights and the Triennial legislation of 1694.

In money matters, the Crown had the power to propose and Parliament had the right to accept or reject (Campion, 1958; May, 1966; Reid, 1967). Because of its experience with the Stuarts raising money ostensibly for one purpose but using it for another, Parliament attempted to keep a much closer tie between the money it approved and how it was used. During the decade of the 1690s, therefore, Parliament gained for the first time the right to audit the executive's use of funds. The need to gain parliamentary approval the following year underpinned a new process of executive accountability for how these funds were spent and thus improved the Crown's adherence to these limits. Similarly, new taxes sought by the Crown, for example, would be supplied only if sufficient support for them and their purpose were to be found in Parliament. The new system ensured that both the Crown and at least a majority of Parliament and their constituents were better off by governmental decisions.[14] By the end of Anne's reign (1714), the treasury was submitting proposed annual budgets for parliamentary consideration, leading one scholar of the period to remark: "We are in the modern age" (Hill, 1980, p. 237).

X.3 THE ROLE OF POLITICAL INSTITUTIONS IN SOVEREIGN DEBT

The central dilemma of sovereign debt concerns how loan agreements are enforced. Private loan agreements in modern Western economies are enforceable in the courts backed by the sanction of the state. When a private individual borrows money for a house, for example, the house typically serves as collateral so that if the buyer defaults on the loan, the lender may seize the house. The nature of sovereignty implies that this type of contractual enforcement is unavailable to those who lend to sovereigns.

In their classic paper on the theory of sovereign debt, Eaton, Gersovitz, and Stiglitz emphasized that the sovereign's *willingness to pay* is the central principle underlying loan agreements (see Bulow and Rogoff, 1989; Eaton *et al.*, 1986. See also Atkeson, 1992; Conklin, 1995; Grossman and van Huyck, 1988; Sargent and Velde, 1995). This section provides an extension to their theory, with the formal results being proved in the appendix.

To see the nature of the sovereign debt problem, assume that the sovereign seeks to finance his operations via debt. The sovereign, *S*, and the lender, *L*, interact as follows (see Figure X.3.1). In period 1, the lender must decide how much debt (*D*) to extend via loans to the sovereign. A loan agreement between the lender and the sovereign takes the form of a promise by the sovereign to repay the loan with interest at rate *i* (that is,

[14] I leave aside here the important question of how well the system of elections worked given the electorate(s) of this period (see, e.g., Plumb, 1967; Hill, 1976; Speck, 1989).

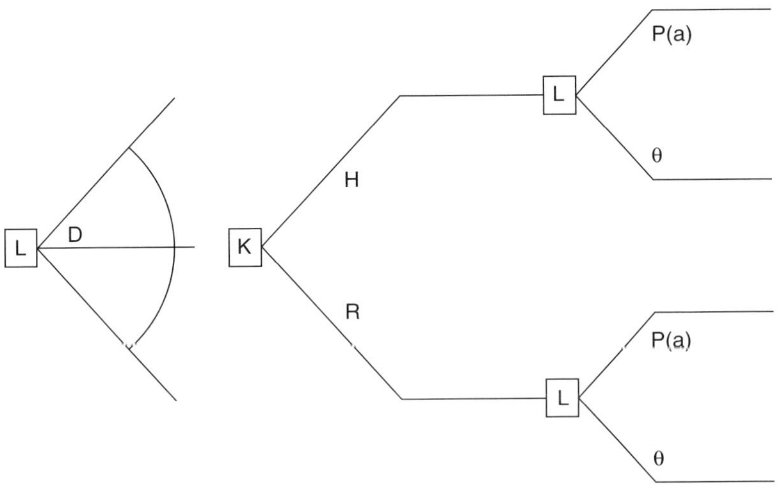

FIGURE X.3.1 The Sovereign Debt Problem

$(1 + i)D$) in the second period. In the next period, the sovereign must decide whether to honor the agreement (H) or to renege (R). The lenders must then decide whether to impose a penalty on the sovereign, where P is the largest credible penalty available to the lender.[15]

A central insight of the theory can be derived from the figure. If P^* is the largest credible penalty that the lender can impose on the sovereign for reneging on the loan agreement, then the sovereign will honor his loan agreement if and only if $D(1 + i) \leq P^*$. This formula determines the maximum size loan the lender is willing to extend, Δ, where $\Delta = P^*/(1 + i)$. The sovereign will renege on any loan larger than Δ. In this theory, limits on the ability of the lender to impose penalties on the sovereign constrains the latter's ability to borrow. Sovereign debt is therefore a theory of *credit rationing*. Even if the sovereign wants to borrow more, once as the credit ceiling equal to Δ, no more credit is available, regardless of the interest rate the sovereign is willing to promise. This implies that credit limits derive from limits on the sovereign, not on the amount of capital available.

Second, if the sovereign desires to borrow more than his credit limit, he stands to benefit from an increase in the magnitude of the penalty that

[15] Three points must be made about this summary of the model. First, this paragraph provides a summary of the players' interaction, not the actual game, which is described in the appendix to this chapter. Second, the nature of credibility, arising from the relevant repeated game, is discussed in the next subsection and is proved formally in the appendix. Finally, in the figure, the penalty, $P(a)$, is written as a function of a parameter, a, which we ignore for the present.

lenders can impose on him. This paradoxical finding is an important insight into sovereign behavior, for many scholars believe that sovereigns always prefer to retain discretion and flexibility. This approach, by contrast, suggests that there are circumstances under which a sovereign would willingly submit to—or even foster—the ability of others to impose penalties on himself. Appropriately structured limits are valuable because they increase the sovereign's access to loans.

Third, a corollary of the second implication is that if "there is no penalty, one observes no lending rather than a rash of loan-contract violations. At its simplest, willingness-to-pay is a theory of rationing, not one of lender losses" (Eaton *et al.,* 1986, p. 488). The inability to impose any penalty implies the absence of sovereign compliance and hence an absence of lending.

Finally, the implications of the change in the penalty are straightforward. If the maximum credible penalty that can be imposed on the sovereign is a function of a parameter, $P(a)$, then changes in the parameter affect the maximum credible loan to the sovereign. Letting $P' > 0$, increases in the parameter, a, increase both $P(a)$ and $\Delta(a) = P(a)/(1 + i)$.

This comparative statics result has striking political implications, for it says that any political institution that improves the ability of lenders to impose credible penalties on the sovereign increases the sovereign's debt limit.

X.3.1 Multiple Lenders and Sovereign Debt

The theory of sovereign debt distinguishes two problems with the credibility of punishments, both deriving from the observation that punishing the sovereign by withholding future funds hurts the lenders as well as the sovereign. Bulow and Rogoff (1989) showed that in certain circumstances this limits the punishment that can be imposed by a lender in the event of a sovereign default. In what follows, we focus on a second credibility problem arising from the problem of multiple borrowers.

To see the political and institutional implications of the theory—and to define the nature of credible penalties—we apply the model of Greif, Milgrom and Weingast (1994). To begin, we note that the previous discussion was unconcerned with the nature of the lender—or, more likely, the community of lenders. To the extent that the penalty to be imposed on the sovereign is the withdrawal of funds available for future loans—that is, a *credit boycott*—then the number of lenders matters considerably. Because it takes only a small portion of lenders to defeat a boycott, a single lender is not plagued by the coordination problem faced by a community of lenders. With many lenders, a boycott potentially becomes difficult to enforce.

The possibility of exclusion from future credit forces a closer look at the lender's problem, for exclusion does not automatically follow a default. This follows because a credit boycott hurts lenders as well as borrowers and there are circumstances in which it is not in the interests of a lender to withhold loans even if a promised repayment has not occurred. Of course, if exclusion is not credible as a penalty, it will not have the required effect on the borrower.

The main problem with a credit boycott as a means of punishing the sovereign arises when there are many potential lenders. Suppose that a sovereign faces a large number of creditors, has loans from several of them, and then defaults on a subset of the loans. Although it might be easy for the lenders who were harmed by a default to refuse to provide new funds, other potential lenders may find it too costly to join the boycott. Because a successful credit boycott is especially costly to the sovereign, he is willing to provide attractive terms in order to induce other lenders to continue to provide funds. As Greif, Milgrom, and Weingast emphasized, inducing third parties to participate in a boycott of this sort is the principal problem facing a community of agents that seeks to influence the behavior of a large party with whom they all transact.

To see the problems with many lenders, we turn to the sovereign's value of debt. We assume that the sovereign can put funds to good use and thus values debt finance. The sovereign's value of the debt is assumed to rise with the size of the debt, but at a decreasing rate (see Figure X.3.2). Technically, this implies that the marginal productivity of capital be positive

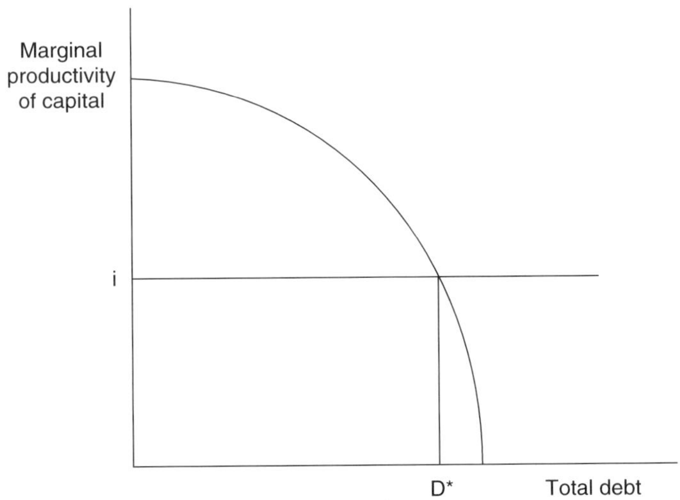

FIGURE X.3.2 Declining Marginal Productivity of Capital

but decreasing. If funds are available at an interest rate of *i*, then the optimal size loan—the loan that maximizes the sovereign's net value—is at D^* where the marginal productivity of the last dollar is exactly equal to the sovereign's cost of borrowing the dollar, or *i*. Were there no limits on the sovereign's credit, he would borrow up to this amount.

Next, assume that individual lenders are small relative to the sovereign. In that case, raising funds to the optimal limit, at D^*, implies that the first few loans are very valuable to the sovereign, but the last few loans are not. The reason is that at at D^*, the sovereign's marginal value of the last loan is exactly equal to its costs and hence has a net value of zero. A potential problem therefore arises for the lenders.

Consider two types of exclusion by creditors and their effect of the sovereign.

Bilateral Exclusion

Bilateral exclusion occurs when a given lender withholds funds only in the event that the lender suffers a default. For a sovereign whose credit is unconstrained, the marginal value of the last lender is zero since the value of the last loan was just equal to its cost. Because these funds are of zero net value to the sovereign, withholding them costs the sovereign nothing. As a consequence, a bilateral mechanism cannot impose sufficient penalty on the sovereign to deter default.

Complete Community Exclusion

In a complete community exclusion, all members of the lending community participate in a boycott if the sovereign defaults against *any* lender. If *all* lenders join the credit boycott in the event of a default, a boycott is quite costly to the sovereign, who then loses the potential value of all loans, not just those marginal loans on which the sovereign has defaulted.

The participation of all lenders in a boycott imposes the maximum penalty on the sovereign in the event of a default, and the preceding results show that a complete boycott provides the best deterrent. Yet complete participation is especially difficult to arrange for two reasons. First, it is costly to the participants, and second, the sovereign has a special interest in defeating a boycott by offering extraordinary terms to lenders willing to defect from a boycott. By offering especially attractive terms to a subset of lenders if they ignore the boycott, both the sovereign and these lenders can be made better off. The possibility of offering especially attractive terms for such loans, however, forces us to inquire what makes the sovereign's promise to repay them credible. The answer again concerns the value of the marginal loan. In the context of a credit boycott, the availability of some funds is of critical value to the sovereign. If only limited funds are available, their value to the sovereign—the marginal productivity of capital—will be the high, implying that their withdrawal is especially costly for sovereign. Therefore, the threat of bilateral exclusion is sufficient to make credible the sovereign's promises to honor loans in violation of a boycott.

In technical terms, Greif, Milgrom, and Weingast's results are as follows (see the appendix). First, there is a subgame perfect equilibrium in which all members of the lending community participate in a credit boycott whenever the sovereign defaults on any one of them. Second, this equilibrium is unlikely to occur in practice because it relies on the sovereign defaulting on any lender who is willing to defect from the boycott. In technical terms, the equilibrium of a community boycott is not renegotiation proof.

Without some means of coordinating their actions and preventing defection from a credit boycott, lenders will have substantial difficulty imposing penalties on sovereigns via credit boycotts. Although a credit boycott may partially succeed, thus imposing a penalty on the sovereign by lowering the amount of available credit, this penalty is substantially less than if all lenders can be induced to participate in a boycott.

X.3.2 Political Institutions and Sovereign Debt

Greif, Milgrom, and Weingast's approach shows that an unorganized community of lenders is unlikely to solve its coordination problem and achieve full community boycotts. Indeed, problems with enforcing penalties via community credit boycotts have played a central role in sovereign finances throughout history. A brief discussion of four historical cases illustrates the central role of creditors, the variable effectiveness of credit boycotts, and sovereign default. First, Veitch's (1986) study of lending in the Middle Ages shows that several episodes follow this pattern. For example, the Jews' financing of England's Edward I worked well as long as they were Edward's principal source of funds. The rise of a second source of funds, Italian bankers, meant that a credit boycott by the Jews would no longer reduce the king's credit to zero. The Italians' interest in replacing the Jews as the English creditors meant that they were willing to establish relations with Edward regardless of what happened to the Jews. The latter thus became marginal lenders, markedly reducing the penalty they could inflict on the king. As a consequence, the king expropriated the Jews' wealth and expelled them from England.[16] Second, Hoffman's (1994) analysis of early modern France suggests a similar problem (see also Bien, 1987; Root, 1989). Prior to the rise of certain credible restrictions on the Crown in the mid and late 17-th century, the Crown was able to play the various financial interests against one another by defaulting against one family while simultaneously

[16] Veitch also argued that Philip IV confiscated the wealth of the Templars under similar circumstances.

raising new funds by offering attractive terms to another family. The consequent limits on the Crown's credit are easily seen from Hoffman's observation that when, under Louis XIV, lenders improved their ability to coordinate their actions in response to a default, the level of credit available to the Crown increased.[17] Finally, analysis of modern third-world debt emphasizes a variant of this problem in which the major banks from the developed nations have devised a system of syndicates to coordinate their behavior in imposing penalties on states that default on loan agreements (see, e.g., Burlow and Rugoff, 1989; Lipson, 1988; Stiglitz and Weiss, 1983).[18] Here too a central problem is to induce other banks to participate in a boycott against a country in default even though making a loan might be quite attractive.

Nonetheless, credible community boycotts are not out of the question. To succeed, the lending community needs some form of organization, one that helps prevent defection. Following the Glorious Revolution in England, two institutional mechanisms provided for this coordination, including the ability of lenders to sanction one another. First, Parliament became a central player in all loans. Prior to 1688, loan agreements allowed the Crown unilateral discretion to adjust the terms. After 1688, parliamentary approval was necessary for adjusting the terms of the loan. Representing England's wealthy elite—those holding most of the sovereign's loans—Parliament could act as an agent of the lenders against the Crown. Parliamentary participation greatly reduced the likelihood that default would occur (North and Weingast, 1989).

Second, at exactly this time (1694), Parliament created the Bank of England, providing additional means to coordinate lenders and thus increasing the penalties available on the sovereign. The bank was given exclusive rights to raise credit for the government, making it illegal for individuals to provide loans under other auspices. The bank also began to *prioritize* loans, that is, to rank loans by seniority whereby, in the event of a default, the least senior loans would be affected first. Prioritizing loans made it harder to default on some loans while raising new credit. Because a new loan would be the least senior, it prevented the government from promising to pay a new lender while withholding payments to an older, more senior one. *Cross-default* clauses also came into use, allowing the bank to declare all loans in default if the government was unable to make good on its promises to any one loan. These mechanisms provided the legal underpinning for the bank to impose a complete credit boycott in the event of a default on *any* of the loans to the government. By centralizing the loan

[17] Spain exhibited a similar pattern in the latter 16th and early 17th centuries (see Conklin, 1995).

[18] The relative abundance of LDC credit in the last 30 years in part reflects the ability of major banks to achieve an effective credit boycott in the event of a default.

decisions in a single intermediary rather than among a large, diffuse community of agents, the bank's charter allowed it to enforce a community credit boycott.[19]

In combination, these institutions had three effects. First, they were able to coordinate the community of lenders, so as to create effective credit boycotts against the sovereign. Second, they were able to increase the penalties on the sovereign beyond that represented by a credit boycott. Third, they mitigated the problem noted by Bulow and Rogoff, namely that a credit boycott also hurts lenders. They did so as follows.

First, loans became acts of Parliament. To change the terms of a particular loan required a new act of Parliament. Second, the Glorious Revolution established that ignoring the lenders' fundamental rights, as defined in the revolution's Bill of Rights, was ground for deposing the sovereign (see Weingast, 1994, for details). This document asserted, among other things, that acts of Parliament were sacrosanct and that violating them threatened the Crown with being deposed.

Thus, the constitutional changes following the Glorious Revolution, critical to preserving Parliament and limited government in England, also influenced the problem of sovereign debt. The new institutions resolved the sovereign debt problem by embedding debt within the principal mechanisms of limited government, Parliament, and the new constitutional rules contained in the Bill of Rights.

X.3.3 Implications for Sovereign Debt

The implications of these institutional changes for sovereign debt can be seen by considering three different *punishment regimes,* that is three different community mechanisms for punishing the sovereign (Table X.3.1). The first is a *partial credit boycott* in which only those members of the community who the sovereign has defaulted withhold funds. As we have seen, this withholds on marginal funds and is not very costly to the sovereign. The

TABLE X.3.1 Three Punishment Schemes

P(0):	Partial Credit Boycott
P(1):	Full Credit Boycott
P(2):	Depose the Sovereign

[19] Of course, creating a single intermediary also raised the problem of potential monopolization of the credit market. This was mitigated in part by an implication of parliamentary government emphasized by Hoffman and Rosenthal (this volume, Chapter 3): Parliament could veto wars not desired by its members. Because the community of lenders and the community seeking wars by and large overlapped, raising the costs of funds by monopolization would reduce the likelihood of success.

second entails a *full community boycott.* Because this punishment withholds all funds from the sovereign, it is very costly. The third punishment regime goes beyond withholding credit from the sovereign to *depose* him, it is yet more costly than withholding all funds. Moreover, deposing the king is less costly to the lenders than a full credit boycott.

This sequence of punishment regimes yields our most important prediction. The sovereign clearly ranks these punishment regimes:

$$P(0) < P(1) < P(2). \qquad (*)$$

Paralleling this ranking, the economic theory suggests that the maximum sustainable debt for the sovereign will also increase. Given that $\Delta = P(a)/(1 + i)$, inequality (*) implies that the corresponding debt limits are ordered similarly:

$$\Delta(0) < \Delta(1) < \Delta(2). \qquad (**)$$

Inequality (**) shows that as the community of lenders is able to impose greater cost on the sovereign, the sovereign's credit limit increases. In particular, *we predict that dramatic increases in the ability to the lending community to impose penalties on the sovereign should lead to dramatic increases in the sovereign's debt limit.*

X.4 THE FINANCIAL REVOLUTION IN ENGLAND

Section X.2 described the institutional changes following the Glorious Revolution. In this section, we discuss their implications for sovereign debt.

Prior to the Glorious Revolution, the English Crown held unilateral authority over the terms of a loan agreement, allowing it to alter the terms without the approval of others. The institutional changes following the revolution provided a much different decision-making process. It did not prevent alterations of the terms of a loan agreement, just unilateral ones by the Crown. Changes after the revolution required approval by Parliament because loans and their terms were authorized by acts of Parliament. Because the main interests providing capital for the loans were represented in Parliament, this meant that renegotiations over loan agreements in effect required the permission of the representatives of the bondholders.[20] The new system implied that debt restructuring be in the interests of *both* sovereign and the bondholders. Because the new institutions gave representatives of bondholders a veto over debt restructuring, bondholders had

[20] Notice that this strikingly parallels the process of renegotiation or "reorganization" of debt in corporate bankruptcy. In the face of potential default, the corporation must seek permission of the bondholders to reorganize the debt payments. This can be to the advantage of the latter, for example, if lower current payments today improve the corporation's chances of long-term profitability.

greater protection than before, reducing the circumstances under which they would be made worse off. Following the theory of sovereign debt, lowering the likelihood of default increased the government's credit limit.

The consequences of this nexus of institutions underpinning government finance—from parliamentary provision of taxes financing debt service and Parliament's ability to limit defaults to the Bank of England's authority as principal intermediary and coordinator of the financial community—provided the foundation for the enormous efficiency of the new fiscal-military state with its ability to finance massive military undertakings (Brewer, 1989; Dickson, 1967; North and Weingast, 1989). Though the French had a larger economy, they did not possess the comparable means of raising capital with which to finance their competition with England.[21]

X.4.1 Sovereign Debt in 17th-Century England

Sovereign debt under the Stuart kings throughout the 17th century illustrates the principles discussed previously. During most of the century the Crown exercised dicretion over loans. As a consequence the Stuarts were remarkably credit constrained, having access to few loans.

The public finances under the late Stuarts (1660–1688) contrast sharply with those following the revolution. Budgets grew somewhat following restoration of the monarchy in 1660. At the time of the revolution, expenditures were approximately £2 million per year, revenue slightly lower, and total debt about the same level. Under the Stuarts, debt rarely exceeded the level of annual revenue.

After 1689, all relevant aspects of public finance grew. During the Nine Years War, annual revenue increased from £1.9 million under James II (1686–1688) to 4.8 million in 1696 (see Table X.4.1). Annual expenditures rose by almost a factor of four, from 2.1 million to 8.0 million. At the same time, the new government ended the war with a debt of £16.7 million, nearly an order of magnitude larger than that it inherited from the Stuarts (Figure X.4.1). Seen from another perspective, although the Stuarts' credit had been constrained to approximately the level of their annual revenue, credit after the Glorious Revolution rose to four times annual revenue. As Figure X.4.1 indicates, the new pattern of debt behavior shows a dramatic and unprecedented break with the past.

The military-fiscal state's striking growth continued over the next century (Table X.4.2). In 1720, for example, just 30 years after the revolution, debt had risen to £54 million, nearly nine times the annual revenue for that year. Revenue, expenditure, and debt rose in each successive war fought

[21] Another aspect of efficient finance concerns the English tax system. As Brewer (1989) emphasizes, taxes on land, for example, achieved a surprising degree of uniformity across the nation. This not only meant an absence of discrimination among constituencies, but a great improvement in efficiency.

TABLE X.4.1 Revenue, Expenditures, and Debt, 1686–1697 (£000s)

Year	Total Revenue	Total Expenditures	Total Military	Total Debt
1686–1688[a]	1914	2111		2.0[b]
1688–1691[c]	8613	11543	8957	3.1
	2871	3848	2986	
1692	4111	4255	3393	3.3
1693	3783	5576	4651	5.9
1694	4004	5602	4490	6.1
1695	4134	6220	4866	8.4
1696	4823	7998	3924	10.6
1697	3298	7915	5989	16.7

[a] Per annum, except for total debt.
[b] From Jones (1978, Chapter 3)
[c] First row of 1688 are totals; second row are per annum.
Source: North and Weingast (1989, Table 3)

during the 18th century. By 1790, on the eve of Britain's military struggle with France, it held a debt of £244 million, nearly fifteen times the annual revenue for that year. It is this capacity for enormous growth in expenditures that Brewer (1989) calls the fiscal-military state.

One final observation is worth noting. Although annual expenditures grew by an order of magnitude over the 100 years following the revolution,

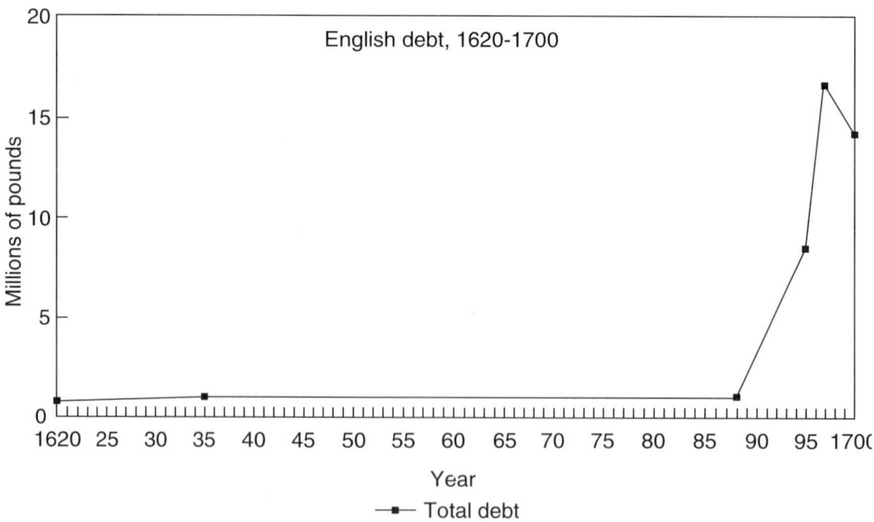

FIGURE X.4.1 English Debt, 1620–1700 (Millions of Pounds) Source: North and Weingast (1989, Table 3)

TABLE X.4.2 Revenue, Expenditures, and Debt, 1686–1697 (£millions)

Year	Total Revenue	Total Expenditures	Total Debt
1686–1688[a]	1.9	2.1	2.0
1688–1691[b]	8.6	11.5	3.1
	2.9	3.8	3.0
1695	4.1	6.2	8.4
1697	3.3	7.9	16.7
1700	4.3	3.2	14.2
1710	5.2	9.7	21.4
1720	6.3	6.0	54.0
1730	6.3	5.6	51.4
1740	5.7	6.2	47.4
1750	7.5	7.2	78.0
1760	9.2	18.0	101.7
1770	11.4	10.5	130.6
1780	12.5	22.6	167.2
1790	17.0	16.8	244.0

[a] Per annum, except for total debt.
[b] First row of 1688 are totals; second row are per annum.
Sources: 1686–1697, Table 1. 1700–1790, Mitchell (1988, Series PF1, PF2, and PF7, respectively).

nearly all the growth in the British state occurred through the military side, including what administration was needed at home to conduct the war and its financing. No interventionist bureaucracy aimed at regulating the domestic economy grew up in parallel with that underpinning Britain's foreign affairs.[22]

X.5 CONCLUSION

Maintaining democracy and the market requires a form of limited government. Throughout history, the restrictions of limited government have been ignored, openly evaded, or simply altered when inconvenient (as North, 1981, 1990, has long emphasized). To survive, the limits inherent in democracy and the market must be self-enforcing on political officials.

[22] Indeed, as I argue elsewhere, the English state was remarkably constrained by a system of federalism that allowed local governments considerable political freedom over local economic conditions (Weingast, 1995). This played a striking role in providing the political foundations for the industrial revolution during the 18th century.

Defining the problem in this way reveals how remarkably ignorant we are about structuring the institutions of government to attain these ends.

To study the problem of self-enforcing limited government, this chapter has focused on a particular aspect of limited government, the mechanisms underlying honorable behavior with respect to debt agreements. The problem of sovereign debt is not only of interest in its own right, but, looking back on the history of economic and political development in Europe, capital markets provide one of the few objective indicators with which to judge the efficacy of changes in institutions underpinning limited government.

The history of early modern Europe shows that regular default is strongly associated with problems of development. In several senses, the evolution of institutions to make these agreements credible proved an important task in Europe's development. By assuring fiscal soundness and access to sufficient funds in times of need, the government was far less likely to have intense, short-term desires for funds leading to arbitrary economic intervention, uncertainty, and political risk. Further, the assurance of limited government in Europe is also associated with the rise of representative institutions.[23] Legislatures provided one means to counterbalance sovereigns, helping to represent the interests of citizens.

These principles can be seen at work with respect to sovereign debt in late 17th and early 18th century England. Prior to the Glorious Revolution, debt repayment remained at the discretion of the Crown, and sovereigns defaulted on loan agreements when they proved inconvenient. As a consequence, the English Crown was highly credit rationed, rarely having a debt above the level of annual public revenue.

The Glorious Revolution not only brought a new king to power, but rewrote the rules of the English state. The broad discretionary powers of the Crown were removed and Parliament was raised to a permanent position of power within the constitutional framework. No longer could the Crown raise money—or an army—without the approval of Parliament. The Revolution Settlement, particularly the Declaration of Rights, laid out a set of conditions which were cause for removing the Crown.

The problem of sovereign debt was embedded within this system, with dramatic, though not necessarily foreseen, consequences. Loans became acts of Parliament, thus requiring a new act of Parliament to alter. Defaulting on a loan thus required the cooperation of Parliament. As representatives, in part, of the lenders, this cooperation was hardly assured. Moreover, the possibility of the Crown ignoring Parliament and defaulting unilaterally threatened a larger sanction, for this represented a clear violation of the laws of Parliament.

[23] This topic is discussed in Schumpeter (1919), North (1981, Chapter 11), and Hoffman and Norberg (1994).

The institutional changes following the Glorious Revolution dramatically increased the penalties that could be imposed on the sovereign following default. The theory of sovereign debt predicts that this increase should, in turn, greatly increase the sovereign's credit limit. The evidence on this prediction is remarkable, with government debt rising by an order of magnitude in just nine years following the revolution. Debt raised during the wars that followed demonstrated that this hardly exhausted the government's credit. Thirty years after the revolution, for example, debt had risen above (estimated) GNP, attaining a debt to annual revenue ratio of nearly ten.

Representative institutions therefore proved central to the fiscal and military success of England following the Glorious Revolution. So too did limited government more broadly, for the absence of the national government's ability to regulate the economy—powers left in large part at the discretion of local governments—played a significant, if unforeseen, role in fostering the industrial revolution (Weingast, 1995).

But this discussion forces us to ask a larger question. If embedding the problem of sovereign debt within the larger constitutional system helped solve the sovereign's commitment problems with respect to debt, what made the constitutional institutions self-enforcing?

The answer is a variant on the principles discussed earlier.[24] Assume that the sovereign must retain the support of at least some proportion of the citizenry to survive, though not necessarily a majority. Further, notice that the natural diversity of circumstances implies that citizens are likely to have widely differing experiences, interests, and values. This observation implies citizens are likely to have differing notions of fundamental rights and hence the definition of a transgression.

The natural diversity of preferences and values implies that universalistic limits on government—ones applying to all citizens—are unlikely to survive. The reason is that the sovereign can take advantage of this diversity and still survive. Like the threat of the withdrawal of the marginal lenders in sovereign debt, the threat of withdrawal of constituents beyond those needed to survive is not harmful to the sovereign. This implies that the sovereign may transgress against what some citizens consider their fundamental rights if other citizens do not deem those as fundamental rights. In short, citizens face a massive coordination problem that hinders their ability to police limits on sovereign behavior.

Considerable evidence supports this view for much of 17th century England, with the sovereign often trampling rights considered fundamental to the Whigs while retaining the support of the Tories (Weingast, 1994). Only late in the century, when a dispute caused the king to turn on his own constituents, did he face a united nation opposed to him. This not only led

[24] This discussion draws on my larger work on this topic (Weingast, 1994).

to his removal, but, as we have seen, a wholesale revision of English institutions. These revisions were designed in part to help solve the coordination problem among citizens.

Prior to crowning William and Mary king and queen, the Whigs and the Tories negotiated over terms of the settlement. Their purpose was to produce a series of universal standards about the limits on government. Although Tories and Whigs still disagreed about values, they could agree about trigger strategies, that is, on what actions should trigger an attempt to depose the king. Here, Parliament, as representative of citizens against a potential hostile and pernicious Crown, became a focal point. Tories and Whigs strongly disagreed about what rights were important (for example, religious freedom versus economic freedom). But all agreed that, to protect these rights, they needed a strong Parliament to counterbalance the king. Put another way, though they disagreed about what rights were fundamental, they could agree on a mechanism for protecting all rights. Hence, the Revolution Settlement made laws of Parliament sacrosanct. In this way, the constitutional revisions served as a new, constructed focal point, helping citizens to respond in concert to violations by the sovereign. The potential withdrawal of total support from the sovereign served as a significant threat, providing the sovereign with considerable incentives to adhere to the prescribed limits. In the words of one prominent scholar of the Glorious Revolution:

> The thirteen points in the Declaration were not just statements of the true nature of the law of the constitution, they were also intended to provide a guideline for the future conduct of government, so that any departure from legality would be instantly signalled, and remedial action could be taken. (Jones, 1972, p. 318)

Limited government in England was thus intimately associated with the rise of representative institutions, for Parliament served as a central focal point in assuring potentially unanimous opposition to the Crown in the event of violations of fundamental rights. That sanction in turn, provided the appropriate incentive system for the Crown to honor these rights, thus assuring self-enforcing limited government.

APPENDIX: APPLICATION OF THE GREIF, MILGROM, AND WEINGAST MODEL TO THE PROBLEM OF SOVEREIGN DEBT

Our model of sovereign debt has two kinds of players: a sovereign and individual lenders. The lenders, identical and large in number, are identified with the points on the interval [0,d]. The sovereign's gross value of debt, d, a given period is $v(d)$. In addition, we assume that, for each unit of debt, the sovereign agrees to pay an interest cost of $i > 0$. Assuming that i represents the true social opportunity cost of capital, then the net social value of debt,

d, is $v(d) - id$. Notice that $U(d) = v(d) - id$ is also the sovereign's payoff from honoring his debt agreements. We assume that debt is valuable to the sovereign, so that v is nonnegative, strictly concave, and differentiable. Moreover, we assume that $f(0) = 0$ and that $v(d) - id$ achieves a maximum at some unique value $d^* > 0$, which we call the *efficient level of debt.*

The payoff to the sovereign from honoring his debt contracts with interest i is $U(d) = v(d) - id$. If the sovereign fails to honor its debt agreements to a fraction of lenders, ϵ, then it saves the interest charge on these loans, $i\epsilon$, and it confiscates these lender's capital, ϵD. Hence, its payoffs on a total debt, d, from cheating a fraction, ϵ, of lenders is $U(d) + \epsilon(D + i)$. Lenders who are not cheated earn i on their loans. Lenders who are cheated lose their capital, l.

This interaction is repeated period after period, and the players' payoffs from the whole repeated game are the discounted sum of the periodic payoffs using discount factor δ. Thus, the sovereign's payoff when the debt is d_t in period t is given by

$$\sum_{t=0}^{\infty} \delta^t[U(d_t) + \epsilon_t(1 + i)] \qquad (1)$$

and the payoffs of the individual lenders are determined similarly as the discounted sum of their periodic payoffs.

The specification of the model captures the idea that lenders are substitutes as far as the sovereign is concerned and each of them is relatively "small." The historical observation that sovereigns could discriminate between lenders is captured through the specification of the sovereign's strategy.

Game 1: Bilateral Reputation Mechanism

Our first model represents the situation of lenders without social or economic organization so that they remain unaware of how the sovereign has treated other lenders. Although this model is surely too extreme to be fully descriptive, it highlights the difficulties faced by individual lenders negotiating with the sovereign on their own.[25]

[25] Readers familiar with either the economics of reputations or the theory of repeated games will recognize that the repetition of the interactions between the sovereign and the individual lenders creates the possibility for reputations to be created that enforce good behavior by the sovereign. The idea is that a lender who is once cheated might refuse to return to the sovereign in future periods, leading to a loss of profits for the sovereign. The effectiveness of this threat depends both on the frequency of trade and the periodic value of the individual lender's trade to the sovereign. If the frequency of trade is sufficiently high and the volume sufficiently low, so that the value of the repeat business of any individual lender to the sovereign is high, the simple reputation mechanism can be effective for providing incentives to the sovereign to protect individual rights. In our model, however, when the volume of trade rises to the efficient level, the value of repeat business falls to zero, so the usual conclusions of the Folk Theorem of repeated games do not apply.

Proposition 1. In no Nash equilibrium of Game 1 does the sovereign honor all debt agreements ($\epsilon_t \equiv 0$) at the efficient level ($d_t \equiv d^*$), regardless of the levels of i or δ.

Proof. Suppose there were such an equilibrium and consider the payoff to the sovereign if it deviates from the equilibrium strategy and cheats a fraction ϵ of the first period lenders. In the initial period, its payoff is $U(d^*) + \epsilon(l + i)$. In subsequent periods, the assumptions of the model imply that the play of at most ϵ lenders is affected. Consequently, at least $l - \epsilon$ lenders lend to the sovereign in each future period, and the sovereign's payoff from treating them honestly is, $\sum\delta^t[U(d^*(l - \epsilon))] = U(d^*(l - \epsilon))/(l - \delta)$. When discounted back to the first period, this sum yields a payoff of $\gamma U(d^*(l - \epsilon))$ where, for convenience, we define $\gamma = \delta/(l - \delta)$. So, the sovereign's total payoff from cheating a fraction ϵ of the lenders in the first period and adhering to the purported equilibrium thereafter is at least

$$U(d^*) + \epsilon(1 + i) + \gamma U(d^*(l - \epsilon)) \tag{2}$$

and this expression coincides exactly with the actual payoff when $\epsilon = 0$, that is, when the sovereign adheres to the purported equilibrium. The derivative of expression (2) with respect to ϵ at $\epsilon = 0$ and $d = d^*$ is

$$(l + i) - \gamma d^* U' = (1 + i) > 0, \tag{3}$$

because $U' = 0$ at d^*. This establishes that the sovereign has a profitable deviation, so that the specified behavior is not consistent with Nash equilibrium.

No mechanism based only on sanctions by those who are cheated can support honest trading at the efficient level, d^*, because, when loans are made to that level, the marginal lender has zero net value to the sovereign. By cheating a few marginal lenders, the sovereign loses nothing in terms of future profits but saves a positive expense in the present period. To support the efficient level of debt, some kind of collective action among lenders is needed.[26]

Game 2: An Uncoordinated Multilateral Reputation Mechanism

In the first game, we treated each lender as negotiating with the sovereign in isolation. Suppose, instead, that the lending community was organized into a number of subgroups, perhaps representing families, clans, or

[26] This result is not an artifact of our specifications of costs. For example, if we had specified that the costs born by the city include some fixed costs per trader (possibly in addition to the proportional costs), the city would have an even stronger incentive to reduce the number of traders, because it bears only a fraction τ of the resulting loss of value but saves all of the service costs. Making costs proportional to value minimizes the distortion in the city's incentives, but still leaves it tempted to seek short-term gains by cutting services at the expense of individual traders when only the bilateral reputation mechanism is at work.

ethnic groups. To represent this, we assume that if a specific lender is ever abused, even in the absence of any organization for information diffusion, some of his peers, especially those in his own group, were likely to learn it. Can this process of limited, uncoordinated multilateral response enable the sovereign to commit himself at the efficient level of debt?

To examine this issue, suppose that an incident in which the sovereign cheats a group of lenders always becomes known to a larger group of lenders. Formally, whenever a set L of lenders is cheated, $L^* \supset L$, each of whom learns of the event. We assume that there is some constant K ($1 \leq K < \infty$) such that if the number of lenders cheated is $\mu(L)$, then the number who learn about the event, $\mu(L^*)$, is no more than $K\mu(L)$: If few lenders are cheated, then proportionately few discover that the event has occurred.

Proposition 2. No Nash equilibrium of Game 2 can support honest sovereign behavior ($\epsilon_t \equiv 0$) at the efficient level of debt ($d_t \equiv d^*$), regardless of the levels of i or δ.

Proof. The proof is essentially the same as for the first proposition, except that the bound on the number who decline to lend in the future is multiplied by K. In particular, (3) is replaced by $(l + i) - \gamma K d^* U' = (1 + i) > 0$.

Violations against a few lenders that are noticed by proportionately few cannot be deterred by a threat of retaliation by just those with firsthand knowledge.

Game 3: Lenders with Coordinating Ability

We have seen that it is impossible for the sovereign and the lenders to sustain an efficient level of debt based only on sanctions applied by small groups. In this subsection, we examine the role of an *organization* for communication and coordination. In our formal model, if the sovereign cheats a set of lenders, L, then the organization is assumed to discover the event and announce a boycott with probability $\alpha(L) \geq \mu(L)$. This specification entails that the more lenders are abused, the more likely is the organization to conclude that some abuse has occurred.

In this game, the organization makes boycott announcements mechanically and without any means of enforcement. Lenders learn the organization's announcement in each period, but they are not forced to heed it. It simply becomes part of the information that is available to them and to the sovereign. Otherwise, the game is the same as Game 1. Despite the organization's lack of enforcement ability, the mere change in information alters the set of equilibria.

Proposition 3. Suppose that

$$d^*(l + i) < \gamma U(d^*). \tag{4}$$

Then, the following strategies form a Markov perfect equilibrium of Game 3[27]: The sovereign does not cheat unless a boycott is announced by the organization; after a boycott is announced, the sovereign cheats any lender who offers to lend. Lenders offer to lend in a given period if and only if no boycott has been announced.

The formal proof is by direct verification. The condition (4) reflects the sovereign's design at the end of period 1, having contracted for the optimal debt, d^*. At that time, the payment due all lenders is $d^*(l + i)$. If he makes this payment, he obtains a future stream of utility valued at $U(d^*)$ per period, or $\gamma U(d^*)$ discounted back to the present. Thus, he will honor his loan agreements if and only if condition (4) holds. It is that fact that accounts for the continued effectiveness of group sanctions even at the efficient level of debt.

As remarked earlier, the equilibrium strategies contain a counterintuitive element: that the sovereign cheats any lender who offers to lend during a credit boycott. It is the lenders' unanimous expectations that the sovereign will behave that way which causes them all to honor the boycott. But why should the sovereign not welcome lenders during a credit boycott, rather than cheating them? Because we are looking at a Markov perfect equilibrium, the sovereign can be expected to cheat embargo-breaking lenders only if it is actually in the sovereign's interest to do so once the credit embargo has been announced. Given the specified strategies, if y lenders violate the boycott and offer their funds, the sovereign expects a payoff of $U(y)$ in the current period and zero in future periods, if it acts honestly. If it cheats, it expects $v(y)$ in the current period and zero in the future, so cheating is, indeed, optimal.

Although the strategies described in Proposition 3 do constitute an equilibrium, the expectations and behavior that they entail seem implausible. The equilibrium requires, for example, that no matter how desperate the sovereign may be for renewed lending relationships once a credit boycott has been announced, the sovereign must nevertheless cheat anyone who ventures to lend with it. In addition, the lenders must expect that behavior. By the equilibrium logic, the sovereign does this because it expects the boycott to take full hold in the next round anyway, so it anticipates that any cooperation it may offer would be fruitless.

This equilibrium behavior does not match the historical facts very well, and it is of doubtful import even as theory, because it supposes that the sovereign and potential embargo breakers play the equilibrium with the lowest possible value for themselves. Similar criticisms have been leveled at the equilibria of other repeated game models, notably by Farrell and Maskin

[27] This is a Nash equilibrium of the game with the properties that (1) the player's strategies at any date depend only on whether a boycott has been announced and (2) each player's strategy at each date maximizes that player's payoff from that date onward, given the equilibrium strategies of the other players.

(1989), Bernheim and Ray (1989), and Abreu and Pearce (1991). None of the alternative concepts that these authors suggest apply directly to our model, but all suggest that it is more reasonable to suppose that some cooperation may be achieved between lenders and the sovereign even after a boycott is announced. As an example, we emphasize the possibility that mutually profitable *bilateral* agreements between the sovereign and individual lenders may be reached even during a boycott. It will be apparent from the logic of the arguments that any other kind of cooperation would lead to qualitatively similar conclusions.

Let us therefore suppose that if some lenders agree to lend to the sovereign despite the credit embargo, they cannot rely on the threat of a *group* boycott to enforce their own claims against the sovereign. What, then, can enforce honest behavior by the sovereign during the boycott? We consider that it is the threat by a cheated lender to withdraw his own future loans. Proposition 1 established that the efficient level of debt, d^*, could not be supported by such an equilibrium, but it leaves open the possibility that some inefficiently low level of debt can be supported. We are therefore led to ask, what is the highest level of debt, d', that can be supported in this way?

Proposition 4. Consider the strategies in which the sovereign cooperates in each period with just those lenders that it has never before cheated and each lender offers to lend in each period if and only if he has not been cheated before. These strategies constitute a subgame perfect equilibrium of Game 1 when the volume of lenders is d and the interest is i if and only if for all $y \leq d$

$$0 \geq l - iy - \gamma y U'(y). \tag{5}$$

Proof. It is obvious that the lenders' strategies are best replies from any point in the history of the game to the strategy of the sovereign, so we need consider only the optimality of the sovereign's strategy.

Beginning with d current lenders, consider the subgame achieved after $d - y$ lenders depart, when there are $y \leq d$ lenders remaining. By cheating a fraction ϵ of the y current lenders, the sovereign's payoff will be $g(\epsilon;y) = v(y) + (l - \epsilon)iy + \epsilon + \gamma U(y(l - \epsilon))$. A necessary condition for the optimality of $\epsilon = 0$ is $\partial g(\epsilon;y)/\partial\epsilon \leq 0$ at $\epsilon = 0$. An easy calculation verifies that this is just the same as condition (5), so the latter condition is necessary for all y.

By the optimality principle of dynamic programming, it is sufficient to show that there is no subgame in which the sovereign would do strictly better by setting $\epsilon > 0$ in the initial period and then adhering to its equilibrium strategy thereafter, given the strategies of the others. If f is concave, then for all y, $g(\epsilon;y)$ is concave in ϵ, so a sufficient condition is that for all y, $\partial g(\epsilon;y)/\partial\epsilon \leq 0$ at $\epsilon = 0$, which is again equivalent to (6), proving sufficiency.

Let d' be the largest solution of (5). The equilibrium described by Proposition 4 suggests an interesting interpretation of the level of debt, d', observed during credit boycotts and explains why some lenders continued to lend but others did not. According to the theory, additional lenders, beyond the number d', would be cheated by the sovereign and would be unable to exact retribution for their losses.

Alternatively, if we think of the level of debt $d < d^*$ during the boycott as being determined by factors outside the model (such as existing alliances or other interests), then condition (5) implies that the maximum interest rate that can be paid and still make it worthwhile for the sovereign increases, the lower is d. This confirms the intuition that a credit embargo breaker may be able to negotiate an unusually attractive deal, because the value of debt per lender ($U(d)/d$) is higher when d is small.

Proposition 4 implies that in the absence of a strong organization—one that can enforce the boycott on its members—the organization cannot credibly threaten to reduce the sovereign to a debt level less than d'.

Game 4: An Organization with Coordination and Enforcement Abilities

The final variant is a game in which the organization has the ability to enforce compliance from the individual lenders. We offer no formal analysis of this case. It is obvious that the only role of enforcement by the organization against member lenders in our formal model is to prevent loans during boycotts. Accordingly, the results are the same as in Proposition 3, but now the lenders participate in the boycott because they are required to do so, rather than because they expect participation to serve their individual interests.

ACKNOWLEDGMENTS

Barry R. Weingast serves as senior fellow of the Hoover Institution and is a professor in the Department of Political Science at Stanford University. The author gratefully acknowledges Bruce Carruthers, James Conklin, Gary Cox, Richard Davis, Raquel Fernandez, Avner Greif, David Haddock, Philip Hoffman, Dierdre McCloskey, Paul Milgrom, Douglass North, Jean-Laurent Rosenthal, and Kenneth Sokoloff for helpful comments.

REFERENCES

Abreu, D., and Pearce, D. (1991). A perspective on renegotiation in repeated games. In *Game Equilibrium Models, Vol. II: Methods, Morals and Markets,* Reinhard Selten (ed.). New York: Springer Verlag.

Atkeson, A. (1991) International Lending with Moral Hazard and Risk of Repudiation, *Econometrica* **59:** 1069–1089.
Bernheim, D. and Ray, D. (1989). Collective dynamic consistency in repeated games. *Games and Economic Behavior* 1 (3 September): 295–326.
Bien, D. (1987). Offices, corps, and a system of state credit: The uses of privilege under the ancient regime. In *The French Revolution and the Creation of Modern Political Culture* (K. Baker, ed.), Vol. 1, pp. 89–114.
Brenner, R. (1976). Agrarian class structure and economic development in pre-industrial Europe. *Past and Present.* **70:** 30–75.
Brewer, J. (1989). *The Sinews of Power.* New York: Knopf.
Bulow, J., and Rogoff, K. (1989). A constant recontracting model of sovereign debt. *Journal of Political Economy* **97,** 155–178.
Campion, L. (1958). *Introduction to the Procedure of the House of Commons,* 3rd ed. Macmillan, London.
Carruthers, B. G. (1990). Politics, popery, and property: A comment on North and Weingast, Journal of Economic History **50,** 693–698.
Carswell, J. (1973). *From Revolution to Revolution: England 1688–1776.* New York: Charles Scribner's Sons.
Conklin, J. (1995). Redistribution and the credibility of sovereign debt, MS. University of Texas, Austin.
Dickson, P. G. M. (1967). *Financial Revolution in England.* New York: St. Martins Press.
Eaton, J.,Gersovitz, M., and Stiglitz, J. (1986). The pure theory of country risk. *European* **30;** 481–513.
Ekelund, R. B., and Tollison, R. D. (1981). *Mercantilism as a Rent-Seeking Society: Economic Regulation in Historical Perspective.* Texas A&M University Press, College Station.
Farrell, J., and Maskin E. (1989). Renegotiation in Repeated Games. *Games and Economic Behavior* 1 (3 September): 327–60.
Greif, A., Milgrom, P., and Weingast, B. R. (1994). Coordination, commitment, and enforcement: The case of the merchant guild. *Journal of Political Economy* **102,** 745–776.
Grossman, H., and van Huyck, J. B. Sovereign debt as a contingent claim: Excusable default, repudiation, and reputation. American Economic Review **78;** 1088–1097.
Hill, B. W. (1976). *Growth of Parliamentary Parties, 1689–1742.* Archon Books, Hamden, CT.
Hill, C. (1980). *Century of Revolution: 1603–1714,* 2nd ed. Norton, New York.
Hochberg, L. (1984). The English Civil War in a geographic perspective. *Journal of Interdisciplinary History.* **14:** 729–750.
Hoffman, P. T. (1994). Early modern France, 1450–1700. In *Fiscal Crises, Liberty and Representative Governments 1450–1789.* (P. T. Hoffman and K. Norberg, eds.). Stanford University Press, Stanford, CA.
Hoffman, P. T., and Norberg, K., eds. (1994). *Fiscal Crises, Liberty, and Representative Government, 1450–1789.* Stanford University Press, Stanford, CA.
Hoffman, P. T., and Rosenthal, J.-L. (1995). [This volume]
Jones, J. R. (1972). *The Revolution of 1688 in England.* Norton, New York.
Levy, B., and Spiller, P. T. (1994). The institutional foundations of regulatory commitment: A comparative analysis of telecommunications regulation. *Journal of Law, Economics, and Organization.* **10:** 201–246.
Lipson, C. (1988). The international organization of third world debt. In *Toward a Political Economy of Development* (pp. 12–46). (Bates, R. H. ed.). University of California Press, Berkeley.
Macaulay, T. B. 1949–1962. *History of England from the Accession of James II.* New York: Harper and Brothers.
May, E. (1906). *Parliamentary Practice,* 17th ed. London. William Clowes and Sons (1st ed., 1844).
Mitchell, B. R (1988). *British Historical Statistics.* Cambridge, MA: Cambridge University Press.

North, D. C. (1981). *Structure and Change in Economic History.* Norton, New York.
North, D. C. (1990). *Institutions, Institutional Change, and Economic Performance.* Cambridge University Press, New York.
North, D. C. (1993). Institutions and credible commitment. *JITE.* **149:** 11–23.
North, D. C. (1996). The paradox of the West. In *The Origins of Modern Freedom,* R. Davis, Ed., Stanford: Stanford University Press.
North, D. C., and Weingast, B. R. (1989). Constitutions and commitment: Evolution of the institutions of public choice in 17th century England. *Journal of Economic History.* **59:** 803–32.
Ordeshook, P. (1993). Constitutional stability. *Constitutional Political Economy* **3,** 137–175.
Plumb, J. H. (1967). *The Growth of Political Stability in England 1675–1725.* London: Macmillan Press.
Przeworski, A. (1991). *Democracy and the Market.* New York: Cambridge University Press.
Reid, G. (1967). *The Politics of Financial Control.* London: Hutchinson University Library.
Root, H. (1989). Tying the King's hands. *Rationality and Society.* **1:** 240–258
Sargent, T., and Velde, F. (1995). Macroeconomic causes and consequences of the French Revolution. *Journal of Political Economy,* **103:** 474–518.
Schumpeter, J. A. (1991[1918]). The Crisis of the Tax State. Reprinted in Richard Swedberg (Ed.), *Joseph A. Schumpeter.* Princeton: Princeton University Press.
Speck, W. A. (1989). *Reluctant Revolutionaries.* Oxford University Press, Oxford.
Stiglitz, J., and Weiss, A. (1983). Incentive effects of terminations. *American Economic Review* **73,** 912–927.
Thirsk, J. (1987). *Agricultural Regions and Agrarian History in England, 1500–1750,* Houndmills, Basingstoke, Hampshire: Macmillan.
Veitch, J. M. (1986). Repudiations and confiscations by the medieval state. *Journal of Economic History* **46,** 31–36.
Weingast, B. R. (1994). *Political Foundations of Democracy and the Rule of Law,* Working paper. Hoover Institution, Stanford University, Stanford, CA.
Weingast, B. R. (1995). The economic role of political institutions: Market-preserving federalism and economic development. *Journal of Law, Economics, and Organization* **11,** 1–31.
Western, J. R. (1972). *Monarchy and Revolution: The English State in the 1680s.* Houndmills, Basingstoke, Hampshire: Macmillan Press.
Williams, E. N. (1960). *The Eighteenth Century Constitution: Documents and Commentary.* Cambridge University Press, Cambridge, UK.
Williamson, O. (1994). *The Institutions and Governance of Economic Development and Reform* (unpublished MS). University of California, Berkeley.

XI

Credible Commitment in the United States: Substantive and Structural Limits on the Avoidance of Public Debt

John N. Drobak

Institutions are crucial to economic growth. These "rules of the game in a society" (North, 1990, p. 3) make economic growth more likely if they create the right incentives, if they establish confidence in the economic system, and if they allow business to achieve productive efficiencies and to realize the gains from trade. Institutions that do otherwise make sustained economic growth impossible. In the history of the United States, the law has been a formal institution that has supported the growth of the economy. Part of that support involved the creation of a general perception that state and local governments "credibly commit" to repay their financial obligations (North, 1990, pp. 50–51, 58–59).

This chapter examines the Supreme Court's attempts to prevent state and local governments from repudiating their debt obligations. The Supreme Court has used two different parts of the Constitution to do that. The contract clause creates a substantive limit on debt repudiation: "No State shall . . . pass any . . . Law impairing the Obligations of Contracts. . . ."[1] This clause applies with full force to all political units of a state, such as towns, public authorities, and public utility districts. Throughout our nation's history, the Supreme Court has vigorously applied

[1] *U.S. Const.*, art. I, § 10, cl. 1.

the contract clause to limit modifications of state debt obligations by legislatures. That has not been true, however, for impairments of government debt obligations resulting from state court decisions, because both the language and purpose of the clause seem to limit its scope to legislative conduct. As a result, the Court has had to deal with judicial impairments of government debt in a different way, based on the federal structure of our government.

Because the Constitution established a federal court system separate from the state courts, the Supreme Court was able to fashion a federal commercial common law as a means of enforcing local contractual obligations in federal court. This federal common law took precedence over any conflicting state court decisions that impaired contract rights. The Supreme Court, in the face of massive repudiations based on state court judgments, used this principle to enforce midwestern railroad bonds throughout the late 19th century. Although these railroad bond cases are mainly derived from the cases establishing the primacy of federal commercial law in federal lawsuits, the cases also appear to be a species of the contract clause doctrine, implicitly extended to judicial impairments. In the 1930s, however, the Supreme Court ended the authority of the federal courts to make their own commercial common law and closed the only method available to police judicial contract impairments. So when the Supreme Court of Washington contorted Washington bond law in order to declare the Washington Public Power Supply System (WPPSS) bonds invalid, the bondholders were left without any way to have that decision reviewed by the United States Supreme Court. As the law stands now, there is no constitutional limitation on the impairment of government debt by state courts.

The first part of this chapter examines the use of the contract clause to control legislative impairments of bond obligations. In passing, the discussion will also touch on the meaning of the contract clause as applied to legislative impairments of private contracts. This part of the chapter will conclude with an analysis and criticism of the claim that the contracts clause is no longer needed today to control legislative impairments of debt obligations, because modern market constraints and political forces are enough to protect bondholders. The second part of the chapter describes the political and social factors that led to the Supreme Court's use of federal court jurisdiction to limit judicial impairments of railroad bond obligations, explains the death of that doctrine, and contrasts the railroad defaults with the WPPSS default. Finally, the conclusion will return to the "institutions" theme by considering whether the impact of the constitutional law is insignificant when compared with all the other factors that affect the riskiness of government investments. The chapter concludes that, even if it is impossible to measure a perceptible change in risk from judicial tolerance of bond repudiation, judicial enforcement of government debt obligations is one small, but important, part of the "rule of law" that is essential for the success of a market system.[2]

XI.1. LEGISLATIVE IMPAIRMENTS

XI.1.1 The Framers' Intent

It is not surprising that many different parts of the Constitution protect property rights. The Framers were wealthy men who wanted to spur economic growth, of which they would be part. They wrote the Constitution to correct economic problems that persisted under the Articles of Confederation, fearing commercial disintegration from state laws that compromised the payment of private debt, by allowing payment in paper currency or commodities (such as cattle, tobacco, or flour) (Wright, 1938, pp. 4–5; Thompson, 1992, pp. 1373, 1380–1381). Shays's Rebellion figured prominently in the Framers' concern, because many were alarmed that it marked the beginning of a trend.[3]

It is difficult to know the precise meaning the Framers intended for the contract clause. The clause first appeared three months into the convention, when it was picked up from the Northwest Ordinance, which had been recently enacted to govern the Ohio territory (Wright, 1938, pp. 6–9). There was little discussion in the convention about the clause; the Committee on Style, which first wrote the clause, left no record of its purpose. It seems that the general view of the Framers was to blame the debtor relief statutes and the related problems on the lack of a stable currency (Wright, 1938, p. 13). Not surprisingly, the clauses dealing with legal tender figured more prominently in both the convention and ratification debates. The contract clause

[2] Before beginning, one qualification is necessary. This chapter does not discuss the impact of the Eleventh Amendment, which, since 1798, has barred most suits against state governments in federal courts. The amendment does not make it impossible to sue states to enforce their debt obligations, although it can make the task extremely difficult. State court is still available for such suits, but, at least until recently, people have feared that state judges would lack the impartiality of federal judges in suits for payments of state debts. Of course, a state can waive the protection of the Eleventh Amendment, just as it can waive sovereign immunity. There are also some limitations to Eleventh Amendment immunity, but it is hard to see how they could apply to a disgruntled creditor of a state. As the discussion in Section XI.2 will illustrate, the amendment does not bar suits in federal court against subdivisions of a state, such as towns and counties. Consequently, the Eleventh Amendment immunity should increase the risk of state, although not local, government bonds.

[3] Some scholars believe that Shays's Rebellion was blown out of proportion in order to generate fears of economic instability that would then lead to support of the new Constitution. George Washington's presence at the Constitutional Convention in Philadelphia was a major reason delegates came, even though the call for a constitutional convention in Baltimore the year earlier had been a failure. Supposedly, Washington was induced to come to Philadelphia by overblown pleas that events like Shays's Rebellion would become common.

appears near the end of the sentence in the Constitution dealing with legal tender, likely signifying its smaller role in dealing with the economic problems.[4]

The brief record of the debate over the contract clause in the convention and its mention in the ratification controversy do give us some generally accepted information about the clause. The clause did not literally mean that all retroactive impairments of contracts were unconstitutional. Several members of the convention expressed their belief that retroactive modifications of contractual obligations were sometimes necessary; no one disagreed (Thompson, 1992, p. 1381). Contemporaneous discussions of the contract clause, often in the ratification debates, show that the proponents of the clause feared the "democratic excesses" typified by Shays's Rebellion, that they believed that many of the debt relief laws were directed at out-of-state creditors who lacked local political power, and that they saw the nation's credit worsening on the world markets as a consequence of these problems (Thompson, 1992, pp. 1382–1383). The supporters of the clause also emphasized the immorality of retroactive impairment of contract obligations.

XI.1.2 19th-Century Opinions

None of the discussions about the contract clause, neither at the Constitutional Convention nor during the ratification debates, ever mentioned the clause as limiting government contracts. Ironically, the first use of the clause by the Supreme Court came in *Fletcher* v. *Peck,*[5] a case in which Chief Justice Marshall ruled that the clause protected contracts to which a state was a party, as well as those between private parties. The case involved Georgia's attempt to annul land grants fraudulently procured from the state as part of the Georgia Yazoo land frauds. In his opinion, Marshall declared that the fraudulent procurement of state land grants from the Georgia legislature was not an appropriate subject for Supreme Court review, but that the legislature's annulment of the grants was within the Court's jurisdiction. As a retroactive impairment of contract rights, the annulment was unconstitutional under the contract clause.

Although the first contract clause case decided by the Supreme Court began the use of the clause as part of the credible commitment for governmental obligations, the vast majority of the 19th-century contract clause cases dealt with government impairment of private contracts. The Marshall

[4] "No state shall enter into any Treaty, Alliance, or Confederation; grant letters of Marque and Reprisal; coin money; emit Bills of Credit, make any Thing but gold and silver Coin a Tender in Payment of Debts; pass any Bill of Attainder, ex post facto Law, or Law impairing the obligation of contracts, or grant any Title of Nobility." *U.S. Const.,* art. I, § 10, cl. 1.

[5] 6 Cranch 87 (1810).

Court steadily developed the clause into the primary constitutional protection of property rights. In large part, this stemmed from John Marshall's strong distrust of state legislatures, coupled with his ardent desire to protect property rights. As one of the leading experts on the contract clause explained:

> By employing a far broader conception of contract than had been prevalent in 1787, and by combining this conception with the principles of eighteenth-century natural law, [John Marshall] was able to make of the contract clause a mighty instrument for the protection of the rights of private property. His personal dominance of the Court, at least until 1827, made it possible for him to give to that clause a breadth of meaning which not only exceeds that intended by the Framers, but also goes beyond the views expressed by Wilson, Paine, the members of Congress who took part in the Yazoo lands debate, and even Paterson and Hamilton. His four great contract opinions written between 1810 and 1819 are among the most important opinions, economic as well as legal, which have ever come from the Supreme Court. (Wright, 1938, p. 28)

The Taney Court continued this use of the contract clause, although it loosened the limits on state legislatures in a number of ways. Probably the best known part of this story stems from the Marshall Court's determination in *Dartmouth College* v. *Woodward*[6] that a corporate charter was a contract protected by the clause, followed eventually by the Taney Court's view that these contracts between firms and a state should be interpreted to give the state the greatest unbridled discretion (e.g., *Charles River Bridge* v. *Warren Bridge*).[7] Very few of the Supreme Court's antebellum contract opinions dealt with governmental financial obligations. The most frequently litigated public contract issue before the Court during this period involved immunity from state taxation. Although the Taney Court followed the Marshall Court in enforcing a state's grant of tax immunity, the Taney Court created the principle that a state could not contract away certain police or regulatory powers that are attributes of state sovereignty (such as the power of eminent domain).[8] This principle grew in importance over the years and foreshadowed the Supreme Court's virtual abandonment of the contract clause as applied to private contracts during the Great Depression.

In *Home Building & Loan Association* v. *Blaisdell,*[9] the 1934 landmark case in which the Supreme Court upheld the constitutionality of a Minnesota law that retroactively extended the time for mortgage redemption, the Court explained that all contracts contained an implied "reservation of essential attributes of sovereign power." Moreover, *Blaisdell*

[6] 4 Wheat. 518 (1819).
[7] 11 Pet. 420 (1837).
[8] *West River Bridge v. Dix,* 6 How. 507 (1848).
[9] 290 U.S. 398, 435 (1934).

adopted a minimal threshold for states to overcome in enacting constitutional impairments. Constitutionality requires only a rational basis for the legislature's interference with private contract rights, very much like the modern, virtually nonexistent, substantive due process limitation on economic regulation.

Most of the cases involving either the repudiation or the alteration of public debt came to the Supreme Court from the 1860s into the 1930s and raised issues of judicial, not legislative, impairments. Those cases will be discussed subsequently. The 19th century was a time, however, of frequent, widespread and massive defaults by state and local governments in their bond obligations. Most arose from the great public works projects of the time—the building of a network of first canals and then railroads across the expanding country. The vast majority of these defaults were eventually compromised and settled. In a few instances, states not only defaulted on their obligations, their legislatures also repudiated them, claiming that their bonds were never legally valid (Thompson, 1992, p. 1407; Goodrich, 1960, pp. 265–297). These repudiations never led to contract clause litigation, however. Beginning in the 1880s, a few cases before the Supreme Court raised the unconstitutionality of tax statutes that impaired municipal bonds. For example, after New Orleans borrowed money as authorized by state law, Louisiana restricted the taxing power of the city so much that it could no longer pay its debt.[10] This, the Court ruled, was unconstitutional under the contract clause. In fact, whenever the issue arose throughout the Supreme Court's two-century existence, which was a rare event, the Court routinely ruled that states could not impair their debt contracts through legislative action.[11]

XI.1.3 The Modern Law of Public Contracts

Only once this century did the Supreme Court permit the alteration of a municipal bond contract by action of a legislature. The case, *Faitoute Iron & Steel Co.* v. *City of Asbury Park,*[12] involved a New Jersey depression-era statute that allowed for the compromise of the bonds of bankrupt municipalities. Upon the approval of 85 percent of the bondholders (and the approval of certain government bodies), all bondholders were obligated to accept the compromise payment. The Supreme Court rejected a contract clause challenge to the statute, noting that the city could not have raised its taxes enough to pay its creditors under the old terms. The composition plan,

[10] *Wolff v. New Orleans,* 103 U.S. 358, 365–368 (1881); see also *Murray v. Charleston,* 96 U.S. 432 (1878) (tax on municipal bonds); *Von Hoffman v. City of Quincy,* 4 Wall. 535 (1867).

[11] *United States Trust Co. v. New Jersey,* 431 U.S. 1, 24 (1977).

[12] 316 U.S. 502 (1942).

which was adopted to help the creditors, actually caused the market value of the bonds to increase sharply.[13]

The Supreme Court last dealt with a bond impairment in 1977, in *United States Trust Co.* v. *New Jersey,*[14] a case that reaffirmed the different approaches under the contract clause for modifications of public and private contracts. *U.S. Trust* dealt with the repeal of a 1962 covenant between New York and New Jersey that, as security for a Port Authority bond issue, expressly limited the ability of the Port Authority to subsidize rail passenger transportation from the Port Authority's revenues. When New Jersey repealed the covenant in 1974, United States Trust sued, alleging that the repeal violated the contract clause. The Supreme Court agreed.

In addressing the question of impairment, the Court observed that the effect of the repeal was uncertain:

> The fact is that no one can be sure precisely how much financial loss the bondholders suffered. . . . [B]ut the question of valuation need not be resolved in the instant case because the State has made no effort to compensate the bondholders for any loss sustained by the repeal. . . . [The covenant's] outright repeal totally eliminated an important security provision and thus impaired the obligation of the States' contract.[15]

Although the Court recognized that the impairment might be constitutional if "reasonable and necessary to serve an important public purpose,"[16] the Court concluded that it, not the legislature, had to determine if the standard was met. As the Court explained, "complete deference to a legislative assessment of reasonableness and necessity is not appropriate because the state's self-interest is at stake."[17] The Court acknowledged that mass transportation, energy conservation, and environmental protection were important state goals, but it nonetheless declined to balance them against the rights of the bondholders. Rather, the repeal had to be both reasonable and necessary. It was not reasonable because "the covenant was specifically intended to protect the pledged revenues and reserves against the possibility that such concerns would lead the Port Authority into greater involvement in deficit mass transit."[18] Although circumstances had changed, the con-

[13] *Faitoute Iron & Steel Co. v. City of Asbury Park,* 316 U.S. 502, 513 (1942). The result in *Faitoute* parallels an aberrational case under the *Hope Natural Gas* doctrine. *Hope* requires utility commissions to set rates at a high enough level to enable regulated utilities to have an opportunity to earn "fair" profits. In *Market Street Railway,* the Court departed from that rule for a streetcar company that was going bankrupt as a result of bus competition [see *Market Street Railway v. Railroad Commission,* 324 U.S. 548 (1945)].

[14] 431 U.S. 1 (1977).

[15] *United States Trust Co. v. New Jersey,* 431 U.S. 1, 19 (1977).

[16] *United States Trust Co. v. New Jersey,* 431 U.S. 1, 25 (1977).

[17] *United States Trust Co. v. New Jersey,* 431 U.S. 1, 26 (1977).

[18] *United States Trust Co. v. New Jersey,* 431 U.S. 1, 32 (1977).

cerns of environmental protection and energy conservation "were not unknown in 1962, and the subsequent changes were of degree and not of kind."[19] The repeal was not necessary because the covenant could either have been less drastically modified or the state could have adopted other, albeit perhaps politically unpopular, means to improve mass transit.[20]

The Court's approach to determining the constitutionality of the bond impairment was in marked contrast to its approach in private contract cases. In the latter, the Court appears to balance the public purposes underlying the impairment against the effects on the parties whose rights are impaired. The balance is stacked in favor of constitutionality, however, with a rational basis for impairment seeming to suffice. For claimed impairments of public contracts, the *U.S. Trust* Court expressed the new standard of "reasonable and necessary." But, more importantly, the Court showed that it does not automatically defer to the legislature when public contracts are involved (Merrill, 1987, p. 597).

Justice Brennan (with Justices Marshall and White) dissented in the case, taking an approach similar to that used for private contract cases. He found the 1962 covenant to be an "effective barrier to the development of rapid transit [in] the port region that squarely conflicts with the legitimate needs of the New York metropolitan community, and will persist in doing so into the next century."[21] He thought the Court's suggested alternatives for funding mass transit unrealistic, and he disagreed with the Court's evaluation of the reasonableness of the impairment and the foreseeability of the mass transit problems.[22] He strongly objected to the finding of impairment, because he believed the bondholders suffered only minimal damage.[23] The entire history of the contract clause, in his view, ran counter to the Court's attempt to check New Jersey's use of the police power. Finally, he concluded that the decision was "markedly out of step" with the prevailing judicial philosophy of deference to the legislature.[24]

The majority of the Court had not deferred to the legislature because the state's self-interest was at stake. As the Court explained:

> A governmental entity can always find a use for extra money, especially when taxes do not have to be raised. If a State could reduce its financial obligations whenever it wanted to spend the money for what it regarded as an important public purpose, the Contract Clause would provide no protection at all.[25]

[19] *Id.*
[20] *United States Trust Co. v. New Jersey,* 431 U.S. 1, 30 (1977).
[21] *United States Trust Co. v. New Jersey,* 431 U.S. 1, 36 (1977).
[22] *United States Trust Co. v. New Jersey,* 431 U.S. 1, 40 (1977).
[23] *United States Trust Co. v. New Jersey,* 431 U.S. 1, 41–44 (1977).
[24] *United States Trust Co. v. New Jersey,* 431 U.S. 1, 59 (1977).
[25] *United States Trust Co. v. New Jersey,* 431 U.S. 1, 26 (1977).

Brennan's response was to point out that the bondholders' financial welfare was adequately policed by both the political process and by the bond marketplace itself.[26] If he is correct in that assessment, it would follow that he is also correct in his belief that there is no need for greater scrutiny of impairments of public, rather than private, contracts.

XI.1.4 Political and Financial Markets

This issue of the efficacy of the political and financial markets, raised by Brennan in one brief paragraph at the end of his dissent, is at the heart of the modern legislative impairment doctrine. One could say that Brennan must be correct because repudiation of state and local debt is so rare. But this is the state of the world with a constitutional contract clause, historically used to enforce public debt obligations. We need to assess, as best we can, the state of a world in which public debt would be policed by only political processes and financial markets. My sense is that the contract clause adds greatly to the restraints imposed by the political and financial markets.

Surely the bond market would quickly and accurately respond to the increased risk of public repudiation. Interest rates should rise dramatically for governmental bodies that renege on their obligations. But a defaulting government would have every incentive to act strategically, claiming that the compromised bonds were somehow unique—perhaps illegal from their inception—so that repudiation could not happen again for a new bond issue. Further, many legislators would be willing to trade a future, uncertain, long-term loss for an immediate, known, short-term gain. Although this type of trade-off is a typical human response, legislators are probably more prone to act this way because their reelection often depends on short-term factors. Any long-term losses are borne by some uncertain group, not by the legislators themselves or, necessarily, their constitutents. These factors make me less confident than Justice Brennan in believing that the bond markets will adequately police legislative impairment of governmental debt. Finally, even if the bond marketplace properly disciplines a reneging governmental body, there may be at least a few spillovers affecting other, reputable governmental bodies who now appear riskier, because they or their bond projects are similar in some way to the culprit. More serious problems arise, however, in the political marketplace.

Justice Brennan did not explain why he believed that the political process adequately protected bondholders.[27] To the contrary, a number of aspects of the political process make it difficult for bondholders to have much influence. There will often be more voters favoring the policies that underlie the bond impairment than voters owning the bonds. Take, for ex-

[26] *United States Trust Co. v. New Jersey,* 431 U.S. 1, 61–62 (1977).

[27] *United States Trust Co. v. New Jersey,* 431 U.S. 1, 62, n. 18 (1977).

ample, the bonds involved in *U.S. Trust Co.* There must have been a tremendous number of voters in New Jersey who would have favored using Port Authority money for mass transit, including many people concerned about the environment. They surely could have outvoted the New Jersey bondholders. Even if we stack the value of the bonds against the number of voters who would favor the covenant repeal (as Brennan implies), it is far from clear that high value gives the bondholders much political clout. It would be virtually impossible for a bond trustee to contribute to political campaigns; to use any of the bondholders' money for this purpose would surely violate the trustee's fiduciary duty. Of course, the bondholders themselves can contribute—to the extent allowed by campaign contribution laws. A large bond issue may be bought and then traded so the bonds end up in the hands of tens or even hundreds of thousands of people. Each bondholder would have a small stake, making large political contributions less likely. There is, however, an even greater impediment to the political power of bondholders.

Governments do not lightly try to avoid their debt obligations. These problems have usually arisen when governments have been pushed to extreme positions, either as a result of a depression or the failure of an expensive capital project (such as a railroad line or a nuclear power plant). Even if the bondholders ordinarily get fair consideration by legislatures, these extreme circumstances make it unlikely that bondholders will be treated fairly. When the problem arises from a failed capital project, the only choices usually available to a legislature are imposing the costs on innocent taxpayers, imposing the costs on innocent bondholders, or sharing between the two groups. It seems to me that bondholders will usually lose that political battle.

These problems with the political and financial markets support the rule of *U.S. Trust Co.* To the extent that the markets work, contract cases will not arise. If the markets do not work, the contract clause serves as the last vehicle for assuring the repayment of public debt—that is, assuring the government's credible commitment for its own debt.

XI.2. JUDICIAL IMPAIRMENTS

Swift v. *Tyson*,[28] an 1842 decision by the Supreme Court, seldom gets the recognition it deserves. This stems in large part from the Supreme Court declaring in 1938 that the Supreme Court itself had acted unconstitutionally in *Swift*.[29] Although by 1938 it made sense to overturn the rule of *Swift*,

[28] 41 U.S. (16 Pet.) 1 (1842).
[29] *Erie Railroad v. Tompkins*, 304 U.S. 64 (1938).

the Supreme Court exaggerated the constitutional defects in the case. *Swift* was a great opinion because it created a nationally uniform commercial law throughout the federal court system by incorporating the principles of the law merchant into federal common law. Justice Story, when he wrote the opinion for a unanimous Court in *Swift,* had hoped that the state courts would follow the federal common law, resulting in a truly uniform commercial law in all courts throughout the country. Although many state courts developed commercial common law that differed from the federal law, the existence of a unified commercial law throughout the federal court system allowed lending, sales, and trade to flow between states in a way that would otherwise have been impossible. *Swift* enabled interstate commerce during an era when the national economy was beginning to grow. By 1938, the states had adopted uniform commercial law through uniform statutes, making nationwide federal commercial common law unnecessary. Consequently, the Supreme Court could overturn *Swift* in 1938, for its slight to both state law and state sovereignty, without harming interstate commerce.

Why the praise of *Swift* in a chapter dealing with government debt? It was the rule of *Swift* that made it possible for the Supreme Court to police judicial impairments of government bond obligations. Recall that the contract clause prohibits states from "passing" laws that impair contracts. Literally the clause seems directed at legislative action. We do not view courts as "passing" laws; today we may say that courts "make" law, while in the 19th century commentators would have viewed courts as "finding" the common law. Further, the economic problems that led to the drafting of the contract clause stemmed from debtor relief measures promulgated by legislatures. Yet courts can do as much damage to contract rights as legislatures. If the Supreme Court wanted to use the contract clause to overturn a judicial impairment, it would have had to confront the barriers imposed by both the language and the history of the clause. The Supreme Court had a way out of this dilemma through a combination of federal diversity jurisdiction and the rule of *Swift.*

The Constitution gives the federal courts jurisdiction over suits between citizens of different states and suits between a state citizen and a subject of a foreign country. In many ways, this grant of "diversity" jurisdiction is a counterpart to the contract clause. Like the contract clause, diversity jurisdiction was created in response to the economic problems of the times. The debtor relief laws raised fears that creditors would not be treated fairly in state courts, particularly out-of-state creditors suing residents of the forum state. Foreign lenders were also fearful that they would be prejudiced in state courts. The difficulty encountered by British creditors after the Revolutionary War, notwithstanding the agreement in the Treaty of Peace to allow their debt repayments, was just one example of the problem.[30] The drafting of the grant of diversity jurisdiction at the Constitutional Convention also supports the view that the jurisdiction was designed to deal with the economic problems. The grant grew out of an earlier proposal that the federal courts hear questions involving "the national peace and harmony" (Borchers, 1993, pp. 92–94). Some delegates to the convention even argued that the grant of diversity jurisdiction made the contract clause unnecessary (Thompson, 1992, p. 1385).

A federal forum would provide some protection to nonresident creditors, but the real protection would come from applying federal law, rather than state law, in the federal court. It appears that the Framers expected federal law to come with the federal forum for certain classes of cases, particularly those involving anticreditor legislation (Borchers, 1993, pp. 97–98). The first Congress enacted the Rules of Decision Act, which specified that "the laws of the several states . . . shall be regarded as rules of decisions in trials at common law in the courts of the United States."[31] The term "laws of the several states" meant the general law throughout the United States. It did not mean that the laws of a particular state should apply in a diversity action in a federal court located in that state. Thus, the rule of *Swift* was consistent with the intent of the Framers and the first Congress.

XI.2.1 The Railroad Bond Cases

The mid-19th century was a time of great excitement over railroads. No midwestern town wanted to miss out on the opportunity to be connected to the coming nationwide railway network. The way to lure a railroad was to support it from the proceeds of bond sales. But too often the railroads never materialized, sometimes due to fraud and sometimes due to incompetence. Then many local governments tried to avoid their financial obligations. A number of state courts aided this process by declaring the bond issues illegal, regardless of conflicting prior state law. The debt repudiations across the Midwest were massive. One commentator estimated that 15 to 25 percent of the outstanding municipal debt was in default after the 1873 depression[32]; another valued the total debt in default somewhere between $100 million to $150 million (Freyer, 1981, p. 60).

The massive defaults rekindled the same fears that existed after the end of the Revolutionary War. To many, the state judicial repudiations were an example of unprincipled democracy. The state courts were made up of

[30] *The Treaty of Peace,* Sept. 3, 1783, art. IV, 8 Stat. 80, 82, specified that "creditors on either side, shall meet with no lawful impediment to the recovery of the full value, in sterling money, of bona fide debts heretofore contracted."

[31] Now codified at 28 U.S.C. § 1652.

[32] G. Hempel, The Postwar Quality of State and Local Debt 18 (1971), quoted in Thompson (1992, p. 1405).

elected judges, who were seen as more prone to follow popular sentiment than legal precedent. In some instances, a state's decision to switch to elected judges was promptly followed by a change of precedent that resulted in bond issues suddenly rendered illegal (Thompson, 1992, p. 1405, No. 188). Further, the repudiations had spillover effects, threatening the national economy by hurting the perceived creditworthiness of all municipal bonds and even many bonds issued by the federal government and by private companies (Thompson, 1992, p. 1411). For example, the House of Baring, which had a relatively sophisticated network for gathering data on the various investments in the United States, had urged Upper Canada to withhold new issues from the British market because its proximity to the United States had given a bad name to Canadian securities (Hidy, 1949, p. 292). Even though Baring and other bankers distinguished between defaulting and creditworthy governmental bodies, many investors lumped all government bonds together. The United States was regarded as a "nation of swindlers" (Hidy, 1949, p. 309).

This problem finally came to the Supreme Court in *Gelpcke* v. *City of Dubuque*,[33] an 1863 diversity case. When Dubuque had issued its railroad bonds in 1857, numerous decisions by the Iowa state courts were consistent in upholding the power of the Iowa legislature to authorize municipal corporations to issue bonds in support of railroads. The enabling act by the Iowa legislature for the Dubuque bonds said: "The proclamation, the vote, bonds issued or to be issued, are hereby declared valid . . . and neither the City of Dubuque nor any of the citizens shall ever be allowed to plead that the said bonds are invalid." Within two years, however, Iowa elected its Supreme Court judges for the first time and those newly elected judges reversed established precedent by holding that the legislature did not have the power to authorize municipalities to issue railroad bonds. When a bondholder sued for unpaid interest (a consequence of Dubuque's economic downturn following the panic of 1857; Fairman, 1971, p. 935), the federal trial court, sitting in diversity, relied on the recent Iowa Supreme Court decision to hold the bonds invalid. On appeal, the United States Supreme Court reversed the decision, ruling that the federal courts had to apply the interpretation of state law that was in effect at the time the bonds were issued. The validity of the bonds could not depend upon a subsequent reinterpretation of state law by the state supreme court.

Gelpcke has puzzled legal scholars because it is not a precise application of the *Swift* doctrine, nor is it precisely a contract clause case. It does not quite fit with *Swift* because the rule of *Swift* should have led the Court either to apply federal commercial law or to defer to the state supreme court in applying state law.[34] By relying on state law rather than federal, the

[33] 68 U.S. (1 Wall.) 175 (1863).

Supreme Court acknowledged that state sovereignty still had some importance under its application of the *Swift* rule. But the Court's reliance on the older, superseded state law showed that the prevention of judicial impairment of government debt was the guiding principle in the case. Although the contract clause was not directly at issue in *Gelpcke,* the Court nonetheless analogized to the clause's limitation on legislative impairment and expanded the rule of *Swift* to create a counterpart for instances of judicial impairment. In a later opinion, which also involved Iowa railroad bonds, the Supreme Court explained:

> We are of the opinion that under the statutes of Iowa, in force when the contract was made, the [plaintiff] is entitled to the remedy he asks, and this right can no more be taken away by subsequent judicial decisions than by subsequent legislation. It is as much within the sphere of our power and duties to protect the contract from the former as from the latter, and we are no more concluded by the one than the other. We cannot in any other way give effect to the contract of the parties as we understand it.[35]

The repudiation of municipal bond obligations happened over and over again. With elected trial and appellate judges in the midwestern states, it was to be expected that many of the bonds were declared void. This was a turbulent problem, but the Supreme Court, constantly relying on the *Gelpcke* doctrine, did all it could to uphold the obligation to pay the municipal bonds. The Supreme Court heard about 300 bond cases in the 30 years after *Gelpcke;* many more were resolved in the lower courts. But the high financial stakes, the injustice felt by taxpayers who had to pay for railroads that never materialized, and the outrage at "probusiness" federal judges led to fierce resistance to enforcement of the bondholders' judgments. The refusal of some local tax officials to raise the money needed to pay the judgments led to further litigation, which established the power of federal judges to compel local tax increases (relevant today in cases requiring local funding, such as school desegregation and prison overcrowding). Some of these tax officials were jailed. Sometimes the resistance led to strategic behavior and occasionally to violence:

> In at least one community in Missouri, an angry mob killed several judges who had signed railroad bonds regarded as fraudulent. Such anger was translated into laws aimed at weakening the bondholders' ability to recover. Iowa and other states attempted to deny railroads and other nonresident corporations the right of doing business within the state unless they agreed not to remove litigation into federal courts. Often, local officials charged with enforcing the creditors' rights resigned

[34] In its opinion, the majority acknowledged that federal courts were usually obligated to follow state decisions construing the state's own statutes, but nonetheless, the Court concluded (in notorious commentary): "We shall never immolate truth, justice and law because a state tribunal has erected the altar and decreed the sacrifice" [*Gelpcke v City of Dubuque,* 68 U.S. (1 Wall.) 175, 200 (1863)].

[35] *Butz v. Muscatine,* 8 Wall. 575, 584 (1869).

> rather than carry out court orders directing the localities to levy taxes to pay off the debts. There were instances of counties reorganizing themselves in attempts to escape payment. State judges, sensitive to their public standing as elected officials, generally sanctioned or ignored these efforts, thereby favoring debtor over creditor. (Freyer, 1981, p. 60)[36]

Regardless of the local resistance to *Gelpcke* and the later cases, the Supreme Court succeeded at maintaining the creditworthiness of municipal bonds. "[B]y the late nineteenth century, municipal bonds were hailed as second only to federal bonds in the security provided—a result the investment houses attributed to continued Supreme Court policing of state judiciaries" (Thompson, 1992, p. 1432).

Even though *Gelpcke* wove the *Swift* rule and the contract clause together, in the 1890s the Supreme Court began a gradual process of separating them.[37] Finally, in 1924, the Court flatly stated that the contract clause did not apply to judicial impairments, notwithstanding "[c]ertain unguarded language" in the railroad bond cases.[38] Finally, in 1934, the Supreme Court implicitly overruled *Gelpcke* when it said that it was bound to follow all state court interpretations of state constitutions and statutes, thereby eliminating the protections afforded bondholders in diversity cases.[39] Despite these changes in the law, a few legal commentators have argued recently that the Supreme Court should extend the contract clause to judicial impairments, resurrecting the essence of *Gelpcke.* In addition, the bondholders who suffered from a judicial repudiation of a huge bond issue in the WPPSS case tried unsuccessfully to get the Supreme Court to hear the case under the contract clause.

XI.2.2 The WPPSS Bonds

The judicial impairment of the WPPSS bonds parallels the 19th-century railroad bond cases. The problem stemmed from a capital project that never materialized, the last two of five nuclear power plants that WPPSS planned to build. WPPSS was an agency of the state of Washington created to produce energy for local municipalities and utilities. Part of the impetus for the massive nuclear power project came from the federal Bonneville Power Authority. Everyone projected increased demand for electricity in the Pacific Northwest, which Bonneville's hydro plants would eventually be unable to fulfill. Bonneville was a strong supporter of nuclear power, as were

[36] Although contemporaneous commentators all viewed *Gelpcke* as fair and the state decisions as biased and threatening to the national economy (see Thompson, 1992, p. 1418, No. 276), a "strong" argument can be made in favor of the state courts, based on the view that earlier state decisions improperly expanded local authority in the initial excitement over railroads (see Thompson, 1992, p. 1413, No. 242).

[37] *Central Land Co. v. Laidley,* 159 U.S. 103, 109 (1895).

[38] *Tidal Oil Co. v. Flanagan,* 263 U.S. 444 (1924).

[39] *Burns Mortgage Co. v. Fried,* 292 U.S. 487, 493–494 (1934).

nearly all federal and state agencies at the time. WPPSS issued the bonds for the project. Although Bonneville indirectly guaranteed the bonds for the first three plants, the bonds for the last two plants were guaranteed by 88 municipalities, public utility districts, and cooperative power agencies located primarily in Washington but also in Idaho and in Oregon. The 88 participants assumed a great share of the risks of the project. Their participation agreement required them to pay WPPSS all the funds necessary to meet the bond obligations, even if the plants were never built. That worse-case possibility turned out to be true. The two plants were canceled after $2.25 billion in bonds had been issued. The WPPSS cancellation resulted from the same problems that befell nuclear projects across the country: the projections of increased energy demand proved false; safety standards increased drastically after the Three Mile Island accident and the "China Syndrome" film scared the public; and construction costs soared, in part, from the need to satisfy the new safety standards but also from the unexpected inefficiencies in constructing such large and complex projects.

During this time of public opposition to nuclear power across the country, immense opposition developed in Washington to the WPPSS project itself and to its costs. This "mass insurgency" stemmed from the realization that some small utility districts faced a 100 percent rate increase within a six-month period; one small town faced a debt of $2,000 per capita as its share of the WPPSS bonds (Sugai, 1987, p. 4). As a result, most of the participants repudiated their obligations. The $2.25 billion in bonds then went into default, by far the biggest default in the history of the municipal bond market.

In the middle of the political turmoil, the Washington Supreme Court released the Washington participants from their obligations by ruling that they had acted beyond their legal authority when they agreed to pay for the plant even if they would never receive any electricity.[40] This was stark judicial impairment of contract obligations; the precedent in Washington and throughout the nation had established the authority of utility districts to "purchase" electricity with this type of financing guarantee. That opinion was followed shortly by the Idaho Supreme Court reaching the same conclusion in order to free the Idaho participants from their obligations. The Supreme Court of Oregon stood fast, however, and ruled that the participants situated in Oregon were bound under Oregon law. With the vast majority of the participants released, the Washington Supreme Court then released the Oregon participants on the basis of mutual mistake and commercial frustration, recognizing that they could not fairly be held responsible for all the participants' obligations.[41]

[40] *Chemical Bank v. Washington Public Power Supply System,* 99 Wash. 772, 666 P.2d 329 (1983).

[41] *Chemical Bank v. Washington Public Power Supply System,* 102 Wash. 874, 691 P.2d 524 (1984).

The Washington Supreme Court's determination that the participants acted beyond their statutory authority and its consequent release of their liability had many similarities to the Iowa Supreme Court's decision in *Gelpcke*. Both decisions were contrary to existing precedent; both decisions were made by elected courts in a time of political turmoil; and both decisions freed local residents from paying for failed, expensive construction projects. In one way, the WPPSS decision was much worse: there was no hint of any impropriety on the part of the WPPSS bondholders, while some of the railroad bondholders were affiliated with the railroads and the construction firms that caused the financial losses. The WPPSS bondholders made these claims when they tried to get the United States Supreme Court to accept an appeal from the Washington court on the basis of the contract clause. The Supreme Court declined to hear the case without any explanation, as is its practice.

The Supreme Court would have had to extend the contract clause to judicial impairments if it were going to reverse the Washington Supreme Court. Given the history of the clause, that would have been a major change in the Court's jurisprudence, but it would not have been an inconceivable change. Nonetheless, even though WPPSS was the largest default of its kind, there was much about the case that made it a poor vehicle for a sea change in doctrine.

Judicial elections today are not as politicized as they were in the Midwest in the 19th century, the defeat of Supreme Court judges in California in the past decade being the rare exception. Most judges and commentators discount the danger of interstate biases in state courts these days. As a result, Congress has considered abolishing diversity jurisdiction. Spillover effects of an isolated bond impairment are less likely today. Bond rating services, analysts and investors are able to identify the risks of particular kinds of bonds and of particular issues. Studies of the bond markets after the WPPSS default showed that the prices of other municipal public power bonds (many in the Pacific Northwest) and of nonpower municipal bonds actually rose by a statistically insignificant amount, relative to Treasury bonds (Peavy and Hempel, 1987, pp. 244–245; see also Smith and Booth, 1985). Nonpower bond offerings by Washington municipalities sold well after WPPSS (Thompson, 1992, p. 1453, No. 483). The lack of a spillover from the WPPSS default may also be a consequence of WPPSS being the public counterpart to the large losses suffered by private investors in nuclear power during this period. There is a long list of the ways equity investors suffered from nuclear power regulation: the delayed opening of the Seabrook plant long after construction was complete, the closure of the new, operational Shoreham plant on Long Island, the frequent refusals by state utility commissions to pass on to the ratepayers the costs of prudent investments in canceled nuclear plants, and the popular referendums that made financing more difficult (such as by disallowing the use of

"Construction Work in Progress" for rate-making purposes), for example. Nuclear power was an intractable economic problem because a combination of factors meant innocent people had to lose money. The WPPSS bonds may have been just another nuclear power investment that investors viewed as a species of its own.

None of these factors does any good for the WPPSS bondholders. The default on the $2.25 billion bonds led, as one would expect, to a massive securities fraud lawsuit against investment advisors, bond counsel, rating services, contractors, architects, engineers—just about everyone involved in any way with the financing or the construction. That suit, along with other claims, ultimately led to settlements that produced about 25 to 30 cents on the dollar of principal. (The interest, totaling billions of dollars, was quickly out of question.) Thousands, probably millions, of people throughout the country suffered financial losses as a result of our country's uncertainty over nuclear power. The WPPSS bondholders were among the worst of those injured. One positive consequence, however, was that the bond market remained strong after WPPSS, despite the federal courts' refusal to help.

XI.3 CONCLUSION

One could argue that there would have been little impact on American economic growth during the 19th century even if the Supreme Court had not been so firm in its limitation on both legislative and judicial impairments of public debt obligations. Throughout the 19th century, the United States was the perfect partner for British and European investors. The massive capital projects in the United States, coupled with an expanding economy, led to a tremendous need for foreign investments. Likewise, British and European capital was abundant, with investors looking for new opportunities. This was the perfect match. Foreign investors, guided by sophisticated bankers, were surely aware of many of the risks that would have manifested themselves in the interest rate and the availability of funds. The 19th century was a time of boom and bust, with rapid growth and severe depressions. Besides the risks from swings in the economic market, public works projects brought their own particular risks. Many were the ordinary business risks involved with construction projects, such as costs exceeding the construction budget (through delays, unexpected construction difficulties, or even fraud), erroneous projections of demand, and project income failing to meet income projections that were reasonable *ex ante.*

The debtor being a governmental body also brought unusual risks in enforcement. The doctrine of sovereign immunity limits suits against a government, although the immunity can be constrained by a constitution or statutes and it can be waived. The Eleventh Amendment meant that federal judges could not decide debt enforcement actions against state governments, although local governments were not similarly protected.[42]

These risks should have led to a higher interest rate or made funds less available. Under this view, one could argue that the risk of government repudiation of public debt, uncontrolled by the judiciary, would add little in terms of an additional risk factor. It is true that foreign investment continued to flow even after the serious defaults by states in connection with canal construction. Compounding this view is the fact that in many instances of judicial enforcement of bond obligations, many innocent taxpayers were forced to pay significant amounts. These lawsuits arose in the context of failed construction projects, circumstances in which some innocent people must pay, regardless of how the lawsuit turns out. Often those at fault are gone or cannot afford to reimburse anything near the full amount of the losses.

Any conclusion of a limited impact of the judicial restraints must be made in the context of our market system, which rests on the rule of law as a foundation. It must be true that a lack of judicial restrictions on government repudiation would have made investments riskier. The only question is whether or not the increased risk would be so small that it would not significantly affect the interest rate or the availability of funds. It may be impossible to quantify risk premiums caused by judicial inaction. Even if the increased risk is very small, the effects would be much larger if the legal foundation were shakier. That is why it is misleading to view the debt repudiation cases in isolation. They should be viewed as one piece of an ongoing legal process that reinforces the efficacy of contracts and creates a solid foundation for a market system. In the case of public repudiation of debt, the case is even stronger for judicial control because politics often plays a major role when a public works project fails. The judiciary is needed to check the tendency of the public to renege on its financial obligations in order to achieve short-term gain. Thus, the constitutional law dealing with public debt repudiation provides one piece to the history of the legal support of economic growth in the United States.

ACKNOWLEDGMENTS

I would like to thank the following people for their helpful comments: Lee J. Alston, Stuart Banner, Dorsey D. Ellis, Jr., Robert E. Gallman, Larry Neal, Norman Schofield and John Wallis.

[42] Throughout history, sovereigns have compromised their own debt by devaluing money. Because the Constitution gives the federal government complete control over the money supply, state and local governments cannot use this tactic.

REFERENCES

Borchers, P. (1993). The origins of diversity jurisdiction, the rise of legal positivism, and the brave new world for *Erie* and *Klaxon*. *Texas Law Review* **72,** 79–133.

Freyer, T. (1981). *Harmony & Dissidence: The Swift and Erie Cases in American Federalism.* New York University Press, New York.

Goodrich, C. (1960). *Government Promotion of American Canals and Railroads 1800–1890.* Columbia University Press, New York.

Hidy, R. W. (1949). *The House of Baring in American Trade and Finance.* Harvard University Press, Cambridge, MA.

Merrill, T. (1987). Public contracts, private contracts, and the transformation of the constitutional order. *Case Western Reserve Law Review* (pp. 597–630) **37,** 597–630.

North, D. C. (1990). *Institutions, Institutional Change and Economic Performance.* Cambridge University Press, Cambridge, UK.

Peavy, J., and Hempel, G. (1987). The effect of the WPPSS crisis on the tax exempt bond market. *Journal of Financial Research* **10,** 239–247.

Smith, R. L., and Booth, J. R. (1985). The risk structure of interest rates and interdependent borrowing costs: The impact of major defaults. *Journal of Financial Research* **8**(2), 83–94.

Sugai, W. H. (1987). *Nuclear Power and Rate Payer Protest: The Washington Public Power Supply System Crisis.* Westview Press, Boulder, CO.

Thompson, B. (1992). The history of the judicial impairment 'doctrine' and its lessons for the contract clause. *Stanford Law Review* **44,** 1371–1466.

Wright, B. F. Jr. (1938). *The Contract Clause of the Constitution.* Harvard University Press, Cambridge, MA.

PART IV

LEARNING, COGNITION, AND RATIONALITY

XII Economic Reason: The Interplay of Individual Learning and External Structure

Andy Clark

XII.1 INTRODUCTION

Much work in economics, the social sciences, and elsewhere takes as its starting point a somewhat unrealistic conception of rationality—a conception that ignores or downplays both the temporal and the situated aspects of human reason. Biological reason, I shall argue, is better conceived as an iterated process of adaptive response made under extreme time pressure and exquisitely keyed to a variety of external structures and circumstances. These external structures and circumstances act as filters and constraints on the spaces of possible real-time responses. Paramount among such structures and circumstances, in the case of human reason, are the cultural artifacts of language and of social and economic institutions. Models of rational decision making need to situate the reasoning agent as just one element in a complex and time-sensitive feedback system in which such external structures play a major role. It is therefore crucial that we understand the complex and mutually modulatory interplay between individual cognition and the extended environmental loops in which it participates. I shall explore a few potential avenues for developing such an understanding including neural network research and multiple time scale simulations.

XII.2 RATIONALITY ON THE HOOF

Human minds were not designed as instruments of unhurried, fully informed reason. They were not designed to adhere to rigid or even consistent preference orderings or to act so as to maximize reward on all occasions. Human minds, it is now widely agreed, are better understood as loci of only *bounded* rationality: reason restricted by a variety of evolutionary and pragmatic factors. There is probably no need to labor this point. But a brief listing of some of the central considerations in favor of a conception of bounded rationality would surely include the following:

1. The observation that human brains often deploy cost-cutting, problem-solving strategies that were more or less reliable in their original ecological settings [e.g., the Wason selection test examples in which abstract and concrete versions of the same logical problem yield very different success rates, (see, e.g., Wason and Johnson-Laird, 1970; Holland *et al.,* 1986), or the Kahneman and Tversky work on persistent errors in statistical reasoning (see, e.g., Kahneman *et al.,* 1982)].
2. The (related) observation that ecologically realistic problems often demand rapid, *real- time responses* (e.g., work on animate vision; see Ballard, 1991; Churchland *et al.,* 1994; Clark, 1995) which may preclude large-scale information gathering, integration, and deduction.
3. The (again related) observation that real-time adaptive behavior may be best served by the construction of *multiple partial models* of the environment without attempting to integrate the information gathered into a consistent whole, or even to translate it into a common central code (e.g., work on autonomous agents and mobile robots; see Brooks, 1991; Clark and Toribio, 1994).

One upshot of this recent explosion of work on bounded, real-time, embodied and environmentally embedded reason is a growing sense of discontent with the image of rational choice as maximizing reward relative to a complete and consistent ordering of preferences (see, e.g., Friedman, 1953; although Friedman insisted that the model should *not* be taken as a claim about individual psychology). This image (which can be extended to embrace conditions of incomplete information and risk; see discussion in Denzau and North, 1996) has been termed the paradigm of *substantive rationality* (see Denzau and North, 1996).

Taken as a psychological theory of individual choice, the substantive rationality model is almost certainly incorrect. Individuals seldom complete a complex and consistent ordering of preferences. Even if they did, reliance on cost-cutting evolved reasoning strategies and the demands of rapid, real-time decision making would probably conspire to undermine the on-line use of such an ordering so as to maximize reward. The individual reasoner, as Herbert Simon (1982) has persuasively argued, is better cast as a quick and dirty satisficer than a cool, well-informed, unhurried classical reasoner.

It is perhaps surprising, then, that neoclassical economics has done as well as it has. Why, given the gross psychological irrealism of its model of human choosing, has traditional economics yielded at least moderately successful and predictive models of, for example, the behavior of firms (in competitive posted price markers) and of political parties, and of the outcomes of double auction experiments (for illuminating discussion, see Satz and Ferejohn, 1994; Denzau and North, 1996)? Why also—on a less optimistic note—has it *failed* to illuminate a whole panoply of other economic and social phenomena? Such notable failures are the failure to model large-scale economic change over time, and the failure to model choice under conditions of strong uncertainty (i.e., cases where there is no preexisting set of outcomes that can be rank ordered according to desirability) (see Danzau and North, 1996). These are fundamental failures insofar as they ramify across a wide variety of more specific cases, such as the inability to model voter behavior, the inability to predict the development of social and economic institutions, and the inability to address the bulk of the choices faced by public policy makers.[1]

The pattern of successes and failures is both fascinating and informative. For the best explanation of the pattern looks to involve a dissociation between cases of what may be termed *highly scaffolded choice* and cases of more weakly constrained individual cogitation. The substantive rationality paradigm, as several authors have recently argued,[2] seems to work best in the highly scaffolded case and to falter and fail as the role of weakly constrained individual cogitation increases. A fully successful economic theory will thus need to address both types of situations and (and this is the crucial move) do so within some overarching framework that enables us to plot the delicate interrelations between the two, that is, to understand how active agents come to construct elaborate forms of social and political scaffolding, which then fundamentally inform their collective problem-solving behavior, and how such scaffolding can itself become transformed by being also the subject of episodes of weakly constrained individual cogitation. In the next section I rehearse the arguments in favor of the hypothesis that neoclassical economics works (insofar as it works at all) only for the highly scaffolded cases. The remaining two sections attempt to sketch a single

[1] The point about voter behavior is forcefully made in Satz and Ferejohn (1994).

[2] I am especially influenced by Satz and Ferejohn (1994) and by Denzau and North (1996).

framework in which interactions between weakly constrained and highly scaffolded choice can begin to be addressed.

XII.3 SCAFFOLDED CHOICE AND MULTIPLE EQUILIBRIA ECONOMICS

Two fundamental distinctions have been invoked to explain the patterns of success and failure reported here:

1. The distinction between cases involving highly scaffolded choice and ones involving only weakly constrained individual cogitation.
2. The distinction between cases involving negative feedback and classical equilibria and those involving positive feedback and multiple or unstable equilibria.

It would simplify matters if these were the same distinctions, differently expressed. Alas, they are at least partially independent, as we shall see.

The idea of highly scaffolded choice is at the heart of important recent treatments by Satz and Ferejohn (1994) and Denzau and North (1996). The common theme is that neoclassical economic theory works best in situations in which individual rational choice has been severely limited by the quasi-evolutionary selection of constraining policies and institutional practices. The irony is explicitly noted by Satz and Ferejohn: "the [traditional] theory of rational choice is most powerful in contexts where choice is limited" (1994, p. 72).

How can this be? According to Satz and Ferejohn, the reason is simple: what is doing the work, in such cases, is not (so much) the individual's cogitations as the larger social and institutional structures in which she is embedded. These structures have themselves evolved and prospered (in the cases where economic theory works!) by promoting the selection of collective actions that do indeed maximize returns relative to a fixed set of goals. For example, the competitive environment of capital markets ensures that, by and large, only those firms that maximize profits survive. It is this fact, rather than facts about the beliefs, desires, or other psychological features of the individuals involved, that ensures the frequent success of substantive rationality models in predicting the behavior of firms. Strong constraints imposed by the larger scale market structure result in firm-level strategies and policies that maximize profits. In the embrace of such powerful scaffolding, the particular theories and worldviews of individuals may at times make little impact on overall firm-level behavior. Where the external scaffolding of policies, infrastructure, and customs is strong and (importantly) is a result of competitive selection, the individual members are, in effect, interchangeable cogs in a larger machine. The larger machine extends way outside the individual and incorporates large-scale social, physical and even geopolitical structures. It is the behavior of this larger machine that traditional economic theory often succeeds in modeling. A wide variety of individual psychological profiles are fully compatible with specific functional roles within such a larger machine. As Satz and Ferejohn have remarked:

> Many sets of individual motivations are compatible with the constraints that competitive market environments place on a firm's behavior. In explaining firm behavior, we often confront causal patterns that hold constant across the diverse realizations of maximizing activity found in Calvinist England and the Savings and Loan Community in Texas.
>
> (1994, p. 79)

By contrast, the theory of consumer behavior is weak and less successful. This is because individual worldviews and ideas loom large in consumer choice and the external scaffolding is commensurately weaker. Similarly, the theory of voting behavior is weak beside the theory of party behavior in electoral competitions. Once again, the parties only survive subject to strong selection pressures that enforce vote-maximizing activity. By comparison, individual choice is relatively unconstrained (see Satz and Ferejohn, 1994, pp. 79–80).

Satz and Ferejohn have suggested that the crucial factor distinguishing the successful and unsuccessful cases (of neoclassical, substantive-rationality assuming theory) is the availability of a structurally determined *theory of interests.* In cases where the overall structuring environment acts to select in favor of actions that are restricted so as to conform to a specific model of preferences, neoclassical theory works. It works because individual psychology no longer matters: the "preferences" are imposed by the wider situation and need not be echoed in individual psychology. Thus, the competitive environment of posted price markets *externally* determines the types of action patterns that will lead to survival and success, and a theory of the "preferences" of the players can be seen not as a theory of individual psychologies but as a reflection of these constraints. Individual psychology is of reduced importance—all that matters is that *whatever* the individual psychological profiles of the players, they must be compatible with this pattern of action selection. The case of political party behavior, likewise, is one in which the overall situation (at least in democratic, two-party electoral systems) selects for parties that act to maximize votes. This external structuring force allows us to impute "preferences" on the basis of the constraints on success in such a larger machine. The constraints on individual voters are much weaker. Hence, real psychological profiles come to the fore, and neoclassical theory breaks down (see Satz and Ferejohn, 1994, pp. 79–80).

This general diagnosis is supported by the analysis of Denzau and North (1996). They have noted that traditional economic theory nicely models choice in competitive posted price markets and in the experimental studies of double auctions. In such cases, they have suggested, certain institutional features play a major role in promoting "maximizing-style" economic performance. By way of illustration, Denzau and North cited fascinating studies by Gode and Sunder (1992). These studies invoke so-called zero intelligence (ZI) traders, that is, modeled agents who do not actively theorize, recall events, or attempt to maximize returns. By constraining such simple agents to bid only in ways that do not yield an immediate loss, an efficiency of 75 percent (measured as "the percentage of sum of potential buyer and seller rents"; Denzau and North, 1996, p. 5) was achieved. Replacing the ZI traders with humans increased efficiency by a mere 1 percent! But altering the institutional scaffolding (e.g., from collecting all bids in a double auction before contracting to allowing simultaneous bidding and contracting) yielded a 6 percent improvement in efficiency. The strong conclusion is this:

> Most efficiency gains in some resource allocation situations may be attributed to institutional details, independent of their effects on rational traders.
>
> (Denzau and North, 1996, p. 5)

The results of the zero intelligence trader experiments are revealing. They clearly demonstrate the power of institutional settings and external constraints to promote collective behaviors that conform to the model of substantive rationality. Such results fit nicely with the otherwise disquieting news that the bulk of traditional economics would be unaffected if we assumed that individuals chose randomly (see Alchian, 1950, cited in Satz and Ferejohn, 1994, p. 76) rather than by maximizing preferences, and that pigeons and rats can often perform in ways consistent with the theory of substantive rationality (see Kagel, 1987, also cited in Satz and Ferejohn, 1994, p. 77)! Such results make sense if it is the scaffolding of choice by larger-scale constraining structures which acts as the strongest carrier of maximizing force. In the extreme limiting cases of such constraint, the individual chooser is indeed a mere cog—a constrained functional role played as well by a ZI trader, a pigeon, a rat, a human trader or, in the worst cases, by a coin-flipping device!

It is important to note that this is *not* to claim (falsely) that highly scaffolded choices will always conform to the norms of substantive rationality. This will only be the case if the institutional scaffolding has itself evolved as a result of selective pressure to maximize rewards and if the economic environment has remained stable or if the original institutional scaffolding itself built in sufficient adaptability to cope with subsequent change. A major question—one at the heart of Douglass North's research agenda—is thus: Under what conditions can such efficient and adaptable institutions evolve?

In sum, traditional economic theory (invoking the substantive rationality paradigm) succeeds wherever individual choice is strongly constrained by social and institutional scaffolding that has *itself* evolved subject to selective pressures to maximize rewards. Outside such highly constrained settings, genuine individual thought plays a greater role, and the psychological irrealism of the substantive rationality model takes its toll.

A seemingly different diagnosis of the pattern of failures of neoclassical economics has been proposed by Brian Arthur. Arthur (1990) has suggested that the successes of neoclassical theory are marked by the operation of processes of negative feedback leading to equilibrium solutions in which buyers and sellers settle on a price that constitutes the most efficient solution for the overall economy. The dynamics of such cases are those of single fixed-point attractors in economic space. Arthur noted that other types of dynamical description may, at times, be more appropriate. The now-classic example is the development of high-technology microelectronics. Here, positive feedback (increasing rather than diminishing returns) can result in economic spaces characterized by multiple equilibria. The process by which a resting point is selected is, in these cases, not one that looks likely to settle at the best solution. Instead, small early biases, amplified by positive feedback, can set the overall system onto a path that becomes increasingly fixed as positive feedback continues to operate. As Arthur pointed out, Betamax video technology may indeed have been superior to VHS format, but once—for whatever reason—the market share of the VHS format edged ahead, processes of positive feedback took over. As video shops stocked more VHS format tapes in response to early market lead, so the choice for new buyers of video equipment became clearer. And as more new buyers chose VHS equipment, so the shops stocking policies became clearer still. The upshot being that VHS cornered the market. In such scenarios, small early advantages (due to luck, advertising, whatever) initiate a tidal wave of gains that quickly locks the market into a particular course—a course largely independent of the objective quality of the product relative to its rivals. In such cases, the initial market system is not characterized by a single point attractor representing an optimal solution enforced by strong negative feedback pushing us away from inferior choices. Instead, the initial space may contain multiple attractors, any one of which could win out if some early chance perturbation should place us within its orbit. Such small chance events are bound to confound economic prediction. At best, we may be better able to formulate science and economic policy, once we recognize the potential for the operation of positive feedback and increasing returns in specific markets.

How, though, do these considerations fit in with our earlier observations concerning highly scaffolded versus weakly constrained choice? In one sense, the positive feedback cases are clearly only weakly constrained. The institutional infrastructure, in such cases, leaves a system's future trajectory quite underdetermined. But the lack of institutional constraints on the outcomes is not, at least in the example cases, generally resolved by a commensurately increased role for individual psychological profiles. Instead, factors external to individual psychological profiles still tend to bear the explanatory burden. For example, Arthur (1990, p. 95) cited the concentration of the electronics industry in Silicon Valley as a possible consequence of a "snowball" effect initiated by the chance geographical positioning of the first few firms to enter that arena. No facts about formal or informal norms of practice determined that location, but neither is it best explained by the individual psychological profiles of the players. Here, it is pure historical and geographical chance, and not institutional scaffolding *or* individual psychology, which sowed the seed that positive feedback dynamics amplified into the dense geographical concentration of expertise we see today.

In one respect, at least, these positive feedback cases thus resemble the highly scaffolded ones: individuals, in both cases, are functioning as cogs in a larger machine. It is the dynamics of the larger machine that is selecting economic outcomes. The difference is just that in the cases where neoclassical theory works best, the dynamics of the larger machine is one of single fixed-point attractors, whereas in the positive feedback cases, it is one of multiple attractors operating in spaces where small early perturbations can lead to strong path fixation. In these latter cases, the events that bear the explanatory burden are the small early perturbations. Such perturbations may be random, due to wider social or geopolitical events, or due to, for instance, a neat marketing idea had by one individual. Even in the case of the neat idea, however, the main explanatory construct will still be the positive feedback dynamics of the overall system. A large proportion of the (important) new range of cases that Arthur and others are studying is thus—like the classical cases—essentially *individual psychology transcending.* The clear indicator of this is once again the fact that the explanatory burden is borne by overall system dynamics in which the microdynamics of individual psychology is relatively unimportant. The multiple equilibria model *could* of course, be applied to the other class of cases too—that is, to cases in which the gross nonpsychological scaffolding is *not* bearing all of the weight. Indeed, it is precisely this class of cases that Arthur turned to in the paper that appears in the present volume. There the focus is on the economic significance of the complex coevolving ecology of *beliefs.* In such an ecology, agents must often try to act in ways that take account of how they predict that others will interpret their own actions, and so on. The simulation tools of complex systems theory, as Arthur noted, may provide our best measure of plotting and understanding such complex and iterated processes of psychological interaction.

How, then, *should* we conceive the role of individual psychology in economic explanation? The key to such an understanding, I believe, lies in seeing how to *couple* psychological effects with the kinds of larger scale system dynamics identified in the preceding discussion. To do so, we must first get a better view of the nature of individual cognition itself.

XII.4 WHAT KIND OF MIND NEEDS A SCAFFOLD?

The moral so far is that the scaffolding matters: the external structuring provided by institutions and organizations bears much of the explanatory burden for explaining current economic patterns. To see where human psychology fits in, let us begin by asking, what kind of individual mind *needs* an external scaffold?

A vital role for external structure and scaffolding is, in fact, strongly predicted by recent work on individual cognition. *Classical* artificial intelligence and information processing psychology tended to downplay any such role. But more recent work in the field of *time-critical adaptive response* posits a much greater reliance on real-world structures, external data stores, and active interventions. (See Clark, 1997, for a review.)

Simon's (1982) notion of bounded rationality was probably the first step in this direction. But although Simon (rightly) rejected the view of human agents as perfect logical reasoners, he remained committed to a basically classicist model of computation as involving explicit rules and quasi-linguistic data structures. The major difference was just the use of *heuristics*, with the goal of *satisfying* rather than optimizing—that is, the use of rules of thumb to find a workable solution, with minimal expenditures of time and processing power.

The reemergence of connectionist (also known as artificial neural networks, or parallel distributed processing) ideas in the last decade or so took us further by challenging classical models of internal representation and of computational process. In place of explicit rules operating on language-like data structures, connectionists posit an intermingling of data and processing supported by a dense parallel architecture of idealized "neurons." Such systems are often trained on examples of a desired input-output mapping and learn (by a process of gradient descent learning) to assign weights (positive and negative numeric values) to the interconnections between the idealized neurons. These weights cause the network to behave as an interpolating associative memory: they enable it to re-create patterns of designed output given fragments of the original inputs and to generalize its knowledge so as to deal with novel cases on the basis of their partial similarity to the training cases.

One feature of neural network learning, to which we will later return, is its rampant path dependence. A compelling series of experiments by Jeff Elman and others (e.g., Elman, 1994) shows that connectionist learning is heavily dependent on the sequence of training cases. If the early training goes wrong, the network is often unable to recover. Thus a specific network proved able to learn complex grammatical rules only if it was previously trained solely on more basic examples highlighting, for example, verb-subject number agreement. Early exposure to the more complex cases of long-distance dependencies, and so forth led it into bad early "solutions" (local minima) from which it was unable subsequently to escape (for a detailed treatment of this case, see Clark, 1993).

For present purposes, however, what matters most is that such networks constitute *fast but limited* systems that in effect substitute *pattern recognition* for reasoning. This, as might be expected, is both a boon and a burden. It is a boon insofar as it provides just the right resources for the tasks humans perform best and most fluently: tasks such as motor control, face recognition, deciphering handwritten zip codes, and so on (for more on these examples, see Jordan *et al.,* 1994; Churchland (1996), Le Cun *et al.,* 1989). But it is a burden insofar as it does not provide an ideal substrate on which to build processes of careful, sequential reasoning, or of long-term planning (see Clark, 1989; Norman, 1986). This is not in itself a bad thing. If our goal is to model human cognition, computational underpinnings that yield a profile of strengths and weaknesses similar to our own are to be favored. And we *are* generally better at Frisbee than at logic. Nonetheless, we *are* able to achieve impressive results using logic, sequential reason, long-term planning, and so on. If we are at root associative pattern recognition devices, how is this competence ever achieved?

Two factors, I suggest, conspire to enable us to rise above our computational roots. The first is our old friend, external scaffolding. The second involves a more tendentious idea, namely, that we are internally driven to reorganize our own knowledge continually in purely exploratory ways. It is the combination of these two factors that (I believe) explains our peculiar degree of communal cognitive success.

Connectionist minds are ideal candidates for extensive external scaffolding. A simple example, detailed in Rumelhart, Smolesky, McClelland, and Hinton (1986), concerns long multiplication. Most of us, they argue, can learn to know at a glance the answer to basic multiplications. Thus we know at a glance that 7 × 7 is 49. Such knowledge could easily be supported by a basic on-board pattern-recognition device. But longer multiplications (for most of us) present a different kind of problem. Asked to multiply 7,222 by 9,422, most of us resort to pen and paper (or calculator). What we achieve, using pen and paper, is a reduction of the complex problem to a sequence of simpler problems beginning with 2 × 2. We use the external medium (paper) to store the results of these simple problems, and by an interrelated series of simple pattern completions coupled with external storage, we finally arrive at a solution. At this point the authors comment that

> This is real symbol processing and, we are beginning to think, the primary symbol processing that we are able to do. Indeed, on this view, the external environment becomes a key extension to our mind.
>
> (Rumelhart, Smolesky, McClelland, and Hinton, 1986, p. 46)

Some of us, of course, go on to learn to do such sums in our heads. The trick in these cases, it seems, is to learn to manipulate a mental model in the same way as we originally manipulated the real world. In such cases we are able to mentally simulate the external arena, and hence, at times, internalize cognitive competencies that are nonetheless rooted in manipulations of the external world (here, cognitive science meets Soviet psychology; see Vygotsky, 1962).

Institutions, firms, and organizations seem to me to share many of the key properties of pen, paper, and arithmetical practice in this example. Pen and paper provide an external medium in which we behave (using basic online resources) in ways dictated by the general policy or practice of long multiplication. Most of us do not know the mathematical justification for the procedure. But we use it, and it works. Similarly, firms and organizations provide an external resource in which individuals behave in ways dictated by norms, policies, and practices; norms, policies, and practices that may even become internalized as mental models. Daily problem solving, in these arenas, often involves locally effective pattern recognition strategies that are invoked due to some external originating prompt (a green slip in the in-tray), discharged in a preset manner, and that leave their mark as further traces (different slips of paper, E-mails, whatever) in the overarching machinery of the firm. It is in these contexts that, in the short term at least, the role of individual rationality can become somewhat marginalized. If the overall machinery has been selected so as to maximize profits, the fact that the individuals are cogs with very bounded forms of rationality will not matter (individual neurons are, if you like, even more restricted cogs, but once organized into brains by natural selection, they too support a grander kind of reason).

Much of what goes on in the complex world of humans may thus, somewhat surprisingly, be understood in terms of so-called *stigmergic* algorithms. A stigmergic algorithm (see Beckers *et al.,* 1994) is one in which actions are strongly determined by external structures that are themselves the *operands* or objects of the actions. The notion originates from studies of termite nest building (see Grassé, 1959; for a more recent discussion, see Bonabeau *et al.,* 1994) in which the termites action is controlled by local nest structure yet results in modifications of that structure, which in turn controls other actions (by itself or others). A nice computational treatment of stigmergy is to be found in the work of Bonabeau and colleagues (1994).

Stigmergic, scaffolded reason is, however, at best, part of the true story. For there is a delicate balancing act in human cognition between stigmergy and scaffolded response, on the one hand, and innovation and integration on the other. It is in understanding the details of this balancing act that we may one day obtain real insight into the longer-term processes by which the external scaffolding of institutions, norms, and practices itself changes and develops. This is the topic of the next and final section.

XII.5 LEAPS AND LEVELS

Processes of innovation and integration appear to operate both at the level of individual learning and, in a curious way, at the level of the cultural scaffolding itself. There is also a very interesting interplay between the shape of individual learning and the various structures that constitute the scaffolding. In this final section, we scout each of these effects in turn.

XII.5.1 Innovation and Integration in Individual Learning

At the very simplest level, standard connectionist gradient descent learning gives rise to what, *from the outside,* can look like a series of radical leaps or discontinuities in acquired knowledge. Nonetheless, such shifts are often a direct consequence of the gradual, gradient descent learning process itself.

The basic way in which simple gradient descent learning can lead to "cognitive leaps" is where the error surface itself contains a sharp gradient. In such cases, a very small change to the internal weights can suddenly lead the network from the top to the bottom of a cliff, with dramatically improved performance making a sudden rapid appearance. In addition, the use of a nonlinear activation function means that small changes to the early weights (between input and hidden units) can make a very large difference to the outputs and hence lead to sudden, dramatic falls in the total sum squared error. Sudden improvements in gross performance can thus result from small changes to the early weights. Nice examples of these and related phenomena are to be found in the work of Plunkett and colleagues (1990) and are further discussed in Clark (1993, Chapter 8).

Such phenomena go some way toward accounting for the rather sudden leaps that are evident in human learning (see especially the developmental psychological literature, e.g., Karmiloff-Smith, 1992). One example of such a leap is the sudden transition from a rote-style representation of a few past tenses to a more systematic and productive representation—a transition that Plunkett and colleagues (1990) successfully modeled using a gradient descent network whose output suddenly alters once the training outputs reaches a critical mass of 40 to 50 verbs. Another example concerns the sudden shifts observed in a beam-balancing task. These include a shift between balance judgments based solely on the weights of items to ones that factor distance from a fulcrum into the judgment. These shifts have been recapitulated in a connectionist network studied by McClelland (1989) and more recently by Schulz (1994).

In such cases, discontinuities in output ("radical new ideas") are undergirded by a smooth continuum of inner computational transitions. But this may not exhaust the tricks of the canny human cognizer. One conjecture [due to Karmiloff-Smith (1992) and pursued further by Clark and Karmiloff-Smith (1994), and Clark (1993)], concerns the possible operation of a process termed "representational re-description." The conjecture is that human learning incorporates an endogenous drive to go "beyond success." Thus imagine a being who has achieved a good working solution to a specific problem. If that being were a standard connectionist network, no further learning would occur. In the absence of error messages, the learning algorithm remains effectively inert. But if that being were a re-describer (it is conjectured), she would take the absence of error as a signal to seek *re-organizations* of her knowledge—reorganizations that might permit greater control, or involve integrating this ability/knowledge with other aspects of her skills and understanding. Karmiloff-Smith has gathered an impressive body of evidence in support of the hypothesis that such processes of re-description occur (evidence from the domains of drawing, number, and physical and social understanding; see Karmiloff-Smith, 1992). As an illustrative example, consider the work in drawing. In a classic series of experiments, Karmiloff-Smith showed how children first internalize a procedure for drawing some familiar and much practiced item (e.g., a man) and then proceed through a series of reorganizations of that knowledge. Each such reorganization increases the flexibility of use of the drawing knowledge allowing more and more innovative changes to be made. Early drawing allows for the deletion and insertion of components (e.g., limbs on a person), but not for the reorientation of parts or the integration of items from another category (e.g., a combination man and airplane). Later on, these more complex changes become possible. The underlying explanation, Karmiloff-Smith has argued, involves the child (or adult) engaging in a process of re-description in which one form of information coding and/or control is re-configured so as to yield another, more flexible encoding (think, for example, of going from a push-down stack to a random access memory).

It remains unclear how best to model such a process using connectionist computational resources. But one possibility currently under investigation involves the use of multiple networks, with successful "expert" networks being subsequently coordinated by "gating" networks so as to support increasingly complex behaviors and to facilitate the reuse of acquired skills and knowledge in new problem domains [see Jacobs *et al.* (1991) for a partial connectionist model, Anderson and Van Essen (1994) for a neurally plausible vision of gating, Damasio (1994) for a link between the gating hypothesis[3] and patterns of cognitive deficit, and Clark (1993, Chapter 8, Clark and Thornton (1996), and Clark and Karmiloff-Smith (1994) for further general discussion of the space of computational options)].

XII.5.2 Incremental Learning and the Second Role of External Scaffolding

One way or another, individual learning is clearly a source of some discontinuities in human ideas and mental models. We have already seen how the presence of various kinds of environmental scaffolding (organizations, institutions, language, external memory devices, etc.) may help to reduce individual cognitive loads and to restrict the scope of individual choice. It seems likely, however, that such scaffolding plays a dual role: it both restricts and *expands* our intellectual horizons. One major way in which it expands them is by enabling the collective exploration of multiple learning trajectories. In this respect, the scaffolding itself can act as the vehicle of a novel kind of cognitive evolution.

Recall the strong path dependence of individual connectionist learning. The use of external memory systems helps ameliorate some of the effects of this path dependence by allowing achieved innovations ("redescriptions") to be transmitted between individuals. This allows the collective construction of representational trajectories that crisscross individual cognizers and hence increase the chance of a good idea finding a viable niche for further development. This is, of course, an old idea. But it is one whose value cannot be fully appreciated except in the context of our increasing understanding of the boundedness and extreme path dependence of individual reason.

The emerging picture fits neatly with Merlin Donald's (1991) exploratory work on the evolution of culture and cognition. Donald recognized very clearly the crucial role of forms of external scaffolding (particularly, of external memory systems) in human thought. But he distinguished two major types of scaffolding, which he termed the mythic and the theoretic. Before the Greeks, Donald claimed, various external formalisms were in use but were deployed only in the service of myths and narratives. The key innovation of the Greeks was to begin to use the written medium to record the *processes* of thought and argument. Whereas previous written

[3] Damasio's term is "convergence zones"—such zones control patterns of activity in multiple spatially distant neural networks.

records contained only myths or finished theories (which were to be learnt wholesale and passed down relatively unaltered), the Greeks began to record partial ideas, speculations with evidence for and against, and the like. This new practice allowed (in our terms) *intermediate level recodings* to be passed around, amended, completed by others, and so forth. According to Donald, what was thus created was

> Much more than a symbolic invention, like the alphabet, or a specific external memory medium, such as improved paper or printing. They founded the *process* of externally encoded cognitive change and discovery.
>
> (1991, p. 343)

One effect of such a process is precisely to ameliorate the detrimental effects of path dependency in individual learning. The path to a good idea can now crisscross individual learning histories, so that one agent's local minima becomes another's potent building block. Even a blind and unintelligent search for productive recodings of stored data will now and again yield a powerful result. By allowing such results to migrate between individuals, culturally scaffolded reason is able to incrementally explore spaces that individual reason could never hope to penetrate (for a detailed, statistically based investigation of this claim, see Clark and Thornton (to appear)).

XII.5.3 The Interplay of Individual Learning and External Structures

The external scaffolding of which we have made so much is, in truth, a strange and various beast. But some of its most interesting manifestations share a core property. Such manifestations relate to their human users in much the way a beneficial parasite relates to its host. For the human user provides a niche to which the scaffolding must adapt. And as the human user changes, so too must the scaffolding, if it is to prosper.

Such vague but suggestive ideas can now be given some admittedly simplistic quantitative and computational flesh. In a recent study, Hare and Elman used a "cultural phylogeny" of connectionist networks to model, in some detail, the series of changes that characterized the progression from the past-tense system of Old English (circa 870) to the modern form. In so doing, they explicitly addressed a number of questions that have clear analogies in the social and economic realms. Thus they wrote:

> The complex inflectional system of OE [Old English] existed for hundreds of years—what permitted that stability in the face of an apparent drive toward simplification? What eventually disrupted that stability and caused the system to change? Can the direction of change be predicted?
>
> (Hare and Elman, 1994, p. 4)

Hare and Elman showed that the historical progression can be modeled, in some detail, by a series of neural networks in which the output from one generation is used as the training data for the next. This process yields changes in the language itself as the language alters to reflect the learning profiles of its users.

Briefly, this is what happens. An original network is trained on the Old English forms. A second network is then trained (though not to asymptote) on the forms produced by the first. This output is then used to train a further network, and so on. Crucially, any errors that one network makes in learning to perform the mappings becomes part of the next network's data set. Patterns that are hard to learn, or items whose form is close to that of other, differently inflected items, tend to disappear. As Hare and Elman put it:

> At the onset, the classes [of verbs] differ in terms of their phonological coherence and their class size. Those patterns that are initially less common or less well-defined are the hardest to learn. And these tend to be lost over several generations of learning. This process snowballs as the dominant class gathers in new members and this combined class becomes an ever more powerful attractor.
>
> (1994, pp. 19–20)

In short, we find a process of positive feedback of the kind described by Arthur (see Section XII.3). But the source of the feedback is located squarely in the specific learning profile of the individual (or, in this case, of the network). By thus studying the interplay between the external data set and the processes of individual learning, Hare and Elman were able to make some very fine-grained,[4] quantitative predictions about the historical progression from Old English to the modern forms. Their account thus goes considerably beyond the common observation that morphological change is somehow driven by analogy, class size, and so on. By factoring a specific model of individual learning into the equation, it becomes possible to understand "what seem to be idiosyncratic analogical effects as inevitable and predictable results of gradient descent learning" (Hare and Elman, 1994, p. 32).

The distance between this kind of work and the social-economic case should not, of course, be underestimated. Where the external structure consists of ideas, or of institutions, the dynamics of change will be importantly different. But the same phenomena of interaction will surely emerge. The content-carrying structures will respond to the particular learning profile of the human agent in ways that favor some ideas over others. Also, processes of positive feedback will kick in to amplify such effects into radical changes

[4] For example, predictions of rare but significant cases of irregularization, in which a once-regular verb falls under the inflectional influence of a phonologically similar, high-token frequency irregular.

in the external intellectual and institutional climate. By better understanding the dynamics of individual learning, we will at a minimum increase our grasp of the possible trajectories of such overall systems.

Crucial to any such understanding will be the use of computational models that incorporate multiple time scales and multiple levels of organization. It is only quite recently that the computational tools, and computational power, necessary for these types of study have become widely available. Work in the area known as "artificial life" is especially pertinent here, combining as it sometimes does the use of individual neural network learning with processes of simulated genetic evolution in small populations of "creatures" (see, e.g., Ackley and Littman, 1994). Such work addresses, albeit in necessarily skeletal form, the interplay between individual learning, collective fitness, and longer-term processes of evolutionary change. The skeptical reader will surely object that it is premature to confront these complex issues while our understanding of the component processes, such as individual learning, remains so poor. But this objection is, I suggest, misplaced. For it may be that even very simple experiments combining multiple time scales and levels of organization will yield a preliminary understanding of the types of dynamics that characterize collections of environmentally embedded learning agents. Such global and transtemporal dynamics may be as fundamental, in their way, as the local dynamics of individual human brains.

XII.5.4 Communities and Communication

As a final example of how computational and cognitive scientific theorizing may shed light on the interplay between pattern-completing individual cognition and the larger scaffolding provided by social organizations and institutions, consider the case described by Hutchins (1995).

Hutchins investigated the collective problem-solving capacity of a small "community" of simple neural networks. Each individual in this community comprised a small number of linked processing units. Each unit coded for some specific environmental feature. Excitatory links connected mutually supportive features, whereas inhibitory links connected mutually inconsistent features. A feature like "is a dog" would thus be coded by a single unit with excitatory links to, for example, "barks" and "has fur" units, and inhibitory links to, for example, "meows" and "is a cat" units (the latter being themselves linked by an excitatory connection). Such networks are known as constraint satisfaction networks.

Once a constraint satisfaction is set up (either by learning or by hand coding), it exhibits nice properties of pattern-completion style reasoning. Thus imagine that the various units receive input signals from the environment. Activation of a few units that figure in a linked web of excitatory connections will yield activity across all the linked units. The input "barks" will thus yield a global activation profile appropriate to the category "dog," and so on. Individual units often "choose" whether or not to respond (become active) by summing the inputs received along various channels and comparing the result to some threshold level. As a result, once a constraint satisfaction network settles into an interpretation of the input (e.g., by having all the dog-feature units become active), it becomes very hard to dislodge it, as the units lend each other considerable mutual support.

This feature of such networks, as Hutchins pointed out, corresponds rather nicely to the familiar psychological effect of confirmation bias, namely, the tendency to ignore, discount, or creatively reinterpret evidence (like a solitary "meows" input), which goes against some hypothesis or model that we already have in place (see, e.g., Wason, 1968). Now imagine a community of constraint- satisfaction networks in which each network has different initial activity levels ("predispositions") and different access to environmental data. Hutchins showed that in such cases, the way in which the internetwork communication is structured makes a profound difference to the kind of collective problem solving displayed.

Surprisingly, what Hutchins (1995, p. 252) found was that in such cases more communication is not always better than less. In particular, if from the outset all the networks are allowed to influence each other's activity (to communicate), the overall system shows an extreme degree of confirmation bias—much more than any one of the individual nets studied in isolation. The reason is that the dense communication patterns impose a powerful drive to rapidly discover a shared interpretation of the data, that is, to find a stable pattern of activity across all the units. The individual nets, instead of giving due weight to the external input data, focus instead on these internal constraints (the need to find a set of activation patterns that does not disrupt the others). As a result, the social group rushes "to the interpretation that is closest to the center of gravity of their predispositions, regardless of the evidence" (Hutchins, 1995, p. 259).

By contrast, if you restrict the level of early communication, this gives each individual network time to balance its own predispositions against the environmental evidence. If internetwork communication is *subsequently* enabled, then overall confirmation bias is actively reduced, that is, the group is more likely to fix on a correct solution than is the average member.

Such results suggest that the collective advantage of a jury over an individual decision may dissipate proportionally to the level of early communication between members.[5] More importantly, however, the example illustrates one more way in which we may begin to understand, in a rigorous

[5] Compare to the Condorcet Jury theorem, which states that if (among other things) juror choices are *independent,* then a majority vote by a jury will be correct more often than an average juror.

manner, some aspects of the delicate interplay between individual cognition and group level dynamics. Such understanding will surely be crucial to a better appreciation of the role of institutional and organizational structures in determining social and economic outcomes, and of the balance between individual cognition and the external scaffolding that it both shapes and inhabits.

XII.6 CONCLUSION: EVERY BRAIN IN ITS PLACE

Classical rule-and-symbol-based artificial intelligence made a fundamental error. It mistook the cognitive profile of the agent *plus* her environment for the cognitive profile of the brain (see Clark, 1989; Hutchins, 1995). The neat classical separation of data and process, of symbol structures and CPU, reflected nothing so much as the separation between the agent and an external scaffolding of ideas persisting on paper, in filing cabinets, or electronic media. Recent models of individual cognition depict the brain as a very different kind of device. They depict it as a loose coalition of pattern completing devices geared to solving real-world problems in real time. To that end, the brain readily exploits external structures to support and amplify its own basic problem-solving capacities.

Biological reason, at the individual level, is thus revealed as a process of iterated, local responses, whose computational costs are reduced by extensive reliance on external structures and circumstances. The successes of classical economics emerge, within this paradigm, as cases that depend largely on the short-term dynamics of responses strongly determined by particular kinds of institutional or organizational structure, namely, structures that have *themselves* evolved as a result of selective pressure to maximize rewards of a certain kind. Individual human reason, in such cases, bears but little of the explanatory burden.

Nonetheless, these external scaffoldings are, in most cases, themselves the products of collective human thought and activity. It is thus in the generation and evolution of the institutional and organizational scaffolding that human psychology may be playing the greatest role. We sketched a few ways in which recent research in computational cognitive science may help us better to understand both the role and gradual evolution of such external structures. And we saw hints of how individual cognitive profiles may interact with different types of social structuring (e.g., various patterns of interpersonal communication) so as to yield different types of collective outcome.

Such hints and sketches barely scratched the surface of a large and difficult project: understanding the way the mind both structures and inhabits a world populated by cultures, countries, organizations, institutions, political parties, E-mail networks, and all the vast paraphernalia of external structures and scaffoldings that guide and inform our daily actions. This large and difficult project, I suggest, demands the application of a wide range of new computational and analytic tools: tools, which, at least in simplified cases, can begin to transform our hints, sketches, and speculations into quantitative demonstrations and to suggest more general overarching dynamical principles. One key to such an improved understanding is the use of computational models that span multiple time scales (individual learning and genetic or cultural evolution) and multiple levels of organization (individuals, populations, and populations-plus-external-scaffolding structures). Many of the tools and skills needed to conduct such investigations are now in place, and a few restricted simulations have already yielded interesting results. At the end of the day, the frontiers of institutional economics may turn out to border rather closely on those of cognitive psychology, cognitive science, and the theory of complex nonlinear systems and neural networks. There is clearly much to learn. Perhaps we should learn it together.

ACKNOWLEDGMENTS

Thanks to Douglass North, Arthur Denzau, Norman Schofield, and John Drobak for support, suggestions, and criticisms.

REFERENCES

Ackley, D., and Littman, M. (1994). Altruism in the evolution of communication. In *Artificial Life* (R. Brooks and P. Maes, eds.), Vol. IV. pp. 40–48 MIT Press; Cambridge, MA.

Alchian, A. (1950). Uncertainty, evolution and economic theory. *Journal of Political Economy* **57,** 211–221.

Anderson, C., and Van Essen, D. (1994). Dynamic routing strategies in sensory, motor and cognitive processing. In *Large-Scale Neuronal Theories of the Brain* (C. Koch and T. Davis, eds.), pp. 271–299. MIT Press, Cambridge, MA.

Arthur, B. (1990). Positive feedbacks in the economy. *Scientific American,* **92,** 99.

Ballard, D. (1991). Animate vision. *Artificial Intelligence* **48,** 57–86.

Beckers, R., Holland, O., and Deneubourg, J. (1994). From local actions to global tasks: Stigmergy and collective robotics. In *Artificial Life* (R. Brooks and P. Maes, eds.), Vol. IV. pp. 181–189. MIT Press, Cambridge, MA. pp. 181–189.

Bonabeau, E., Theraulaz, G., Arpin, E., and Sardet, E. (1994). The building behavior of lattice swarms. In *Artificial Life* (R. Brooks and P. Maes eds.), Vol. IV. pp. 307–312. MIT Press, Cambridge, MA.

Brooks, R. (1991). Intelligence without representation. *Artificial Intelligence* **47,** 139–159.

Churchland, P. M. (1996). The Engine of Reason, the Seat of the Soul (MIT Press: Cambridge MA).

Churchland, P., Ramachandran, V., and Sejnowski, T. (1994). A critique of pure vision. In *Large-Scale Neuronal Theories of the Brain.* (C. Koch and J. Davis, eds.). 23–60. MIT Press, Cambridge, MA.

Clark, A. (1989). *Microcognition: Philosophy, Cognitive Science and Parallel Distributed Processing.* MIT Press, Cambridge, MA.

Clark, A. (1993). *Associative Engines: Connectionism, Concepts and Representational Change.* MIT Press, Cambridge, MA.

Clark, A. (1995). Moving minds: Situating content in the service of real-time success. In *Philosophical Perspectives* (J. Tomberlin, ed.), Vol. 9. 89–104. (Ridgeview, CA)

Clark, A. (1997). *Being There: Putting Brain, Body and World Together Again.* MIT Press, Cambridge, MA.

Clark, A., and Karmiloff-Smith, A. (1994). The cognizer's innards: A psychological and philosophical perspective on the development of thought. *Mind & Language,* 8:487–519.

Clark, A., and Thornton, C. (to appear). Trading spaces: Connectionism and the limits of learning. *Behavioral and Brain Sciences.*

Clark, A., and Toribio, J. (1994). Doing without representing? *Synthese* **101,** 401–431.

Damasio, A. (1994). *Descartes' Error.* Grosset, Putnam, NY.

Denzau, A., and North, D. C. (1996). *Shared Mental Models: Ideologies and Institutions.*

Donald, M. (1991). *Origins of the Modern Mind.* Harvard University Press, Cambridge, MA.

Elman, J. (1994). Learning and development in neural networks: The importance of starting small. *Cognition* **48,** 71–99.

Friedman, M. (1953). *Essays in Positive Economics.* University of Chicago, Chicago.

Gode, D., and Sunder, S. (1992). *Allocative Efficiency of Markets with Zero Intelligence (ZI) Traders: Markets as a Partial Substitute for Individual Rationality,* Working Paper No. 1992–16. Carnegie-Mellon Graduate School of Industrial Administration, Pittsburgh, PA.

Hare, M., and Elman, J. (1994). *Learning and Morphological Change.* Center for Research in Language, University of California at San Diego.

Holland, J., Holyoak, K., Nisbet, R., and Thagard, P. (1986). *Induction.* MIT Press, Cambridge, MA.

Hutchins, E. (1995). *Cognition in the Wild.* MIT Press, Cambridge, MA.

Jacobs, R., Jordan, M., and Barto, A. (1991). Task decomposition through competition in a modular connectionist architecture: the what and where visual tasks. *Cognitive Science* **15,** 219–250.

Jordan, M., Flash, T., and Arnon, Y. (1994). A model of the learning of arm trajectories from spatial deviations. *Journal of Cognitive Science* **6,** 359–376.

Kagel, J. (1987). Economics according to the rat (and pigeons too). In *Laboratory Experimentation in Economics: Six Points of View* (A. Roth, ed.). pp. 94–115. Cambridge University Press, New York.

Kahneman, D., Slovic, P., and Tversky, A. (1982). *Judgement Under Uncertainty.* Cambridge University Press, Cambridge, UK.

Karmiloff-Smith, A. (1992). *Beyond Modularity: A Developmental Perspective on Cognitive Science.* MIT Press/Bradford Books, Cambridge, MA.

LeCun, Y., Boser, B., Denker, J. S., Henderson, D., Howard, R., Hubbard, W., and Jackal, L. (1989). Back propagation applied to handwritten zip code recognition. *Neural Computation* **1** (4), 541–551.

McClelland, J. L. (1989). Parallel distributed processing—Implications for cognition and development. In *Parallel Distributed Processing—Implications for Psychology and Neurobiology.* (R. Morris, ed.). pp. 104–139. Clarendon Press, Oxford, UK.

Norman, D. (1986). Reflections on cognition and parallel distributed processing. In *Parallel Distributed Processing* (J. McClellan, D. Rumelhart, and T. P. R. Group, eds.), (Vol. 2, pp. 110–146). MIT Press, Cambridge, MA.

Plunkett, K., Marchman, V., and Knudsen, S. L. (1990). *From rote learning to system building: Acquiring verb morphology in children and connectionist nets.* Paper presented at the Proceedings of the 1990 Connectionist Models Summer School.

Rumelhart, D., and McClelland, J. (1986). On learning the past tenses of English verbs. In *Parallel Distributed Processing: Explorations in the Microstructure of Cognition* (J. McClelland, D. Rumelhart, and T. P. R. Group, eds.), Vol. 2, pp. 216–271. MIT Press, Cambridge, MA.

Rumelhart, D., Smole-sky, P., McClelland, T., and Hinton, G. (1986). Schemata and Sequential Thought Processes. In PDP Models in J. McClelland and D. Rumelhart (Eds.) *Parallel Distributed Processing: Explorations in the Microstructure of Cognition* (MIT Press, Cambridge, MA) pp. 7–58.

Satz, D., and Ferejohn, J. (1994). Rational choice and social theory. *Journal of Philosophy* Vol. 9:102:71–87.

Schulz, T. (1994). The challenge of representational redescription. *Behavioral and Brain Sciences* **17,** 728–729.

Simon, H. (1982). *Models of Bounded Rationality,* Vols. 1 and 2. MIT Press, Cambridge, MA.

Vygotsky, L. (1962). *Thought and Language.* MIT Press, Cambridge, MA.

Wason, P. (1968). Reasoning about a rule. *Quarterly Journal of Experimental Psychology* **20,** 273–281.

Wason, P., and Johnson-Laird, P. (1970). A conflict between selecting and evaluating information in an inferential task. *British Journal of Psychology* **61,** 509–515.

XIII

Beyond Rational Expectations: Indeterminacy in Economic and Financial Markets*

W. Brian Arthur†

One of Douglass North's great gifts is his ability to see over the horizon in economics—to see what is coming in economic theory before economic theorists are themselves quite aware of the changes looming. Thus, in the last few years, North has squeezed insights for economic history from several successive new ways of thinking: transaction-cost economics, theoretical institutional economics, increasing-returns economics. If North were a speculator, investing in ideas, it would pay handsomely to follow his long-term choices. Now Doug North predicts that issues of cognition will become crucial to economic thinking (Denzau and North, 1994; North, 1997), and once again even to theorists it is not obvious why. The purpose of this chapter is to explain why North is again the smart money—why economists and economic historians need to take cognition seriously, not as an adjunct to theorizing, but as basic to our understanding of economic decision making and its consequences for economic markets.

The standard way to look at the economy is to view it in physical terms as a collection of activities, technologies, and needs, all interacting though a

* This paper appeared earlier under the title "Complexity in Economic and Financial Markets," in *Complexity,* 1, 20–25. Reproduced by permission.
† Citibank Professor, Santa Fe Institute, Santa Fe, New Mexico.

market system peopled by decision-making agents such as firms, banks, consumers, and investors. A very different way—the one I want to explore here—would be to view the economy in psychological terms: as a collection of beliefs, anticipations, expectations, and interpretations, with decision-making and strategizing and action-taking predicated upon these beliefs and expectations. Of course, the two views are related. Activities follow from beliefs and expectations. And beliefs and expectations are mediated and sculpted by the physical economy they find themselves in.

Why might a psychological or cognitive view of the economy be useful? Economic agents make their choices based upon their current beliefs or hypotheses (I will use these terms along with the jargon terms *expectations* or *predictions*) about future prices, or future interest rates, or competitors' future moves, or the future character of their world. And these choices, when aggregated, in turn shape the prices, interest rates, market strategies, or world these agents face. The beliefs or hypotheses that agents form in the real economy are largely individual and subjective. They are often private. And they are constantly tested in a world that forms from their and others' actions—a world that is ultimately formed from their and other agents' subjective beliefs. Thus at a sublevel, we can think of the economy ultimately as a vast collection of beliefs or hypotheses, constantly being formulated, acted upon, changed, and discarded, all interacting and competing and evolving and coevolving, forming an ocean of ever-changing predictive models-of-the-world. This view is useful because it forces us to think about how beliefs create economic behavior—and how economic outcomes create beliefs. And it leads to different insights. Beyond the simplest problems in economics, this ecological view of the economy becomes inevitable. And it leads to a world of complexity.

The customary way to handle predictive beliefs in economic analysis is to assume identical agents who possess perfect rationality and arrive at shared, logical predictions or expectations about the situation they face. When these expectations induce actions that in aggregate create a world that validates them as predictions, they are in equilibrium and are called *rational expectations.* Assuming rational expectations is useful if the purpose is to demonstrate logical equilibrium outcomes and to analyze their consequences. But in the real world, rational expectations break down easily. If some agents lack the computing power to deduce the posited outcome, or if some arrive logically at different conclusions from the same data (as they might in a pattern recognition problem), or if there is more than one rational expectations equilibrium with no means to coordinate which is chosen, then some agents may deviate in their expectations. And if some deviate, the world that they cocreate may change, so that others should logically predict something different and deviate too. And so rational expectations unravel easily. Unless there are special circumstances, they are not robust.

There is a game in economics that illustrates this unraveling of rational expectations beautifully. It is the Guessing Game, where N players choose a number between 0 and 100, and the winner is the one closest to two-thirds of the average guess. Obviously here, beliefs of what constitutes a good guess depend on one's view of others' beliefs of what constitutes a good guess. Now, uniform predictions of zero would constitute rational expectations—they would be self-validating in that if agents expected other agents to choose zero they should also choose zero. Therefore expectations that everyone will choose zero would be in equilibrium. No other real number, if chosen by all, would constitute an expectational equilibrium. But does this mean that zero will necessarily be chosen? If I, as a reference player, suspect that some players—or even one player—may choose nonzero, then logically I ought to choose nonzero. Likewise if I believe that others believe that someone may choose nonzero, I will deduce that they too will choose nonzero. Thus beliefs that some may choose nonzero lead others to expect nonzero and choose nonzero. The game leads to a self-referential sequence of "If they choose x, I and others should choose y. But if I and others choose y, they will have to choose z." There is no closure here, and ultimately beliefs or expectations in this game are deductively indeterminate, no matter how logical or rational the agents are.[1]

Consider as a second example my El Farol Problem or Bar Problem (Arthur, 1994). One hundred people must decide independently each week whether to show up at their favorite bar (*El Farol* in Santa Fe, say). The rule is that if a person predicts that more that 60 (say) will attend, he will avoid the crowds and stay home. If he predicts fewer than 60, he will go. This seems innocuous. But it destroys the possibility of long-run shared expectations. If all believe *few* will go, than *all* will go, thus invalidating these expectations. And if all believe *many* will go, *no one* will go, invalidating those expectations. Predictions of how many will attend depend on others' predictions, and others' predictions of others' predictions. Once again there is no rational means to arrive at deduced *a priori* predictions. Predictively, the problem is indeterminate, and other means must be sought to analyze its likely outcome.

These two problems are of course toy problems, concocted, like the famous Prisoner's Dilemma, to make a point. But they illustrate a founda-

[1] A typical way to avoid such indeterminacy is to assume that agents follow a sequence of "deductive" inferences by which they reason that other agents will choose smaller and smaller numbers in preplay, arriving "logically" at zero. But this fails on two grounds. First, rational expectations is a *static* concept: it assumes no sequence of deductions. Second, such a sequence of inferences would itself be nonrobust: if I suspect that even one agent will falter in the sequence or will disbelieve that others will follow this sequence of thought, it will again collapse. It will again produce indeterminacy. For a readable account of logical unraveling in the Guessing Game when played with actual human subjects, see Nagel (1994).

tional difficulty in economics. Where economic outcomes form in part from agents' expectations, then the expectations that some agents might form depend on the expectations they believe that others might form, and the expectations *these* might form depend on the expectations they believe the first group might form. Expectation formation can thus become self-referential. The problem of logically forming expectations then becomes ill-defined, and rational deduction finds itself with no bottom ground to stand upon. This indeterminacy of expectation-formation is by no means an anomaly within the real economy. On the contrary, it pervades all of economics and game theory.

What do we as humans do in cases like this? If a decision problem presents itself to us only once, our predictions and actions depend largely on what is currently in our minds. But if the situation is repeated, as humans, we tend with high reliability to follow a well-known logical procedure. As the situation is replayed regularly, we look for patterns, and we use these to construct temporary expectational models or hypotheses to work with. We carry out localized deductions based on these hypotheses and act on them. As feedback from the repeated plays comes in, we strengthen or weaken our beliefs in our current hypotheses, discarding some when they cease to perform and replacing them as needed with new ones. In other words, to use Tom Sargent's phrase (1993), we act as economic statisticians, using and testing and discarding simple expectational models to fill the gaps in our understanding. Such behavior is perfectly logical—in fact, on a microscale it is the scientific method. But as logic it is not deductive, but *inductive.*[2]

XIII.1 FINANCIAL MARKETS

To see that expectation formation matters, and that circularity in the formation of expectations is not merely an academic worry, let us look in some detail at a major arena of real economic activity, financial markets, and within them the formation of stock market prices.

One of the major puzzles in finance is that academic theorists, by and large, see markets differently from the way traders or practitioners do. The academic view sees investors as perfectly rational. It follows from the assumption of rationality that all usable information is discounted into current prices. Thus markets are efficient. Thus it is not possible to obtain speculative profits via technical trading (using past prices to forecast future prices) or other means. Temporary bubbles and crashes cannot occur, other than as adjustments to market news. (The information that might cause

[2] For a full account of induction, see Holland *et al.* (1986). For earlier versions of induction applied to asset pricing, to decision problems, and to the El Farol problem, see Arthur (1992, 1994). Sargent (1993) applies an inductive approach to problems in macroeconomics.

such swings would be discounted into the price instantaneously.) Further, such notions as a "market psychology" are absurdities. The theory lends useful insight into the workings of financial markets. But it is by no means shared by traders themselves. They, in contrast, tend to see markets as offering speculative opportunities. Many believe that technical trading is profitable, and that "market psychology" and herd effects unrelated to market news can cause bubbles and crashes. Some traders and financial writers even see the market itself as possessing "moods," sometimes describing it as "nervous," or "sluggish," or "jittery."

Which side is correct? Empirically this is hard to settle. Markets do turn out to be reasonably efficient. But statistics show that trading volume and price volatility in real markets are a great deal higher than the standard theory predicts (Shiller, 1981). Statistical tests also show that technical trading can produce consistent, if modest, long-run profits (Brock *et al.,* 1991). And the crash of 1987 showed dramatically to traders and economists alike that sudden price changes do not always reflect rational adjustments to news in the market (Cutler *et al.,* 1989).

Let us begin our examination of financial markets by looking at the standard theory. Full-dress models (for example, Lucas, 1978) are complicated, but at their core is a simple logic (as in Diba and Grossman, 1988) which I will lay out, ignoring extraneous technicalities. In essence, this logic is going to say there is a natural (or fundamental) valuation at any time of a stock, and *given that all investors share the expectational model that produces this valuation,* it will be realized and will therefore be in rational expectations equilibrium. The difficulty will come with the stipulation "given that all investors share the expectational model that produces this valuation." Once we look at *how* investors might come to share this expectation, or how they might form a good expectational model, the solution will unravel and we will have to turn to inductive reasoning to resolve stock pricing behavior.

So let us now go into the standard argument in some detail. Assume that at any time t, N investors can purchase shares in a single security, a stock say, and this provides unknown-in-advance stochastic payoffs or dividends $\{d_t\}$, exogeneously determined. Investors place the remainder of their wealth in a risk-free asset, a T-bill say, that pays a constant r units per period. Market information I_t (economic indicators, rumors, historical price data, Reuters news, and the like) is available at time t, which may suggest the direction the dividend may move. On the basis of this information, the theory has each investor deciding at each time how much wealth to allocate between the stock and the T-bill. What interests us is not this allocation, but how the stock price forms and moves in the resulting market.

Let us go through the standard reasoning in this simple case to arrive at a theory of stock price formation and movement. Assume *homogeneous* investors who use the available information I_t identically in forming unbiased expectations $\{E[d_{t+k}|I_t]\}$ about future dividends at times $t + k$. We can show as follows that such investors can reach deductive conclusions about the market price. Suppose the stock is bid for each day in an auction among these identical investors. It is a simple exercise (Diba and Grossman, 1988) to show that its price will settle at the level:

$$p_t = \beta(E[p_{t+1}|I_t] + E[d_{t+1}|I_t]), \tag{1}$$

where $E[p_{t+1}|I_t]$ is the investors' shared expectation of tomorrow's price. This tells us that a share of the stock today is worth tomorrow's price plus any intervening dividend, discounted by the factor, $\beta = 1/(1 + r)$, which reflects that a dollar tomorrow is worth β dollars today if invested overnight in the T-bill. In other words, today's stock price p_t, is arbitraged to a value that reflects its current expected worth or *fundamental value,* given the shared beliefs derived from the information I_t.

But today's price is still not fully determined. It depends upon our investors' expectation of tomorrow's price $E[p_{t+1}|I_t]$. How do our infinitely rational investors form this expectation? They may take mathematical expectations across the above arbitrage equation as it will play out tomorrow (i.e., with time index $(t + 1)$),

$$E[p_{t+1}|I_t] = \beta(E[p_{t+2}|I_t] + E[d_{t+2}|I_t]). \tag{2}$$

But this process leaves the expectation of the price in two days' time, $E[p_{t+2}|I_t]$, unknown. In fact, by repeating this operation for all times from $t + 2$ onward, substituting future price expectations backward and eventually into (1), our rational investors can eliminate all price expectations, and settle the current price simply as

$$p_t = \sum_{k=1}^{\infty} \beta^k E[d_{t+k}|I_t]. \tag{3}$$

These deduced beliefs that the stock's price are the discounted summation of the values $E[d_{t+k}|I_t]$ (the expected valuation of the future dividend stream) are unbiased and will on average be upheld. They therefore constitute a rational expectations equilibrium. Such beliefs will, of course, fluctuate day by day as the information I_t changes, and so the daily price moves randomly, yielding the random-walk character noted in the popular Wall Street literature.

We now have a rational-expectations theory. But we have paid a price for it. It is valid only under certain, highly singular conditions. Our deductive solution requires (i) that our investors possess identical, known, unbiased expectations of future dividends $E[d_{t+k}|I_t]$; (ii) that these agents are perfectly rational; (iii) that they know that the price at each time will be formed by arbitrage as in (1); and (iv) that they also know that (i), (ii), and (iii) are known and accepted by all.

In passing let us note the implications of this reasoning that were mentioned earlier. Because we assume that dividend expectations are unbiased, prices at each time on average reflect "correct" or fundamental value so speculative profits are not available except by luck. Thus any information contained in past prices, say, or in news, cannot generate profits—it would already be discounted in the price. Therefore the market is efficient and technical trading (using past prices to forecast future ones) cannot generate consistent profits. Price crashes (and temporary bubbles) are ruled out as well: sudden bad news is instantaneously fully reflected in the price, and can therefore not cause a snowball effect. These ideas—whether correct or not—are buried deep in our half-conscious notions of how financial markets operate.

Let us now redo the pricing exercise, more realistically this time. In particular, let us drop condition (i) and instead assume our N investors are heterogeneous—each possibly differs from the others. We will ask how intelligent price and dividend expectations might be formed, given such heterogeneity.

As mentioned, the available shared information I_t consists of past prices, past dividends, trading volumes, economic indicators, rumors, news, and the like. But these are merely qualitative information plus sequences of data points, and *there may be many different, perfectly defensible statistical ways* based on different assumptions and different error criteria to use them to estimate future dividends (Arthur, 1992; Kurz, 1991). The information I_t is a Rorschach inkblot, as it were, and so there is no objective means for one investor to know other investors' expectations of future dividends. Neither is there an objectively laid-down expectational model upon which differing investors can coordinate. We immediately enter the dilemma pointed out earlier in the Guessing Game. Given that I do not know others' expectations, and that I know they will form them on the basis of *their* expectations of others' expectations, how can I form mine?

Let us follow the story logically and watch it unravel. Assuming individual expectations $E_i[d_{t+1}|I_t]$ and $E_i[p_{t+1}|I_t]$ (now indexed for investor $i = 1,2, \ldots, N$), the same argument as before yields the arbitrage equation[3]:

$$p_t = \beta \sum_i \frac{1}{N} (E_i[p_{t+1}|I_t]) + E_i[d_{t+1}|I_t]). \tag{1'}$$

[3] For details of the pricing model that yields this arbitrage equation, see Arthur *et al.* (1996). I assume here that agents use identical forecasting variances, which simplifies the expressions but in no way negates the argument.

Once again, this contains expectations of tomorrow's price. But how can agent i form this expectation? He must either act subjectively, or alternatively try to deduce it by applying the pricing equation (1′) to period $t + 1$:

$$E_i[p_{t+1}|I_t] = \beta E_i\left[\sum_j \frac{1}{N}(E_j[p_{t+2}|I_t] + E_j[d_{t+2}|I_t])\right]. \tag{2'}$$

This calls for agent i's expectations of *everyone's* expectations of the dividend and price at time $t + 2$. Substituting for *this* price expectation in turn yields

$$E_i[p_{t+1}|I_t] = \beta E_i\left[\sum_j \frac{1}{N}\left(E_j[d_{t+2}|I_t] + \beta E_j\left[\sum_k \frac{1}{N}(E_k[p_{t+3}|I_t] + E_k[d_{t+3}|I_t])\right]\right)\right]. \tag{4}$$

This leads agent i into taking into account his expectations of others' expectations of others' expectations of future dividends and prices. Keynes (1936) famously remarked upon this when he pointed out that valuing stocks called for taking into account "what average opinion expects the average opinion to be." Expectation formation by deduction is now facing severe difficulties. There is no objective means by which others' dividend expectations can be known, and the repeated iteration of subjective expectations of subjective expectations merely widens the uncertainty and never comes to closure.

Worse, the situation here leads to instability. As we see in (2′), investor i's expectation of the price at $t + 1$ depends on his ideas of other investors' expectations of the price at $t + 2$. Thus the sense he makes of the Rorschach pattern of market information I_t is influenced by the sense he *believes* others may make of the same pattern. If he believes that others believe the price will increase, he will revise his expectations to anticipate upward-moving prices (in practice helping validate such beliefs). If he believes others believe a reversion to lower values is likely, he will revise his expectations downward. All we need to have self-reinforcing suspicions, hopes, and apprehensions rippling through the subjective formation of expectations (as they do in real markets) is to allow that I_t contains hints—and imagined hints—of others' intentions.

Under heterogeneity, deductive logic leads not just to indeterminate expectations but also to unstable ones.

Notice the difficulty depends in no way on investors being limited in their reasoning powers. It merely says that, given differences in agent expectations, forming deductive expectations becomes indeterminate. Therefore even infinitely rational investors cannot form expectations in a deductive way. Our investors can be arbitrarily intelligent, yet be unable to implement deductive rationality.

XIII.2 LIFE IN AN OCEAN OF EXPECTATIONS

We have seen that deductive reasoning unravels if we take expectation formation seriously. How then might our inductive approach fare? And given the innate complication of dealing with not just one expectational model but an ocean of beliefs, how might its implications be studied?

To study asset pricing under inductive reasoning, John Holland, Blake LeBaron, Richard Palmer, Paul Tayler, and I have created a stock market on the computer—an artificial market peopled by investors who are individual, artificially-intelligent computer programs that can reason inductively (Arthur *et al.*, 1997). In our market-within-the-machine, each artificial investor acts as a market statistician and continually creates multiple "market hypotheses"—subjective, expectational models—of what moves the market price and dividend.[4]

These expectational models are simple mathematical expressions based on past dividends and prices and conditioned to "recognize" particular states of the market. For example, in words a model might be "If today's price is higher than its average in the last 100 days, predict that tomorrow's price will be 3 percent higher than today's." Each agent possesses many such models and can therefore have different predictive hypotheses that "recognize" different states of the market. Each acts on his most accurate model or hypothesis that applies to the current market state. Some expectational models perform well in predicting price and dividend movements. These are retained and acted upon in buying and selling decisions. Others perform badly and are dropped. The agents use the genetic algorithm to produce new forecasting models from time to time (by recombining and mutating those of theirs that work well), as well as to replace poorly performing ones. The agents learn both from discovering useful new expectational models or beliefs and from finding the ones within their current set that perform well.

The market price of course forms endogeneously from the bids and offers of the agents, and thus ultimately from their beliefs. And so the computerized market is its own self-contained, simple, artificial financial world.

In the experiments we carry out with this computerized market, we typically use 100 artificial investors each with 60 expectational models. Thus there are at any time 6,000 expectational models. This is hardly an "ocean" of expectations, but it is still a sizable tidal pool. To see how these beliefs might feed upon each other and coevolve in this pool, consider expectational models that predict an upward trend. If such expectations appeared by random generation in several agents' sets of expectational models, and if prices trended upward by chance driven by an upward dividend, these

[4] For a noncomputational evolutionary approach to asset pricing, see Blume and Easley (1990). They assume arbitrary but fixed expectations and investment strategies that compete.

trend expectations would become validated and would cause buying behavior, furthering the trend and possibly producing a temporary price bubble. Thus trend expectations in sufficient density in the population of expectations are mutually reinforcing.[5] Suppose the price showed sinusoidal swings of period K unrelated to dividend. Then expectations that tomorrow's price at time $t + 1$ equals that at $t - K + 1$ would become validated. But use of such expectations would cause buying at the bottom of the cycle and selling at the top, and this would arbitrage the cycle away and render such cyclical expectations inaccurate. Cyclical expectations in combination would therefore be mutually negating and would disappear from the pool of beliefs. Expectations that price follows fundamental value would be valid as long as they were held by others. But if price were trending upward above fundamental value, and others believed the price rise would continue, this might temporarily lead to the continuation of the trend, so that fundamentalist beliefs might be rendered inaccurate.

From this we see that expectations—like species—can come and go in the ocean of beliefs. They can mutually reinforce or mutually negate each other. And they form a coevolving ecology of beliefs. The situation is similar to that of Lindgren's (1991) beautiful study of coevolving strategies in the Prisoner's Dilemma. In our actual market a huge variety of beliefs can in principle be generated. How then does the ecology organize itself? How do fundamentalist beliefs fare? And do technical trading beliefs gain a footing? Does the outcome in our experimental market validate standard financial theory or the traders' view?

Our findings are still preliminary. But it appears that the academic view and the traders' view are both upheld, but under different conditions, or in different regimes.

If we start our traders off with identical, fundamental-value expectations (by setting the parameters of all their expectational models to reproduce prices that validate these expectations), we find that deviating, nonfundamentalist expectations cannot get a footing. If a large majority of investors believe the fundamentalist model, the resulting prices will validate it, and deviant predictions that arise by mutation in the population of expectational models will be rendered inaccurate. Thus in our market, the homogeneous rational expectations equilibrium of the standard literature is evolutionarily stable: it cannot be invaded by small numbers of deviating expectations. The standard finance theory, under these special circumstances, is upheld.

[5] In an interesting set of papers, De Long and colleagues (1990) and Shleifer and Summers (1990) show analytically that certain expectations can be self-fulfilling, so that herd effects or positive feedbacks can be demonstrated. Typically they have two groups of homogeneous traders with fixed expectational models.

If, however, we start our traders off *in an exactly identical market,* except that their initial expectations are randomly distributed uniformly about the fundamentalist ones, we find that trend-following beliefs that appear by chance have enough density to become self-reinforcing in the ecology of beliefs. The situation here is reminiscent of that in certain theories of the origin of life. If a sufficient density of small nucleotide molecules appears in the soup or ocean of molecules, they can become mutually reinforcing and "take off" (Eigen and Schuster, 1977) into a set of mutually sustaining molecules that constitute primitive life. Similarly, if expectations appear that are mutually reinforcing, they too can "take off." The market "comes to life." Now, in our artificial financial world, these trend-following expectations should cause temporary price bubbles and crashes to occur, and such swings are indeed observable in the price series. Thus we can restate all this by saying that, in this initially heterogeneous expectations regime, using past prices to forecast future ones—technical trading—becomes an emergent property.

We also find that the market possesses a nontrivial *psychology.* We can define this as the collection of market hypotheses (or expectational models or mental beliefs) that are being acted upon at a given time.

We believe (and yet need to validate statistically) that in this regime no stationary equilibrium is reached. There are indications that if we "freeze" successful agents early on and inject them back into the system much later, they do no better than average: the market has evolved and moved on as new strategies are discovered from time to time that exploit the earlier winning strategies so that the latter no longer succeed. Of course, we find no evidence of market "moods." But from time to time we do see agents being torn between beliefs that a price trend will continue upward and beliefs that a downturn is imminent—hints of conjoined "greed" and "fear," the source of nervousness in real markets.

In the data that our inductive-expectations market generates, we also observe a curious statistical phenomenon that is a signature of actual financial markets. This is GARCH (Generalized AutoRegressive Conditional Heteroscedastic) behavior. GARCH behavior means in essence that there are periods of persistent high volatility (or high variance) in the price series followed randomly by periods of persistent low volatility. Persistence of high or low volatility makes no sense in the standard theory. But in our evolutionary market, prices might continue in a stable pattern for quite some time—implying low price volatility—until new expectations are discovered that exploit that pattern. Then there will be swift changes of *gestalt,* swift readjustments in expectations that change the market itself and cause avalanches of further change. Volatility will become high and remain so until such change is absorbed. GARCH behavior is statistically measurable in our price series and resembles that shown in actual financial markets. By contrast, the initially-homogeneous-expectations regime—as assumed by standard theory—displays no GARCH signature.

To see these phenomena, note that we have no need to invoke "irrationality" or "behaviorism" or "investor sentiment" (cf. Thaler, 1993). They follow simply from the subjective-inductive nature of belief formation.

We can conclude that given sufficient homogeneity of (unbiased) beliefs, the standard equilibrium of the literature is upheld. In this regime the market in a sense is "dead." As the dial of heterogeneity of initial beliefs is turned up, the market undergoes a phase transition and "comes to life." It develops a rich psychology and displays phenomena regarded as anomalies in the standard theory but observed in real markets. The inductive, ecology-of-expectations model we have outlined is by its definition an *adaptive non-linear network* (Holland, 1988). In its heterogeneous mode it displays complex, pattern-forming, non-stationary behavior. We could therefore rename the two regimes or phases *simple* and *complex*.

We conjecture that actual financial markets live within the complex regime.

XIII.3 COGNITION, THE ECONOMY, AND HISTORY

An economy of course, does indeed consist of technologies, actions, markets, financial institutions, and factories—all real and tangible. But behind these, guiding them and being guided by them on a subparticle level, as it were, are beliefs: the subjective expectations, multiple hypotheses, and half-hoped anticipations held by real human beings. Beliefs can be mutually reinforcing or mutually competing. They can arise, get a footing, become prominent, fall back, and disappear. They can be generated privately by theoretical reasoning or by pattern recognition, and they can be transmitted from one agent to another. They shape in aggregate the macroeconomy. They give rise to the movements of financial markets. They direct flows of capital internationally. They govern strategic behavior. They govern investment. Beliefs are the DNA of the economy, and they are present everywhere. When beliefs form an ocean of interacting, competing, arising and decaying entities, occasionally they simplify into a simple, homogeneous equilibrium set. More often they produce complex, ever-changing patterns. Within the most significant parts of the economy, interacting, nonequilibrium beliefs are unavoidable, and with these so is a world of complexity.

This cognitive view of the economic behavior applies also to economic history. History emerges from the lives and actions of peoples, their wars and extended wars, their treaties and agreements, their movements and migrations, their new technologies and institutions and polities and ways of living. But all these are predicated upon and arise from interpretations of the world and beliefs of how it operates. And the historical circumstances of any particular period support only certain interpretations and cognitions. Thus in history as in the economy, beliefs arise and compete and linger and decay. And so cognition and historical action coevolve, and as with cognition and economic action, they coevolve in a predictively indeterminate way. Beliefs and actions in history cannot be separated. They must be simultaneously understood and interpreted. Their intermingling in history produces complex, ever-changing patterns.

Within history, interacting, nonequilibrium beliefs are unavoidable, and with these so is a world of complexity. Once again, Douglass North is prescient.

ACKNOWLEDGMENTS

I am grateful to John Casti, John Drobak, John Holland, David Lane, Blake LeBaron, Douglass North, Richard Palmer, Martin Shubik, and George Soros for discussions and comments on the arguments in this chapter.

REFERENCES

Arthur, W. B. (1992). On Learning and adaptation in the economy. *Santa Fe Institute Paper* **92-07-038.**

Arthur, W. B. (1994). Inductive behavior and bounded rationality. *American Econonmic Review* **84,** 406–411.

Arthur, W. B., Holland, J. H., LeBaron, B., Palmer, R., and Tayler, P. (1997). Asset pricing under endogenous expectations in an artificial stock market. Forthcoming in *The Economy as an Evolving, Complex System II,* (W. B. Arthur, S. Durlauf, D. Lane, Eds.) Addison-Wesley, Reading, MA.

Blume, L., and Easley, D. (1990). Evolution and market behavior. *Journal of Economic Theory* **58,** 9–40.

Brock, W., Lakonishok, J., and LeBaron, B. (1991). Simple technical trading rules and the stochastic properties of stock returns. *Santa Fe Institute Paper* **91-01-006.**

Cutler, D. M., Poterba, J. M., and Summers, L. H. (1989). What moves stock prices? *Journal of Portfolio Management* pp. 4–12.

De Long, J. B., Shleifer, A., Summers, L. H., and Waldmann, R. J. (1990). Positive feedback strategies and destabilizing rational speculation. *Journal of Finance* **45.**

Denzau, A., and North, D. C. (1994). Shared mental models: Ideologies and insititutions. *Kyklos.* **47**(1), 1–31.

Diba, B. T., and Grossman, H. I. (1988). The theory of rational bubbles in stock prices. *Economic Journal* **98,** 746–754.

Eigen, M., and Schuster, P. (1977). The hypercycle: A principle of natural self-organization. *Naturwissenschaften* **64,** 541.

Holland, J. H., Holyoak, K. J., Nisbett, R. E., and Thagard, P. R. (1986). *Induction.* MIT Press, Cambridge, MA.

Holland, J. H. (1988). The global economy as an adaptive process. In *The Economy as an Evolving Complex System* (P. W. Anderson, K. J. Arrow, and D. Pines, eds.), pp. 117–124, Addison-Wesley; Reading, MA.

Lindgren, K. (1991). Evolutionary phenomena in simple dynamics. In *Artificial Life II* (C. Langton *et al.*, eds.), pp. 295–312, Addison-Wesley; Reading, MA.

Keynes, J. M. (1936). *General Theory of Employment, Interest and Money.* Macmillan, London.

Kurz, M. (1991). On the structure and diversity of rational beliefs. *Santa Fe Institute Paper* **91-02-013.**

Lucas, R. E. (1978). Asset prices in an exchange economy. *Econometrica* **46,** 1429–1445.

Nagel, R. (1994). Reasoning and learning in guessing games: An experimental investigation. Ph.D. Dissertation, University of Bonn.

North, D. C. (1997). Some fundamental puzzles in economic history. In *The Economy as an Evolving, Complex System II* (W. B. Arthur, S. Durlauf, and D. A. Lane, eds.). Addison-Wesley, Reading MA.

Sargent, T. J. (1993). *Bounded Rationality in Macroeconomics.* Oxford University Press, New York.

Shiller, R. J. (1981). Do stock prices move too much to be justified by subsequent changes in dividends? *American Economic Review* **71,** 421–436.

Shleifer, A., and Summers, L. H. (1990). The noise trader approach to finance. *Journal of Economic Perspectives* **4,** 19–33.

Thaler, R. H. (1993). *Advances in Behavioral Finance.* Russell Sage Foundation, New York.

XIV Making Use of Treacherous Advice: Cognitive Progress, Bayesian Adaptation, and the Tenacity of Unreliable Knowledge

Paul A. David
Warren C. Sanderson

XIV.1 CAVEAT LECTOR

The ensuing discussion embarks upon a rather idiosyncratic speculative venture into a vast, difficult, but surely important territory for historical social scientists. Our topic might be described in abstract terms as being concerned with human learning behaviors and the roles of cognitive understanding (and misunderstanding) in the evolution of control over complex and imperfectly observed stochastic processes. From this description one could reasonably surmise that this chapter is one among a growing number of recent works belonging to the genre of *evolutionary epistemology.* Although that label certainly is applicable to our inquiry into the influences of evolutionary processes upon human cognition, in the present usage it must be read as referring only to the proposition that conceptual change is an evolutionary process, or can be modeled usefully as such.[1] Nothing in the following pages addresses the preoccupations of the other branch of inquiry in the evolutionary epistemology literature, which has been concerned with the epistemological implications that might follow from the

[1] This follows the distinction drawn by Bradie (1986) in an illuminating review of the literature on evolutionary epistemology. The most fully worked out account of conceptual change in modern science as an evolutionary process is that provided by Hull (1988).

fact of the human organism's evolutionary origins.[2] But, even thus delimited, our general subject matter should hold some considerable interest for students of the history of the interplay between ideas and material civilization.

In these pages, however, we explore only a particular and very narrow tract of that broad field. The concrete domain of research reported on here concerns the historical development of knowledge about human reproductive physiology in relationship to the intentional control of fertility within marital unions. Perhaps this is a sufficiently interesting matter to stand on its own, but we present it as an exercise in what might be called "applied metonomy"—a mode of inquiry predicated on belief in the possibility that significant attributes of the whole can be revealed by close examination of one, albeit small part. The route we are following onto the terrain of the cognitive scientists, therefore, has been cautiously chosen. It eschews anything close to a frontal approach to the general problem of the relationship between changes in economic agents' states of knowledge and individually or socially adaptive mechanisms in their observable behaviors. That is, indeed, the "big issue" which we may be able to illuminate by reflection on some of the more generic conclusions that can be extracted from a specific historical case study.

Were it feasible, proper implementation of a research strategy designed to exploit the principle of metonomy in this instance would call for the assembling of a large multidisciplinary team, recruited from the ranks of experts in cognitive science, epistemology, the sociology of knowledge, behavioral psychology, and the history of science and technology, as well as from economics and demography. Evidently, the capabilities of the much smaller exploratory party undertaking this expedition are considerably more limited than the metasubject deserves. Therefore, perhaps the most that should be expected on this occasion is a different view of the connections, and the lacunae, between processes of cognitive evolution and behavioral adaptations in economic and demographic history—as seen from an unexpected and admittedly rather eccentric angle.

To be more concrete, the historical inquiry we refer to was launched quite a number of years ago, when we were actively engaged in research on

[2] Waters (1990) referred to the view that the growth of knowledge should be modeled as an evolutionary process as the "model version" of evolutionary epistemology, and he contrasted it with the "implications version," the latter of which he associated particularly with the suggestions advanced by epistemologists such as Quine (1969) and Kornblith (1985), to the effect that natural selection has given us cognitive mechanisms that have a tendency to produce true beliefs. Waters (1990, pp. 80–81) made a persuasive case for "naturalizing" epistemology by pursuing cognitive science and then working out "the philosophical implications of discoveries to be made in psychology, linguistics, artificial intelligence and neurology," rather than by pondering "the evolutionary origins of mechanisms we do not yet understand."

the efficacy of rudimentary fertility control techniques and their role in the American population's 19th-century transition to family limitation.[3] At the time, this entire topic lay far outside the usual ambit of economists and economic historians, and so the keen interest we developed in the efficacy of the particular class of contraceptive practices that were referred to during the 19th century as "safe-period" methods must have seemed more than a little recherché—even to our colleagues in demography. Some consciousness of this attitude in others, undoubtedly, contributed to heightening our concern to not lose sight of the generalizable issues—the metaproblems, so to speak—in the welter of fascinating particulars. Of the latter there was no shortage, for, as we discovered, the precursors of the modern "rhythm method" had a long and curious history, about which more will be said, anon. Fortunately, what we learned about it also turned out to be so intriguing in its possible larger significance that it has remained a topic of our recurring ruminations and conversations over many years, at least long enough to warrant our attempt now to discourse upon it in public.

XIV.2 PARTICULARITIES AND GENERALITIES: AN EVOLUTIONARY OVERVIEW

A part of what was so interesting, undeniably, had to do with the history of beliefs regarding the biology of human sexual reproduction. It quite alters one's sense of the chronology of "modernity" to realize at how recent a date medical scientists succeeded in dispersing most of the pall of confusion and misapprehensions that previously had enshrouded the physiology (let alone the endocrinology) of the processes of ovulation and conception in humans. At the same time, one wonders how it was possible for the basic facts about the periodicity of ovulation to have remained a mystery for so great a portion of human experience.

Another part of the topic's interest lay in the more technical, methodological aspects of analyzing processes of learning and adaptive behavior under random reinforcement. These had to do with the approach we took in attempting to discover whether the sheer lack of accurate physiological knowledge had prevented women from deriving any substantial degree of contraceptive protection by employing "safe-period" methods, which some of them testified to having done during the era before more reliable modern conceptive techniques were available. It occurred to us to try to answer

[3] Commencing with the formation of the Stanford Project on the History of Fertility Control in 1976, this larger program of research was conducted by the authors and several generations of graduate students in the Stanford University Department of Economics. The studies of particular relevance here are discussed in David and Sanderson (1978a, b, 1986) and David *et al.* (1988).

that question by constructing a stochastic computer simulation model that would—in a comparatively costless way—permit a quantitative exploration and evaluation of the possibilities of constrained experience-based (trial-and-error) learning about the rhythm of ovulation and susceptibility to impregnation. The relevant constraints on such a process we took to be twofold in nature. One set would stem from the fundamental lack of understanding about the physiology of reproduction and the other from limitations that necessarily would be imposed on individual experimental action in this field—by the participants' other motivating concerns. Principal among the latter, we were ready to suppose for the purposes of the analysis, would be a desire to manage the "regime" of coition (and, specifically, the distribution of the times when sexual intercourse occurred within the intermenstruum) so as to minimize the expectation of a conception.

In building a model of sequential "regime adaptation," we thus were soon obliged to consider the problem of the cognitive limitations under which experience-based inferences and consequent behavioral adaptations would have to proceed. These we characterized in two ways: (1) *maintained beliefs* about the existence and nature of a monthly interval during which a woman would be at the peak of her susceptibility to the risk of impregnation from unprotected intercourse and (2) *mutable and adaptable beliefs* concerning the location of that interval within the intermenstruum. The representation of cognitive evolution as the sequential updating of beliefs concerning those matters, following Bayesian principles of inference to guide the trial-and-error process of learning, was then a comparatively straightforward step to take in the formal modeling exercise. To suppose that revision of such beliefs would induce adaptations in the goal-seeking behaviors of the individuals who held them, so that the time distribution of coition might correspondingly be modified, also was (for economists) a quite natural conceptual sequel.

The upshot of this was a simple model that qualified as "evolutionary," although not so in the strict Darwinian sense. The touchstone of an evolutionary process is that whatever can exist at each point in time remains strictly bounded by that which existed previously; genetic processes of evolution are those in which the contents of the gene pool sets the limits on the genetic material that can be phenotypically expressed in the next generation. So, as often is said, in matters biological, Nature is obliged to solve her problems largely with materials that already are on hand.[4] A thoroughly

[4] Various implications of importance, which economic theorists concerned with evolutionary processes might absorb from this simple observation, are to be found in Gould (1980, Chapter 1), and Crick (1988, pp. 137–142). Although insufficiently appreciated by many economists who employ the evolutionary metaphor in modeling technological change, this point holds even in regard to genetic mutations; for, at every point in time, the overwhelming number of mutant genes are those already latent in the gene pool.

Darwinian evolutionary process is one that can be said, following the usage made popular by Campbell (1959, 1960), to depend on some mechanism involving "blind variation and selective retention"—irrespectively of whether the subject of evolution is a gene-governed biological trait or a cultural "meme." Our simple model of behavioral optimization under uncertainty, where actions are conditioned on beliefs concerning states of the world that are sequentially revised on the basis of the observable realization of the stochastic process, thus qualifies as "evolutionary." It also features selective retention of beliefs and consequent patterns of behavior, although the hypothesized mechanism of selection has nothing to do with the principle of "inclusive fitness" that operates in Darwinian natural selection; rather the opposite, for it involves the retention of beliefs that are consistent with consequential actions that are functionally adaptive to the extent of serving the (myopic) goal of minimizing the monthly conditional expectation of a pregnancy. On its face, therefore, the adaptive process we modeled is *intentional,* and, as its evolutionary mechanism involves the intertemporal transmission of *acquired* behavioral traits, it might be said to view more closely to the formulation of Lamarck than to that of Darwin. Whether or not it is really more illuminating, however, to see the process of selection as representing Lamarckian *instructionism,* rather than strict Darwinian *selectionism,* is an issue of interpretation that turns out to be rather subtle, and can best be left for later consideration.[5]

What is beyond question is that whether one focuses on the individual's belief structures (concerning the timing of ovulation) or the associated behavioral regimes (concerning the timing of intercourse) as being the memes in this microlevel evolutionary process, from the point at which the process begins, variations in the memes over which selection takes place will not be blind. Such evolution as may occur is driven by a conscious cognitive process of interpreting "the data," and optimizing, and reoptimizing the be-

[5] In the views on evolution held by the French botanist Jean-Baptiste Pierre Antoine de Monet, le Chavalier de Lamarck (1744–1829), the motive forces for evolutionary change are the needs of living organisms and the activities they engage in to satisfy them, which results in the acquisition of characteristics that are heritable by the next generation and so leads to the development of more complex organisms (see, e.g., Hull, 1988, pp. 86–88). Whereas in *Darwinism,* heritiable variations that are the subject of natural selection arise spontaneously, produced by mechanisms that are "blind" in regard to the processes of selection, *Lamarckian* evolutionary theory would accommodate processes of "instruction" by experience (subsuming imaginative perception, cognitive learning, memory, and purposive alteration of design) as sources of variations that can be propagated from one generation to the next. Of course, Lamarckism contravenes the "central dogma" of molecular biology, according to which genetic information is transmitted only from nucleic acid to protein or other products and never passes in the opposite direction.

havioral regime subject to the constraints of the agents' currently prevailing information states. It is of interest to ask whether there are conditions under which this kind of rational, evolutionary learning procedure could permit the user effectively to control fertility within a finite reproductive life span. But also, we would like to know whether or not in doing so it would perform in a way that was qualitatively superior to a strictly Darwinian evolutionary process of adaptation. The possibility of answering such questions by numerical simulations, as has been intimated, motivated our efforts to construct a computable model.

When it came to trying to implement this research program concretely, by specifying our stochastic learning model, we soon were forced to reconsider carefully the formulation that initially had been chosen for the maintained portion of the agents' beliefs about the (physiological) states of the world with which they were having to contend. We had started from a suitably modern, medically informed specification of the objective processes that our hypothetical couples would be trying to control. But we were then driven toward ever-less-complicated suppositions about reality, in order to reduce to plausibly manageable levels the computational burden of the implied Bayesian information processing procedure. The emergence of this latter class of considerations, and the existence of an elegantly simple and intuitively appealing solution to the problem, was not at all obvious to us at the outset. Moreover, these considerations cast the problem of modeling "bounded rationality"—and the related issue of the possible origins of "rational heuristic strategies" more generally conceived—into what struck us at the time as a rather interesting new light. And so it still seems.

The following sections of this chapter provide details of the two arresting aspects of the research journey that has just been recalled. Section XIV.3 starts with a bit of the history of safe-period methods and the puzzles that they raise. From there we move on to discuss briefly, in Section XIV.4, some psychological and socioeconomic conditions pertinent to effective individual learning behaviors. Section XIV.5 provides an informal description of our model of sequential Bayesian modification of beliefs and consequent behavioral adaptation, and the several ways in which it is possible to characterize learning within this quantitative framework. (Details of the model's formal specifications, and the basis for our parameterization of the objective biological component of the stochastic simulation structure, are relegated to Appendices A and B, respectively.) Section XIV.6 reports and comments on what the simulation studies revealed about individual and population-level adaptation in fertility control, and the relationship of the latter to the evolution of beliefs held regarding the rhythm of ovulation and the time pattern of susceptibility to impregnation in the human female.

The chapter concludes in Section XIV.7 by pointing to several broader, generic themes upon which these findings might be seen to have a more-or-less direct bearing: (1) the relationship between cognitive and behavioral evolution in a population and the implications of changes in conditions for experimentation; (2) deeper connections that may exist between evolutionary models that appear to feature Lamarckian instructionism and those that are built on strictly Darwinian selectionist principles; and (3) a suggested bounded rationality view of cognitive progress, as involving the co-evolution of information processing capabilities and the selection of computationally expedient heuristics. Such provocations may entice or incite others to help in discovering whether or not some larger pearl of wisdom eventually can be formed around the particular granule of sand that has been both irritating and intriguing us for so many years.

XIV.3 SAFE-PERIOD PUZZLES: TREACHEROUS ADVICE AND FUNCTIONAL MYTH

The idea that the menstrual cycle of the human female contains a period of peak susceptibility to impregnation, and the complementary notion of a safe or sterile period, has a long history. It is well known that these notions have figured more or less explicitly in the conceptual structures and patterns of behavior found by ethnographers among the peoples of various preliterate cultures. They also appeared in the systematic gynaecological writings of Soranus of Ephesus (98–138 A.D.), and his followers in the West, down to the modern age.[6] The immediate legacy that this venerable tradition left to medical writers in the 19th century, unfortunately, was largely one of confusion about the timing of ovulation and the location of the so-called sterile period. Soranus had started from the perfectly plausible supposition that menstruation in the human female was an estrous event, a conjecture that, however correct and well founded it might be in observational evidence from domesticated animals, just happens to be completely wrong in the case of the higher primates. Nevertheless, the citation of ancient authority in medical writings, as in other matters, served to propagate erroneous beliefs, namely, that there was a fertile period that was coincident with menstruation, and that the period of minimal susceptibility to conception must therefore occur somewhere toward the middle of the intermenstruum. This was only one among manifold misapprehensions concerning

[6] Cf. Himes (1970), index references to "Sterile Period"; Hopkins (1965, esp. p. 134), gave an alternative translation of the references made by Soranus to the period "suitable for conception."

the physiology of reproduction, many of them tracing back to Hippocrates and Aristotle, that remained current in the West for more than a millennium.

For decades after the startling late 17th-century discovery of the viviparous ovum by Reinier de Graff (1641–1673), and the reports of microscopic observations of the spermatozoa by his fellow Hollander, Antoine van Leeuwenhoek (1632–1723), ancient beliefs, such as the one which held that the human foetus was the product of "semen" contributed by the two sexes, continued to be affirmed in theses submitted to the Faculty of Medicine in Paris. Pierre Darmon (1981) has entertainingly described the flourishing of such fables during the 17th and 18th centuries and the profusion of prescriptions compounded from them as how best to conceive boys or girls, as needs might be. Darmon attributes these baroque fantasies to escapist reactions on the part of medical professionals and lay people alike, reflecting their frustrating and persisting bafflement concerning the details of the procreative process. On the question of whether generation was a "secret of nature" that man some day would be able to uncover, even Voltaire and *L'Encyclopédie* of Diderot remained pessimistic.

The durability of human confusion over what today we deem to be rather basic facts about the physiology of procreation, especially among the supposedly learned whose opinions have been recorded for us to reflect on, is truly sobering. Coming to the early 19th century, one finds that the influential work by Charles Knowlton, *Fruits of Philosophy* (1841), for example, reiterated Soranus's conviction that conception was most likely to occur in the days *immediately following* menstruation (cf. Knowlton, 1841, p. 16, cited by Hopkins, 1965, p. 134).[7] In England and the United States, the perpetuation of the belief that ovulation and menstruation were physiologically related and temporally coincident events, quite naturally, led some 19th-century authorities on birth prevention to instruct their readers to confine sexual intercourse to the midmonth period (cf. eg., Ashton, 1865, pp. 14–15, and more influentially, Stockham, 1887, pp. 29, 324–326).

Not all the medically informed advice published on the subject of the safe period was quite so bad, however. Along with their mistaken belief

[7] Knowlton was the first modern proponent of douche as a contraceptive and did not advocate continence during the susceptible period (as he delimited it). Bergues *et al.* (1960, pp. 116–119), discussed the writings of Pouchet (1847) on the safe period and the 18th-century European medical literature upon which he drew—both of which are slighted in Himes (1970).

about the timing of ovulation, some experts came to hold the equally erroneous theory that, following ovulation, the ovum survived in the female reproductive tract and remained capable of being fertilized for a very considerable span of time. The most cautious among them therefore counseled, as a method of avoiding pregnancies, complete abstention from coitus throughout the fourteen days following the cessation of the menses.[8]

When considered *in toto,* therefore, the information emanating from physicians, and other authorities during the 19th and the early 20th centuries as to the whereabouts of the safe period had a rather diabolical cast to it. Recipients who took to heart the urgings of extreme caution, and so foreswore coition before the 18th day of the menstrual cycle, would indeed have had scant chance of conceiving children, whereas, those couples who deemed it adequate to avoid only the supposed period of maximum susceptibility (in the week following the menses) would thereby be directed to resume sexual relations at just the point in the month when the woman was most likely to be ovulating.[9]

The roots of this exquisitely treacherous 19th-century advice obviously lay in the medical profession's persisting ignorance of the parameters of the ovulatory cycle in humans. It was not until the physiological discoveries based on lapryscopic observations by Ogino and Knaus, in 1931 and 1933, respectively, that the safe period method began to be placed on scientific foundations; these reflected a growing consensus that ovulation was a periodic event in human females, and that there was enough regularity about it to describe *the* rhythm of ovulation. In recognition of this important and comparatively recent qualitative shift, historians concerned with voluntary fertility limitation practices in the West generally have followed the lead of Norman Himes (1936–1970) in supposing that the historical antecedents of

[8] Cf. *American Physician* (1855, pp. 59–61), and Lewis (1874, pp. 94–98), among American writers on birth prevention, and the earlier influential work of the Frenchman Pouchet (1847). Still other theories led to equivalently antinatal recommendations. The rather unorthodox views of Drysdale (1854, p. 348), who described the sterile period as an interval commencing two or three days before the menses and ending on the eighth day following, continued to claim some adherents among respectable purveyors of birth prevention advice in England (cf. Himes, 1970, pp. 234–235 on Drysdale, and H. A. Albutt's *The Wife's Handbook,* 1878). On the other hand, opposing suppositions about the coincidence of ovulation with menstruation were so widely held that it is not difficult to understand why Drysdale's message was garbled by some other writers, who relabeled as the susceptible period the exact interval he described as "sterile" (cf. Himes, 1970, p. 232, n. 71, on the inversion of Drysdale by "M.G.H.", the anonymous author of *Poverty: Its Causes and Cure,* c. 1854–1861).

[9] Cf. Hartman (1962) for extensive discussion and references on the actual location of the period of susceptibility within the normal menstrual cycle.

the modern rhythm method essentially had no contraceptive value worthy of consideration.[10]

The reasoning upon which this conclusion seems to rest is not unassailable, as one may see by pausing to ask why anything so putatively useless as the so-called premodern safe period should have had so wonderful a career. Current expert opinion on the diffusion of contraceptive methods might suggest that a technique that was likely to yield its users an enormously variegated set of outcomes, ranging in this case from extremely effective contraception to perversely quick pregnancies, would not be easy to promote and therefore would not be likely to establish itself even among the members of a population who actively sought means of limiting their fertility. Yet, archival records have been found of interviews conducted around the turn of the 19th century on U.S. university campuses, in which some of the married female respondents to questions about their sexual and reproductive behaviors volunteered that, among the various contraceptive techniques they had employed, the safe-period method had been used—and to good effect.[11]

Cast into this frame of reference, the history just reviewed presents the appearance of a paradox, in that the treacherous nature of the practices to which it led notwithstanding, belief in the safe period as a method of contraception became widely diffused geographically and persisted in Western societies over a considerable stretch of time. This, however, is a paradox that is more contrived than real. It arises from the failure to distinguish explicitly between the principle of seeking the woman's period of minimal (or maximal) susceptibility to impregnation, and the various specific recommendations that have been made as to where to look first. The historians of medical contraception and family limitation have tended to

[10] Cf. the references to Himes' (1970) treatment of the safe period presented previously. When Himes' monumental work was first published (1936), however, the discovery of the rhythm of ovulation was a recent thing, and his discussion of the historical literature in regard to the safe period—unlike his approach to other contraceptive practices—was dominated by a concern for the scientific accuracy of the various authors' views on the time of ovulation, rather than the differing contraceptive value of each of the several major brands of advice that were offered. Himes' (1970, pp. 182–185) survey of the "effective" methods of contraception found in European folk medicine and folk beliefs also rather pointedly excludes all forms of the safe period.

[11] In the survey responses dating from the 1890s, the "safe period" was the second most frequently mentioned method of contraception after "douche." Cf. David and Sanderson (1978a, 1986, pp. 317ff.) for further details relating to demographic aspects and the statistical representativeness of the so-called Mosher Survey sample, a collection of some 48 interviews (involving 44 individual women) conducted by Clelia Duel Mosher during 1892–1896, 1913, and 1920 at the Stanford University and during 1897–1900 at The Johns Hopkins University. The contents of the Mosher Papers were first described by Degler (1974) and a largely accurate transcription of the manuscript interview records is available in MaHood and Wenburg (1980).

identify the premodern safe period method as a static array of conflicting and erroneously informed recommendations, contrasting this with the modern, scientific rhythm method. In so doing, they have overlooked the possibility that the informal practice of *searching* for the elusive safe period could in itself constitute an effective means of controlling individual fertility.

There is a fable of La Fontaine that seems apposite to this argument.[12] "The Laborer and His Children" relates the story of an old man who tells his offspring that the farm they are to inherit from him contains a buried treasure. "I do not know where it is," he admonishes them, "but if you work hard and leave no stone unturned, you will find it." As soon as the father dies, the children begin digging in an effort to unearth their fortune. Alas, they fail to locate any buried treasure, But, as a consequence of their furious digging, the soil of the farm is turned over thoroughly, the weeds are uprooted, and the next crop they sow yields a bounteous harvest. Thus, the myth of a buried treasure, being linked to an injunction to search for it, rewards the belief in the efficacy of the actions it has prompted.

The central point seems worth restating in terms more direct than those of the foregoing allegory. During the 19th century, as has been seen, good advice on how to implement the safe-period method was interspersed with bad advice, but the various recommendations as to the location of the sterile period were not issued simultaneously. Furthermore, they could not in any event have been applied simultaneously by a couple desirous of averting pregnancies. At the individual level such recommendations only could be implemented, and their outcomes monitored, one at a time. Some "good" experiences might be sufficient for belief in the utility of the general approach to be sustained in the population at large, even though "bad" experiences would have left others in doubt.

A puzzle emerges, nevertheless. Inasmuch as some versions of the safe-period method, when rigorously applied, would have rivaled the anovulant pill and IUD in use effectiveness, the question one well might ask is: Why did not those "good" versions drive the others from the field? Indeed, if birth control advice that incorrectly located the safe period within the menstrual cycle could be quickly modified or discarded on the basis of personal experience of their untoward consequences, would it ultimately matter which particular version of the method people had accepted when they commenced the practice? Perhaps it was through a similar process of experience-based revision that some 19th-century medical practitioners had come to extend the proscribed interval, eventually ad-

[12] T. Kuran (1994) refers to the same fable in a connection that is different from the one at hand, yet related to it in a general sense.

vising against sexual intercourse during the two weeks following the end of menstruation and correspondingly adjusting their theories about the viability of the human ovum. These, and some other largely unnoticed puzzles concerning the history of fertility control beliefs and practices, can be approached by treating the primitive rhythm method as a *process*—a search or learning process, to be concrete—and analyzing the opportunities it could have provided for effective, fertility-limiting adaptations at the microbehavioral level.

It might be thought that this tack could be followed by undertaking an essentially epidemiological inquiry, that is, by reexamining the findings of past surveys of contraceptive practice for evidence of a tendency for the more efficacious versions of the safe-period strategy to be selected. There is a difficulty with this, however. By modern standards, the requirements for the adaptive practice of primitive rhythm methods are so minimal that such behavior need hardly have been noticed or formally identified by surveys intended to discover which contraceptive methods were in widespread use.[13] The formal aspect of the modern rhythm method consists in the various procedures whereby a woman may establish a strong prior belief about the location of her time of ovulation, just as the formal aspects of the safe-period methods prescribed by medical authorities before the 1930s consisted in blanket injunction against coitus during certain portions of the menstrual cycle. It is quite possible, however, to envisage an adaptive rhythm method in which the woman begins with "diffuse" priors—the absence of focused beliefs about the likeliest location of her susceptible period. Any subsequent pattern of periodic continence that became established, even though it proved highly effective in reducing the probability of an unintended conception, would be likely to pass unnoticed in an inventory of formal contraceptive practices.

Even in the contemporary context, where it would be feasible to pursue an epidemiological approach by designing special surveys of the practice of periodic continence, it still appeared to us altogether more fruitful to adopt an analytical approach, and begin by modeling learning behavior with *primitive* versions of the rhythm method. By indicating the circumstances in which adaptations of a primitive method are likely to become ef-

[13] Worse still, the basic design of such surveys generally renders them biased instruments, in the sense that when they collect individual histories, they gather reports of the abandonment of some *formal* version of the rhythm method but have no provision for recording *informal* personal adaptations that might have replaced it. Himes' (1970, p. 183) conclusion (on the basis of his own survey findings) that there was virtually no retention of the safe period as a method of contraception among English working-class women during the 1920s should be reconsidered in this light. So too should the similar conclusions derived from the more widely known British survey results presented by Lewis-Fanning (1949, pp. 8–9).

fective—either for pronatal or for antinatal purposes—the analytical and numerical simulation approach may provide further guidance in identifying which groups within historical populations might have been able to regulate their fertility with the help of a rudimentary safe-period method. That information, in turn, would shed fresh light on how it was that the functionally adaptive idea of a fertile period and a safe period, conjoined with the mythic location of the latter in midcycle, could have been preserved and jointly propagated through the centuries. That, at least, was our rationale for the inquiry now to be described.

XIV.4 SPECULATIONS: THE ROLE OF PSYCHOLOGICAL AND SOCIOECONOMIC CONDITIONS IN ADAPTIVE SAFE-PERIOD REGIMES

Learning through purposive experimentation is a peculiarly human activity. It is bound therefore to reflect in some measure the particular material, social, and cultural circumstances in which human beings find themselves, as well as the conceptual apparatus, attitudes, and personality traits that individuals bring to a potential learning situation. In further developing the idea that adaptive modification in the implementation of a contraceptive strategy could contribute significantly to reducing completed fertility (at least among couples who at some early stage of their marital union had committed themselves to the goal of family limitation), it will not be possible to ignore completely socioeconomic and psychological influences on the course of such learning behavior. Nor would we regard as most useful a theory of adaptive contraception in which, by design, those influences—or some representations thereof—remained of only negligible importance among the determinants of average use effectiveness. Rather, we seek here to articulate some mechanisms that might cause learned contraceptive effectiveness to be governed ultimately, if not proximately, by modes of individual behavior, and structures of personal belief which may be thought of as differing among various identifiable population groups. Fortunately, an informal consideration of what such an activity would have to entail (in order for it to have any significant contraceptive value) will suffice to suggest several reasonably direct and intuitively appealing hypotheses about the potential influence of personal and societal factors in this connection.

For this purpose, it helps to pose the problem vividly: would it be possible for a woman who sought to avert pregnancies to learn to avoid unprotected coitus around the time she normally was ovulating, even though she had only the experience of her own, finite reproductive life span to guide her? Our imaginary subject would have to proceed by observing the consequences of following different regimes of sexual intercourse, regimes which differed in respect to the temporal distribution of coition within her "month." At the same time, it may be supposed, she would be trying to make use of whatever information she had been able to obtain in this fashion and would therefore be following whichever regime of unprotected coition currently appeared least likely to result in a pregnancy.

This simple scenario rests on an imposing number of implicit empirical premises. Consider how much already has been taken for granted in supposing the existence of the social circumstances that would permit pursuing a sustained trial-and-error experiment such as the one just contemplated. We must presuppose that, between our imagined woman and her mate(s), there is some unanimity of purpose, or at least of action, directed to controlling fertility. Beyond that, even an informal safe-period method is not likely to work without substantial compliance by the partners in the tacit agreement to avoid coitus on days that at least one of them had reason to deem "unsafe."[14]

It is therefore with deliberation that we refer, hereinafter, to the woman as the decision-agent who undertakes to implement the primitive safe-period method of contraception. Notice that she must believe in the existence of a period of peak susceptibility to impregnation and surmise that it will be possible to control her fertility by regulating her sexual activities. She also must keep a simple daily chronology in which the ultimate point of reference is not some event or events occurring in the external world, but an identifiable point in her menstrual cycle, say, the onset or the cessation of the menses. Were her monthly cycle extremely regular, the collinearity of such events with periodic natural or social phenomena—phases of the moon, the succession of weekdays and weekends, and so forth—would make such record keeping easier and compatible with rather

[14] Of course, unanimity of action could arise from the dominance of one of the partners and need not entail any real mutual agreement on the objective; but in such circumstances the regulation of reproductive activities by the female partner would seem to be the critical condition. Much could be written on this point, but it will be sufficient to note that without his partner's assent or cooperation the male would be at a distinct informational disadvantage in attempting to chronicle the occurrence of coition in relation to the events of the menstrual cycle. As a surrogate for this degree of mutuality, either of the partners might refuse participation in coitus at an "unpropitious" time; but for stable marital unions, it seems necessary that some minimally acceptable social formula be found for unilateral refusals—such as the invocation of "a headache." We shall not deal here explicitly with the possibility that coitus may be refused unconsciously on supposed days of high risk, through psychosomatic mechanisms that translated heightened anxieties about the chance of pregnancy into temporary physical (and on that account acceptable) indisposition to participate in sexual intercourse. It may be noted, however, that if such anxieties were experience based and focused, rather than diffuse, this mechanism would function in much the same way as the conscious, goal-seeking process portrayed in our model.

less self-preoccupation and less heavy reliance on calendars or equivalent aids to memory.[15]

If the foregoing indicates the minimal requirements for purposive practitioners of this particular method of contraception, what further conditions or modes of behavior would favor learning to employ the primitive rhythm technique more successfully? *A priori* considerations would suggest three such conditions: (1) regular record keeping, (2) relatively low coital frequency, and (3) comparatively diffuse prior beliefs as to the location of the period of peak susceptibility. Taking them in turn, it is possible quickly to sketch the intuitive reasoning underlying these several conditions and to venture some conjectures about the societal and personal circumstances in which each might be expected to materialize.

First, the role of record keeping appears to be rather straightforward as far as the qualitative effects of regularity (or its absence) are concerned.[16] If information is lost through failure to chronicle the timing of intercourse in a month preceding a pregnancy, or subsequently is discarded as a basis for action when the woman once again becomes susceptible to impregnation, the learning process will have been interrupted. In other words, the probability of another pregnancy will not have been altered by virtue of the incremental experience represented in the last pregnancy. Although this may be somewhat less obvious, the information that a particular pattern of periodic continence did *not* (in a given month) lead to a conception also is of value in modifying the woman's views as to the comparative safety associated with the regime of intercourse. One question, of course, is how quan-

[15] All this should suggest that at the outset the possible historical relevance of the entire scenario is restricted implicitly to only certain cultural and class milieus. Even where a firm, consistent desire on the part of the couple to limit their fertility has been stipulated, suitable candidates for the adaptive practice of a primitive version of the rhythm method would not be found among women whose prior socialization and psychological development had left them personally dominated, lacking in a strong sense of self-identity and in the capacity to assert some substantial control over the terms of their marital lives. Well-educated women of the upper middle class and elite strata of western European society and their counterparts in the United States during the 19th century thus appear to be especially eligible candidates for the learning role envisaged by our scenario. The same probably could be said, however, in regard to other female-implemented discretionary methods of averting pregnancies. See David and Sanderson (1986) for evidence consistent with this supposition.

[16] It will become evident from Section XIV.5.1 that extensive record keeping and the use of formal menstrual calendars are not really required; recalling only the prior beliefs about the time patterns of susceptibility and the actual regime of coitus that was followed in the month just passed, and noting whether or not a pregnancy ensued, would be sufficient. Brodie (1994, Chapter 1) presents evidence that there were at least some married women in postbellum 19th-century America who kept careful menstrual calendars and explained how their interest in phrenology—by suggesting that the character of one's child would be determined by the circumstances of its conception—also encouraged some women to record dates of intercourse and potential impregnation.

titatively important an effect such information losses would have in degrading the effectiveness of this adaptive method of control.

Second, the potential importance of coital frequency in determining how much useful information can be extracted from each month's experience may be readily appreciated by considering the polar cases. Were sexual intercourse held on every day of the month, the occurrence of a conception would be uninformative as to which days within the month were "responsible." At the opposite extreme, instances of isolated coitus would make it possible to identify and subsequently avoid days when—on at least one occasion and therefore possibly on others—the woman proved susceptible to impregnation. Understanding what happens in the range between these two extremes, evidently, would better enable us to evaluate the influences on contraceptive effectiveness that might be exercised by factors impinging on the level of coital frequency. Cultural practices and social circumstances may be held to govern the modal level of coital frequency, causing it to change only gradually (from cohort to cohort) in any reasonably stable society. Yet there must be individual variations around that social norm, and these may be affected by a multitude of personal factors, including attitudes toward pregnancy and child rearing. These can be viewed as setting coital frequency as a parameter of the learning process for the individual experimenters.[17]

What one would like to know in the present connection is how the frequency of coitus affects the ability to change (i.e., to adapt) the timing of intercourse in a nonrandom fashion that reduces the expected frequency of unintended conceptions. A natural means of evaluating these informational effects, at any specified level of coital frequency, would be to compare the expected frequency of unintended conceptions when adaptive rhythm was being practiced with the expected frequency of (unintended) conceptions under the assumption that the timing of coition within the month remained purely random and independent from one month to the next. The existence of significant information effects when intercourse is infrequent would imply that practitioners of adaptive rhythm methods could employ *"periodic continence"* (or partial abstinence) in a manner that was more effective in averting unwanted pregnancies than simply making the same reduction in the monthly frequency of *randomly timed* coitus.

[17] Abstracting from the particular case at hand, one may see that coital frequency (when viewed as a parameter of the microlevel learning process) is analogous to some culturally or technologically defined feature of the trial-and-error learning context that affects the possibility of drawing useful inferences from a "black box" approach, in which only inputs and outputs are observed. David (1975, Chapter 1) conjectured that in industrial processes some factor-proportions may be more conducive than others to technological progress through "learning by doing," and David *et al.* (1988) showed that the Bayesian model of adaptive behavior described here may be reinterpreted in a way that substantiates further such a conjecture.

Third, in regard to prior beliefs about the location of the susceptible period, it seems clear enough that the more firmly held are one's views, the greater the weight of conflicting evidence (accumulated in the form of accidental pregnancies) that would be required to dispel them. Success in learning, measured in terms of unwanted conceptions averted, thus will depend on the character of those initial beliefs, as well as the tenacity with which they are held: couples who proceeded on the supposition that it was "safe" to have unprotected coitus midway through the woman's menstrual cycle would be likely to obtain strong counterindications at a comparatively early point in their marital history. If we were interested in the influence of the couple's initial belief structure on their completed fertility, it would be necessary to take account of both the pronatal (or antinatal) character of the initial regime of intercourse that it leads them to adopt and the rapidity with which they are led to modify their pattern of periodic continence.

But, instead of immediately confounding these two effects, it is better to begin by isolating the influence of the revision process. We can do so by considering situations in which the couple's initial views about the most likely location of the safe period have a *neutral* direct effect on fertility. That is to say, the initial beliefs would indicate neither a pronatal nor an antinatal pattern of periodic continence, but instead would reflect ambivalence (or indifference) between all the alternative regimes of intercourse consistent with a given frequency of coitus within the month. Now, in situations where the women had not already ruled out the possibility that ovulation might occur at any point in her menstrual cycle, the foregoing neutrality condition would be satisfied when she had perfectly diffuse prior beliefs concerning the rhythm of ovulation. By "diffuse priors" we mean that, in evaluating the various imaginable periodic patterns of susceptibility to impregnation, she starts with a mental *tabula rasa:* she assigns equal probability to *all* the alternative theories regarding the location of her period of peak susceptibility. It must be borne in mind that in positing diffuse priors and thereby suppressing the influence of the formal-advice aspects of primitive rhythm methods (i.e., the authoritative views as to the safe period's location), we shall be allowing the information informally obtained through experimentation to have maximal potency in modifying behavior regarding the pattern of periodic continence.

XIV.5 BOUNDED BAYESIAN ADAPTATION: A SIMULATION MODEL OF STOCHASTIC LEARNING

The following describes a Bayesian strategy for conceptions by selecting regimes of sexual intercourse that minimize the subject expectation of pregnancy, doing so myopically, for each successive trial. In this routine, prior probabilities assigned to alternative states of the world are updated on the basis of the outcome of each month's experience—a "state of the world" being a particular time profile of the hazard of a conception, corresponding to the location of the date of ovulation in the woman's monthly cycle. We will use the term *Bayesian Adaptive Rhythm (BAR)* when referring to the generic method of averting pregnancies by "sampling" and using the conditional likelihoods of the observed outcomes to revise beliefs about the location of the safe period. BAR is to be distinguished from the modern rhythm method(s), which rely on information about basal temperature and other physiological indicators to predict the occurrence of ovulation.

Our model falls within a very broad class of statistical learning models that have been investigated by mathematical psychologists (Suppes and Atkinson, 1960; Atkinson *et al.,* 1965) Described in their parlance, the sequence of events for each monthly trial of a series proceeds like this: at the beginning of each month (trial), a stimulating situation is presented, and the subject responds to the stimulus with one or another of a set of alternative actions or "responses" (which in this case correspond to the implementation of a selected regime of intercourse for the month). The trial terminates with the occurrence of one of a set of outcomes (announcement of a pregnancy or the absence thereof). The underlying specification of a Bayesian strategy for the choice of a regime gives rise to the possibility that is assumed in statistical learning theory—namely, that is other parameters of the situation are held fixed there will be a course of learning determined by the trial outcomes.

To continue in the language of the so-called stimulus-sampling models of learning behavior, the reinforcement serves to connect elements in the set of stimuli with particular responses; stimuli thus connected are said to be "conditioned" to the response. In the mathematical formalization of these theories, one major set of axioms relates the probabilities of responses to the proportion of conditioned elements in the stimulus sample. A second major set of axioms specifies how those elements change their state of conditioning as a result of the occurrence of events. The place of the latter is occupied in the present model by the (Bayesian) rules for the updating of priors, and the place of the former axioms is taken by the rules specifying that regimes be selected so as to minimize the current *a priori* expectation of a pregnancy.

Unlike the majority of the statistical learning models that have been submitted to formal analysis and experimental tests, the structure of the learning algorithm we present here does not conform to axioms of path independence. Being strictly Bayesian, the model is recursive: the probabilities of a response at every moment in time are functions of the preceding *sequence* of response probabilities and of the intervening consequences of each probabilistic trial. This history is distilled and compactly summarized by the current beliefs of the agent—her assignment of *a posteriori* subjective probabilities to alternative conceivable states of the world. Although it is possible to set up the model so that there exists a direct mapping from the *a posteriori* distribution of beliefs (about the time pattern of ovulation) to the choice of a regime of coitus, and thence to an objective probability of conception, the "state space" of the *a posteriori* distributions is potentially infinite. Therefore, although the mathematics of homogeneous Markov chains has been used to good effect in studying other kinds of stochastic learning, it is not the best tool for analyzing the detailed properties of this Bayesian statistical learning process. To study our non-Markovian variety of a path-dependent dynamical system, we can more conveniently resort to numerical analysis by using stochastic simulation methods.[18]

XIV.5.1 Structure of the Constrained Bayesian Adaptive Rhythm (BAR) Model

Abstracting from the full complexity of biological realities, we may proceed by representing the intermenstruum as a vector comprising a fixed number of ordered elements; specifically, there will be T elements, arranged in sequence corresponding to the days of the "month"; following convention, these are numbered from 1 beginning with the day of the onset of menstruation. A "rhythm of susceptibility" is our term for the $1 \times T$ vector whose elements describe the woman's subjective estimate of the risk that (an observable) conception would result from her having unprotected sexual intercourse on that day of the month. Each such imaginable profile of susceptibility, or rhythm, describes a state of the world. But, there will be some restrictions maintained upon conceivable, or, as we may more precisely label them, *admissible* states of the world—those to which the woman assigns positive *a priori* subjective probabilities, $A^0 > 0$.

The vector(s) describing an *i*-th rhythm of susceptibility, $\tilde{\theta}^i$, must satisfy some very general restrictions, but to these we add a set of further restrictions. These restrictions are described formally in Appendix A. Having been imposed in a specific invariant form (detailed in mathematical terms in Section A.2 of Appendix A), these restrictions function as maintained hypotheses; they consistently delimit the set of possibilities that the learning agent regards as worthy of serious consideration. One may think of them as representing a particular model of the biology, one has been chosen with an eye to the computational feasibility of implementing a BAR strategy. Inasmuch as we envisage such a model of the world being formed largely in ignorance of the actual biological processes of ovulation, fertilization, and conception, there is no reason to suppose that the objectively "true" state

[18] On the mathematics of Markov learning models particularly, see Suppes and Atkinson (1960). Dynamical systems with non-Markovian transition probabilities, and their relationship to "strongly historical" processes are discussed in David (1988); the special significance of advances in computational methods for the study of path-dependent economic phenomena is noticed in David (1993).

of the world—as far as concerns the time pattern of susceptibility within a representative menstrual cycle—would necessarily be included among the subset S comprising the admissible rhythms.[19]

A regime of coitus, analogously, is represented as a $1 \times T$ vector whose ordered elements signify whether or not coitus is held on the given day of the month. Thus, in jth regime, the time pattern of unprotected coitus is described by a permutation of 0 and 1 elements forming the vector $\phi_j = (\phi_1, \phi_2, \ldots \phi_t \ldots \phi_T)$, where $\phi_t = 1 \equiv$ coition; $\phi_t = 0 \equiv$ no coition. The regime index is $j - (1, \ldots \binom{T}{\tau})$, where T, the number of days on which intercourse is held, is simply

$$\tau = nT = \sum_{t}^{T} \phi_{t}.$$

The parameter n, namely the woman's coital frequency *rate,* will be restricted in this discrete application of the model to regular fractions in the interval (0,1); it is assumed that effectively only one act of coitus can occur on any day, and the maximum number is limited to T.

As was noted previously, we shall be concerned here with the performance of a constrained form of BAR, in which the hypothetical woman (user/experimenter) is restricted throughout the period of the experiment to choosing from among the set of all possible regimes of intercourse only those for which the monthly frequency of coitus, τ is identical. If the maximum number of coition days available in the month is $T' \leq T$, then $n = \tau / T'$ corresponds to the coital frequency *rate.*[20] Effects of parametric variation in coital frequency (τ) can be readily studied using this model, and we will do this by simulating the performance of the constrained BAR algorithm over a standard duration of 264 months, that being taken as the full reproductive life span for a woman who married at the age of 24.

Given the *a priori* probability, $A^o{}_i$, that the woman attaches to the proposition that the ith rhythm of susceptibility depicts the true state of her world, and given any jth regime of coition, it is possible to ascertain the corresponding subjective probability of a conception, P_{ij}. This probability

[19] Indeed, for reasons shortly to be indicated, the admissible rhythms in our implementation are greatly simplified and so exclude the more complex biological reality. The important formal implication of thus setting the *a priori* probability of the true state to zero is that there is then nothing in our model that guarantees that the Bayesian algorithm will converge on any one among the set of admissible states of the world.

[20] In our implementation of the model, the assumption that there is a taboo on sexual intercourse during a 4-day interval of menstruation (at the end of the 28-day month) reduces T' to 24 days. This assumption is consistent with the evidence of the Mosher Survey and with the diary of Mary Pierce Poor discussed by Brodie (1994, Chapter 1).

value is the product of the two magnitudes, l_{ij}, the likelihood of a conception ensuing from choice of the *j*th regime under the *i*th rhythm of susceptibility (i.e., state of the world), and $A^o{}_i$ the *a priori* probability assigned to that rhythm. Then the monthly expectation of a conception conditional on the selection of the *j*th regime can be calculated by summation of the P_{ij} over all the admissible rhythms.

By evaluating these expectations for every possible regime, the hypothetical woman can choose the regime that minimizes her monthly subjective expectation of a pregnancy. For each cycle she also will observe whether or not a conception has ensued. Given that information, the conditional likelihoods $l_{ij} \in L_{ij}$ may then be used to compute the *a posteriori* probabilities of the rhythms of susceptibility—by Bayesian revision, or updating the priors A^o to obtain A'. The formal details of this procedure are set out in Appendix A. On the basis of the revised set of priors thus obtained, the regime for the following month can be selected, and so on.

The interaction between this cognitive-behavioral algorithm and the objective stochastic process that determines the actual time profile of susceptibility, and the probabilistic outcomes of coital acts in the regime selected, is schematically summarized by the flow diagram in Figure XIV.5.1. As is indicated there, certain biological conditions, affecting the objective levels and timing of fecundability in the woman, must be specified for the purposes of computationally assessing the learning algorithm's efficacy. Whether the woman's *a priori* understanding of those processes allows these conditions to be represented with reasonable accuracy among the set of admissible rhythms may, of course, be a matter of crucial importance for the ultimate success of a Bayesian strategy of learning. Hypotheses that are wholly excluded from consideration cannot be evaluated by analysis of empirical data.

It usually is not feasible to consider seriously every conceivable state of the world. Can the foregoing model of learning be thought to be plausible when we examine it from the latter standpoint? Even were one predisposed (as we believe most economists will be, at least for the sake of their discourse) to accept the rationality postulates of expected utility maximization that underlie the present characterizations of the agents' motivation and behavioral constraints, there remains the problem of implementing the resulting program of control in real time. Notice that given the T days in the month of which τ might be assigned as coition days, there would be $T!/(T - \tau)!\ (\tau)!$ possible regimes among which to choose. Thus, given a 28-day month in which a menstrual period taboo on sexual intercourse removed 4 days from the set of those available, when the coital frequency rate is as low as one-sixth ($\tau = 4$), there will be 10,626 regime permutations to evaluate at the start of each month. When n is one-third, so that coitus is to occur 8 times per month (rather closer to the rate observed among married white

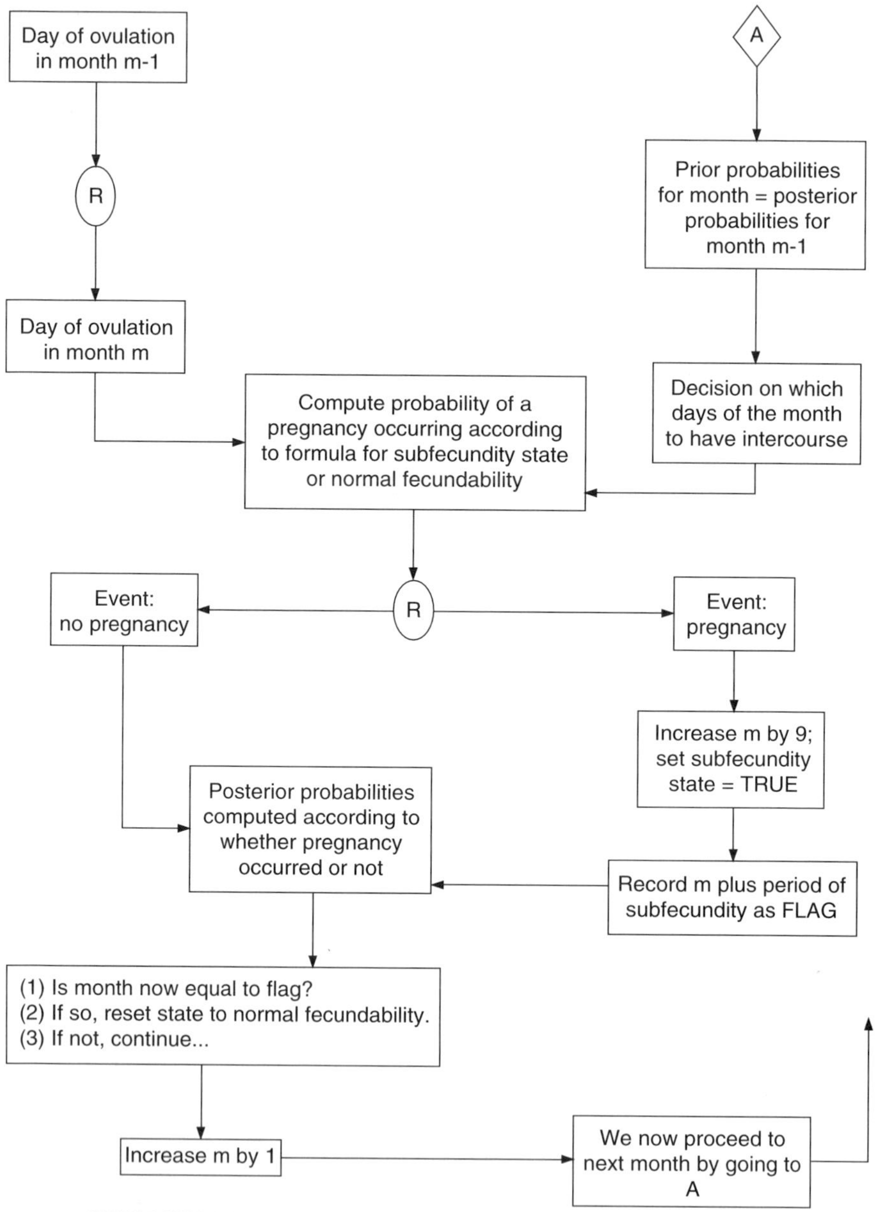

FIGURE XIV.5.1 Schematic of computational model for evaluating BAR.

women in the age range 25–34 in the U.S. population during the 1970s[21], the number of possible regime combinations rises to 735,471! The computational requirements for this trial-and-error learning scheme would appear to be so burdensome that one scarcely could imagine it to have any bearing on human behavior, either in the present or the past. It has been remarked that merely having to undertake the arithmetic entailed would produce a strong antinatal effect.

This is the issue in regard to which our inquiry took on a third intriguing aspect: the choice of the maintained, *a priori* restrictions on the states of the world turns out to be of critical importance in determining whether or not information processing *per se* becomes a binding constraint. In pursuing this point, we have proved that there exists at least one simple and quite reasonable restriction on the admissible states of the world—that is, on the form of the rhythms of susceptibility that would be considered—sufficient to reduce the whole procedure to a computationally trivial *heuristic* learning algorithm and yet preserve strict adherence to the rules of Bayesian inference.[22] The trick in doing this is the choice of a simple "model of the biology"—an *a priori* structural specification that is, in effect, the maintained hypothesis for the entire learning experiment. A drastically simple conjecture is one that uniquely associates every admissible rhythm of susceptibility with a single (peak) day of susceptibility within the intermenstruum. With maintained *a priori* restrictions of that form, it can be shown that the conditional expectation of a conception, $E(c_j)$, for the month in question is minimized by avoiding coitus on the days that the woman believes most strongly to be ones of peak susceptibility.

The intuition for this is quite simple. Because each "rhythm" is associated with one possible day of peak susceptibility, the woman's "priors," or subjective probabilities on rhythms correspond to subjective evaluations of the relative "dangerousness" of unprotected coitus on the associated days of hypothesized peak susceptibility. To implement a Bayes Exact heuristic algorithm, therefore, it is sufficient to rank all the days of the intermenstruum according to the woman's subjective estimate of their "dangerousness" and allocate the days of coition accordingly by starting with the "least dangerous" and moving upward through the ranking as far as is necessary (see Appendix A: Sections A.4 and A.5).

Thus, as the discussion at the end of Section XIV.4 anticipated, implementing this formulation of the algorithm requires only some minimal

[21] For further discussion of contemporary findings from the National Fertility Surveys on coital frequency within marriage, and comparisons with historical sample data, see David and Sanderson (1986).

[22] See the appendix for the restrictions that satisfy these conditions. A proof built on these formal specifications of the model is available in David *et al.* (1988), but, in consideration of space limitation, its analog has been omitted here.

record keeping: a woman using BAR must keep track of the days on which coitus occurred (but only during the preceding month); and she must remember the subjective probabilities she held at the start of that month in regard to the alternative (admissible) rhythms of susceptibility. Nothing more.

XIV.5.2 Specifying the Objective Process—The Relationship of "Reality" to Beliefs

To appreciate the nature of the computation-simplifying restrictions that are placed on beliefs about the nature of the stochastic process that our hypothetical agents are attempting to manage, it is best to start from the "objective" component of the model—the part that we specified with the intention of capturing at least something of the complex biological "realities."

There is a substantial literature on the timing of fecundability in humans, which divides roughly into two branches. The biological branch focuses attention on the complexities of the interactions of egg life, sperm life, ejaculate volume, sperm motility, and the like. The epidemiological branch of the literature is concerned with attempts to infer time patterns of fecundability from observations of coital patterns and conception frequencies, without explicit reference to those underlying biological processes. Unfortunately, the two branches suggest somewhat different patterns of human fecundability. The parameters of our adaptive learning model have been chosen to be roughly consistent with the picture presented by the reproductive biologists, in part because this structural approach allows us greater flexibility and realism in simulation work than could be attained by distilling the reduced-form results of the epidemiological studies.[23]

Appendix B sets out the underlying structural specifications governing the fecundability states of the hypothetical woman in our simulation model and the resulting parameter values that are used in all the simulations. Rather than seeking to closely mimic the individual subprocesses of ovulation, menstruation, fertilization, and nidation (or implantation of the fertilized ovum in the lining of the uterus) leading up to a conception, this part of the model aims to capture some of the stochastic complexities governing the dynamics of the woman's fecundability state in a computationally parsimonious fashion. Thus, we make a radical simplification by assuming a menstrual cycle of invariant duration (28 days), within which there will be an invariant duration of menstruation (4 days). The date of ovulation, however, moves randomly month by month, always cycling within the bounds

[23] A further consideration was our impression that among the latter investigations there was less consensus in conclusions than modern reproductive biology has managed to obtain. The persisting difficulties of drawing sharp inferences from epidemiological data, of course, are a part of the story of the unreliability of many of the premodern safe-period prescriptions.

set by the 13th and 16th day of the woman's month. Because we allow, realistically, for the occurrence of a conception as a consequence of an isolated act of unprotected intercourse two full days preceding the time of ovulation, in any randomly drawn month there is a positive hazard for fecundability on each of the 6 days in the interval stretching from day 11 to day 16 of the standard intermenstruum.[24]

Specification 1. In any given month, fertilization leading to a conception may result from coitus on any one of three consecutive days, the day of ovulation and the two days preceding.

The maintained beliefs of the women represented in our simulation experiments, however, are far simpler in their view of the way that their susceptibility to impregnation varies from day to day within any month, and from one month to the next. As has been already noted, in describing the restrictions imposed on their admissible rhythms of susceptibility, we discovered that the BAR algorithm's computational feasibility could be assured by supposing that the individuals engaged in learning remained ignorant about these details of their ovulatory cycle and of their implications for the actual month-to-month variations of the "true rhythm of susceptibility." We assume that the woman believes she has one particularly susceptible day in her "month" when the probability of a conception is $\overline{\theta}$, and 27 days on which there is a (negligibly) low probability of conception, ϵ.

As a consequence of this greatly simplified model of the world, the task of executing a strictly Bayesain information processing routine is reduced to almost trival dimensions. The assignment of *a priori* probabilities to each member of the set of admissible rhythms is rendered equivalent to the formation of a simple index, ranking each of the 28 days of the woman's month according to her subjective evaluation of the inherent "danger" that a conception would ensue were she to have unprotected coitus on that day. Regime optimization to minimize the risk of a conception then may be achieved by following a so-called packing algorithm for allocating the τ days of coitus in the month, starting with the least (subjectively) dangerous and proceeding as far as required toward days of higher rank.

[24] To capture the possibility of the spermatozoa staying motile in the female's reproductive tract for periods as long as 60 hours following ejaculation, whereas the released ovum remains in a "fresh" state for fertilization for approximately 12 hours, we attach positive (albeit reduced) probability of conception occurring as a result of isolated coitus preceding the ovulation day by 48 hours. See the table in Appendix B. This accords roughly with the physiological data summarized by Hartman (1962). "Fecundability," as used in the text and Appendix B, refers to the conditional *daily* probability of a conception resulting from unprotected coitus held on the specified day, and on no other day of the month, for a randomly chosen month in the life of a woman who is ovulating (i.e., not pregnant and not undergoing lactational amenorrhea).

Furthermore, as is pointed out in Appendix A (Section A.5), under these same conditions the conditional likelihoods for the occurrence and non-occurance of a pregnancy also become very simple to calculate, which makes it no trouble at all to carry out the Bayesian computation of an *a posteriori* distribution. The latter operation, it will be recalled, is the equivalent of revising the woman's prior index of inherent dangerousness of the days in her month. To do that in a consistent and statistically correct fashion requires only the systematic application of one or the other of a pair of *constant* multipliers: one of these must be applied to proportionally raise the relative dangerousness rating of the coition days in the month when a pregnancy has ensued; the other is applied to proportionally reduce the relative rating of the month's non-coition days, when a pregnancy does not ensue.[25] The choice of the exact Bayesian values for those multipliers is a bit more of a challenge, as they depend in a complicated way on the woman's maintained subjective evaluation of how easy or difficult it would be for her to become pregnant by having unprotected coitus on her day of peak susceptibility—which is to say, on her belief about the level of $\overline{\theta}$ in relation to ϵ.

Were one to ask what is the "objective" magnitude what would represent a "correct" guess at the value of the parameter $\overline{\theta}$ in this *a priori* specification of $\tilde{\theta}^i$, an approximate answer can be obtained by computing the probability that a single act of coitus on the susceptible day would result in a conception. The six possible susceptible days, for which the respective susceptibility or fecundability levels are indicated by the table in Appendix B, would be selected with equal likelihood if the woman's priors on the admissible rhythms were "diffuse," which is what will be the assumed initial condition of a learning sequence. We thus can use those parameter values (from Appendix B, Section B.2) to obtain the following estimate:

$$\overline{\theta} = \sum_{t=11}^{16} \phi_t/6 = 0.06.$$

In the simulation experiments reported here we have set the woman's maintained beliefs to coincide with this "best approximation to the truth," and it should be borne in mind that this eliminates one potential source of confusion that could becloud the trial-and-error process of learning.[26] Still,

[25] The modest amount of algebra required to state this rigorously, along with the other propositions in this paragraph, is relegated to Appendix A. Proofs have been omitted here in the interest of brevity, but they are given in David *et al.* (1988).

[26] The direction and magnitude of discrepancies between maintained beliefs about the mean level of fecundability and the objective level, can influence the effectiveness of BAR, as it affects the speed of response to unwanted outcomes. But this is a more complicated matter that must be left for treatment on another occasion.

there are many other notable points of divergence between the assumed form of the maintained beliefs and the objective, biological reality specified in the model. Over the course of her reproductive life, the woman's observations of outcomes of different regime choices (i.e., whether or not a pregnancy ensues) are treated by her as independent random events. This is the simplest way for her to process the available data, especially considering the supposition that she does not know about the mechanism governing the timing of ovulation. The objective component of the model, as we have noted, is constructed in a way that causes the assumption of independence to be violated in actuality: the day of ovulation in each month was assumed to depend in part on the day of ovulation in the previous month. This misperception of the nature of the randomness in the objective process creates a realistic source of confusion, making the woman's learning task that much more difficult.

Another feature of the model's specifications will contribute further to such confusions. After a child is conceived we assume that a woman enters a period of subfecundity lasting for three months, during which time the schedule describing the objective conditional probabilities of a conception is reduced by 75 percent. Although we make this reduction ostensibly to allow for the effects of lactational amenorrhea, we assume that the woman remains unaware of the possibility that her susceptibility to impregnation would be lowered in that way by breast-feeding her newborn and that the couple's return to a normal regime conjugal relations was not inhibited by any taboo on sexual intercourse during lactation. The model further augments the element of confusion that safe-period practitioners would have had to cope with, by allowing women to begin revising her priors on the rhythm of susceptibility in the months immediately following the birth of a child as if her normal level of fecundability had been immediately reestablished—even though that is inconsistent with the actual suppositions made by many women in the past.

The question that must now be considered, before turning to the results of the simulations themselves, is: What kinds of effective "learning" should we be looking for in this inquiry? In view of the tight cognitive bounds that have been placed upon the learning agents model of the process they are trying to control, it will be important for us to allow for distinctions between cognitive progress and other kinds of learning.

XIV.5.3 Alternative Characterizations of Learning within the BAR Model

The behaviorist approach to learning generally considers any change in behavior to be "learning," whether or not it is adaptive, desirable for certain purposes, or in accordance with any other such normative criteria. Under this approach, learning is taken to be complete simply when certain kinds of stability—not necessarily stereotypy—are obtained in observable behaviors.[27] Although there are attractive aspects in such an approach, the premise of our investigation is that learning should produce changes that *are* adaptive, in the sense of being consistent with the hypothetical agent's antinatal goals.

Proceeding in this spirit we shall speak of adaptive changes that may occur in either or both contraceptive behavior, and effective control, corresponding to Learning Definitions 1, and 2, respectively:

Learning Definition 1 (Contraceptive Behavior). Trial-to-trial changes in the probability of responses (constrained regime choices) that progressively reduce the monthly probability of conception below the levels that would obtain under a regime of randomly timed coitus.

Learning Definition 2 (Effective Control). Progressive antinatal deviation of the sequence of actual births from that which would be expected under a regime of randomly timed coitus.

Two points are to be noticed regarding these definitions. First, both address the dynamic aspect of learning in that they are concerned with changes that would occur over time. The conception probabilities can be viewed as an evaluation (from the antinatal perspective) of the "dangerousness" of the regime of coitus that had been selected for the month in question, and their time path thus provides a convenient summary indicator of *behavioral* adaptation.

Of course, it is also possible to evaluate the degree of adaptive change by reference to transversal measures computed for the entire span of the experiment. In the case of Definition 1, the transversal measure would be the overall reduction achieved—at a constant, parametrically specified coital frequency—in the monthly probability of conception, starting from the level implied by randomly timed intercourse. In the case of Definition 2, the corresponding transversal measure is simply the expected number of births averted, again with reference to the number of births expected were the monthly regimes of coitus to have been selected randomly throughout the whole time span considered.

The second point to be noticed is that were we to undertake a very large number of replications of each (full life) simulation experiment, there would be no substantive difference between the characterizations of learning provided by Definitions 1 and 2; the Central Limit Theorem applies

[27] See Suppes and Atkinson (1960) for discussion of the approach of Bush and Mosteller (1955) among other pioneers of mathematical learning theory.

here, so that Law of Large Numbers guarantees these two measures would reveal exactly the same thing about the effects of learning. Looking at the sequence of monthly conception probabilities (Definition 1), rather than the average sequence of conception outcomes, however, does makes more sense when one is limited to a small number of replications. The reason is that the Definition 2 measures will contain an additional component of "noise" arising from sampling errors in the realization of the probabilistic process of conception (leading to a birth). The latter source of noise, however, is more attenuated in its effect upon the transversal measures that correspond to Definition 2, namely, expected cumulative births, and births averted. Those summary indicators have an additional virtue in being more readily interpreted and related to the objective of family limitation. Thus, both Definition 1- and Definition 2-type measures of learning will be worth considering.

In contrast with the focus of the foregoing notions of adaptation in behavior (and its consequences), it is possible within the framework of our model also to characterize a cognitive form of learning. Once again we have a choice, in this case between taking a relativist and an absolutist stance in regard to knowledge. The former might consider the assignment of higher and higher subjective probabilities to *any* small, and not internally discordant subset among the conceivable states of the world as representing a process of cognitive evolution. The absolutist stance, however, would insist that such evolutions be deemed "learning" only when they proceed in the direction of attaching greater credibility to states of the world that are objectively true. Embracing this latter position, we should then be obliged to accept a third characterization of learning:

Learning Definition 3 (Cognitive Evolution). The convergence of the agent's "priors" regarding her rhythm of susceptibility to the "true" pattern in the day-specific probabilities of a conception ensuing from unprotected coitus.

Now it will be recalled that the true state of the world is more complicated than any among the set of admissible rhythms in our Bayesian algorithm. As a result of this, the wording of Definition 3 poses something of a problem: perfect convergence of the woman's *a posteriori* distribution of probability on her true rhythm of susceptibility is too much to expect when the admissible rhythms exclude the "true" state of the world. Movement toward significantly greater correlation between beliefs and reality, therefore, is a more reasonable way to assess cognitive evolution in keeping with the sense of Definition 3. It is quite feasible, however, to construct both sequential and transversal indicators of the degree of conformity between beliefs and reality that could be expected to emerge through the trial-and-error learning process.[28]

In the context of the present model, individual cognitive evolution in the general sense of Definition 3 implies behavioral adaptations in the sense of Definition 1, because regimes are chosen to minimize the *a priori* expectation of pregnancy. But notice that the reverse is not true. It is quite possible that within a finite reproductive life span, a woman may learn to avert pregnancies precisely in the behaviorist sense captured by Definitions 1 and 2, yet not make any significant progress toward discovering the true time pattern of ovulation and her consequent rhythm of susceptibility to impregnation. With this, however, there also comes the dual possibility that erroneous cognitive states can become deeply entrenched beliefs when they are consistent with functional adaptations in human behavior.

This latter remark should underscore the point that in investigating this model we really were not interested in the possibility of a Bayesian strategy being successfully applied to the discovery of the modern rhythm method by an epidemiological approach, rather than by the physiological approach that actually was pursued successfully by Ogino and Knaus in the 1930s. Rather, we posit the Bayesian strategy because it offers a familiar and appealingly rational basis on which to develop a computationally tractable algorithm describing path-dependent stochastic learning behaviors that co-evolve with a structure of beliefs about the natural world. We conjecture that qualitatively similar results also can be obtained with many other algorithms that are statistically less well founded, but which might be justified as arising from psychologically more plausible heuristic procedures for processing information acquired sequentially, in the manner of trial-and-error experimentation.

XIV.6 OVERVIEW OF THE SIMULATION RESULTS

The simulation results enable us to address the issue of the effectiveness of learning in each of the several senses just identified and to see how behavioral adaptations and cognitive evolution are affected by parametric

[28] In the simplified specifications detailed by the Appendix, each of the admissible rhythms is characterized by the placement of the (single) spike of susceptibility on a different day of the month. The subjective evaluation placed on the *i*th rhythm being the true state of the world thus becomes, in effect, the probability that she assigns to the truth of the hypothesis that *i*th day is her (single) day of nonnegligible susceptibility. The current state of her subjective assessment of the risks of conceiving, for each day in her month, can then be found by taking the convolution of the distribution of her "priors" on the set of admissible rhythms with her maintained beliefs as to the inherent peak and nonpeak levels of the conception-hazard rate characteristic of every "rhythm" in the admissible set.

variation in the coital frequency rate. For this purpose, six different levels of coital frequency (τ), ranging from 2 to 12 times per month in increments of 2, were specified as an invariant aspect of the regime of intercourse whose time pattern was optimized, and reoptimized, sequentially on a month-by-month basis. Every reproductive life span in these simulations lasts for 264 months, or 22 years, representing the approximate average duration of a woman's exposure to the risks of childbearing if she entered an uninterrupted marital union at age 24–25. The statistical results reported in Tables XIV.6.1–XIV.6.4 and Tables XIV.7.1–XIV.7.2 are based on the samples constituted from the first 50 simulated cases of *mothers,* that is, women for whom one or more births were recorded over the course of their reproductive life span.[29]

Although it is possible to investigate the effects of varying other parametric settings in the model, especially those describing the maintained beliefs as to the maximum and minimum levels of the woman's inherent fecundability (θ and ϵ, respectively), these were held fixed, so that the subjective evaluation of fecundability is always $\hat{\theta} = 0.06$ throughout the simulation runs reported her. That value was chosen to coincide with the point estimate implied by the specifications of the model's objective, biological component: it is the mean probability that a single act of coitus on a susceptible day would result in a conception.[30] Loosely expressed, the latter assumption comes down to our having chosen to let the hypothetical woman correctly guess (at the beginning of her reproductive life span) the mean level of here susceptibility to conceive when unprotected coitus occurs on a "dangerous day." At the same time, however, it should be recalled that we suppose that she begins without any particular convictions about where such a day might be situated within her "month." In every run of the simulation model, then, the woman is assumed to start with completely diffuse priors regarding the set of admissible rhythm of susceptibility. Inasmuch as that is tantamount to believing each day in the intermenstruum to be an equally

[29] It should be noted that no allowance has been made for the possibility of the conceptus being aborted spontaneously. Stillbirths, similarly, are excluded outcomes. Thus, in our model, every conception translates into a live birth.

[30] The monthly probability of 0.06 compounds the monthly probabilities of conception resulting from coitus on a given "susceptible" day, with the probability that the given day is a fertile day for the month in question. See the discussion accompanying the text table in Section XIV. 5.2. It may be recalled that we specified there that a woman may conceive as a result of having unprotected coitus at any time within a three-day interval, which terminates with the day of ovulation. As our simulation allows the day of ovulation to range randomly within a four-day interval (from one month to the next), over the course of the woman's life there are six days in her standard month(s) on which conception is possible, even though in any given month of our simulated life spans there will be only three "fertile" days.

likely candidate for being her peak day of susceptibility, the regime optimization routine initially allocates the days of coitus randomly over the 24 days of the cycle (the first available day, following the cessation of menstruation, always being day 5).

XIV.6.1 Behavioral Adaptation and Effective Control

We may start by looking at the summary, transversal measures of effective control that correspond to learning in the sense of Definition 2. Table XIV.6.1 (and Figure XIV.6.1, which is derived from it) compares the average numbers of births to a woman who follows a BAR-guided routine consistently, at each of the alternative coital frequencies that are indicated; also shown are the corresponding outcomes that would be expected were the timing of intercourse in the regime to have been selected randomly. The difference between the two cases yields an evaluation of "effective control" in terms of the mean number of births averted. In these terms, BAR is shown quite clearly to be an "effective" method: the mean number of births averted is positive, and statistically significantly so, over the whole range of coital frequencies displayed in the table.

Indeed, BAR ($\hat{\theta} = 0.06$) turns out to be not simply effective, but remarkably effective in reducing (marital) fertility when the frequency of coitus is maintained at levels below six times per month ($\tau = 6$). A woman engaging in a regime of randomly timed sexual intercourse at $\tau = 4$ could expect 8.22 births in 22 years of exposure, whereas, by adhering to BAR under the same conditions, she could expect as few as 2.12 births! Moreover,

TABLE XIV.6.1 Number of Births per Mother during Reproductive Life of 264 Months: Simulation Samples of 50 Mothers

Invariant monthly frequency of coitus	Randomized monthly regime:		BAR ($\theta = 0.06$)		Incremental births averted per mother due to BAR ($\theta = 0.06$)	
	Mean	Std. dev.	Mean	Std. dev.	Mean difference	Pooled std. dev.
2	5.62	1.38	1.54	0.80	4.08	0.23
4	8.22	1.57	2.12	1.38	6.10	0.30
6	10.18	1.62	4.66	3.30	5.52	0.52
8	11.28	1.54	8.72	3.61	2.56	0.55
10	12.70	1.23	9.52	3.61	3.18	0.54
12	12.90	1.04	11.54	2.56	1.36	0.39

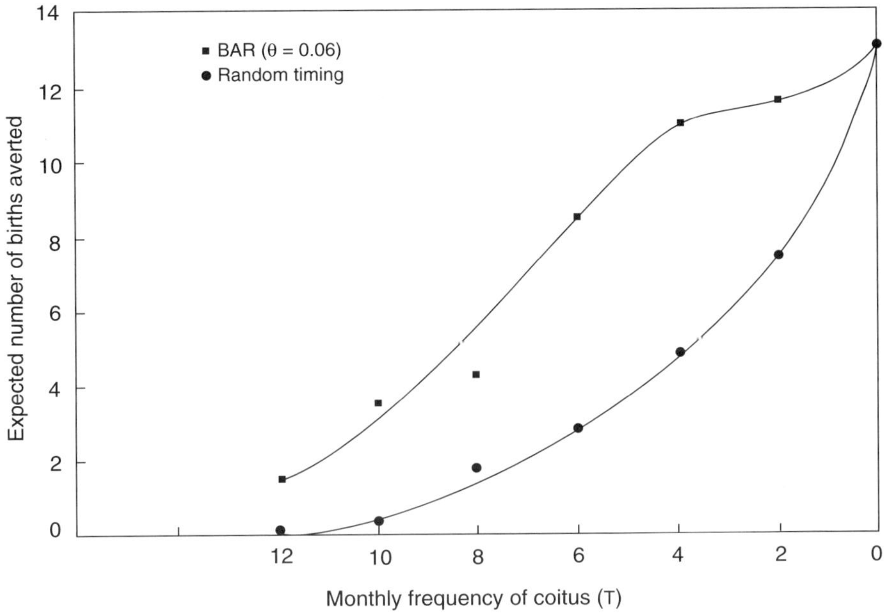

FIGURE XIV.6.1 Simulation results for Bayesian adaptive rhythm method: expected numbers of births averted (runs of 50 sample lives, each of 264 months in duration). Note: Data plotted in the figure are averages of births averted per mother; in simulation results for regimes of randomly timed coition, the number of mothers always equaled the number of women (50). Source: Table XIV.6.1

when using BAR at the lower levels of coital frequency, the standard deviation of her completed fertility is found to be just the same, if not smaller, than that which would be generated by selecting the time pattern of coition in a random fashion. Although the variance is larger in relation to the mean of completed fertility, the much lower average number of children ever born is not obtained at the cost of any absolute enlargement of the margin of uncertainty surrounding the outcome.[31]

Quite obviously, fertility can be reduced by simply lowering the monthly frequency of randomly timed coitus. But the relationship between

[31] To be sure, we recognize that the reduction in coital frequency required to achieve this may be viewed as a "cost" of a different kind. The relationship between the middle-class Victorian ideology of marital sexual continence, and successful family limitation employing rudimentary contraceptive techniques, is explicitly discussed in David and Sanderson (1986, esp. pp. 359ff.).

those two variables is quite nonlinear—a point that is often not appreciated but shown plainly by Figure XIV.6.1. In order for any substantial decreases in completed fertility to be achieved simply by a reduction of coital frequency, it is necessary to curtail the latter to levels ($\tau \leq 4$) far below those observed among modern married women.[32] With BAR, however, there is a powerful differential learning effect, reflected in the rise of the mean number of births *averted* to a maximum before those extremes of conjugal restraint are reached. As may be seen from the rightmost column of Table XIV.6.1 (and graphically in the difference between the curves plotted in Figure XIV.6.1), the birth-averting effect attributable to BAR-guided behavioral adaption becomes strongest when coital frequency moves into the range between six and four times per month.

These simulation results substantiate fully the conjectures offered on intuitive grounds (above, in Section XIV.4), namely, that there would have to exist a coital frequency rate in the interval between 1 and 0 that was optimal for eliciting information about the timing of the woman's susceptibility, and that this learning optimum would be bounded away from rates closely approaching 0 by the infrequency with which any conceptions would occur at those low levels.

The dynamic adaptation process (learning, in the sense of Definition 1) that produces those outcomes is more directly reflected in the measures presented by Table XIV.6.2. For every given coital frequency level, it is possible to compute a simple index of the objective "dangerousness" of the regimes that the woman selects—where the "danger" involved is that of an unwanted conception. We do this by first calculating an intercourse regime score, IRS_m for the month in question.[33] With this measure, an intercourse regime score of unity corresponds to "maximal dangerousness," which would be obtained were the selected regime to schedule unprotected coitus on every one of the six days of the woman's month on which it would be possible (within her life span) for a conception to occur. A score of zero, ob-

[32] It may be noted, however, that coital frequency averaging around 4 times per month are reported by the married middleclass women (aged 25–34) who were included in the pre-1913 Mosher Survey interviews (see David and Sanderson, 1986, for further discussion).

[33] This measure is defined as follows:

$$IRS_m = \sum_{i=1}^{T} \phi_{mi}\theta^*_i,$$

where ϕ_{mi} is an element of the intercourse regime vector ϕ_m; θ^*_i is an element of the vector of objective "susceptibilities" probability of becoming pregnant from a single act of intercourse on day i, standardized so that the ϕ^*_i sum to unity; T is the length of the month in days (=28).

TABLE XIV.6.2 Time Path of Intercourse Regime Adaptation with Bar ($\theta = 0.06$) for Stimulated Groups of 50 Mothers All Starting with Diffuse Priors

	Index of regime dangerousness:[a] 100 = Most dangerous (least 'safe') regime possible with given τ			
	Coital frequency (τ) = 4		Coital frequency (τ) = 8	
Month of reproductive union	Mean	Std. dev.	Mean	Std. dev.
1	29.8*	15.8	33.0*	15.8
2	11.6*	16.2	29.6	16.5
49	5.8*	10.9	24.1	15.7
73	3.0*	6.4	23.4	15.7
97	2.6*	5.8	21.9	14.8
121	1.9	5.6	22.9	15.0
145	1.3	4.0	23.8	16.4
169	0.5	1.4	20.2	13.4
193	0.5	1.4	22.6	16.0
217	0.5	1.4	21.4	14.8
241	0.5	1.4	21.1	14.6
264	0.5	1.4	20.6	14.3

[a] For women pregnant at indicated date, the regime index is calculated for the following postpartum regime of intercourse.
* Significantly greater than mean index values for months 217, 241, and 264 at 95% confidence level.

viously enough, would obtain when intercourse did not take place on any of those objectively feasible days for a conception.[34]

Table XIV.6.2 shows that—with the initial regime always having been one selected at random—the index of dangerousness starts out in the neighborhood of 30–33 percent of the maximum level, regardless of whether coital frequency is at four or at eight time per month. Further, some statistically significant contraceptive adaptation in behavior is achieved in both

[34] The table in Appendix B.2 shows that among all possible regimes in which $\tau = 6$, the one that assigns days 11 through 16 as coitus days would generate the maximum average probability of a conception (in a randomly chosen month). This conception probability is 0.36 ($= 0.06 \times 6$) and is the normalization constant that sets the maximal regime score to unity, corresponding to the index value 100 in Table XIV.6.2. Although no higher maximum than this is attainable with regimes in which τ exceeds 6, the highest "relative dangerousness" index possible with $\tau = 4$ is 86 [$= (0.31/0.36) \times 100$]; with $\tau = 2$, it is 50 [$= (0.18)/0.36) \times 100$]. The likelihood of hitting the bound at 86 by random assignment (at the start of the BAR process) of 4 days of coitus, out of the 24 days "available," is sufficiently small that a unique normalization, rather than a τ-specific normalization, was used to present the results in Table XIV.6.2.

cases by the 14th year (169 months) of adherence to BAR. Yet, when $\tau = 8$, no significant learning in this sense occurs after the second month, on average; whereas with $\tau = 4$, significant adaptive changes in the regime of coitus continue to occur, even after the sixth year (73rd month). Indeed, by that point in the woman's marital history, the mean index of the dangerousness of her selected regime has been reduced to approximately a tenth of its initial magnitude, and the process does not stop there. Further statistically significant adaptations cut that monthly probability of conception again, by a factor of 5, eventually reducing it to the negligibly small level attained by the time her union has begun its 14th year (month 169).[35]

XIV.6.2 Bounded Cognitive Evolution

The foregoing *behavioral* adaptations on the part of our simulated populations of BAR users suggest that at the low end of the range of coital frequencies, at least, it is possible for a woman's cognitive state to evolve toward a more accurate view of her rhythm of susceptibility, and therefore of the true timing of ovulation specified in our model. Given the Bayesian strategy of control being deployed, changes in the woman's regime of intercourse must be driven by changing beliefs expressed in terms of *a priori* probabilities assigned to the alternative (admissible) states of the world. Hence, we should inquire directly about what the representative woman will have learned in the cognitive sense of Definition 3.

It is useful to distinguish between two facets of the problem of the bounded nature of cognitive evolution within the framework of our model. The first has to do with whether or not statistically significant cognitive evolution is taking place, whereas the second addresses the question of how closely it is possible to come to discovering "the truth"—remembering the maintained restrictions that information-processing constraints have placed on the admissible set of rhythms.

Table XIV.6.3 is designed to illuminate the first issue. Correlations can be computed between the objective rhythm of susceptibility and the subjective *a priori* probabilities assigned to the occurrence of the peak of sus-

[35] Notice that the statistically significant differences indicated (by *) in Table XIV.6.2 between the mean level of the dangerousness index attained toward the end of the reproductive life span, that is, averaging the values for months 217, 241, and 264, applies also to the difference between the scores for month 169 and scores at earlier months. This is the case for regime selection when coital frequency is 8, as well as when it is 4. In the latter case, however, by month 169 the absolute monthly probability of a conception has been reduced to a quite small magnitude—[$.005 \times (0.36) =$] .0018, implying that the probability of having an unwanted conception in the course of a year is 0.02. With coital frequency at 8, the corresponding mean probability of a conception occurring during the 14th year (month 169 being the first month of that year) is more than 20 times larger than the latter magnitude—that is, as high as 0.40.

TABLE XIV.6.3 Proportion of Mothers (50 cases) Whose Priors Exhibit Statistically Significant Positive Correlation with the "True State" (Rhythm of Susceptibility) after 264 Months of Reproductive Life with BAR ($\theta = 0.06$) Regime

	Statistical significance (error) levels:		
	10 percent	**30 percent**	**50 percent**
		Beginning-of-life priors*	
	0.14	0.24	0.44
Invariant monthly frequency of coitus		**End-of-life priors**	
2	0.56	0.78	0.98
4	0.46	0.84	0.98
6	0.46	0.82	0.96
8	0.32	0.74	0.94
10	0.48	0.72	0.96
12	0.38	0.86	0.96

* These proportions are calculated from the *finite* correlation coefficients (28 days of data) that can be computed for subjects who (all) start with diffuse priors.

ceptibility on the corresponding days of the month. The columns of the table show the proportion of cases in each simulation sample of 50 mothers for which the degree of correlation is statistically significant at the beginning and at the close of the reproductive life span. At the end of the initial month of the process, which starts out in every instance with the woman having diffuse priors, the proportion of women whose *a posteriori* evaluations and the true rhythm of susceptibility are correlated at a statistically significant level should conform quite closely with what one would expect to find purely as a result of chance. There cannot have been much opportunity for the Bayesian inferential engine to have done much work within its first cycle of operation. So, if we picked a confidence level of 90 percent, we should expect to find that only 10 percent of the cases would, essentially by random chance, have turned out to be "significantly" correlated. From the 14 percent figure that appears in the top row of Table XIV.6.3, it is seen that the correlation analysis of the output from all the first months in all the simulation runs does, indeed, comes close to matching that (large sample) expectation.[36] This, and the corresponding proportions for the beginning-of-life priors, can be taken as the benchmarks appropriate to each statistical

[36] Similarly, sampling errors result in small deviations between the theoretically expected proportions found for significant beginning-of-life correlations at the 30 percent and 50 percent error levels of significance, namely 24 percent and 44 percent, respectively.

confidence level. It is against these benchmarks that we must gauge the extent of the significant cognitive evolution that takes place by the time that the representative woman reaches the close of her reproductive life span.

From Table XIV.6.3 just such evaluations can be made for conjugal lives lived at each of the six fixed monthly frequencies of coitus. Focusing on what can be said with a reasonably high level of confidence (the 10 percent significance level), it appears that in the lower range of coital frequencies (τ in the 2–6 range) the end-of-life priors show significant correlation in about half of the cases in each simulation run, that is, in 46 to 56 percent of the lives. Comparing that to the initial benchmark figure, one would have to say that in only 30 to 40 percent of the 50 cases simulated did the individual experience *significant cognitive evolution* in the course of trial-and-error learning. Considering how remarkably well these same groups of (identical) women are found to have done by the criteria of behavioral adaptation, their poor average performance in the cognitive domain is rather a surprise. Also striking is the fact that whereas reduced coital frequency made a big difference in terms of behavioral adaptation and effective control (Learning Definitions 1 and 2), there appears to be no Learning Definition 3 counterpart of that effect in the results displayed by Table XIV.6.3.

To get a sense of how much of the truth those who do learn in this way are able to uncover, Table XIV.6.4 shows the results of our computation of the coefficients of rank correlation (Kendall's Tau B, corrected for ties) between the *a posteriori* probabilities associated with the admissible rhythms of fecundability at the end of each woman's reproductive life, and the true fecundability ranking of the days of the month (according to the specification for the model's objective component). Were the women of our simulated world able to converge in their beliefs on a close approximation to the structure of the stochastic process governing their fecundability, we would

TABLE XIV.6.4 Proportions of Mothers (50 Cases) Whose End-of-Life Priors Exhibit Significant Rank Correlation with "True" Rhythm of Susceptibility, after 264 Months of Reproductive Life with BAR ($\theta = 0.06$) Regime

Invariant monthly frequency of coitus	Proportions for whom the probability of achieving a higher rank correlation score (Kendall's Tau B) is less than or equal to:		
	10 percent	30 percent	50 percent
2	0.80	0.86	0.90
4	0.62	0.88	1.00
6	0.48	0,84	0.96
8	0.26	0.70	0.94
10	0.54	0.76	0.86
12	0.50	0.86	0.80

expect to be able in general to reject the null hypothesis that there was no correlation between their objective susceptibilities on each day of the month and their *a posteriori,* end-of-life estimates of those inherent conception risks. The proportion of cases in which the null hypothesis (no positive rank correlation) could be rejected at the 10, 30, and 50 percent error levels of significance are displayed, respectively, in the three columns of Table XIV.6.4.

Once again focusing on the statistics for first and most conservative error level, it is found that only at the lowest two coital frequencies (2 and 4) was it possible in significantly more than half the cases to extract information about the rhythm of susceptibility from the trial-and-error process. The very best performance in this dimension is obtained with coital frequency drastically reduced to the twice-monthly level: 80 percent of that sample of 50 mothers attained a rank correlation score exceeding that which could be expected to occur purely by chance in 10 percent of the cases. At the higher coital frequency level ($\tau = 4$), which was found to be near optimal for behavioral adaptation and effective control of fertility under the guidance of BAR, the proportion drops to only 0.62, implying that in only roughly half of the 50 cases did the correlation scores attained at the end-of-life represent an improvement on the state of biological understanding that could have been arrived at purely by chance.

What these experiments have brought out most starkly is that while it is possible to use the bounded BAR algorithm quite effectively, on the average, as a method of family limitation, the practitioners as a group would remain very confused about the timing of the fertile and safe periods within the intermenstruum. A result of this kind can occur in our model because the woman is motivated to learn about the timing of ovulation only to the extent that it helps her to avoid becoming pregnant. Should she happen upon a set of beliefs, (i.e., priors) which, though far from the truth , nonetheless enabled her successfully to avert any further births, her beliefs about the safe period will never converge any closer toward the truth. For these rational adaptive agents, the operative truths toward which they are myopically driven is simply "whatever works."[37]

This aspect of our finding is most intructive. It sheds light on the history of popular and medical confusion surrounding the safe period and at the same time provides some rational grounds for the historical persistence of faith in the potential efficacy of such a method of regulating marital fertility. In performing this explanatory service, however, the divergence between BAR's performance in the behavioral and cognitive domains has set

[37] It sometimes is said that such an attitude toward sufficiency in "knowledge" distinguishes the stance of the professional engineer from that of the scientist. But for us to characterize our hypothetical BAR-using women as "family limitation engineers" would be to venture into territory that is likely to prove doubly hazardous.

a new and unanticipated question for us to puzzle over: How does cognitively bounded BAR manage nonetheless to control fertility so tightly?

This question can be given a sharper, quantitative form by considering the following illustrative calculations. It has been seen that when the coital frequency level is maintained at four times per month, approximately half of a population of BAR users will have learned something about the rhythm of susceptibility by the end of their reproductive career. Let us then suppose that the gain in knowledge thus acquired yielded so precise an approximation to the true rhythm of susceptibility that these cognitive learners were enabled to cease having any conceptions after giving birth to a first child. Further, let us suppose that at the other extreme those women whose end-of-life priors were still not significantly correlated with the true rhythm of susceptibility would have done no better to have selected all their coital regimes at random. From Table XIV.6.1 we see that with the hypothesized coital frequency ($\tau = 4$), the latter group on average should have ended up with a completed fertility of 8.22, whereas the group of cognitive learners, *ex hypothesis,* would average 1.0 birth apiece. As the groups are of equal size, the average number of births per mother for the whole of this imagined population, therefore, ought to have been 4.61, which is just the arithmetic average of the respective group means for the number of children ever born. Yet, as a glance back at Table XIV.6.1 will confirm, BAR at the indicated coital frequency ($\tau = 4$) actually manages to limit the mean number of births in the corresponding population of *mothers* to a mere 2.21, far below the level of average completed fertility that the foregoing calculations would lead one to anticipate.

XIV.6.3 How Does Bounded BAR Do It?

How then is this mysterious power of cognitively bounded BAR to be explained? Evidently, the algorithm must be working in a way that does not entail a tight coupling at the microlevel between correct knowledge and correct action; that is, between understanding what is going on—in the sense of possessing either a good structural model of the underlying process or an accurate empirically induced reduced-form approximation of it—and being able successfully to avoid regimes in which coitus occurs during the "fertile" period of the month. The key to the mystery lies in an often overlooked generic feature of Bayesian adaptive routines, all of which have embedded within them the following primitive but powerful rule: "Stay with a winner."

Staying with a winner, which in the context of BAR means not abandoning a regime that has just avoided generating a conception, is the behavioral consequence of the fact that in response to contraceptive successes the woman's priors undergo revision in a direction that raises the subjective evaluation of the *relative* dangerousness of those days on which coitus did not take place during the month preceding. Re-optimization of the regime on the basis of the *a posteriori* evaluation thus causes the same regime to be repeated whenever it has yielded a success in the previous trial. Regime selections that initially met with a run of successes will tend to become locked in. Correspondingly, agents whose initial regime choices issued in unwanted outcomes eventually will be pushed by the revision of their priors to discard such regimes in favor of others that come to appear as less "dangerous."

The tendency, therefore, must be for an *ensemble* of agents who are BAR users to be propelled (although the nature of the process would, perhaps, be conveyed more precisely by the phrase "jiggled and jostled") toward the subset of *comparatively antinatal* regimes by the reactions of individual agents to contraceptive failures. Being functionally adaptive with reference to the individual agents' goals, the members of the subset of relatively safe regimes also possess the property that their selection will cause the agent's behavior to stabilize—thereby incidentally fulfilling the behavioral psychologists minimalist criterion for the completion of learning. As a larger and larger proportion of the ensemble becomes thus stabilized in relatively safe regimes, the average monthly probability of a conception must be reduced.

At the macrolevel, such diminution gives rise to the impression of a process of continuous learning on the part of a representative (contracepting) agent. The insights imparted by the evolutionary metaphor are not inaptly invoked at just this point: we were to think of the collection of regimes that were in use in each month by the ensemble of agents as constituting a population (of memes), the BAR routines followed by the agents could be viewed as a mechanism that drives the regime population to evolve in the (desired) antinatal direction by differentially selecting and retaining for use those regimes that were relatively safe. It is important to stress that in this evolutionary formulation the population, but not necessarily any of its constituent members, is doing the learning.

To see that this evolutionary mechanism works much more swiftly, and therefore more effectively in controlling fertility within a finite time span, when the level of coital frequency is low, we may now turn to consider the statistics presented in Table XIV.6.5. The proportion of women who remain childless at the end of a continuous 264-month span is shown there as a function of the invariant monthly frequency of coitus. Each of the three columns of the table does this for a different population, but fundamentally they all make the same point: the lower the coital frequency rate, the more likely it is that one will be able, purely by chance, to avoid unprotected sexual intercourse on those days (in a month chosen at random) on which the probability of a conception is relatively high. The column at the extreme right shows the theoretically calculated proportion of cases in which a random distribution of coitus within the intermenstruum would avoid hitting one (or more) of the six possible susceptible days in an infinite lifetime of

TABLE XIV.6.5 Proportion of Women Remaining Childless at End of 264-Month Reproductive Life

Invariant monthly frequency of coitus (τ)	Random sample of 150 lives, stimulates with BAR ($\theta = 0.06$)	In sample of lives containing first 50 mothers, simulated with BAR ($\theta = 0.06$)	Expected frequency of safe regime being chosen initially $\prod_{k=0}^{\tau}\left\{\frac{(24-6)-k}{(28-4)-k}\right\}$
0	1.000	1.000	1.000
2	.600	.515	.554
4	.293	.342	.228
6	.113	.123	.138
8	.060	.038	.022
10	.030	.019	.013
12	.000	.000	.007

independent monthly trials. Supposing these proportions to describe the expected frequency of randomly landing in a "safe" regime in the first month of the woman's married life, we see that for monthly coital frequencies below six there is an appreciably high chance of her becoming locked in to a perfectly antinatal regime by subsequent BAR-driven revisions of her initially diffuse priors.

The simulation results for the proportion of childless women found in runs of 150 lives with BAR, at each of the invariant coital frequencies indicated, are shown in the left-hand column of the table. They closely match the theoretical calculations, with some deviations due to sampling errors arising from the stochastic workings of the model. In the middle column we report the corresponding proportions, as calculated from the respective simulation runs that yielded the first 50 *mothers* for each parametric level of τ.[38] It is seen that even with the greater possibilities of divergences due to sampling errors, the agreement with the theoretical probabilities remains quite close. One observation that should be made in connection with the picture emerging from Table XIV.6.5 bears on the reading of the results reported earlier, on the basis of the statistics for the mothers in our simulation samples. Inasmuch as the latter ignore the impact on childlessness, strictly speaking, they *understate* the efficacy of combining BAR with lower coital frequency as a means of achieving lower levels of completed fertility; the understatement entailed is particularly pronounced when coital frequency is in the range $\tau \leq 6$. For example, Table XIV.6.1 shows that the average

[38] Thus, to be concrete, at coital frequency 4 it was necessary to perform simulation runs for 76 lives in order to accumulate 50 women who did not remain childless after the 264th month: the proportion childless is therefore 26/76 = .342.

number of births to mothers who consistently used BAR at coital frequency $\tau = 4$, was 2.12, whereas we now can see that after correcting for the theoretical probability of childlessness, the average figure can be put at 1.63 for all *women* (because the corresponding expected fraction of mothers among all women is 0.772). A corollarly implication, however, is that expected numbers of birth averted *per woman,* due to learning with BAR, is somewhat lower than those shown by Table XIV.6.1 and Figure XIV.6.1 for the low end of the range of coital frequencies.[39]

Coming now to the nub of the present question, Table XIV.6.5 tells us that the "stay with a winner" rule embedded within BAR will be likely to come into operation more rapidly at lower coital frequencies, especially when the routine starts from a position in which the woman's priors are diffuse. To grasp the reason for this intuitively, consider that in the event that an unlucky choice at the beginning of the process produced quick pregnancy, the ensuing updating of the woman's belief will lead her, when intercourse is resumed, to select a regime that previously had not been tried. Then, as coital frequency is *ex hypothesis* held to the same low level as before, the odds of choosing a safe regime out of the hitherto untried days must be even better than before, on average. This is so because, in the first instance, the odds would have been those shown in the right-hand column of Table XIV.6.5 as being determined purely by chance when coition on the days that gave rise to the first conception had not been excluded.

To be sure, the inertial tendencies of the "stay with a winner" kernel of Bayesian adaptation can become a drawback in certain circumstances, making it a something of a double-edged sword for the individuals who seize upon this mode of learning. Suppose that a woman who by chance had selected a potentially quite dangerous regime was favored by a succession of rare contingencies and so escaped conceiving a child. In the course of the associated sequential updating of her priors, she would be led to believe quite firmly that her past regime was a relatively safe one, compared to the others that had remained untried; and so, she would regard persisting in the selection of that previous regime to be the best way (myopically) to minimize the monthly expectation of a pregnancy. It could then require the ex-

[39] The proportional reduction of the average completed fertility rate for all women decreases as coital frequency increases, so that it is only .987 at $\tau = 8$. The effect of these adjustments, starting at coital frequency 2, therefore, yields the following figures for the average numbers of children born to all women using BAR: 0.991, 1.63, 4.01, 8.53. To obtain the corresponding figures for the expected number of births averted, similar adjustments can be made to the data for mothers in Table XIV.6.1. The resulting estimates for births averted due to BAR are, for $\tau = 2, \ldots, 8$: 1.81, 4.71, 4.75, 2.50. Note that, with this in mind, when discussing the coital frequencies that were optimal for "learning" with BAR, we were careful to place these in the range of between 4 and 6 times per month, rather than literally following the figures computed for the case of *mothers* in Table XIV.6.1.

perience of repeated unwanted conceptions (and time-consuming pregnancies) before her subjective evaluations of the relative "dangerousness" of the days associated with the regime were raised sufficiently to eradicate the erroneous beliefs that had been acquired in the course of her early experience. Only at that point would she be cognitively liberated to select a different regime. As unhappy a tale as this is for the individuals involved, instances in which a woman's family limiting efforts will be largely vitiated by her accidental imprisonment in the grip of her early history must themselves be very much the exception when coital frequency is low. For the latter itself serves to reduce the probability of randomly selecting an initial regime so as to include coitus on a day of peak susceptibility.

The mystery is now thoroughly dispelled: BAR "works" at low coital frequency because, under those conditions, the odds favor the formation of functionally adapted behaviors that stabilize as rationalized habits. This is so, even though we have seen that an individual's persistence in such goal-satisfying behaviors is not only quite compatible with the holding of cognitive convictions that are objectively false, but that it also may cause such myths and fantasies to become more and more deeply entrenched in the minds of those who are guided by them.

XIV.7 CONCLUSIONS AND PROVOCATIONS

Cognitive evolution that proceeds within a Bayesian decision-theoretic framework is a path-dependent process, and so, when coupled to myopic optimizing behaviors, it will generate perceptible hysteresis effects in actions and observed consequences. At each stage in the process, those acting under the instruction of their *a priori* views have made themselves, in effect, creatures of a potentially tenacious past—a past that will have been distilled down and incorporated into their prevailing subjective evaluations of alternative hypotheses about the nature of the world with which they have to contend.

In this way, historical experiences—whether in the form of belief structures instilled in them by others, or acquired unconsciously, or consciously formed from personal observation of the temporal association between particular actions and sequelae—are able to lay down a (boundedly) rational basis for behaviors that come to resemble habits. Whether the resulting transiently, or permanently stabilized patterns of behavior truly qualify as habits is beside the point here; what matters is that they are habitlike, even to the extent that the actions entailed are conditioned on beliefs that grow more and more difficult to cast off quickly. Thus they are able to persist even after they have revealed themselves to be responsible for the recurrence of unwanted consequences. This is "sunk cost hysteresis"—in the realm of cognitive evolution. That functional habits, rather than dysfunctional ones, will emerge from such a process is not, however, merely a matter of luck. Good fortune in trial-and-error learning can be systematically favored more strongly by some learning environments than by others, as the preceding analysis of the effect of parametric changes in the frequency of unprotected coitus has demonstrated.

The general terms in which the foregoing conclusions are formulated is meant to suggest that their relevance is not confined to the particular problem in the history of contraceptive knowledge and practices. What has been brought to light by the inquiry seems to have a much wider validity, pertaining to many other contexts involving a reciprocal and mutually reinforcing interplay between cognitive evolution and behavioral adaptation.

It may be thought that to have established this point is enough, and that it is not really warranted to go beyond the quantitatively grounded and analytically straightforward summary propositions that we have just set out. But, such self-restraint is difficult, for there are several still larger issues that already have been touched upon in the preceding pages and to which it seems worth devoting some concluding reflections of a more speculative nature.

XIV.7.1 Instructionist versus Selectionist Mechanisms in Evolution

The intertwined cognitive changes and behavioral adaptations that we have examined here appear unambiguously to be classifiable as evolutionary mechanisms of the Lamarckian *instructionist* rather than of the strict neo-Darwinian variety. New regime configurations in our simulation model cannot be represented (after the first month) as having emerged through "blind variation," which is what the Darwinian paradigm of evolution strictly requires. Instead, these regimes (considered now as memes) merge, and are available to be replicated in subsequent use, through a process that is definitely Lamarckian in spirit. They are reshaped by the responses of the goal-seeking individual agent to the outcomes of interactions between her past choices of behavior and the objective (stochastic) environment represented by her rhythm of susceptibility. In view of the intentional manner in which it operates, however, this process qualifies as Lamarckian in spirit but not as "natural instructionism." Indeed, a *rational* course of cognitive evolution is the purpose behind the calculation of likelihoods and the revision of priors in the Bayesian process; just as the selection of regimes follows from the intention to minimize the expectation of an unwanted conception.

All that seems very clear, and it may be found helpful thus to locate our simulation model with reference to the crisp taxonomic boundaries that separate Lamarckian from Darwinian evolution. In actuality, however, the character of the underlying evolutionary process responsible for the adaptive performance of the BAR algorithm is considerably fuzzier than this exercise in classification would suggest. We already have pointed out that it is the "stay with a winner" rule buried in the Bayesian routine that enables BAR to manage so successfully to avert births for the representative woman in the population. It remains now to observe that with one simple modification we can effect what may seem to be a profound alteration in the character of the learning model, transforming Lamarckian BAR into a purely Darwinian evolutionary process and yet not substantially changing its adaptive properties.

It is easy enough to replace the subroutines for the monthly revision of priors and the regime optimization in the model (see Figure XIV.5.1), substituting an altogether simpler routine that, similarly, responds to successes and failures in the avoidance of conceptions. This routine is based on the rule: "Win Stay, Lose Start Again" (WSLSA). Beginning, as before, from a regime chosen at random, it will retain the initial selection so long as a conception does not occur, but when coition is resumed following a birth, the new regime will be, again, chosen randomly. This would be a ruthless policy, indeed, in labor relations—discarding faithful servants who have had a long record of success as soon as they revealed themselves to be fallible, even if it does permit the possibility of their being reinstated by random draw. In the context of our rather different application, it might be supposed that the failure of control, by ushering in the condition of pregnancy, would effect the erasure of all memory of the woman's antecedant priors—a form of maternal amnesia that returned her beliefs to their original, diffuse state. Evaluating the performance of WSLSA by simulations comparable with those we examined for BAR show what can be achieved in this context with a purely Darwinian process of adaptation based on the "blind variation and selective retention" of regimes.

By comparing the performance of WSLSA against a perfectly random process of regime choice, as we have done in Table XIV.7.1, one can see how powerful is the fertility reducing effect that comes just from the selective retention feature of BAR—furnished by its mimicry of a "stay-with-a-winner" policy. The average numbers of births averted among mothers using WSLSA exhibits the same sensitivity to parametric variations in coital frequency as that found in the simulations of BAR. To determine how important the non-Darwinian, cognitive adaptation component of BAR is for its adaptive performance (in the same transversal measures corresponding to Learning Definition 2), we may examine Table XIV.7.2 and Figure XIV.7.2, wherein the expected number of births averted with WSLSA are matched against the figures for BAR (from Table XIV.6.1). *Mirable dictu,* even though it had been found that something approaching half of the population of BAR practitioners were undergoing significant cognitive evolution

TABLE XIV.7.1 Effect of the Pure Darwinian (WSLSA) Adaptive Strategy: Number of Births per Mother during Reproductive Life of 264 Months in Simulation Samples of 50 Mothers

Invariant monthly frequency of coitus	Randomized monthly regime		WSLSA*		Incremental births averted per mother due to WSLSA	
	Mean	Std. dev.	Mean	Std. dev.	Mean difference	Pooled std. error of estimate
2	5.62	1.38	2.20	1.39	3.42	0.28
4	8.22	1.57	2.58	1.83	5.64	0.34
6	10.18	1.62	4.36	2.83	5.82	0.46
8	11.28	1.54	8.20	3.55	3.08	0.54
10	12.70	1.23	10.34	3.45	2.36	0.52
12	12.90	1.04	11.56	2.68	1.34	0.40

* The WSLSA strategy rerandomizes after each birth, but thereafter remains invariant (up until the next birth). Hence: **W**in **S**tay, **L**ose **S**tart **A**gain.

of some sort, the intentional, cognitively guided component of this algorithm is seen not to be making much of a difference at all in the behavioral domain. At the very lowest coital frequency level, it is true, adding the information processing and optimization subroutines that transform WSLSA into BAR improves performance—by 20 percent in terms of expected births averted per mother (i.e., the proportional gain recorded relative to the performance of WSLSA). But when coital frequency is moved into the range between four and six times per month, this differential vanishes completely; indeed, with τ in the range between six and eight, BAR does slightly, although not significantly, worse than its Darwinian counterpart.

TABLE XIV.7.2 Incremental Effect of Bayesian (BAR) versus Darwinian (WSLSA) Strategy upon Mean Number of Births Averted during Reproductive Life of 264 Months: Simulation Samples of 50 Mothers

Invariant monthly frequency of coitus	Difference in means between BAR ($\theta = 0.06$) and WSLSA	Pooled standard error of the difference
2	0.66	0.277
4	0.46	0.324
6	−0.30	0.615
8	−0.52	0.716
10	0.82	0.706
12	0.02	0.524

Source: Computed from Tables XIV.6.1 and XIV.6.6.

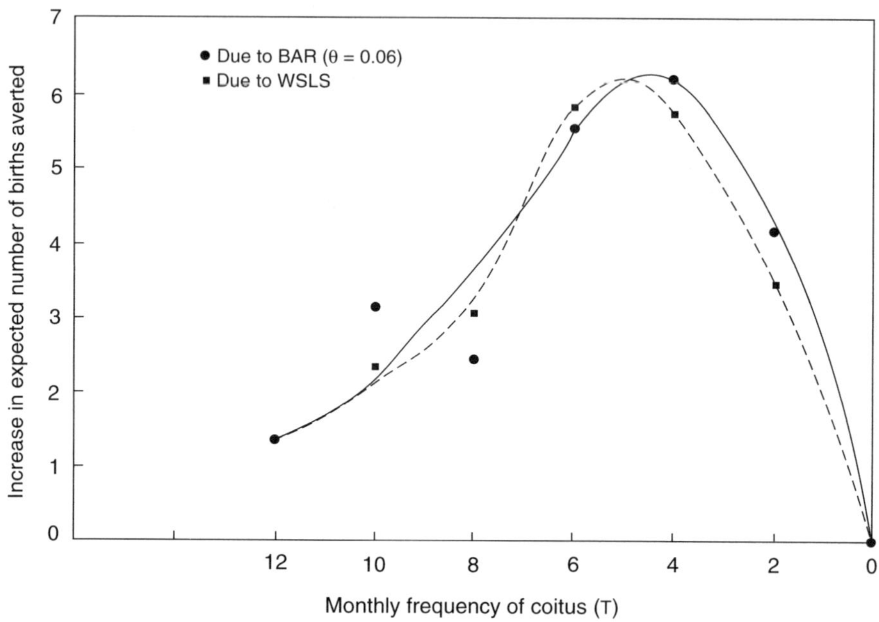

FIGURE XIV.7.1 Bounded Bayesian Learning versus Darwinian Adaptive (WSLS) behavior: Comparison of simulation results for expected number of births averted (runs of 50 sample lives, each of 264 months in duration).

Note: Data plotted in the figure below are averages of births averted per mother; in simulation results for regimes of randomly timed coition, the number of mothers always equaled the number of women (50). The curves are hand drawn, disregarding deviations produced by sampling errors in simulations for coital frequencies 8 and 10.

Source: Table XIV.6.2

Two morals might be drawn from these revelations. The first is that advances in knowledge, empirically grounded on inferences from trial and error in a myopic control process, cannot be a big help when you are restricted in both the number of trials you can undertake and the states of the world you can imagine as worth considering. This, then, is not a new point, but one that serves to re-emphasize the propositions advanced in the preceding section. The second, and perhaps more contentious, lesson would seem to be that in social science invocations of evolutionary metaphors, the effort spent in carefully distinguishing non-biological processes that are Lamarckian from those that are properly Darwinian may be misplaced and reflective of analogical rather than analytical reasoning. What appears here, at least outwardly, to be a classically instructionist mechanism of a thoroughly intentional sort has turned out to be effectual only to the extent that its operation mimics the workings of Darwinian selectionism. At least it is worth bearing in mind that there can be contexts where the instructionist-selectionist distinction is operationally far less important than would be suggested by the amount of paper and ink that has been devoted to it in the literature of evolutionary epistemology. It is a distinction that is likely to be worth insisting upon when cognitive evolution must undergird behavioral adaptation, but that is something to be demonstrated, rather than simply presumed.

XIV.7.2 Advances in Knowledge and Improvements of Learning in History

For students of the past, the domain of our findings' relevance would seem to be especially broad. Throughout much of human history, and indeed until very recent times in a number of important fields of human endeavor—the control of disease and other biological processes being especially notable but scarcely unique among these—the quest for practical knowledge has been heavily dependent upon trial-and-error learning in situations resembling those stylized by our stochastic simulation model. That is to say, people have of necessity engaged in processes of causal inference from their observations, and have been obliged to do so in situations that left them handicapped by a one or more of a variety of constraints: (1) where pure experimentation was limited or denied to them by perceptions that such a strategy would conflict with their other purposes, or normative values; (2) where the possibilities of discovering the true state of the world though such procedures were closely circumscribed by maintained *a priori* suppositions about seemingly secondary aspects of the phenomenon under examination; and (3) where much of the motivation for seeking knowledge about the natural world rest on the hope of acquiring it *and* being able to benefit from its application within a time span that was comparatively short.

Of course, the point in the foregoing formulation is to emphasize the limitations on myopic learning-by-doing, the kind that Arrow (1962) first brought to the attention of economists seeking insight into endogenous mechanisms of technological change. This is a less rosy perspective on the large role that cognitively and materially bounded trial-and-error adaptation had to play in permitting people in the past to improve their ability to control their natural and social environments. And the view grows still darker when one focuses on the severe and "costly" constraints that needed to be accepted, in certain features of "the learning environment"(here represented most notably by the parameter τ), in order that significant gains in discretionary control of fertility might be achieved (by adapting the timing of coitus). Even so, it must be acknowledged that what was learned in a behavioral sense would not seem safely transferable to situations that appeared superficially the same, but might be critically different in some respects that had remained very imperfectly understood.

To be sure, the Bayesian adaptive procedure has been found to permit remarkably effective adaptations in behavior, and fertility, even under constraining conditions that cause cognitive evolution to remain quite tightly circumscribed. Hence, it is possible to read our findings as support to those behaviorists, many economists included, who generally are skeptical about the value of modeling "learning" explicitly as a cognitive activity. But quite the opposite conclusion actually is warranted. It should be clearly understood that to be obliged to act myopically on what you have just "learned" through your previous action is a strategy that is dominated by one of learning first, through implementing an experimental design, and only then, after a period devoted to gathering data, trying to infer and select the best course for actual implementation (cf. Rothschild, 1974). The possibility of making a switch to that superior learning mode, from hand-to-mouth adaptive modes of the sort with which our analysis has been concerned, represents an important transition in the historical emergence of the knowledge-based economy.

Such transitions, which doubtless have occurred in different areas of human endeavor at different times in the past, would repay closer investigation than they have received hitherto. Indeed, though developing a better understanding of what could not be learned in the behavioral domain (via myopic learning by doing), economic historians may be able to evaluate the magnitude of the economic gains and the improvements of human well-being in other dimensions that properly are attributable to the ascendance of organized scientific research and development as the modern mode of knowledge-based innovation and endogenous economic growth.

One cannot help but come away from an analysis of constrained trial-and-error learning, such as the one essayed here, without a sharpened appreciation for the repercussions in the sphere of cognitive evolution that were permitted by historical changes in certain of the conditions of material culture. Among the sorts of developments that spring readily to mind in connection with the secular relaxation of the constraints on "learning while doing" are those that had the effect of shortening the real-time duration of the learning cycle; of multiplying the opportunities to impose experimental controls; of increasing the ability of individuals and organizations to finance, learning by controlled experimentation. All manner of institutional innovations can be seen to have had significant and inadequately appreciated side consequences in encouraging the decoupling of experimentation from the restrictions of simultaneously having to meet pressing, day-to-day material need. No less noteworthy in this connection would have been the growing importance of forms of economic activity that provided learning environments that were protected from disruption and more and more amenable to standardization. The latter must have greatly increased the scope for beneficial application of the behavioral rules upon which individual learning sequences had (successfully) stabilized. In short, one unexpectedly arrives via this somewhat roundabout route at a renewed awareness that much remains to be studied about the linkages between secular economic change and the systematic application of the emerging methods that have come to be associated with the pursuit of knowledge by means of modern science.

XIV.7.3 Cognitive Limitations, Information Processing and the Origins of Heuristics

It is reasonable enough to suppose that heuristic procedures fundamentally originate in the cognitive limitations of human agents. We have been concerned with the limitations of the sorts of heuristics that are resorted to in processing data and analyzing decision problems. These sometime take the form of rules of thumb that are consciously employed by the individual problem solver and, in other cases, are deeply, and even invisibly embedded in the routines followed by human organizations for collecting, filtering, and analyzing data to extract information on which discretionary control will be conditioned. Those limitations, indeed, may be at the root of perceptual distortions of the sort that have been identified by behavioral psychologists as "framing biases," "salient aspect" comparisons in multidimensional choice situations, and the like. Certainly, one may justifiably label as cognitive deficiencies the manifold difficulties that ordinary people display in grasping elementary concepts of probability and in applying such notions to everyday decision problems. The latter they nonetheless proceed to answer by some means or other, often quite incorrectly, as has been shown by Tversky and Kahneman (1974), and Kahneman *et al.* (1982).

One troublesome aspect of the view that heuristics arise through cognitive errors is that it leads to the same conundrum that causes many economists to hang back from embracing the implications of the concept of bounded rationality. It then allows them go to on modeling individuals and firms as if they behaved as thoroughly informed rational maximizers, even when they are presented with overwhelming psychological evidence that, when people are asked to solve decision problems involving probabilities, more often than not they make conceptual errors or fail to do sums right. The economists who acknowledge the evidence cling nevertheless to models that ignore it, on the ground that there are just too many ways for fallible agents to make mistakes, and no *a priori* principle seems available on which to justify selecting one rather than another flawed heuristic as the standard analytical model. A theory of bounded rationality that could offer more guidance in characterizing how people and organizations proceed when confronted with complex problems surely would be of use in breaking this methodological logjam.

The modeling exercise described in the preceding pages does not constitute such a theory. But it may have stumbled on a useful way to think about the formation of heuristic procedures, one that is close to the spirit of Henry Simon's original observations about rationality being bounded by cognitive constraints on decisions analysis. Limitations on computational capability, as well as on information collection, storage, and retrieval, may preclude attempting to base decisions on representations of the world that reflect the full range of its perceived complexities. As mathematical theorists in the natural sciences know well, and as practicing engineers publicly profess, there is an art of simplifying that enables people to use manageable quantities of data to extract information upon which to base real-time predictions and action. Rules of thumb that are inexact, but nonetheless have practical utility in that way, might then arise from the effort to simplify the problem to the point of ready computability. In our simulation model, by grossly simplifying the representation that the decision agents give to the time pattern of fecundability within the intermenstruum, the updating of priors in strict Bayesian fashion is rendered equivalent to an easily implemented heuristic procedure.

Of course, as we have seen, to have misspecified the models of the world (in the way that Appendix A details) is likely to be a serious handicap when it comes to making progress in understanding the processes that one is trying (with some success) to manage. Furthermore, an outside observer who had a inkling of the true complexity of the underlying process could justifiably scoff at the lack of statistical sophistication manifested in the reduced form algorithm. Such an observer might not even perceive the strict Bayesian properties of a routine that was described as nothing more than ranking the days of the intermenstruum according to a subjective evaluation of their inherent "dangerousness;" even more misguided might appear the mechanical modification of those rankings depending on the outcomes that ensued from acting upon them. Nevertheless, the feasible Bayesian heuristic to which those simplifications led, turned out to be usable to very good effect, on average, in attaining the agent's family limitation goals. It therefore would fulfill a minimal consistency requirement for its continuation in practical usage.

By extrapolation from this particular case, we may badly state the following hypothesis: At any point in the history of an organization or a culture, rational economic agents needing to manage complex technical and social processes (the underlying structure of which is incompletely known to them) will, as a rule, be found to be relying on heuristics and decision rules that had been formed by framing some model of the world so as to render feasible the necessary "calculations". Such implementable rules may far outlive the conditions under which they were formed, especially when, as Arrow (1972) has noted, they become embedded in the ritualized operating procedures of social organizations. Codes and information channels are notably durable, become easier to work with more frequent usage, and represent large sunk costs for the organizations in question. As David (1994) suggests, that alone may enable the organization to withstand for some time the competitive pressures from new entrants, even when the latter possess superior capabilities in gathering and processing information to support their internal decision processes.

Proceeding from this line of speculation, a potentially fruitful research approach in the study of cognitive evolution, therefore, would be to examine "computability and tractability" of information management requirements, as an attribute for which theories are selected for implementation in a given, technologically constrained environment. Further, under this hypothesis, one would consider major technical and organizational advances that relaxed the constraints imposed on information processing as having potentially profound cognitive repercussions, analogous to those of catastrophic shifts in the natural environments of biological species. Such "environmental" transformations affecting the costs of acquisition and analysis of relevant data could render totally obsolete large portions of the existing array of computational routines, thereby causing the associated scientific theories, management heuristics—along with the people adept in implementing these—to be dislodged from the cultural, economic, and political niches into which they had been selected.

It would appear from the foregoing excursion that, at some points, the frontiers of the new institutional economics extend into the less familiar reaches of historical demography and the economic history of knowledge. By journeying more frequently in these strange borderlands, we eventually may come to a better understanding not only of many intriguing arcana, but of such matters as the long-run implications of the information revolution that is taking place around us.

ACKNOWLEDGMENTS

There are some long-standing intellectual debts of gratitude that we are pleased to have the opportunity to acknowledge in connection with this paper. Our original demographically motivated research received financial support under a grant from the National Institutes of Health (NIH R01 HD 17288-01/02). David benefited from the opportunity to first become acquainted with the work of psychologists on Markovian and other models of learning while he was a fellow of the Center for Advanced Study in the Behavioral Sciences in Stanford, California, during 1978–1979. Subsequent research along these lines, in connection with applications of Bayesian learning to problems of industrial design, was supported under a National Science Foundation grant to the Stanford Center for Economic Policy research (IRI-8814 179-02/03). Our intellectual indebtedness on many points is acknowledged in the footnotes and references, but only imperfectly so. An important contribution, which the latter utterly fail to record, was made by W. Edward Steinmueller during 1978–1979 when, in his capacity as a graduate student research assistant in the Stanford Economics Department, he wrote and ran the computer programs that produced the statistical analysis of the stimulation model results reported here (Sections XIV.6 and XIV.7). Subsequently, as a friend and academic colleague, Steinmueller generously shared his mature insights and reflections on the substantive meaning of the computations that he diligently executed so long ago. Of more recent origin is our indebtedness to Christopher Bliss, for bringing Pierre Darmon's engaging book to our notice, and to John M. Ziman and other participants in the epistemology group meetings held in London during 1995 under the sponsorship of the Renaissance Trust, for bibliographic guidance and critical discussions of the large and rapidly growing literature on evolutionary epistemology. Undoubtedly, they saved us much time and averted many embarrassing mistakes. John Drobak's blend of editorial skill and patience materially improved the present exposition. We claim full responsibility for the errors of commission and omission that remain.

APPENDIX A

A.1 Model Notation

t	: index of days in the intermenstruum
T	: number of days in the intermenstruum
τ	: number of events (days) of coitus in the intermenstruum, a parameter
n	: coital frequency rate $n = \tau/T$; $(1 - n)$ is the rate of periodic abstinence
θ_t	: hazard for conception when coitus occurs on the ith day
$\tilde{\theta}^i$	: The ith inherent rhythm of susceptibility, a $1 \times T$ vector representing the inherent probabilities of conception for each of the T days in the intermenstruum
$A^o(\tilde{\theta}^i)$	: *a priori* subjective probability of the ith rhythm of susceptibility $\tilde{\theta}^i$
$A'(\tilde{\theta}^i)$	: *a posteriori* subjective probability of the ith rhythm of susceptibility $\tilde{\theta}^i$
ϕ_t	: binary variable defined on the days, which takes the value 0 if there is no coitus on the tth day of the month; and 1 if coitus occurs on the tth day
$\tilde{\phi}_j$	: the jth regime of intercourse, a $(1 \times T)$ vector comprised of the elements ϕ_t
$\tilde{\phi}^{\tau}_{*}$	: an element of the set of regimes characterized by τ, which also satisfies the condition: min $E(c_j)$
l_{ij}	: the conditional likelihood of a pregnancy, given the ith rhythm of susceptibility and jth configuration
$E(c_j)$	: the *a priori* expectation of a pregnancy conditional on the jth regime being selected

A.2 Maintained Restrictions on the "Admissible" Rhythms of Susceptibility

The vector(s) describing an ith "rhythm of susceptibility", $\tilde{\theta}^i$, must satisfy certain general restrictions:

(1) In $\tilde{\theta}^i = (\theta_1, \theta_2, \ldots, \theta_T)$, $0 \leq \theta_t \leq 1$ for t $= (1, \ldots, T)$.

Defining θ to be the set of all vectors formed by all permutations of the possible values of θ_t over the days $(1, \ldots, T)$, and letting $S \in \theta$ denote the "admissible rhythms of susceptibility," a subset comprising the $\tilde{\theta}^i$'s for which the transformation $A^o(\tilde{\theta}) > 0$, then we impose

(2) The prior general restriction on rhythms of susceptibility: $\tilde{\theta}^i \in S$.

Our rules for forming S are simple. We interpret θ_t as a discrete random variable and impose a further restriction that admissible rhythms be generated by canonical permutation of a symmetric unimodal rhythm of susceptibility.

(i) First, we formally define $S = \overline{S}$, where $\overline{S} \in \theta$ s.t. If $\tilde{\theta}^i \in \overline{S}$ then $\exists$ a canonical permutation of $\tilde{\theta}^i$, say $\tilde{\theta}^v$, s.t. $\tilde{\theta}^v \in \overline{S}$.

(ii) Since for computational ease it is desirable that $\overline{S}$ take the form of limiting the (discrete) values that θ_t may assume, we impose the most extreme nontrivial restriction:

(3) Only two values of the day-specific inherent hazards of a conception are considered:

$$\theta_t \in ({}_1\theta, {}_2\theta) \text{ for } t = (1, \ldots, T),$$

in which case $\overline{S}$ contains as many as $T(T-1)$ admissible rhythms (vectors $\tilde{\theta}^i \in \overline{S}$).

(iii) A final restriction on S that proves computationally useful is to limit the number of days of the month on which $\theta \neq {}_1\theta$ may occur. Note that if this number lies anywhere in the set $(1, \ldots, T-1)$, and the restrictions described in (i) and (ii) also hold, then $\overline{S} \in \theta$ has only $s = T$ vector elements.

These restrictions on the admissible rhythms of susceptibility really amount to maintained priors about the pattern of intermenstrual variation in susceptibility. We shall say that the distributions of θ_t through the month must be (1) symmetrical and unimodal, in that they are generated by a phase-shift of some standard distribution in which there is a single day of maximum inherent risk of conception, and (2) of the form in which $\theta_t = \overline{\theta}$ for the vector's ith element and ϵ for all others. This says that the woman firmly believes there is one day of peak conception risk ($\overline{\theta}$) within the intermenstruum that remains the same from month to month—save for the months in which she is pregnant, of course—but it is uncertain as to where exactly it falls within her "month."

A.3 Subjective Probabilities on Admissible Rhythms

Being uncertain, she nonetheless can form subjective probability evaluations of each of the admissible rhythms that might be her actual rhythm:

$$A^o \left({}^{\mu}_{\theta} l \right) = A_o^{\,t}$$

is defined formally as a transformation that expresses the *a priori* (subjective) probability over the states described by $\tilde{\theta} i \in \overline{S}$ whose size is s.

This $A_o^i \in A_o$ whose size is s, and the transformations must satisfy the conditions

$$A_o^{\,i} \leq 1 \text{ and } \sum_{i}^{s} A_o^{\,i} = 1.$$

A.4 Regimes of Coitus and Regime Optimization

A.4.1 Regimes

A "regime" of coitus is represented as a $1 \times T$ vector whose ordered elements signify whether or not coitus is held on the given day of the month. Thus, in jth regime, the time pattern of unprotected coitus is described by a permutation of 0 and 1 elements forming the vector $\overline{\phi_j} = (\phi_1, \phi_2, \ldots \phi_t, \ldots \phi_T)$, where $1 =$ coition, $0 =$ no coition. The regime index is $j = (1, \ldots \binom{T}{\tau})$, where T, the number of days on which intercourse is held, is simply

$$\tau = nT = \sum_{t}^{T} \phi_t.$$

(Note that in discrete simulation applications of the model, the parameter n is restricted to regular fractions in the interval (0,1); it is assumed that effectively only one act of coitus can occur on any day, and the maximum number is limited to T.)

A.4.2 Regime Optimization Criterion

Given the *a priori* probability, $A^o{}_i$, and any *j*th regime of coition, it is possible to ascertain the corresponding subjective probability of a conception, P_{ij}:

$$P_{ij} = [l_{ij}]A_o{}^i = Pr[c \mid \tilde{\theta}^i, \tilde{\phi}_j]A^o\,(\tilde{\theta}^i).$$

Then, the monthly expectation of a conception conditional on the selection of the *j*th regime can be calculated as follows:

$$E(c_j) = 1 - \sum_{i=1}^{T} [\prod_{t=1}^{T} (1 - \phi_{jt}\,\tilde{\theta}_t)]A^o\,(\tilde{\theta}^i),$$

since

$$\sum_{i=1}^{T} A_o^{\,i} = 1.$$

By evaluating these expectations for every possible regime, the hypothetical woman can choose the regime that minimizes her monthly subjective expectation of a pregnancy.

A.5 Bayesian Revision of Priors

For each regime chosen, it can be observed whether or not a conception has ensued. The conditional likelihoods $l_{ij} \in L_{ij}$ may then be used to compute the *a posteriori* probabilities of the rhythms of susceptibility—by Bayesian revision, or updating the priors A^o, to obtain A'. Formally, invoking Bayes' rule, the *a posteriori* probability of the *i*th rhythm is found from the expression

$$A'(\tilde{\theta}^i) = \frac{(l_i)\,A^o\,(\tilde{\theta}_i)}{\sum_{i=1}^{s} (l_i)\,A^o\,(\tilde{\theta}^i)} \quad \text{when a conception has occurred;}$$

and from the expression

$$A'(\tilde{\theta}^i) = \frac{(1 - l_{ij})\,A^o\,(\theta^i)}{\sum_{i=1}^{s} (1 - l_{ij})\,A^O(\tilde{\theta}^i)} \quad \text{when no conception has occurred in the month past.}$$

Given the restrictions specified in Section A.2, subjective probabilities A^o correspond to subjective evaluations of the relative "dangerousness" of unprotected coitus on the respective days (of hypothesized peak susceptibility). To implement a Bayes' exact heuristic algorithm it is therefore sufficient to rank all the days of the intermenstruum according to the woman's subjective estimate of their "dangerousness."

A proof of this is omitted here, but can be found in David Sanderson and Steinmueller (1988). The key is to consider first the subjective likelihood function under the foregoing restrictions $S = \overline{S}$, s.t.,

$$\theta_t \in ({}_1\theta = \epsilon, {}_2\theta = \bar{\theta}),$$

and $\theta_t \neq {}_1\theta$ on only one day of T possible days, where $0 < \epsilon < \bar{\theta}, 1$. Only two values of l_{ij} need then be considered:

$$l_{ij} = \begin{cases} l_+ = 1 - (1 - \bar{\theta})(1 - \epsilon)^{\tau - 1} \\ l_o = 1 - (1 - \epsilon)^{\tau} \end{cases}.$$

The first option applies if regime j entails coitus on the ith day, and the second if not. It then follows that $E(c_j)$ can be expressed as a weighted sum of the A^o for the days on which coitus occurs, from which the minimization rule derives directly.

Bayesian updating of the priors, using these likelihoods, can be achieved by proportional rescaling of the initial index of "dangerousness" for the month in question, using a pair of constant multipliers. Concretely, denote by (ρ_c^{υ}) the multiplier that proportionally *raises* the "dangerousness rating" of coition days *relative* to days on which coitus was omitted in the event of a pregnancy, and by ($\rho_N^{\upsilon *}$) the dual multiplier, which *lowers* the relative "dangerousness rating" of the coition days when no pregnancy occurs. Then, following David Sanderson and Steinmueller (1988, para. 10), it can be proved that the relevant pair of multipliers for the present model must be given by

$$\rho_c^{\upsilon *} = \frac{1 - (1 - \theta)\,(1 - \epsilon)^{\tau - 1}}{1 - (1 - \epsilon)^{\tau}}$$
$$\rho_N^{\upsilon *} = \frac{(1 - \tilde{\theta})}{(1 - \epsilon)}.$$

APPENDIX B THE OBJECTIVE BIOLOGICAL COMPONENT OF THE SIMULATION MODEL

B.1 Structural Specifications

The structural component of the simulation model (see Figure XIV.5.1) that governs the fecundability states of the hypothetical woman is based on the following specifications:

Specification 1. In any given month fertilization leading to a conception may result from coitus on any one of three consecutive days, the day of ovulation and the two days preceding.

Specification 2. A menstrual cycle is always 28 days long and the menstrual flow's duration always last for 4 days. These are assumptions made for the sake of simplicity, not realism. In actuality, the length of menstrual cycles varies from cycle to cycle, and the position of the day of ovulation and the duration of menstruation itself may also vary within a cycle to some extent.

Specification 3. The day of ovulation varies month by month, but always remains within a given consecutive range of days. In order to take the latter variations into account while keeping the cycle at a fixed length, we describe the behavior of the day of ovulation with four parameters, a, b, c, and d. Let v_t be the day in the month in which ovulation occurs. We assume that v_t is in the closed interval $[a, b]$. Further, we assume that v_t and v_{t+1} are not serially independent of one another and posit the following stochastic motion: Letting $R(c,d)$ be an observation randomly drawn from a uniform distribution defined over the closed set of integers from c to d, then

$$
\begin{aligned}
v_{t+1} &= v_t + R(c,d) && \text{if } v_{t+1} \leq b \\
v_{t+1} &= a + (v_t + R(c,d) - b) && \text{otherwise.}
\end{aligned}
$$

Letting the first day of the menses be counted as Day 1, our simulations are generated using the parameter values $a = 13$, $b = 16$, $c = 0$, and $d = 1$.

Specification 4. In the female reproductive tract, sperms gradually lose their ability to fertilize an ovum. For our simulations we assume that the probability of conception from a single act of intercourse on the day preceding ovulation is 0.5 times the probability of conception from a single coitus on the day of ovulation. Similarly, coition two days before ovulation produces 0.25 times the probability of a conception for a coitus on the day of ovulation. These assumptions are roughly in accord with the biological literature (e.g., Hartman, 1962).

B.2 Parameter Values: Mean Daily Hazards for "Fecundability"

The "true," day-specific probabilities of conception from a single act of intercourse to which these specifications will give rise, *on the average,* are set out in tabular form as follows:

Objective Probabilities of Conception from Isolated Coitus on Various Days of the Menstrual Cycle*

	Possible ovulation days							
	1–10	**11**	**12**	**13**	**14**	**15**	**16**	**17–28**
Probability of a conception	0.00	0.01	0.04	0.09	0.09	0.08	0.05	0.00

*Note: These probabilities are not independent from month to month, because of the autocorrelation in the location of the day of ovulation.

Source for Table: We let Ψ_t be the probability of a conception resulting from intercourse on day *t:*

$$\Psi_t = \theta_o \sum_{k=0}^{2} q_{t+k}\,\lambda\,(k),$$

where q_{t+k} is the probability that day $t + k$ is the day of ovulation. The numbers in the table are generated with this formula and the following specifications:

$$\lambda_o = 1; \lambda_1 = 0.5; \lambda_2 = 0.25;$$
$$\theta_o = 0.2;$$
$$q_1 = \ldots = q_{12} = q_{17} = \ldots = q_{28} = 0.0;$$
$$q_{13} = q_{14} = q_{15} = q_{16} = 0.25.$$

REFERENCES

Albutt, H. A. (1878). *The Wife's Handbook,* 3rd ed. W. J. Ramsay, London.

American Physician (1855). *Reproductive Control, Or a Rational Guide to Matrimonial Happiness . . . , by an American Physician.* Cincinnati, OH.

Arrow, K. J. (1962). The Economic Implications of Learning by Doing, *Review of Economic Studies,* 29(2): pp 150–168.

Arrow, K. J. (1972). *The Limits of Organization.* Norton, New York.

Ashton, J. (1865). *The Book of Nature.* Brother Jonathan Office, New York.

Atkinson, R. C., Bower, G., and Crothers, E. J. (1965). *Introduction to Mathematical Learning.* Wiley, New York.

Bergues, H. *et al.* (1960). *La prévention des naissance dans la famille,* Cahier No. 35. Institut National d'Études Demographiques (INED), Paris.

Bradie, M. (1986). Assessing evolutionary epistemology. *Biology and Philosophy* **1,** 401–459.

Brodie, J. F. (1994). *Contraception and Abortion in 19th-Century America.* Cornell University Press, Ithaca, NY.

Campbell, D. T. (1959). Methodological suggestions from a comparative psychology of knowledge processes. *Inquiry* **2,** 152–182.

Campbell, D. T. (1960). Blind variation and selective retention in creative thought as in other knowledge processes. *Psychological Review* **67,** 380–400.

Crick, F. (1988). *What Mad Pursuit: A Personal View of Scientific Discovery.* Basic Books, New York.

Darmon, P. (1981). *Le mythe de la procréation à l 'âge baroque.* Éditions du Seuil, Paris.

David, P. A. (1975). *Technical Choice, Innovation and Economic Growth.* Cambridge University Press, Cambridge, UK.

David, P. A. (1988). *Path-Dependence: Putting the Past into the Future of Economics,* Tech. Rep. No. 533. Institute for Mathematical Studies in the Social Sciences, Stanford University, Stanford, CA.

David, P. A. (1993). Historical economics in the long run: Some implications of path-dependence. In *Historical Analysis in Economics* (G. D. Snooks, ed.), Chapter 2. Routledge, London.

David, P. A. (1994). Why are institutions the "Carriers of History"? *Structural Change and Economic Dynamics* **5**(2), 205–220.

David, P. A., and Sanderson, W. C. (1978a). The effectiveness of nineteenth-century contraceptive practices: An application of microdemographic modelling approaches. In *International Economic History Association, Seventh International Economic History Congress: Edinburgh, 1978,* pp. 60–70. University of Edinburgh Press, Edinburgh.

David, P. A., and Sanderson, W. C. (1978b). The role of experience and adaptive behavior in contraceptive efficiency. *Stanford Project on the History of Fertility Control,* Working Paper No. 1. Stanford University Department of Economics, Stanford, CA (December).

David, P. A., and Sanderson, W. C. (1986). Rudimentary contraceptive methods and the American transition to fertility control, 1855–1915. In *Long-Term Factors in American Economic Growth* (S. L. Engerman and R. E. Gallman, eds.), NBER Studies in Income and Wealth, Vol. 51, Chapter 7. University of Chicago Press, Chicago.

David, P. A., Sanderson, W. C., and Steinmueller, W. E. (1988). *Bounded Bayesian Learning and Performance Improvement in Complex Production Processes: A Stochastic Simulation Approach,* Research-IOIP Project Research Memorandum. Stanford University Center for Economic Policy, Stanford, CA. (Original draft, 1978)

Degler, C. N. (1974). What ought to be and what was: Women's sexuality in the nineteenth century. *American Historical Review* **79,** 1467–1490.

Drysdale, G. R. (1854). *Physical, Sexual and Natural Religion: By a Student of Medicine.* E. Truelove, London.

Gould, S. J. (1980). *The Panda's Thumb.* Norton, New York.

Hartman, C. G. (1962). *Science and the Safe Period.* Williams & Wilkins, Co., Baltimore.

Himes, N. E. (1970). *Medical History of Contraception* (Shocken paperback edition, with a new preface by C. Tietze). Shocken, New York.

Hopkins, K. (1965). Contraception in the Roman Empire. *Comparative Studies in Society and Science* **8,** 124–151.

Hull, D. L. (1988). *Science as a Process: An Evolutionary Account of the Social and Conceptual Development of Science.* University of Chicago Press, Chicago.

Kahneman, D., Slovic, P., and Tversky, A., eds. (1982). *Judgment under Uncertainty: Heuristics and Biases.* Cambridge University Press, Cambridge, UK.

Knowlton, C. (1841). *Fruits of Philosophy or the Private Companion of Young Married People.* London.

Kornblith, H. (1985). What is naturalized epistemology? In *Naturalizing Epistemology* (H. Kornblith, ed.), MIT/Bradford, Cambridge, MA.

Kuran, T. (1994). Cognitive limitations and preference evolution. *Journal of Institutional and Theoretical Economics.*

Lewis, D. (1874). *Chastity, or Our Secret Sins.* Philadelphia.

Lewis-Fanning, E. (1949). *Report on an Enquiry into Family Limitation and Its Influence on Human Fertility During the Past Fifty Years.* Papers of the Royal Commission on Population, Vol. 1. London.

MaHood, J., and Wenburg, K. (1980). *The Mosher Survey: Sexual Attitudes of 45 Victorian Women.* Arno, New York.

'M.G.H.' (c. 1854–1861). *Poverty: Its Causes and Cure.* London.

Pouchet, F. A. (1847). *Théorie positive de l'ovulation spontanée, et de la fécundation des mammifères et de l'espèce humaine.* J. B. Ballière, Paris.

Quine, W. V. O. (1969). Natural kinds. In *Ontological Relativity and Other Essays* (W. V. O. Quine, ed.), Columbia University Press, New York.

Rothschild, M. W. (1974). Searching for the lowest price when the distribution of prices is unknown. *Journal of Political Economy* **82,** 689–711.

Stockham, A. B. (1887). *Tokology.* Sanitary Publishing Co., Chicago.

Suppes, P., and Atkinson, R. C. (1960). *Markovian Learning Theory* (Stanford Mathematical Studies in the Social Science). Stanford University Press, Stanford, CA.

Tversky, A., and Kahneman, D. (1974). Judgment under uncertainty: Heuristics and biases. *Science* **185,** 1124–1131.

Waters, C. K. (1990). Confessions of a creationist. In *Evolution, Cognition and Realism: Studies in Evolutionary Epistemology* (N. Rescher, ed.), pp. 79–89. University Press of America, Lanham, MD.

Index